Time Out London

Contents

D1827410

Time Out Group Limited
Universal House
251 Tottenham Court Road
London W1T 7AB
Tel   + 44 (0)20 7813 3000
Fax   + 44 (0)20 7813 6001
Email guides@timeout.com
www.timeout.com

Editorial
Editor Simon Coppock
Additional editorial Ros Sales,
Yolanda Zappaterra
Editorial Director Sarah Guy
Management Accountant Margaret Wright

Design
Art Director Anthony Huggins
Designer Thomas Havell
Group Commercial Senior Designer
Jason Tansley

Picture desk
Picture Editor Jael Marschner
Picture Researcher Ben Rowe
Freelance Picture Researcher Lizzy Owen

Advertising
Managing Director of Advertising
St John Betteridge
Advertising Sales Deborah Maclaren, Helen
Debenham @ The Media Sales House

Marketing
Head of Circulation Dan Collins

Production
Production Controller Katie Mulhern-Bhudia

Time Out Group
Chairman & Founder Tony Elliott
Chief Executive Officer Tim Arthur
Publisher Alex Batho
Group IT Director Simon Chappell
Group Marketing Director Carolyn Sims

Contributors

Sections in this guide were written and
researched by Carol Baker, Simon Coppock,
Peter Watts, Yolanda Zappaterra.

The editor would like to thank the Time Out
London team and all contributors to the *Time
Out London* guide, whose work forms the basis
for parts of this magazine.

Cover photography Sandra Raccanello/
4Corners Images.

Printed and bound by Wyndeham [Roche] Ltd.

Leicester Square

LONDON FOR VISITORS 2014/15

Features

London in Focus

Bus Some Moves

East End Interiors

Diary

Out & About

Explore

Consume

Arts & Entertainment

Hotels

Essentials

London in Focus

The Shed

Theatre of dreams

The new man at Britain's finest playhouse will have much to do to match his predecessor.

Only a truly brave soul would follow in the footsteps of Nicholas Hytner, whose curatorial track record at the helm of the National Theatre (*see p107*) has been daunting, to say the least. Hytner's series of blockbuster West End transfers include *The History Boys* and *War Horse*, both of which became hit movies. And even as government subsidies drop, he has managed to keep the private money and ticket receipts rolling in.

Luckily, the man who's been associate director alongside Hytner since 2011 has, in layman's terms, form. Rufus Norris cut his teeth as an associate director at the Young Vic (*see p108*) in 2002, before moving to the National to successfully direct works across all its spaces. He revived modern classics such as James Baldwin's *The Amen Corner* and Wole Soyinka's *Death and the King's Horseman* on the huge rotating stage of the Olivier; for the intimate Cottesloe stage, he put on the extraordinary musical *London Road* by Alecky Blythe and Adam Cork, built from interviews with the ordinary residents of an Ipswich street inhabited by a serial killer; and, most recently, he was behind the multi-generational drama *Table* by Tanya Ronder in the temporary Shed.

> ## In layman's terms, Rufus Norris has form

The latter venue is typical of the National's Hytner-era inventiveness. Faced with the closure of the Cottesloe as part of an extensive redevelopment programme that will see that stage reopen as the Dorfman Theatre in autumn 2014, along with a Clore Learning Centre and the Max Rayne Centre for production and design, the National simply opened a new venue: the temporary Shed – yes, that upside-down red piano stool on the South Bank – to host more experimental plays, largely under the oversight of Norris.

With its rough-sawn timberboard cladding, Haworth Tompkins' big red Shed has been such a hit, both as an arresting counterpoint to the board-formed concrete of Denys Lasdun's original National Theatre complex and as a performance space, that it's now likely to be on site until at least 2017. But will Norris? He's received acclaim for his recent film directorial debut *Broken*, which won Best Film at the British Independent Film Awards last year, and has described cinema as a terrific medium, so it may be that his theatre stewardship will be a lot shorter-lived than Hytner's 12-year marathon stint.

Still, before the master departs in 2015, there are many goodies to be savoured – among them ten world premières – including new plays by Tom Stoppard and David Hare, and revivals of classic plays by Euripides (*Medea*, starring Helen McCrory) and Shaw (*Man and Superman*, starring Ralph Fiennes).

Some kind of paradise

Will luxury tourists find their Shangri-La 52 floors above London Bridge?

While Irish folk everywhere celebrated St Patrick's Day on 17 March 2014, London's high-fliers were at their own exclusive party for the launch of the tallest hotel in Western Europe. The shindig marked the day bookings opened for the latest Shangri-La Hotel (www.shangri-la.com/london), nestled loftily on floors 34 to 52 of Renzo Piano's 87-storey Shard (see p21). From May, guests will be able to gaze down on the proletariat from 125m up; if they can bear to wait until June, they can do so from London's highest infinity pool on level 52. Still not enough? From September you'll be able to splurge on one of the three suites.

The hotel features a stunning two-floor sky lobby, with its dizzying staircase lit by floor-to-ceiling windows. Above it, 202 guestrooms and suites on levels 36 to 50 will sit beneath that handily located pool, all of them with full-height picture windows, marble-clad bathrooms with heated floors, Acqua di Parma toiletries and, our favourite futuristic touch, mirrors with integrated TV screens. At £450, even the cheapest room will be beyond the budget of most. But Ting, the signature restaurant and lounge on level 35, will serve authentic Asian specialities and afternoon teas in the lounge at a fraction of the price. Or, if you want to celebrate in serious style, the 52nd floor Gong will be serving champagne and cocktails in the city's highest bar.

More than toys for boys?

The Imperial War Museum reopens for the 1914 centennial.

Creating a war museum that's not exclusively of interest to small boys, their dads and their granddads is no mean feat, but the splendid Imperial War Museum (see p16) has managed to achieve it effortlessly. As with all its branches, the London arm of the museum, whose focus is on the history of 20th-century conflict, intelligently brings together art, artefacts, interactive and immersive displays – and, of course, plenty of big guns and planes – to not only inform and educate, but also to represent life during wartime in a spirited, engaging way that offers something for everyone.

This summer, after a six-month closure for a major revamp, the IWM will reopen for the centenary of the Great War in July 2014. The museum will feature a whole raft of new displays and spaces, all of them continuing the IWM's focus on telling stories as much through the voices of protagonists as historians.

Brand-new World War I galleries will bring together everything from a Sopwith Camel biplane and Mark V tank to personal love letters, souvenirs from the Front, photographs, art and film. An interactive table will offer insight into the mind-boggling production scale needed to assist the war effort and keep the troops fed, and a recreated trench complete with soundscape will evoke daily life for the troops.

The museum will wisely retain some aspects of its illustrious past – notably the soaring atrium. Fans worried that the splendid objects displayed prior to the closure will have been ditched can take heart: the reconfigured space – designed by Foster + Partners – will see nine iconic objects, including a Harrier, Spitfire and V2 rocket, suspended from the ceiling, along with modern equipment, including a Reuters Land Rover that was damaged by a Gaza rocket attack, littering the ground. New terraces above will reveal more of the collection, taking visitors through key stories from World War II and curated displays telling the stories of later conflicts, including Northern Ireland, Iraq and Afghanistan.

Excitingly for art-lovers, the museum will host the largest retrospective of British First World War art for 100 years: 'Truth and Memory' (until March 2015) promises more than 120 paintings, sculptures, prints and drawings, including work by Paul Nash, Percy Wyndham Lewis, CRW Nevinson and Stanley Spencer. The theme of 'truth' will be covered by artists who experienced life on the frontline, first-hand, while 'memory' will focus on how British art commemorated the conflict, helping to form the collective memory of the Great War as we know it today.

AMAZING ANNIVERSARIES
From Hoxton Overground station, the Geffrye (see p48) doesn't look like much, but this superb museum of domestic interiors is not only 100 years old – but 300 years old too. 2014 marks the centennial of the museum's opening – and the tricentennial of the founding of the almshouses that now contain it.

DOESN'T GROW ON TREES
Just when you thought all the creatives had high-tailed it north into Dalston, the Silicon Roundabout grabbed a bit of iCrazy back. Old Shoreditch Station café (1 Kingsland Road, E2 8DA, 7729 5188, www.jaguarshoes.com) opened the UK's first Bitcoin ATM... just as online currency exchange Mt Gox collapsed.

TOP MODELS
Everybody's favourite eccentric London house, the Sir John Soane's Museum (see p28), is planning to reconstruct the architect's Model Room. Having resisted the temptation for nearly 20 years, Soane transformed his late wife Eliza's bedroom into a showcase for his miniaturised buildings in 1834. It should reopen in 2016.

IT'S ELECTRIFYING!
Our mayor certainly has some out-of-the-box ideas. There's that cable car (see p49) joining up bits of the capital that no one needs to travel between; there's the new bus (see p6) that overheats in summer; and now there's a proposal to modify Boris Bikes (see p122) – get fit, London! – by adding electric motors to help you get up north London's hills without too much effort.

Berners Tavern

Social eating

The talent behind some of the finest dining in town.

With the news that he'll be taking over the City eyrie in Tower 42 (*see p27*) once occupied by Gary Rhodes (a Michelin star winner at the age of just 26 and pretty much the first British celebrity chef), chef-patron Jason Atherton's extraordinary run of success continues. In the space of just a few weeks in 2013, he opened two restaurants – first the Social Eating House (58-59 Poland Street, W1F 7NR, 7993 3251, www.social eatinghouse.com), then Berners Tavern (*see p56*) – both of which secured rare five-star ratings from our food editor.

It isn't easy to open a spate of new restaurants in quick succession and maintain high standards, but Atherton has grown rapidly from sorcerer's apprentice to Gordon Ramsay at Maze to himself being the magician. His first solo venture was Pollen Street Social (8-10 Pollen Street, W1S 1NQ, 7290 7600, www.pollen streetsocial.com), where Atherton's philosophy of 'deformalised fine dining' was established: decor that's smart but approachable, dishes grounded in French and English tradition but embellished with occasionally esoteric – often international – side notes of texture and taste.

Atherton then opened up a kind of superbistro just opposite, Little Social (5 Pollen Street, W1S 1NE, 7870 3730, www.littlesocial.co.uk), which neatly caught on to the neo-bistro trend in the capital.

But it has been with the Social Eating House and Berners Tavern that his playful and appealing dishes have really come to the fore, in the careful hands of, respectively, Paul Hood and Phil Carmichael. At the Social, the smoked duck 'ham', egg and chips is a dish typical Pollen Street Social's inventiveness, with 'ham' cured and smoked from duck breast on the premises, served with a breadcrumbed duck egg that's molten in the middle, but with an aroma of truffle oil. It's an object lesson in delivering umami – savouriness, the taste that enhances other flavours.

Refreshingly zingy presentation, inventiveness, imagination and attention to detail are all trademarks of *école de* Atherton. At the Social Eating House, if you visit the basement (where the duck smoker as well as the loos are housed), you can even take a quick peek at how it's all done: look through the glass-walled private dining room towards the kitchen, in full view of the 'chef's table', and you'll see Hood and his team working their magic with a spell-like calm.

The future at Foyles

London's definitive bookshop begins another chapter.

In the mid 1980s, Foyles (*see p79*) wasn't just the worst bookshop in London – it was probably the worst in the world. Founded in 1903, the shop was run from 1945 by charming but thoroughly autocratic Christina Foyle, daughter of the founder.

She would sack anyone who'd worked at the shop for six months, lest they acquire an improved contract. She would move staff from their areas of specialist knowledge, so they'd be less tempted to browse at work. Notoriously, to prevent too many staff having access to cash, she introduced a quasi-Stalinist double queuing system – you took your book to a desk, swapped it for a ticket, paid the ticket at a second desk, then collected your purchase from a third. Foyles had massive stock, but few staff knew where books were – they were shelved by publisher, not author or subject. No wonder a competitor felt able to run a series of posters saying: 'Foyled again? Try Dillons'.

Still, she kept Foyles in operation until her death in 1999 – the year, incidentally, that Dillons folded. 'In her 80s,' her *Guardian* obituary noted, 'she was still reading at least a book a day, drinking only champagne and declining even to try to cook.'

But the most surprising twist was yet to come. After a decade of shrewd management, Foyles became the most impressive independent bookshop in London, winning awards for its wide range of stock and clued-in, friendly customer service.

And now it's time to change again. With Central St Martins art school having decamped to Granary Square (*see p30*), bigger premises suddenly became available in the art deco building next door at 107-109 Charing Cross Road. Huge picture windows either side of the new building's entrance used to house installations by the students; now they will be where Foyles' Art and Design Department is situated. There is a wonderful central atrium, and the stage of the former Assembly Hall (once graced – perhaps disgraced – by the Sex Pistols) will be the Children's section. Fiction will be on what was a ballroom floor, peered down upon from Cookery, Travel and Lifestyle on a mezzanine above. And a gallery, café and events space will crown the building either side of the atrium.

One thing has remained certain: at the centre of the shop will be, as there always were, shelves of thousands of wonderful books.

Clockwise from left: the celebratory silver 'Boris Bus'; Mayor Boris Johnson; the restored 'Battle Bus'.

Bus some moves

Why focus on 2014? asks Peter Watts. For real Londoners, it's always the year of the bus.

In 2009, the gonzo cartoonist Ralph Steadman held a typically whimsical competition inviting people to design a symbolic gateway to London, a monumental piece of architecture that would announce to any visitor that they had arrived in one of world's leading capitals. The winning entry was an eye-catching arch based on Edwin Lutyens' Thiepval Memorial to the Missing of the Somme in France that was made entirely out of stacked Routemaster buses. As one of the judges, architect Sir Terry Farrell, noted, it 'cleverly picks up on what is probably the most iconic object that represents London'. And so it is. This is the city of Big Ben, of the London Eye, of St Paul's Cathedral – but its most popular icon is a humble bus.

Even though 2014 has been designated the Year of the Bus by the Mayor of London, this could be said of just about any year in London, where the bus is venerated like the cow in Mumbai. 'London buses are the pulsing red arteries of the capital, 24-hours a day, 364 days of the year and they play an undeniably important role in the city's economy,' enthuses Mayor Boris Johnson (pictured), and while the Tube is relatively simple to comprehend and master, it's use of the bus that separates the confirmed Londoner from the dilettante. As Johnson

notes, while the Tube and train make up the bones of London's skeleton, it's the bus that acts as the blood cell, bringing life to parts of the city that are not touched by the underground and where tourists rarely tread.

This is what the Year of the Bus has been designed to celebrate – and there's no better way to join in than to hop on board a bus yourself (we recommend the No. 15, which allows you to ride a classic Routemaster from Trafalgar Square to the Tower of London).

The strength of street knowledge

The London bus is more than just a functional feature of London infrastructure, it is a colourful and charismatic creation, travelling illogical but beloved routes that allow Londoners to see parts – and people – of their city that would otherwise remain faceless. The bus may sometimes take an inordinate amount of time to reach its destination, but it still serves to make London smaller, filling in the gaps between A and B, and anything that makes this unwieldy city more manageable is bound to go down well with locals. With the Tube network shutting down at midnight, the bus is also essential in allowing London to maintain a 24-hour economy, with a series of night buses shuttling night workers and party animals around the capital.

It helps that it looks good too, particularly the beloved Routemaster, which was first unveiled 60 years ago and rapidly became one of the city's most cherished emblems, featuring in numerous films and television programmes as a shorthand symbol for the city in everything from episodes of Dr Who to Nancy Sinatra album covers. The Routemaster still engenders such strong feelings that in 2008, three years after it had been withdrawn, it was being used as a political vehicle, helping in a roundabout way to secure the election of Mayor Johnson. When a 48-hour Tube strike was called in early 2014 and bus routes were buckling under the strain, commuting Londoners were delighted to see old Routemasters pressed back into service at their time of need.

Johnson, being a history buff and despite his fondness for anti-French soundbites, probably knows that the bus was a French invention. The first buses – carriages carrying several passengers travelling a designated route on a pre-planned timetable – were created in the 18th century by a Frenchman, M. Omnes, who named them the 'omnibus', a Latin pun on 'all for every one' based on his own name.

The omnibus was brought to London by George Shillibeer, a London-born coachmaker who had been working in

Paris developing carriages that could transport up to two-dozen people at a time. On 4 July 1829 the first 'Shillibus' travelled along the New Road between Paddington and Bank, costing 1s 6d for those sitting inside and 1s for passengers who travelled on the open roof. The bus was pulled by three horses and could carry up to 18 passengers, travelling four times daily in each direction.

So intense was demand that within a few years, there were 90 such vehicles travelling up and down the road at three-minute intervals. Conductors became notorious for their ability to cram as many people on board as possible. London was a heavily congested city, and by 1850 the streets were packed with 200,000 travellers who used horse, private coach and hansom cab, as well as 150 different omnibus routes to get around a city that was ringed by seven mainline railway termini, all of which dumped passengers on the outskirts of the city as railway companies were forbidden from building stations in the very centre.

In 1855, an Anglo-French enterprise was established in Paris with a view to acquiring the many private omnibus companies operating in London. This became the London General Omnibus Company, which dominated the bus network before it joined London Transport in 1933. At this point, the bus joined tube, tram and rail in an integrated transport system. In recent years, the bus has become even more popular. Passenger numbers have doubled since 2000, with 2.3 billion passengers travelling 490 million kilometres on around 700 routes – more than New York and Paris put together.

The Year of the Bus

This is what the Year of the Bus will acknowledge. At the heart will be a couple of anniversaries, the first tying into the nation's centenary commemorations for the outbreak of Word War I. In 1914, London's B-Type bus was used to transport troops to the frontline for the start of the war – and one of these few remaining vehicles, dubbed the 'Battle Bus', has been restored in khaki livery for the anniversary. More than 1,000 B-Types were used in the war. The B-Type was built especially for use in London, and manufacturers continued with this philosophy for half a century, designing buses equipped to deal with London's huge demand and stop-start traffic. The first motor buses were licensed in 1897 but horses remained in use until 1916, and for a while steam-powered buses were also used – 184 of them in 1914. Gradual improvements in tyres, engines and staircases allowed buses to get bigger, so that when the NS was introduced in 1923 it could hold 52, and even had a roof on the upper deck.

The Battle Bus will feature in the London Transport Museum's exhibition, 'Goodbye Piccadilly – from the home front to the Western front', which runs until 8 March 2015 and looks at the massive social

change accelerated by the outbreak of the war, its impact on London life and the role London's buses and bus drivers played on the Western Front. Other bus-related events at the museum include a symposium on 'The social history and cultural significance of the London bus' on 18 October 2014, which will examine whether the London bus changed the world in areas from female emancipation to design. The museum also contains several classic old buses in its permanent collection, along with other bus-related ephemera. Other Year of the Bus events include a cavalcade of historic London buses doing a lap of honour around the London streets.

Among the buses in this procession will be the Routemaster, which was first unveiled 60 years ago in 1954 and went on to become the most recognisable and popular bus in the world. The Routemaster is distinguished by its jaunty, rounded front and the open rear platform that allowed Londoners to hop on or off when the bus was stationary – or even when it was clipping along at quite a pace. Although the Routemaster was controversially phased out in 2005, it was retained on two Heritage Routes – the 9 and 15, which passed several London landmarks and were popular with tourists. But these routes are now under threat. Routemasters will be removed from the 9 in July 2014, and campaigners fear the 15 will follow suit, bringing London's relationship with its most beloved bus to a teary end.

That is partly because of the cost of maintaining these aged, rattling Routemasters, but also because the Mayor believes London has a new icon to promote, his New Bus For London, which Transport for London have named the New Routemaster but most Londoners call the Boris Bus. This bus was the outcome of Johnson's chord-striking pre-election pledge that he would re-introduce a Routemaster-style bus to the London streets. The Boris Bus, designed by Thomas Heatherwick, duly arrived in 2012 to replace the 'bendy bus' – single-deck, high-capacity, articulated buses that Johnson argued were more suitable for a 'Scandinavian airport' than the streets of London.

The chief distinguishing feature separating the Boris Bus from other London buses is that, like the Routemaster, it has an open rear platform and conductors – although the rear platform closes in the evening (all day on some routes) and conductors are not allowed to sell tickets and are expected to stop people getting on or off between the designated stops. The Boris Bus is also a lot more bullish-looking than the stylish Routemaster and can get hot during the summer. Still, more are being rolled out – including one painted silver to mark the Year of the Bus – and Boris buses are already in operation on six routes across capital, including the old No. 9 Heritage route. Whether it will ever replace the Routemaster in popular affection remains to be seen.

> **The bus rapidly became a cherished emblem.**

ON THE BUS
Five ways to enjoy the London bus.

1 LONDON TRANSPORT MUSEUM
The LTM (see p31) is located in the old flower hall at Covent Garden. The museum dates back to the early 1900s, when London General decided to preserve old buses, so the bus features strongly in its collection. A number of them can be seen on display, along with related ephemera plus bus-themed gifts from the shop.

2 HERITAGE ROUTE
The No. 15 (Heritage) is the last route on which you can catch a Routemaster (pictured below). It's a popular route with tourists, shuttling between the Tower of London and Trafalgar Square via St Paul's and the City. The route is also served by ordinary buses, so you may need to wait for your Routemaster.

3 NEW ROUTEMASTER
The Boris Bus has begun to roll out across London, with 600 in service by 2016. It's a green bus, using diesel-electric hybrid technology, and is a fairly stylish – if over-sized – attempt to redraw a classic. In 2014, the Boris Bus was serving routes 9, 11, 24, 38, 148 and 390, which between them cover all points of the compass.

4 NIGHT BUS
Travelling on one of London's night buses is a rite of passage for any young Londoner, who won't let a Tube network that closes at midnight get in the way of their fun. Night buses –numbers prefixed with an 'N' – run similar routes to their daylight equivalent, but often with extensions into unfamiliar territory. There are also several 24-hour services.

5 LONDON TRANSPORT MUSEUM, ACTON DEPOT
Given space limitations in Covent Garden, many of the LTM's larger objects are kept in the Acton depot, which can be visited for monthly guided tours as well as themed open weekends. There are 370,000 items here, including many buses.

At home in the East End

The amazing interiors at House of Hackney in Shoreditch.

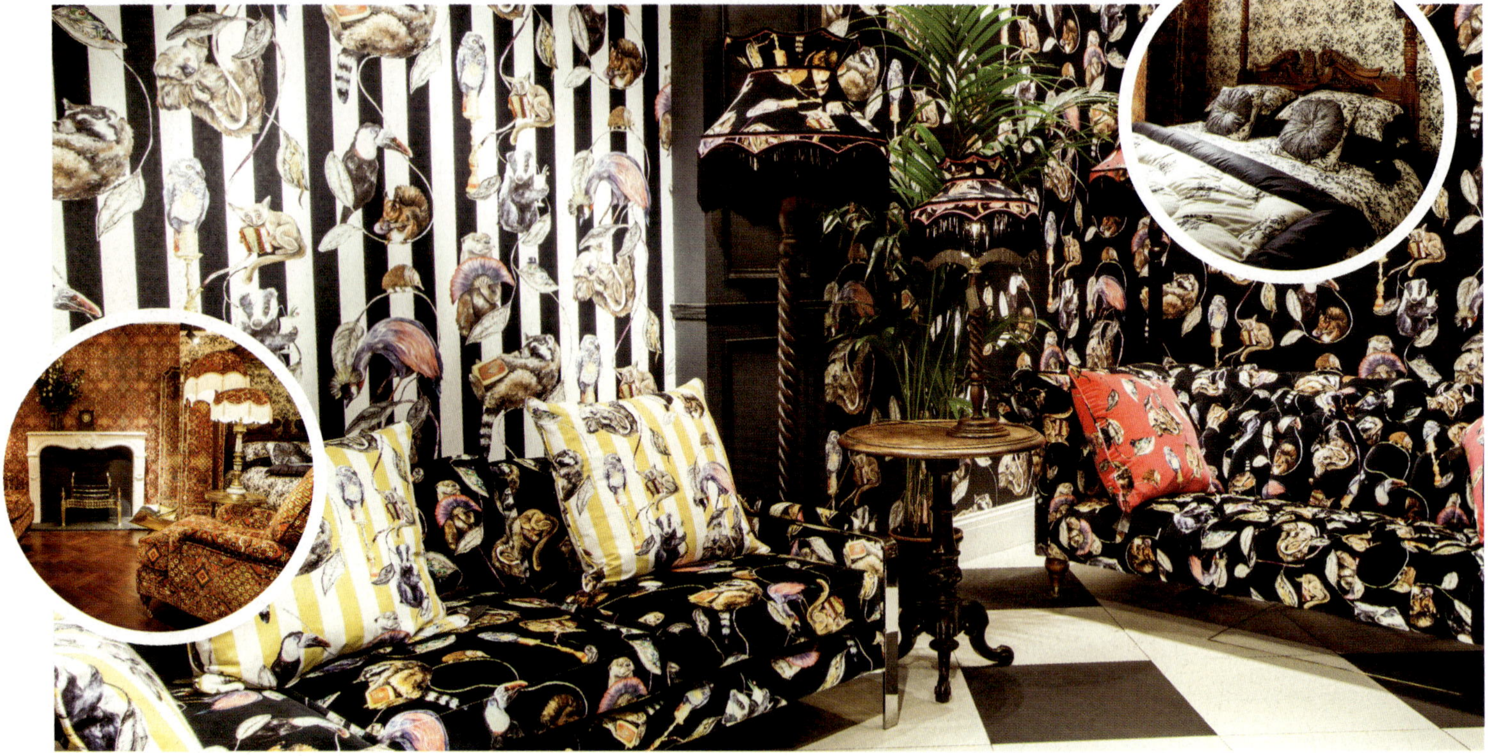

House of Hackney has made its first home, unsurprisingly, in its namesake borough – with an ambitious flagship store in the heart of Shoreditch that is likely to become a stop-off destination for in-the-know fashion tourists from all over the world.

It started as an interiors label, but with founders (and couple) Frieda Gormley and Javvy M Royle both hailing from fashion backgrounds, it was only natural that their London-inspired prints (Dalston Rose, Hackney Empire – both of which nod to the charms of the local area) should make their way first on to clothing and accessories, and more recently diversifying across everything from washbags and notepads to crockery.

When the label's first shop opened in summer 2013, it was one of the most gorgeous retail establishments to land in London in years – bedecked in the deliberately over the top juxtapositions of print-on-print-on-print that have made the brand's name. The entrance to the store is full of plants – luxury florists Wild at Heart have sublet the front of the shop. That sets the tone for the place, with things getting increasingly nature-obsessed as you glide across black polished floors, surrounded by rose wallpaper, prints of palms and bees, and more.

Downstairs you'll find furniture: generously proportioned sofas and plump leopard-print armchairs cheek-by-jowl with chaises longues and scattered with floral cushions – all decorated in more-is-more combinations of print and texture.

The entire range of House of Hackney's beautiful prints is here – represented upstairs in rolls of paper, fabric, trays, mugs, fashion and collaborative designs with brands like Puma. But it isn't just about hot-right-now prints – the brand has a laudable focus on products that are made in England, and as far as possible made in London.

Gormley confesses that the brand was partly inspired by her own boredom with the ubiquity of IKEA-style minimalism. Certainly you'll find none of that here: instead, the floral theme established by that fragrant entrance is picked up on sweatshirts, bikinis, cups and saucers all over the first floor.

And although most shoppers will walk away with a teacup rather than a suite of furniture, they'll be taking home a little piece of England. A little piece of England that's exactly how we'd like it to look.

BEST OF THE REST *More sensational stores in east London.*

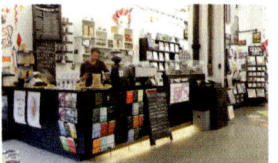

ROUGH TRADE EAST

Best for... in-store gigs

Rough Trade East (*see p88*) is a retailer of expertly curated vinyl, CDs and books. It also contains a café and a purpose-built stage, with standing room in front. In-store gigs usually kick off at 7pm and wristbands are obtained by pre-ordering a CD.

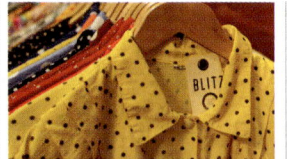

BLITZ

Best for... quality vintage gear

Blitz (*see p87*) is a veritable department store of vintage wonders, spread over all the floors of an old furniture factory. From trunks stuffed with silk scarves to racks on racks of denim sorted by shade, you'll find it all. There's even a coffee bar.

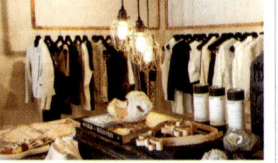

CELESTINE ELEVEN

Best for... luxury labels

This dreamy boutique and treatment room (*see p87*) is a good measure of how much Shoreditch has changed. Tena Strok was a stylist before launching this whopping lifestyle store on a quiet backstreet in summer 2013.

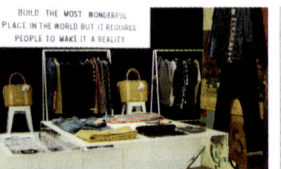

GOODHOOD STORE

Best for... edgy clothes with a sense of humour

This off-beat indie outfit (*see p87*) has spawned a pair of shops, a creative agency, a thriving online store and a Shoreditch cult for five-panel caps. The store sells premium fashion brands to young 'creatives'.

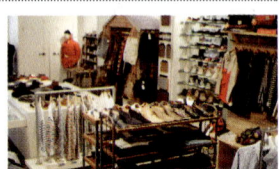

PRESENT

Best for... quality menswear

Present (*see p88*) is a mini-department store for men, stocking rare brands, heritage labels and clever, in-house staples. The price range varies hugely, and the store is constantly reworked and stocked up with gem after gem.

HOUSE OF HACKNEY/CELESTINE ELEVEN: ROB GREIG, ROUGH TRADE EAST: MING TANG-EVANS, BLITZ: MICHAEL FRANKE, GOODHOOD STORE: ROSS TREVAIL

When in London, dine out with the stars.

HACHÉ

www.hacheburgers.com

Diary

Notting Hill Carnival. See p12.

Plan your perfect weekend

Your guide to what happens when: from flower shows to rock festivals.

Forget about British reserve. Festivals and events play ever more elaborate variations on the age-old themes of parading and dancing, nowadays with ever-larger sprinklings of arts and culture. Some are traditional, some innovative, from the outdoor spectacle of the Greenwich & Docklands International Festival to the splendid ritual of the Changing the Guard. Weather plays a part in the timing, with a concentration of things to do in the summer, but the city's calendar is busy for most of the year. Indeed, some of the most enjoyable events take place in winter – Bonfire Night, for example.

In addition to the rich array of annual events, the resounding success of the 2012 Olympic and Paralympic Games has been followed by a plethora of high-profile one-off sporting events. Over the next couple of years, watch out for a visit from the Tour de France (7 July 2014; www.letour.2014

stage3.com), the Rugby World Cup (18 Sept-31 Oct 2015; www.rugbyworldcup.com) and a busy programme of cricket internationals (www.ecb.co.uk) that includes two home Test matches (the classic five-day format) against India (Lord's, 17-21 July 2014; the Oval, 15-19 Aug 2014). Our nautical spirit is recognised by the start of the Venture Offshore Cup (7 June 2014; www.ventureoffshorecup.com), a powerboat race to Monte Carlo, and the graceful Royal Greenwich Tall Ships Regatta (5-9 Sept 2014; www.royalgreenwich.gov.uk/tallships).

All year round

For the **Changing the Guard**, *see p14* **Stunning Ceremonials**.

Ceremony of the Keys
Join the Yeoman Warders after-hours at the Tower of London as they ritually lock the fortress's entrances

in this 700-year-old ceremony. You enter the Tower at 9.30pm and it's all over just after 10pm, but places are hotly sought after – apply at least two months in advance; full details are available on the website. *Tower of London, Tower Hill, the City, EC3N 4AB (3166 6278, www.hrp.org.uk). Tower Hill tube or Tower Gateway DLR. Date 9.30pm daily (advance bookings only).*

Gun Salutes
There are gun salutes on many state occasions – see the list of dates given above for a complete breakdown of when the cannons roar out. A cavalry charge features in the 41-gun salutes mounted by the King's Troop Royal Horse Artillery in Hyde Park at noon (it takes place opposite the Dorchester Hotel; *see p116*), whereas, on the other side of town, the Honourable Artillery Company ditches the ponies and piles on the firepower with its 62-gun salutes (1pm at the Tower of London).

If the dates happen to fall on a Sunday, the salute is held on the following Monday. *Green Park, Mayfair & St James's, W1; Tower of London, the City, EC3. Dates 6 Feb (Accession Day); 21 Apr & 14 June (Queen's birthdays); 2 June (Coronation Day); 10 June (Duke of Edinburgh's birthday); 14 June (Trooping the Colour); State Opening of Parliament (see p11); Lord Mayor's Show (see p14); Remembrance Sunday (see p14); also for state visits.*

Spring

League Cup Final
Less prestigious than the FA Cup, the League Cup is a knockout football competition with a 50-year history – but widely regarded as the annual trophy that's 'better than nothing'. Still, the winners do get to play in the UEFA Europa League. *Wembley Stadium, Stadium Way, Middx HA9 0WS (www.capitalonecup.co.uk). Wembley Park tube or Wembley Stadium rail. Date early Mar.*

Kew Spring Festival
Kew Gardens is at its most beautiful in spring, with five million flowers carpeting the grounds. *Kew Gardens, Surrey TW9 3AB (8332 5655, www.kew.org). Kew Gardens tube/rail, Kew Bridge rail or riverboat to Kew Pier. Admission £16; £14 reductions; free under-17s. Date early Mar-May.*

National Science & Engineering Week
From the weird to the profound, this annual week of events engages the public in celebrating science, engineering and technology. *7019 4937, www.britishscience association.org. Date mid Mar.*

St Patrick's Day Parade & Festival
Join the London Irish out in force for this annual parade through central London followed by toe-tapping tunes in Trafalgar Square. Held on the Sunday closest to 17 March. *7983 4000, www.london.gov.uk. Date mid Mar.*

Oxford & Cambridge Boat Race
Blue-clad Oxbridge students (dark blue for Oxford, light blue for Cambridge) race each other in a pair of rowing eights, as they have done since 1829. Experience the

GOOD FRIDAY
FRI 18 APR 2014
FRI 3 APR 2015

EASTER MONDAY
MON 21 APR 2014
MON 6 APR 2015

MAY DAY HOLIDAY
MON 5 MAY 2014
MON 4 MAY 2015

SPRING BANK HOLIDAY
MON 26 MAY 2014
MON 25 MAY 2015

SUMMER BANK HOLIDAY
MON 25 AUG 2014
MON 31 AUG 2015

CHRISTMAS DAY
THUR 25 DEC 2014
FRI 25 DEC 2015

BOXING DAY
FRI 26 DEC 2014
MON 28 DEC 2015

NEW YEAR'S DAY
THUR 1 JAN 2015
FRI 1 JAN 2016

excitement from the riverbank – along with 250,000 other fans. *River Thames, from Putney to Mortlake (www.theboatrace.org). Putney Bridge tube, or Barnes Bridge, Mortlake or Putney rail. Date Apr.*

La Linea
A contemporary Latin music festival, featuring everything from brass bands to flamenco guitar, held over a fortnight in April. *www.comono.co.uk. Date early Apr.*

Virgin London Marathon
One of the world's elite long-distance races, the London Marathon is also one of the world's largest fundraising events – nearly 80% of participants run for charity, so zany costumes abound among the 36,000 starters. Held on a Sunday. *Greenwich Park to the Mall via the Isle of Dogs, Victoria Embankment & St James's Park (7902 0200, www.virginlondonmarathon.com). Blackheath & Maze Hill rail (start), or Charing Cross tube/rail (end). Date mid Apr.*

FA Cup Final
The oldest domestic knockout tournament is an annual highlight for many international football fans. For all that the competition – which began in 1871 – has lost a little lustre for the top teams, who all fear being defeated by lowly opposition, it retains the capacity to surprise. *Wembley Stadium, Stadium Way, Middx HA9 0WS (www.thefa.com/thefacup). Wembley Park tube or Wembley Stadium rail. Date mid May.*

Covent Garden May Fayre & Puppet Festival
All-day puppet mayhem (10.30am-5.30pm) devoted to celebrating Mr Punch at the scene of his first recorded sighting in England in 1662. Mr P takes to the church's pulpit at 11.30am. Held on a Sunday. *Garden of St Paul's Covent Garden, Bedford Street, WC2E 9ED (7375 0441, www.punchandjudy.com/coventgarden.htm). Covent Garden tube. Date mid May.*

State Opening of Parliament
Pomp and ceremony attend the Queen's official reopening of Parliament after its recess, an event that marks the formal beginning of the Parliamentary year. She arrives (at about 11.15am) and departs in the state coach, accompanied by troopers of the Household Cavalry. *Palace of Westminster, SW1A 0PW (7219 4272, www.parliament.uk). Westminster tube. Date May.*

Chelsea Flower Show
Elbow through the huge crowds to admire perfect blooms, or get ideas for your own plot, with entire gardens laid out for the show, as well as tents packed with endless varietals. The first two days are reserved for Royal Horticultural Society members and tickets for the open days can be hard to come by. On the final day, the display plants are sold off to the public from around 4.30pm. *Royal Hospital, Royal Hospital Road, Chelsea, SW3 4SR (www.rhs.org.uk). Sloane Square tube. Date late May.*

Epsom Derby
The world's most famous horse race on the flat, the Derby, is run over a distance of one and a half miles, but crowd-watching is a large part of the fun, with the race accompanied by all manner of hoopla. *Epsom Racecourse, Epsom Downs, Surrey KT18 5LQ (01372 726311 information, 0844 579 3004 tickets, www.epsomdowns.co.uk). Epsom Downs or Tattenham Corner rail. Date early June.*

Summer

Spitalfields Music Summer Festival
A series of mainly classical concerts in June, based at Christ Church Spitalfields, as well as local venues including Shoreditch Church and Spitalfields Market. The festival returns in December each year. *7377 1362, www.spitalfieldsmusic.org.uk. Date June.*

Field Day
One of the best music festivals in London, with a leftfield booking policy. Acts range from weird pop and indie rock to underground dance producers and folk musicians. *Victoria Park, Victoria Park Road, Hackney, E3 5SN (www.fieldday festivals.com). Date June.*

London Festival of Architecture
An entertaining mix of talks, discussions, walks, screenings and other events, always gathered under a punchy theme. *www.londonfestivalofarchitecture.org. Date June.*

Meltdown
The Southbank Centre invites a guest artist to curate a fortnight of gigs, films and other events. David Bowie, Ornette Coleman, Richard Thompson and Patti Smith are among the previous curators (2014 has UNKLE's James Lavelle). *Southbank Centre, Belvedere Road, Southbank, SE1 8XX (www.southbankcentre.co.uk). Date mid June.*

Opera Holland Park
A canopied outdoor theatre hosts a season of opera, including works aimed at children. *Holland Park (7361 3570, www.operahollandpark.com). Date June-Aug.*

Open Garden Squares Weekend
Secret – and merely exclusive – gardens are thrown open to the public for this horticultural shindig. You can visit roof gardens, prison gardens and children-only gardens, as well as a changing selection of those tempting oases railed off in the middle of the city's finest squares. Some charge an entrance fee. *www.opensquares.org. Date mid June.*

Tennis: Aegon Championships
The pros tend to treat this week-long grass-court tournament as a summer warm-up session for Wimbledon (see p12). *Queens Club, Palliser Road, West Kensington, W14 9EQ (7386 3400, www.queensclub.co.uk). Barons Court tube. Date mid June.*

see p12

TOP TIP!
Get with it
The free *Time Out* magazine has highlights of each week's festivals and events. See the website, www.timeout.com, for comprehensive listings.

Royal Ascot
Major races include the Ascot Gold Cup on the Thursday, which is Ladies' Day. Expect sartorial extravagance from natty shoes to fancy hats. *Ascot Racecourse, Ascot, Berks SL5 7JX (0844 346 3000, www.ascot.co.uk). Ascot rail. Date mid June.*

Greenwich & Docklands International Festival
This annual week of outdoor arts, theatre, dance and family entertainment is consistently spectacular. Events take place at the Old Royal Naval College and other sites, including Canary Wharf and Mile End Park. *8305 1818, www.festival.org. Date late June.*

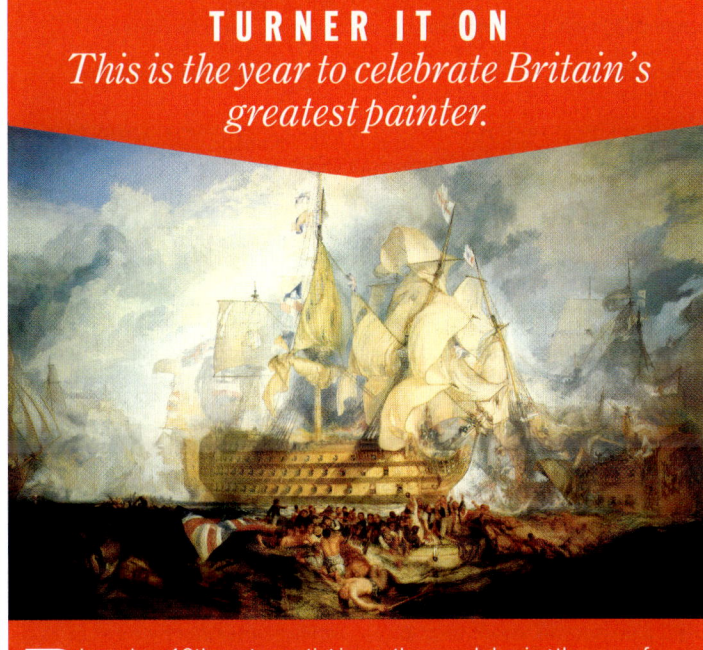

TURNER IT ON
This is the year to celebrate Britain's greatest painter.

Bizarrely, a 19th-century artist is posthumously having the year of his life – but then Joseph Mallord William Turner was no ordinary painter. He almost single-handedly revolutionised the art – with a commitment that reputedly on one occasion saw him lashed to the mast of a ship in order to capture a storm at sea. Turner's lifelong fascination with the ocean is the focus of 'Turner and the Sea' (until 21 Apr 2014) at the National Maritime Museum (*see p50*), while 'Late Turner: Painting Set Free' (10 Sept 2014-25 Jan 2015) at Tate Britain (*see p40*) explores his increasing visual radicalism. There's even to be a Mike Leigh-directed biopic, called *Mr Turner* and starring Timothy Spall as the great man, due for release by eOne in 2014.

Pride London

LIFT (London International Festival of Theatre)
An extraordinary number of performances (nearly 90 in just under a month), under the inspirational directorship of Mark Ball. *7968 6800, www.liftfest.org.uk. Date June.*

Pride London
A week-long celebration of the LGBT community, with the Parade held on the Saturday. In 2014 the Parade on 28 June commemorates the 45th anniversary of the Stonewall Riots in New York. *www.prideinlondon.org. Date late June.*

City of London Festival
A wide array of classical in a variety of genres, with an emphasis on classical music and jazz. Many concerts are held in unusual venues, and there's always a strong programme of free events. *0845 120 7502 tickets, www.colf.org. Date late June-mid July.*

Wimbledon Tennis Championships
Getting into Wimbledon requires considerable forethought. Seats on the show courts are distributed by a ballot, which closes the previous year; enthusiasts who queue on the day may gain entry to the outer courts – and even get rare tickets for Centre Court. You can also turn up later in the day and pay reduced rates for seats vacated by spectators who've left the ground early. *All England Lawn Tennis Club, Church Road, Wimbledon, SW19 5AE (8971 2700, www.wimbledon.org). Southfields tube. Dates 23 June-6 July 2014; 29 June-12 July 2015.*

Lovebox Weekender
Expect some of the best names the London nightlife scene has to offer, over two days in myriad themed stages, tents and arenas. *Victoria Park, Victoria Park Road, Hackney, E3 5SN (www.mamacolive.com/lovebox). Date mid July.*

Somerset House Summer Series
Somerset House welcomes an array of big and generally pretty mainstream acts for approaching a fortnight of open-air shows. *Somerset House, the Strand, WC2R 1LA (7845 4600, www.somersethouse.org.uk/music). Temple tube. Date July.*

BBC Proms
The Proms overshadow all other classical music festivals in the city, with around 70 concerts, covering everything from early music recitals to orchestral world premières, and from boundary-pushing debut performances to reverent career retrospectives. BBC Radio 3 plays recordings of the concerts. *Royal Albert Hall, Kensington Gore, South Kensington, SW7 2AP (0845 401 5040, www.bbc.co.uk/proms). Date mid July-mid Sept.*

Camden Fringe
An eclectic bunch of new, experimental shows, staged by everyone from experienced performers to newcomers. *www.camdenfringe.org. Date late July-Aug.*

Prudential RideLondon
This cycling festival encourages around 50,000 people to don branded fluorescent vests and ride an eight-mile traffic-free circuit from Buckingham Palace to the Tower. Competitive races also form part of the weekend's festivities. *7902 0212, www.prudentialride london.com. Date early Aug.*

Carnaval del Pueblo
This vibrant outdoor parade and festival is more than just a loud-and-proud day out for South American Londoners: it attracts people from all walks of life (as many as 60,000, most years) looking to inject a little Latin spirit into the weekend. *Burgess Park, Southwark, SE5 7QH (www.carnavaldelpueblo.co.uk). Elephant & Castle tube/rail. Date early Aug.*

London Mela
Thousands flock to this exuberant celebration of Asian culture, dubbed the Asian Glastonbury. You'll find urban, experimental and classical music, circus, dance, comedy, food and children's events. *Gunnersbury Park, Ealing, W3 (7387 1203, www.londonmela.org). Acton Town or South Ealing tube. Date late Aug.*

Notting Hill Carnival
Two million people stream to Europe's largest street party, full of the aromas, colours and music of the Caribbean. Massive mobile sound systems dominate the streets with whatever bass-heavy party music is currently hip, but there's plenty of tradition from the West Indies too: calypso music and a spectacular costumed parade. *Notting Hill, W10, W11 (www.thenottinghillcarnival.com). Ladbroke Grove, Notting Hill Gate or Westbourne Park tube. Date end Aug.*

Tetley's Challenge Cup Final
Rugby league is mainly played in the north of the country, but for the Challenge Cup Final the north heads south, bringing boisterous, convivial crowds to Wembley Stadium for some hard-tackling action. *Wembley Stadium, Stadium Way, Middx HA9 0WS (www.thechallenge cup.com). Wembley Park tube or Wembley Stadium rail. Date late Aug.*

Autumn

London African Music Festival
A wonderfully eclectic affair, held over a fortnight in September. Recent performers have included Osibisa (from Ghana), Modou Toure (Senegal) and Hanisha Solomon (Ethiopia). *7328 9613, www.joyfulnoise.co.uk. Date Sept.*

Mayor's Thames Festival
A giant party along the Thames, this month of events is London's largest free arts festival. It's a family-friendly mix of carnival, pyrotechnics, art installations, river events and live music alongside craft and food stalls. The highlight is the last-night lantern procession and firework finale. *Between Westminster Bridge & Tower Bridge (7928 8998, www.thamesfestival.org). Blackfriars or Waterloo tube/rail. Date Sept.*

Tour of Britain
Join spectators on the streets of the capital for a stage of British cycling's biggest outdoor event. *www.thetour.co.uk. Date mid Sept.*

Open-House London
An opportunity to snoop round other people's property, for one weekend only. Taking part are more than 500 palaces, private homes, corporate skyscrapers, pumping stations and bomb-proof bunkers, many of which are normally closed to the public. *3006 7008, www.open-city.org.uk. Date mid Sept.*

London Literature Festival
LLF combines superstar writers with stars from other fields: architects, comedians, sculptors and cultural theorists examining anything from queer literature to migration. *Southbank Centre, Belvedere Road, South Bank, SE1 8XX (7960 4200, www.southbankcentre.co.uk). Waterloo tube/rail. Date mid Sept-mid Oct.*

Great River Race
More interesting than the Boat Race (*see p10*), the Great River Race sees an exotic array of around 300 traditional rowing boats (including skiffs, canoes, dragon boats and Cornish gigs) from around the globe racing in the 'river marathon'. Hungerford Bridge, the Millennium Bridge and Tower Bridge are all good viewpoints. *River Thames, from Millwall Docks, Docklands, E14, to Ham House, Richmond, Surrey TW10 (8398 8141, www.greatriverrace.co.uk). Date late Sept.*

TOP TIP!
In the know
The Lord Mayor is a City officer, with no power outside the City of London; don't confuse him with the Mayor of London, currently Boris Johnson.

American Football: NFL
The NFL took a regular-season fixture out of North America for the first time in 2007 – it was a huge success, and immediately became an annual fixture. In 2012, the Jacksonville Jaguars announced they would play a home game here for the four seasons up to 2016.
Wembley Stadium, Stadium Way, Middx HA9 0WS (www.nfluk.com). Wembley Park tube or Wembley Stadium rail. Date late Sept-early Nov.

London Film Festival
The most prestigious of the capital's film fests – in fact, the key film festival in the country. Nearly 200 new British and international features are screened each year, mainly at the BFI Southbank and Leicester Square's Vue West End, and there's always a smattering of red-carpet events for the celebrity-crazed.
www.bfi.org.uk/lff. Date Oct.

Big Draw
Engage with your inner artist at the month-long Big Draw, using anything from pencils to vapour trails.
8351 1719, www.campaign fordrawing.org. Date Oct.

Dance Umbrella
A leading international dance festival, featuring a range of events (many free) in unusual spaces.
7407 1200, www.danceumbrella.co.uk. Date Oct.

Diwali
A celebration of the annual Festival of Light by Hindu, Jain and Sikh communities.
Trafalgar Square, WC2 (7983 4100, www.london.gov.uk). Charing Cross tube/rail. Date Oct/Nov.

Winter

London to Brighton Veteran Car Run
The London to Brighton is a sedate procession southwards by around 500 pre-1905 cars. The first pair trundles off at sunrise (around 7-8.30am), but you can catch them a little later crossing Westminster Bridge, or view them on a closed-off Regent's Street the day before the event (11am-3pm).
Departs Serpentine Road, Hyde Park, W2 2UH (01483 524433, www.veterancarrun.com). Hyde Park Corner tube. Date early Nov.

Bonfire Night
Britain's best-loved excuse for setting off fireworks: the celebration of Guy Fawkes's failure to blow up the Houses of Parliament in 1605. Check the dedicated page at www.timeout.com for a list of public displays – several are free, and many charge only a nominal entry fee.
Date 5 Nov & around.

Lord Mayor's Show
This big show marks the traditional presentation of the new Lord Mayor

STUNNING CEREMONIALS
London is a past master when it comes to parades and marching bands.

On alternate days from 10.45am (www.royal.gov.uk has the details), one of the five Foot Guards regiments lines up in scarlet coats and tall bearskin hats in the forecourt of Wellington Barracks; at exactly 11.27am, the soldiers start to march to Buckingham Palace, joined by their regimental band, to relieve the sentries there in a 45-minute ceremony for the Changing of the Guard.

Not far away, at Horse Guards Parade in Whitehall, the Household Cavalry mounts the guard daily at 11am (10am on Sunday). Although this ceremony isn't as famous as the one at Buckingham Palace, it's more visitor-friendly: the crowds aren't as thick as they are at the palace, and spectators aren't held far back from the action by railings. After the old and new guard have stared each other out in the centre of the parade ground, you can nip through to the Whitehall side to catch the departing old guard perform their hilarious dismount choreography, a synchronised, firm slap of approbation to the neck of each horse before the gloved troopers all swing off.

As well as these near-daily ceremonies, London sees other, less frequent parades on a far grander scale. The most famous is Trooping the Colour, staged to mark the Queen's official birthday on 13 June (her real birthday is in April). At 10.45am, the Queen rides in a carriage from Buckingham Palace to Horse Guards Parade to watch the soldiers, before heading back to Buckingham Palace for a midday RAF flypast and the impressive gun salute from Green Park.

Also at Horse Guards, on 3-4 June, a pageant of military music and precision marching begins at 7pm when the Queen (or another royal) takes the salute of the 300-strong drummers, pipers and musicians of the Massed Bands of the Household Division. This is known as Beating the Retreat (7414 2271, tickets 7839 5323).

for approval by the monarch's justices. The Lord Mayor leaves Mansion House in a fabulous gold coach at 11am, along with a colourful procession of floats and marchers. At 5pm, there's a fireworks display on the river.
7332 3456, www.lordmayorsshow.org. Date early Nov.

Remembrance Sunday Ceremony
Held on the Sunday nearest to 11 November – the day World War I ended – this solemn commemoration honours those who died fighting in the World Wars and later conflicts; 2014 marks the centenary of the start of the Great War. The Queen, the prime minister and other dignitaries lay poppy wreaths at the Cenotaph. A two-minute silence at 11am is followed by a service of remembrance.

Cenotaph, Whitehall, Westminster, SW1, Charing Cross tube/rail. Date early Nov.

London Jazz Festival
Covering most bases, from trad to free improv, this is the biggest London jazz festival of the year, lasting the best part of a fortnight.
7324 1880, www.londonjazz festival.org.uk. Date mid Nov.

Christmas Celebrations
Of the big stores, Fortnum & Mason (*see p83*) still creates enchantingly old-fashioned Christmas windows. Otherwise, though, skip the commercialised lights on Oxford and Regent's streets and head, instead, for smaller shopping areas such as St Christopher's Place, Bond Street, Marylebone High Street and

Covent Garden. It's traditional to sing carols beneath a giant Christmas tree in Trafalgar Square – an annual gift from Norway in gratitude for Britain's support during World War II – but you can also join in a mammoth singalong at the Royal Albert Hall (*see p106*), enjoy the starry choral Christmas Festival at St John Smith Square (*see p106*) or an evocative carol service at one of London's historic churches. London's major cathedrals all, naturally, celebrate Christmas with splendid liturgies and music.
Covent Garden (0870 780 5001, www.coventgardenlondonuk.com); Bond Street (www.bondstreet association.com); St Christopher's Place (www.stchristophersplace.com); Marylebone High Street (7580 3163, www.marylebonevillage.com); Trafalgar Square (www.london. gov.uk). Date Nov-Dec.

Spitalfields Music Winter Festival
See *p11* Spitalfields Music Summer Festival.
Date Dec.

New Year's Eve Celebrations
The focus of London's public celebrations has officially moved from overcrowded Trafalgar Square to the full-on fireworks display launched from the London Eye and rafts on the Thames. You have to get there early for a good view. Those with stamina can take in the New Year's Day Parade in central London the next day (www.londonparade.co.uk).
Date 31 Dec.

London International Mime Festival
Theatrical magic in many forms, from haunting visual theatre to puppetry for adults.
www.mimefest.co.uk. Date Jan.

Chinese New Year Festival
Launch the Years of the Sheep (19 Feb 2015) and Monkey (8 Feb 2016) in style at celebrations that engulf Chinatown and Leicester Square. Lion dancers gyrate alongside a host of acts in the grand parade to Trafalgar Square, while the restaurants of Chinatown get even more packed than usual.
Around Gerrard Street, Chinatown, W1, Leicester Square, WC2, & Trafalgar Square, WC2 (7851 6686, www.thelondonchinatown.org.uk). Leicester Square or Piccadilly Circus tube. Date Feb.

Six Nations Tournament
This major rugby union tournament for the northern hemisphere teams sees England take on Wales, Scotland, Ireland, France and Italy, with some fixtures played at home in the code's headquarters at Twickenham.
Twickenham Stadium, Rugby Road, Middx TW1 1DZ (8892 2000, www.rfu.com). Dates Feb-Mar.

Explore

Museums, galleries and great days out

Explore

Tower Bridge. *See p27.*

Discover London

An ancient city with a relish for 21st-century architecture.

London has some amazing sights. We're blessed with no fewer than four UNESCO World Heritage Sites: the **Tower of London** (*see p27*), the cluster of fine buildings round Parliament Square in **Westminster** (*see p38*), soothing **Kew Gardens** (*see p52*) and, above all, the numerous attractions in **Greenwich** (*see p50*).

Yet none of them are even London's key tourist destination. That honour is reserved for the **South Bank** (*see right*), where you'll find Tate Modern, Shakespeare's Globe and the Southbank Centre, although the three world-class museums of **South Kensington** (*see p43*) – the V&A, Natural History Museum and Science Museum – run it close. And now we've neglected the **British Museum** (*see p29*), Trafalgar Square and the **National Gallery** (*see p38*)… the problem with London is there's too much to see. Time to get out there to start enjoying the overload.

The South Bank

An estimated 14 million people come this way each year, and it's easy to see why. Between the **London Eye** and **Tower Bridge**, the south bank of the Thames offers a two-mile procession of diverting, largely state-funded arts and entertainment venues and events, while also affording breezy, traffic-free views of the succession of landmarks ('Big Ben', St Paul's, the Tower of London) on the other bank.

THE SOUTH BANK

Thanks to the sharp turn the Thames makes around Waterloo, **Lambeth Bridge** lands you east of the river, not south, opposite the Tudor gatehouse of **Lambeth Palace**. Since the 12th century, it's been the official residence of the Archbishops of Canterbury.

The palace is not normally open to the public, except on holidays. The church next door, St Mary at Lambeth, is now the **Garden Museum**.

The benches along the river here are great for viewing the **Houses of Parliament** opposite, before things get crowded after **Westminster Bridge**, where London's major riverside tourist zone begins. Next to the bridge is **County Hall**, once the seat of London government, but currently home to the **Sea Life London Aquarium** and the **London Dungeon**; they are due to be joined in summer 2015 by a new DreamWorks attraction **Shrek's Far Far Away Adventure**. In front of all three attractions, in full view of the lovely new **Jubilee Gardens**, the wheel of the **London Eye** rotates.

South, beyond Waterloo, the **Imperial War Museum** will come into its own for the 2014 centenary of the start of World War I.

Garden Museum

The world's first horticulture museum fits neatly into the old church of St Mary's. A 'belvedere' gallery contains the permanent collection of artworks, antique gardening tools and horticultural memorabilia, while the ground floor is used for interesting temporary exhibitions. In the small back garden, the replica of a 17th-century knot garden was created in honour of John Tradescant, intrepid plant hunter and gardener to Charles I; Tradescant is buried here. A stone sarcophagus contains the remains of Captain William Bligh of the mutinous HMS *Bounty*. *Lambeth Palace Road, SE1 7LB (7401 8865, www.gardenmuseum. org.uk). Lambeth North tube. Open 10.30am-5pm Mon-Fri; 10.30am-4pm Sat. Admission £7.50; £3-£6.50 reductions; free under-16s.*

Hayward

This versatile gallery has no permanent collection, but runs a good programme of temporary exhibitions, with a particular taste for participatory installations: Antony Gormley's fog-filled chamber for 'Blind Light', a rooftop rowing boat for group show 'Psycho Buildings', a kind of informal university for the arts at the 'Wide Open School', even an exhibition that contained no art. There are free contemporary exhibitions at the inspired Hayward Project Space, and the Concrete café-bar. *Southbank Centre, Belvedere Road, SE1 8XX (0844 875 0073, www. southbankcentre.co.uk). Embankment tube or Waterloo tube/rail. Open 10am-6pm Mon-Wed, Sat, Sun; 10am-8pm Thur, Fri. Admission varies; check website for details.*

Imperial War Museum

IWM London has decided on a major refit – by Foster & Partners architects – in time for the centenary of World War I, which means it will be closed until July 2014. The museum provides a compelling, frequently hard-hitting history of armed conflict since World War I, as well as many excellent, long-running temporary exhibitions aimed at children. *Lambeth Road, SE1 6HZ (7416 5000, www.iwm.org.uk). Lambeth North tube or Elephant & Castle tube/rail. Open 10am-6pm daily. Admission free. Special exhibitions prices vary.*

London Dungeon

This jokey celebration of torture, death and disease (book your tickets online to keep prices down) takes visitors through a dry-ice fog past gravestones and hideously rotting corpses to experience the nastiest sides of the last 1,000 years of London history. Expect an actor-led medley of boils, projectile vomiting, worm-filled skulls and scuttling rats for the Black Death, gory skulduggery from the likes of Guy Fawkes and Jack the Ripper, and any number of unspeakable royals doing unspeakable things – Henry VIII prominent among them. *County Hall, Westminster Bridge Road, SE1 7PB (0871 423 2240, www.the dungeons.com). Westminster tube or Waterloo tube/rail. Open Term-time 10am-5pm Mon-Wed, Fri; 11am-5pm Thur; 10am-6pm Sat, Sun. School holidays 10am-7pm Mon-Wed, Sat, Sun; 11am-7pm Thur. Admission £18.50-£25.20; £16.95-£19.80 reductions.*

London Eye

Here only since 2000, the Eye is already up there with Tower Bridge and 'Big Ben' as one of the capital's most postcard-friendly tourist assets. Assuming you choose a clear day, a 30-minute circuit on the Eye affords predictably great views of the city. Take a few snaps from the comfort of your pod and your sightseeing's done.

The Eye was planned as a temporary structure but its removal now seems unthinkable. Indeed, the wheel's popularity is such that owner Merlin Entertainments has seen fit to future-proof its investment: each of the wheel's 32 pods (one for every London borough) now has a touchscreen to guide you around the vista. *Jubilee Gardens, SE1 7PB (0870 500 0600, www.londoneye.com). Westminster tube or Waterloo tube/rail. Open times vary; check website for details. Admission £19.95; £12.60-£17.96 reductions; free under-4s.*

Sea Life London Aquarium

This is one of Europe's largest aquariums and a huge hit with kids. The inhabitants are grouped by geographical origin, beginning with the Atlantic, where blacktail bream swim alongside the Thames Embankment. The 'Rainforests of the World' exhibit has introduced poison arrow frogs, crocodiles and piranhas. The Ray Lagoon is still popular, though touching the friendly flatfish is no longer allowed (it's bad for their health). Starfish, crabs and anenomes can be handled in special open rock pools instead, and the clown fish still draw crowds. There's a mesmerising Seahorse Temple, a tank full of turtles and enchanting Gentoo peguins. The centrepieces, though, are the massive Pacific and Indian Ocean tanks, with menacing sharks quietly circling fallen Easter Island statues. *County Hall, Westminster Bridge Road, SE1 7PB (0871 663 1678, tours 7967 8007, www.sealife.co.uk). Westminster tube or Waterloo tube/ rail. Open term-time 10am-7pm daily. School holidays 10am-8pm daily. Admission £21.60; £15.90 reductions; £75 family; free under-3s.*

BANKSIDE

In Shakespeare's day, the area known as Bankside was the centre of bawdy Southwark, neatly located just beyond the jurisdiction of the City fathers. As well as playhouses such as the Globe and the Rose, there were the famous 'stewes' (brothels) presided over by the Bishops of Winchester, who made a tidy income from the fines they levied on the area's 'Winchester Geese' (or, in common parlance, prostitutes). There's less drinking, carousing and mischief-making here these days, but the area's cultural heritage remains alive thanks to the reconstructed **Shakespeare's Globe** and, pretty much next door to it, **Tate Modern**, a former power station that's now a powerhouse of 20th-century art.

Spanning the river in front of the Tate, the **Millennium Bridge** opened

British Museum

Critic's choice

1 **British Museum** A superb gathering of artefacts from every civilisation. *See p29.*

2 **Museum of London** The whole story of London, from its ancient beginnings to our own strange times. *See p24.*

3 **Tate Britain** Compellingly rehung, the first Tate is ace for British art. *See p40.*

4 **Houses of Parliament & Westminster Abbey** The birthplace of modern democratic government. *See p38.*

5 **Sir John Soane's Museum** An eccentric little house where every corner is crammed with treasures. *See p28.*

6 **St James's Park** Within sight of Buckingham Palace (*see p41*) play pelicans, ducks and swans. *See p41.*

7 **Victoria & Albert Museum** Astoundingly rich collection of design and applied art through the ages. *See p45.*

8 **Royal Botanic Gardens, Kew** Leafy acres and huge Victorian glasshouses. *See p52.*

9 **Greenwich** A world-class maritime museum, a planetarium and a sailing ship. *See p50.*

10 **Wellcome Collection** Bizarre, artful and information-packed exhibitions. *See p30.*

The South Bank & Bankside

BRITISH MUSEUM: DAN BRECKWOLDT

© Copyright Time Out Group 2014

in 2000, when it became the first new Thames crossing in London since Tower Bridge (1894). Its early days were fraught with troubles; after just two days, the bridge was closed because of a pronounced wobble, and didn't reopen until 2002. Its troubles long behind it, the bridge is an elegant structure; a 'ribbon of steel' in the words of its conceptualists, architect Lord Foster and sculptor Anthony Caro. Cross it and you're at the foot of the stairs leading up to St Paul's Cathedral (*see p23*); to its left, the massively refurbished Blackfriars rail station not only has a brand-new entrance on the south bank of the river, but runs train platforms right across the river on the podiums of an earlier version of **Blackfriars Bridge**.

Continue east past the Globe and Southwark Bridge and you'll reach the **Anchor Bankside** pub (34 Park Street, 7407 1577). Built in 1775 on the site of an even older inn, the Anchor has, at various points, been a brothel, a chapel and a ship's chandlers. The outside terrace offers fine river views.

All that's left of the Palace of Winchester, home of successive bishops, is the ruined rose window of the Great Hall on Clink Street. It stands next to the site of the bishops' former Clink prison, where thieves, prostitutes and debtors all served their sentences; it's now the **Clink Prison Museum** (1 Clink Street, SE1 9DG, 7403 0900, www.clink.co.uk). Around the corner is the entrance to the wine showcase **Vinopolis** (1 Bank End, SE1 9BU, 7940 8300, www.vinopolis. co.uk). At the other end of Clink Street, St Mary Overie's dock contains a terrific full-scale replica of Sir Francis Drake's ship, the **Golden Hinde**.

Golden Hinde
This meticulous replica of Sir Francis Drake's 16th-century flagship is thoroughly seaworthy: the ship has even reprised the privateer's circumnavigatory voyage. You can visit by means of a self-guided tour, but if you've got kids it's much more fun to join in on a 'living history' experience (some overnight): participants to dress in period clothes, eat Tudor fare and learn the skills of a seafarer; book well in advance. *Pickfords Wharf, Clink Street, SE1 9DG (7403 0123, www.goldenhinde.com). London Bridge tube/rail. Open 10am-5.30pm daily. Admission £7; £5 reductions; £20 family; free under-4s.*

Shakespeare's Globe
The original Globe Theatre, where many of William Shakespeare's plays were first staged and which he co-owned, burned to the ground in 1613 during a performance of *Henry VIII*. Four centuries later, it was rebuilt not far from its original site, using construction methods and materials as close to the originals as possible, and is now open to the public for tours throughout the year (allow 90 minutes for the visit). During matinées, the tours go to the site of the Rose (21 New Globe Walk, SE1 9DT, 7261 9565,

www.rosetheatre. org.uk), built by Philip Henslowe in 1587 as the first theatre on Bankside; red lights show its original position.

Under the adventurous artistic directorship of Dominic Dromgoole, the Globe is also a fully operational theatre. From 23 April, conventionally regarded as the Bard's birthday, into early October, Shakespeare's plays and the odd new drama are performed. There's also a brand-new Jacobean theatre on the premises, which opened in 2014; *see p106* **Shadow Plays**. For more on the Globe as a theatre, *see p107.*
21 New Globe Walk, SE1 9DT (7401 9919, www.shakespeares-globe.org). Blackfriars tube/ rail or Southwark tube. Open Exhibition Feb-Oct 9am-5.30pm daily; Nov-Jan 10am-5.30pm daily. Globe Theatre tours daily, Rose Theatre tours Mar-Oct, check website for details. Admission £13.50; £8-£12 reductions; £36 family; free under-5s.

Tate Modern
Thanks to its industrial architecture, this powerhouse of modern art is awe-inspiring even before you enter. Built after World War II as Bankside Power Station, it was designed by Sir Giles Gilbert Scott, architect of Battersea Power Station. The power station shut in 1981; nearly 20 years later, it opened as an art museum, and has enjoyed spectacular popularity ever since. The gallery attracts five million visitors a year to a building intended for half that number; the first fruits of work on the immensely ambitious, £215m TM2 extension opened in 2012: the Tanks, so-called because they occupy vast, subterranean former oil tanks, will stage performance and film art. As for the rest of the extension, a huge new origami structure, designed by Herzog & de Meuron (who were behind the original conversion), will gradually unfold above the Tanks until perhaps 2016, but the work won't interrupt normal service in the main galleries.

Tate Modern

In the main galleries themselves, the original cavernous turbine hall will be used to jaw-dropping effect once again from 2015 when a new series of sponsored installations begins. Beyond, the permanent collection draws from the Tate's collections of modern art (international works from 1900) and features heavy hitters such as Matisse, Rothko and Beuys – a genuinely world-class collection, expertly curated. There are vertiginous views down inside the building from outside the galleries, which group artworks by movement (Surrealism, Minimalism, Post-war abstraction) rather than theme. *Bankside, SE1 9TG (7887 8888, www.tate.org.uk). Blackfriars tube/ rail or Southwark tube. Open 10am-6pm Sun-Thur; 10am-10pm Fri, Sat. Tours 11am, noon, 2pm, 3pm daily. Admission free. Temporary exhibitions vary.*

BOROUGH TO TOWER BRIDGE
At Clink Street, the route cuts inland, skirting the edge of the district of Borough. The landmark here is the Anglican **Southwark Cathedral** (7367 6700, www.southwark.anglican. org), formerly St Saviour's and before that the monastic church of St Mary Overie. Shakespeare's brother Edmund was buried in the graveyard; there's a monument to the playwright inside. Just south of the cathedral you'll find the roof of **Borough Market**, a busy food market dating from the 13th century, although with its new glass-fronted premises you'd hardly think so. There's still plenty of Victorian ironwork to enjoy. The market is wholesale only for most of the week, but hosts London's foodiest public food market (*see p75*) on Thursdays, Fridays and Saturdays (when it gets very crowded). It's surrounded by good places to eat and drink. Not far away, the **George** (77 Borough High Street, 7407 2056), London's last surviving galleried

coaching inn, still peers out gently over its cobbled courtyard.

With the **London Dungeon** having moved from Tooley Street to County Hall (*see p16*), fans of gore should head to similarly jokey **London Bridge Experience** (2-4 Tooley Street, SE1 2SY, http:// thelondonbridgeexperience.com) or the more interesting and no less grisly **Old Operating Theatre, Museum & Herb Garret**, with its body parts and surgical implements. But nothing can compete with the monstrous, impressive 1,016-foot **Shard** development, towering over London Bridge station.

Design Museum
Exhibitions in this former banana warehouse focus on modern and contemporary design. The temporary shows run from major installations to design artefacts, from architects' travel photographs to retrospectives of key theorists of the built environment. The Blueprint Café has a balcony overlooking the Thames, and the museum shop is excellent. The museum has ambitious plans to move to the former Commonwealth Institute in west London, which should be completed in 2015. *Shad Thames, SE1 2YD (7403 6933, www.designmuseum.org). Tower Hill tube or London Bridge tube/rail. Open 10am-5.45pm daily. Admission £17; £8.50-£12 reductions; free under-12s.*

HMS Belfast
This 11,500-ton 'Edinburgh' class large light cruiser is Europe's last surviving big gun World War II warship. A floating branch of the Imperial War Museum, it makes an unlikely playground for children, who tear around its complex of gun turrets, bridge, decks and engine room. The *Belfast* was built in 1938, ran convoys to Russia, supported the Normandy Landings and helped UN forces in Korea before being decommissioned. *Morgan's Lane, Tooley Street, SE1 2JH (7940 6300, www.iwm.org.uk). London Bridge tube/rail. Open Mar-Oct 10am-6pm daily. Nov-Feb 10am-5pm daily. Admission £15.50; £12.40 reductions; free under-16s (must be accompanied by an adult).*

Old Operating Theatre, Museum & Herb Garret
The tower that houses this reminder of the surgical practices of the past used to be part of the chapel of St Thomas's Hospital. The operating tools on display look more like torture implements, and there are bunches of herbs and quack remedies a plenty. Visitors enter via a vertiginous spiral staircase to inspect a pre-anaesthetic operating theatre dating from 1822, with tiered viewing seats for students. *9A St Thomas's Street, SE1 9RY (7188 2679, www.thegarret.org.uk). London Bridge tube/rail. Open 10.30am-5pm daily. Admission £6.50; £3.50-£5 reductions; £13.90 family; free under-6s. No credit cards.*

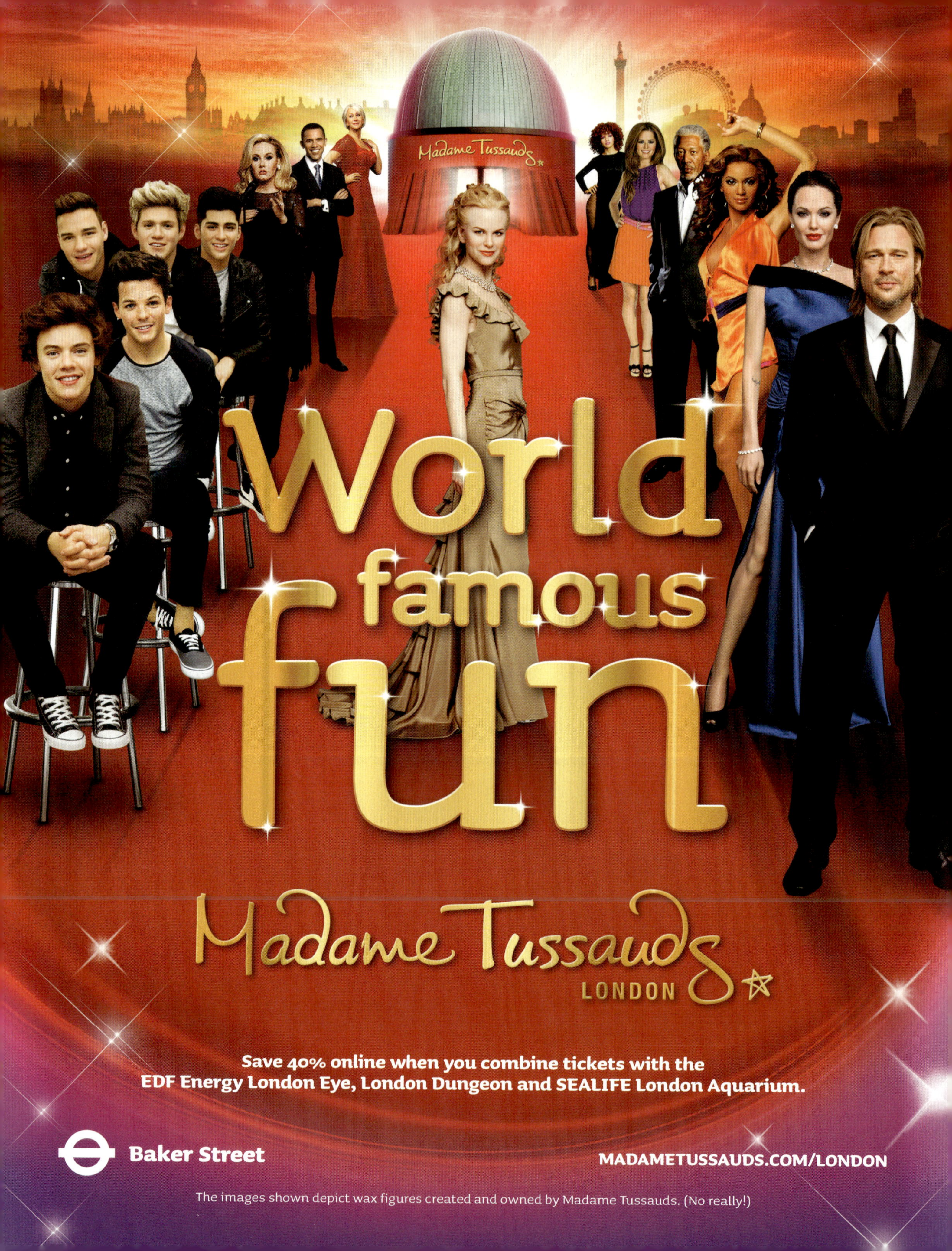
Madame Tussauds
World famous fun
Madame Tussauds
LONDON
Save 40% online when you combine tickets with the
EDF Energy London Eye, London Dungeon and SEALIFE London Aquarium.
Baker Street
MADAMETUSSAUDS.COM/LONDON
The images shown depict wax figures created and owned by Madame Tussauds. (No really!)

Shard

You can't miss the Shard – which is, after all, the point. It shoots into the sky 'like a shard of glass' – to use the words of its architect, Renzo Piano. Already by 2010, when the building was still a skeleton, it had overtaken One Canada Square ('Canary Wharf') as London's tallest building. And it kept going: in 2011, it became the tallest building in the EU, but even then had still to reach its full height. Finally, in 2012, when its 217-foot, 500-tonne spire was winched into place, it topped out at 1,016 feet. The Shard's claims to be the tallest are relative: it's beaten in Moscow, the Arab Emirates and across South-east Asia. But this slim, slightly irregular pyramid is the centrepiece of views from right across London. High-speed lifts whisk passengers up to stunning 360°, 40-mile views.

32 London Bridge Street, SE1 9SS (www.theviewfromtheshard.com). London Bridge tube/rail. Open 10am-8.30pm daily. Admission £24.95; £18.95 reductions; free under-4s.

The City

The City's current fame merely as the financial heart of London does no justice to its 2,000-year history. Here Romans founded the city they called Londinium, building a bridge to the west of today's London Bridge. Here were a forum-basilica, an amphitheatre, public baths and the defensive wall that still defines what we now call the Square Mile (an area, in fact, of 1.21 square miles).

Although the City has just over 9,000 residents, 330,000 people arrive each weekday to work as bankers, lawyers and traders, taking over 85 million square feet of office space. Tourists come, too, to see St Paul's Cathedral and the Tower of London, but there's much else besides. No area of London offers quite so much in so small a space. Roman ruins? Medieval? Iconic 21st-century offices? You're in the right place.

TEMPLE & THE INNS OF COURT

At its western end, the arterial Strand (*see p31*) becomes Fleet Street at **Temple Bar**, the City's ancient western boundary and once the site of Wren's great gateway (now in Paternoster Square beside St Paul's; *see p23*). A newer, narrower, but still impressive wyvern-topped monument marks the original spot. The area has long been linked to the law, and here stands the splendid neo-Gothic **Royal Courts of Justice**. On the other side of the road, stretching almost to the Thames, are the several courtyards that make up **Middle Temple** (7427 4800, www.middle temple.org.uk) and **Inner Temple** (7797 8250, www.innertemple.org.uk), two of the Inns of Court that provided training and lodging for London's medieval lawyers. Anybody may visit the grounds, but access to the grand, collegiate buildings is for lawyers and barristers only.

The site was formerly the headquarters of the Knights Templar, an order of warrior monks founded in the 12th century to protect pilgrims to the Holy Land. The Templars built the original **Temple Church** in 1185, but fell foul of Catholic orthodoxy during the Crusades and their order was disbanded.

Almost due south of Temple Bar, alongside Middle Temple, is the fabulous **Two Temple Place**.

Two Temple Place

The pale Portland stone exterior and oriel windows here are handsome – but the interior is extraordinary. Built as an estate office in 1895 to the close specifications of William Waldorf Astor, Two Temple Place now opens to the public three months a year with great exhibitions of 'publicly-owned art from around the UK', arranged by an up-and-coming curator. Ring the bell and you're warmly welcomed by volunteers into a house with decor that combines sublime, extravagant craftsmanship with a thorough lack of interest in coherence: there's even a medieval-style Great Hall on the first floor. During exhibitions, there's a good café on the ground floor.

2 Temple Place, WC2R 3BD (7836 3715, www.twotempleplace.org). Temple tube. Open Late Jan-mid Apr 10am-4.30pm Mon, Thur-Sat; 10am-9pm Wed; 11am-4.30pm Sun. Admission free.

FLEET STREET

Without Fleet Street, the daily newspaper might never have been invented. Named after the vanished River Fleet, Fleet Street was a major artery for the delivery of goods into the City, including the first printing press, which was installed behind **St Bride's Church** (Fleet Street, EC4Y 8AU, 7427 0133, www.st brides.com) in 1500 by William Caxton's assistant, Wynkyn de Worde, who also set up a bookstall in St Paul's churchyard. London's first daily paper, the *Daily Courant*, rolled off the presses in 1702; in 1712, Fleet Street saw the first of innumerable libel cases when the *Courant* leaked the details of a private parliamentary debate.

By the end of World War II, half a dozen offices were churning out scoops and scandals. Most of the newspapers moved away after

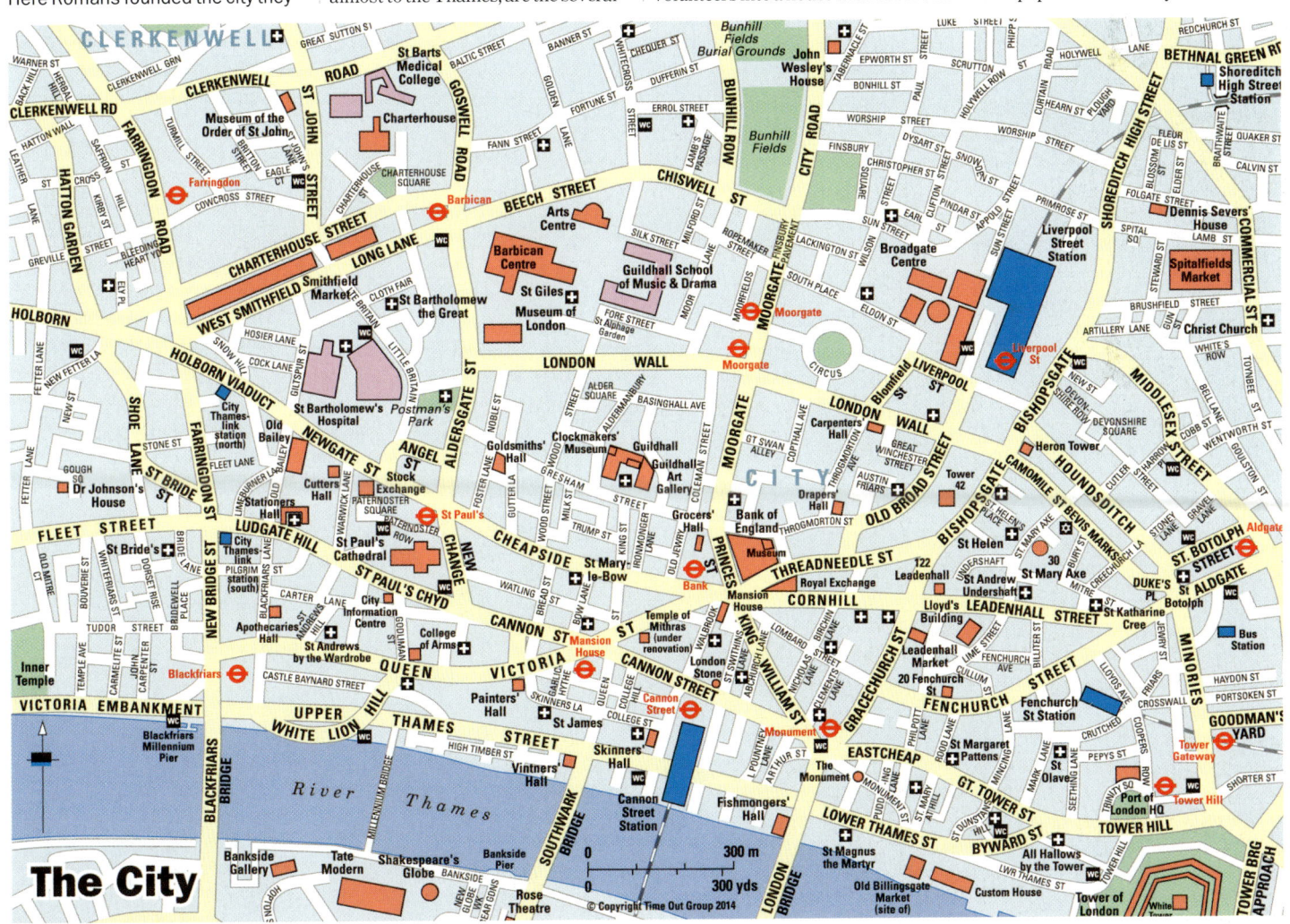

The City

Rupert Murdoch won his war with the print unions in the 1980s; the last of the news agencies, Reuters, finally followed suit in 2005. Until recently, the only periodical published on Fleet Street was a comic, the much-loved *Beano*. However, in 2009, left-wing weekly the *New Statesman* moved into offices around the corner from Fleet Street on Carmelite Street. Relics from the media days remain: the Portland-stone **Reuters building** (no.85), the Egyptian-influenced **Daily Telegraph building** (no.135) and the sleek, black **Daily Express building** (nos.121-128), designed by Owen Williams in the 1930s and arguably the finest art deco building in London.

At the top of Fleet Street itself is the church of **St Dunstan-in-the-West** (7405 1929, www.stdunstaninthe west.org; closed Sat & Sun, except for services), where the poet John Donne was rector in the 17th century. The church was rebuilt in the 1830s, but the eye-catching clock dates to 1671. The clock's chimes are beaten by clockwork giants who are said to represent Gog and Magog, tutelary spirits of the City. Next door, no.186 is the house where Sweeney Todd, the 'demon barber of Fleet Street', reputedly murdered his customers before selling their bodies to a local pie shop. The legend, sadly, is a porky pie: Todd was invented by the editors of a Victorian penny dreadful in 1846.

Fleet Street was always known for its pubs; half the newspaper editorials in London were composed over liquid lunches, but there were also more literary imbibers. If you walk down Fleet Street, you'll see **Ye Olde Cheshire Cheese** (no.145, 7353 6170), a favourite of Dickens and Yeats. In its heyday, it hosted the bibulous literary salons of Dr Samuel Johnson, who lived nearby at 17 Gough Square (**Dr Johnson's House**). It also had a famous drinking parrot, the death of which prompted hundreds of newspaper obituaries. At no.66, the **Tipperary** (7583 6470) is the oldest Irish pub outside Ireland: it sold the first pint of Guinness on the British mainland in the 1700s.

Dr Johnson's House

Famed as the author of one of the first – as well as the most significant and unquestionably the wittiest – dictionaries of the English language, Dr Samuel Johnson (1709-84) also wrote poems, a novel and one of the earliest travelogues, an acerbic account of a tour of the Western Isles with his biographer James Boswell. You can tour the stately Georgian townhouse off Fleet Street where Johnson came up with his inspired definitions – 'to make dictionaries is dull work,' was his definition of the word 'dull'. The house has been open to the public since 1911. *17 Gough Square, off Fleet Street, EC4A 3DE (7353 3745, www.dr johnsonshouse.org). Chancery Lane tube or Blackfriars tube/rail. Open May-Sept 11am-5.30pm Mon-Sat. Oct-Apr 11am-5pm Mon-Sat. Tours by arrangement, groups of 10 or more*

only. Admission £4.50; £1.50-£3.50 reductions; £10 family; free under-5s. Tours £3.50. No credit cards.

ST PAUL'S & AROUND

The towering dome of **St Paul's Cathedral** is, excluding the 'Big Ben' clocktower, probably the definitive symbol of traditional London. It was also an architectural two fingers to the Great Fire and, later, the Nazi bombers that pounded the city in 1940 and 1941. Beside the cathedral, you enter redeveloped Paternoster Square through Wren's statue-covered **Temple Bar**. It once stood at the intersection of Fleet Street and the Strand (*see p31*), marking the boundary between the City of London and neighbouring Westminster. The archway was dismantled as part of a Victorian road-widening programme in 1878 and became a garden ornament for a country estate in Hertfordshire, before being installed in 2004 in its current location, as the gateway between St Paul's and Paternoster Square. South of St Paul's, steps cascade down to the **Millennium Bridge**, which spans the river to Tate Modern (*see p18*).

East of the cathedral is the huge **One New Change** shopping mall (*see p76*). Designed by French starchitect Jean Nouvel, its most interesting aspects are a gash that gives views straight through the building to St Paul's and, for a fine roof-level panorama, the sixth-floor public terrace and bar-restaurant. Meekly hidden among the alleys behind it, you'll find narrow Bow Lane. At one end sits **St Mary-le-Bow** (7248 5139, www.stmaryle bow.co.uk; open 7am-6pm Mon-Thur; 7am-4pm Fri), built by Wren between 1671 and 1680. The church bell's peals once defined anyone born within earshot as a true Cockney. At the other end of Bow Lane is **St Mary Aldermary** (7248 9902, www.moot. uk.net; open 9am-6pm Mon-Fri). With a pin-straight spire designed by Wren's office, this was the only Gothic church by him to survive World War II. Inside, there's a fabulous moulded plaster ceiling and original wooden sword rest (London parishioners carried arms until the late 19th century). Roman coins are sold here to fund renovation work, and it's home to a modern monastic community.

Built on the site of the infamous Newgate prison to the north-west of the cathedral is the Central Criminal Court, known to almost everyone as **Old Bailey** (corner of Newgate Street & Old Bailey, EC4M 7EH, 7248 3277, www.cityoflondon.gov.uk). A remnant of the prison's east wall can be seen in Amen Corner, but it is the gilded statue of blind (meaning impartial) justice on the roof that marks out Britain's most famous criminal court, site of Oscar Wilde's trial, among many others.

St Paul's Cathedral

The first cathedral to St Paul was built on this site in 604, but fell to Viking marauders. Its Norman replacement, a magnificent Gothic structure with a 490ft spire (taller than any London building until the 1960s), burned in the Great Fire. The current church was commissioned in 1673 from Sir Christopher Wren as the centrepiece of London's resurgence from the ashes. Modern buildings now encroach on the cathedral from all sides, but the passing of three centuries has done nothing to diminish the appeal of London's most famous cathedral. Start with the exterior. Over the last decade, a £40m restoration project has painstakingly removed most of the Victorian grime from the walls and the extravagant main façade looks as brilliant today as it must have when the last stone was placed in 1708. The vast open spaces of the interior contain memorials to national heroes such as Wellington and Lawrence of Arabia. There are also more modern works, including a Henry Moore sculpture and temporary Arts Project displays of major contemporary art. The Whispering Gallery, inside the dome, is reached by 259 steps from the main hall; the acoustics here are so good that a whisper can be bounced clearly to the other side of the dome. Steps continue up to first the Stone Gallery (119 tighter, steeper steps), with high external balustrades, then outside to the Golden Gallery (152 steps), with its wonderful, giddying views.

Before leaving St Paul's, head down to the maze-like crypt (through a door whose frame is decorated with skull and crossbones), which contains a shop and café and memorials to such dignitaries as Alexander Fleming, William Blake and Admiral Lord Nelson, whose grand tomb is right beneath the centre of the dome. To one side is the small, plain tombstone of Christopher Wren himself, inscribed with the epitaph, 'Reader, if you seek a monument, look around you'.

As well as tours of the main cathedral and self-guided audio tours (which are free), you can join tours of the Triforium, visiting the library and Wren's 'Great Model' (pre-book on 7246 8357, £22 incl admission). *Ludgate Hill, EC4M 8AD (7236 4128, www.st pauls.co.uk). St Paul's tube. Open 8.30am-4pm Mon-Sat. Galleries, crypt & ambulatory 9.30am-4.15pm Mon-Sat. Tours of cathedral & crypt 10am, 11am, 1pm, 2pm Mon-Sat. Admission Cathedral, crypt & gallery (incl tour) £16; £7-£14 reductions; £39 family; free under-6s.*

NORTH TO SMITHFIELD

North of St Paul's Cathedral on Foster Lane is **St Vedast-alias-Foster** (7606 3998; open 8am-5.30pm Mon-Fri; 11am-4pm Sat), another finely proportioned Wren church, restored

after World War II using spare trim from other churches in the area. Off nearby Aldersgate Street, peaceful **Postman's Park** contains the Watts Memorial to Heroic Sacrifice: a wall of ceramic plaques, each of which commemorates a heroic but doomed act of bravery.

Further west on Little Britain is **St Bartholomew-the-Great**, founded along with **St Bartholomew's Hospital** in the 12th century. Popularly known as Bart's, the hospital treated air-raid casualties throughout World War II; shrapnel damage from German bombs is still visible on the exterior walls. Scottish nationalists now come here to lay flowers at the monument to William Wallace, executed in front of the church on the orders of Edward I in 1305. Just beyond St Bart's is the fine ironwork of Smithfield Market.

NORTH OF LONDON WALL

From St Bart's, the road known as **London Wall** runs east to Bishopsgate, following the approximate route of the old Roman walls. Tower blocks have sprung up here like daisies, but the odd lump of weathered stonework can still be seen poking up between the office blocks, marking the path of the old City wall. You can patrol the remaining stretches of the wall, with panels (some barely legible) pointing out highlights on a route of two miles. The walk starts near the **Museum of London** and runs to the Tower of London.

The area north of London Wall was reduced to rubble by German bombs in World War II. In 1958, the City of London and London County Council clubbed together to buy the land for the construction of 'a genuine residential neighbourhood, with schools, shops, open spaces and amenities'. What Londoners got was the **Barbican**, a vast concrete estate of 2,000 flats that feels a bit like a university campus after the students have gone home. Casual visitors may get the eerie feeling they have been miniaturised and transported into a giant architect's model, but design enthusiasts recognise the Barbican – with its landmark saw-toothed towers – as a wonderful example of 1970s Brutalism.

The main attraction here is the Barbican arts complex, with its library, cinema, theatre and concert hall, plus an art gallery and the Barbican Conservatory (open noon-5pm Sun & bank hols), a steamy greenhouse full of tropical plants. Marooned amid the towers is the only pre-war building in the vicinity: the restored 16th-century church of **St Giles Cripplegate** (7638 1997, www.stgilescripplegate.com; open 11am-4pm Mon-Fri), where Oliver Cromwell was married and John Milton interred.

North-east of the Barbican on City Road is **Bunhill Fields**, the nonconformist cemetery where William Blake, the preacher John Bunyan and novelist Daniel Defoe are buried.

TOP TIP!

Save your pennies
As soon as you arrive – get an **Oyster card** (*see p120*). For the tube, buses and the DLR, Oyster pay-as-you-go fares are always the cheapest.

Museum of London

A five-year, £20m refurbishment came to completion in 2010 with the unveiling of a thrilling lower-ground-floor gallery that covers the city from 1666 to the present day. The new space features everything from an unexploded World War II bomb, suspended in a room where the understated and very moving testimony of ordinary Blitz survivors is screened, to clothes by the late Alexander McQueen. There are displays and brilliant interactives on poverty (an actual debtor's cell has been reconstructed, complete with graffiti), finance, shopping and 20th-century fashion, including a recreated Georgian pleasure garden, with mannequins that sport Philip Treacy masks and hats. The museum's biggest obstacle had always been its location: the entrance is two floors above street level, hidden behind a dark and rather featureless brick wall. To solve this, a new space was created on the ground floor, allowing one key exhibit – the Lord Mayor's gold coach – to be seen from outside.

Upstairs, the chronological displays begin with 'London Before London', where artefacts include flint axes from 300,000 BC, found near Piccadilly, and the bones of an aurochs. 'Roman London' includes an impressive reconstructed dining room complete with mosaic floor. Windows overlook a sizeable fragment of the City wall, whose Roman foundations have clearly been built upon many times over the centuries. Sound effects and audio-visual displays illustrate the medieval, Elizabethan and Jacobean city, with particular focus on the plague and the Great Fire.
150 London Wall, EC2Y 5HN (7001 9844, www.museumoflondon.org.uk). Barbican or St Paul's tube. Open 10am-6pm daily. Admission free; suggested donation £5.

St Paul's Cathedral. See p23.

BANK & AROUND

Above Bank station, seven streets come together to mark the symbolic heart of the Square Mile, ringed by some of the most important buildings in the City. Constructed from steely Portland stone, the Bank of England, the Royal Exchange and Mansion House form a stirring monument to the power of money: most decisions about the British economy are still made within this small precinct. Few places in London have quite the same sense of pomp and circumstance.

Easily the most dramatic building is the **Bank of England**, founded in 1694 to fund William III's war against the French. It's a fortress, with no accessible windows and just one public entrance (leading to the **Bank of England Museum**). The outer walls were designed in 1788 by Sir John Soane, whose own museum can be seen in Holborn (*see p28 **Sir John Soane's Museum***). Millions have been stolen from its depots elsewhere in London, but the bank itself has never been robbed. Today, it's responsible for printing the nation's banknotes and setting the base interest rate. On the south side of the junction is the Lord Mayor of London's official residence, **Mansion House** (7626 2500, www.cityoflondon.gov.uk, group visits by written application to Diary Office, Mansion House, Walbrook, EC4N 8BH, or by phone), an imposing neoclassical building constructed by George Dance in 1753. It's the only private residence in the country to have its own court and prison cells for unruly guests. Just behind Mansion House is the superbly elegant church of **St Stephen Walbrook** (7626 9000, www.ststephenwalbrook.net; open 10am-4pm Mon-Fri), built by Wren in 1672. Its gleaming domed, coffered ceiling was borrowed from Wren's original design for St Paul's; other features include an incongruous modernist altar, sculpted by Sir Henry Moore.

To the east of Mansion House is the **Royal Exchange**. It's the Parthenon-like former home of the London Stock Exchange, founded back in 1565 to facilitate the newly invented trade in stocks and shares with Antwerp. In 1972, the exchange shifted to offices on Threadneedle Street, thence to Paternoster Square in 2004; today, the Royal Exchange houses expensive shops and restaurants.

South-east of Bank on Lombard Street is Hawksmoor's striking, twin-spired church of **St Mary Woolnoth** (7626 9701; open 9.30am-4.30pm Mon-Fri), squeezed in between what were 17th-century banking houses. Only their gilded signboards now remain, a hanging heritage artfully maintained by the City's planners. The gilded grasshopper at 68 Lombard Street is the heraldic emblem of Sir Thomas Gresham, who founded the Royal Exchange and Gresham College.

A short walk down Queen Victoria Street leads to the eroded foundations of the **Temple of Mithras**, built by Roman soldiers in AD 240-250 - the remains are rather unimpressive.

Further south, on Cannon Street, is the **London Stone,** easily missed and preserved behind a grille in the wall. Depending on who you talk to, it marks the Romans' measuring point for distances across Britain, it's a druidic alter or it's just a lump of rock. Nearby on College Hill is the late Wren church of **St Michael Paternoster Royal** (7248 5202; open 9am-5pm Mon-Fri), the final resting place of pantomime hero and real-life Lord Mayor, Richard 'Dick' Whittington.

North-west of the Bank of England is the **Guildhall**, the City of London headquarters. 'Guildhall' can either describe the original banqueting hall or the cluster of buildings around it, of which the **Guildhall Art Gallery**, the **Clockmakers' Museum** (Aldermanbury, EC2V 7HH, 7332 1868, www.clockmakers.org) and the church of **St Lawrence Jewry** (7600 9478, www.stlawrencejewry.org.uk; open 8am-5pm Mon-Fri), opposite the hall, are also open to the public. St Lawrence is another restored Wren, with an impressive gilt ceiling. Within, you can hear the renowned Klais organ at lunchtime organ recitals (usually from 1pm Tue).

Glance north along Wood Street to see the isolated tower of **St Alban**, built by Wren in 1685 but ruined in World War II and now an eccentric private home. At the end of the street is **St Anne & St Agnes** (7606 4986; open 10.30am-5pm Mon-Fri, Sun), laid out in the form of a Greek cross.

Bank of England Museum

Housed inside the former Stock Offices of the Bank of England, this engaging and surprisingly lively museum explores the history of the national bank. As well as ancient coins and original artwork for British banknotes, the museum offers a rare chance to lift nearly 30lbs of gold bar (you reach into a secure box, closely monitored by CCTV). After a three-month refurb in early 2014, the museum emerged with a new display of curiosities gathered from the bank's vaults.
Entrance on Bartholomew Lane, EC2R 8AH (7601 5545, www.bankofengland.co.uk/museum). Bank tube/DLR. Open 10am-5pm Mon-Fri. Admission free. No credit cards.

Guildhall Art Gallery

The City of London's gallery contains numerous dull or unimpressive portraits of royalty and long-gone mayors, but also some wonderful surprises, including a brilliant Constable, some superbly camp Pre-Raphaelite works and a number of absorbing paintings of London, from moving depictions of war and melancholy working streets to the likes of the grandiloquent (and never-enacted) George Dance plan for a new London Bridge. The collection's centrepiece is the massive *Siege of Gibraltar* by John Copley, which spans two entire storeys of the gallery. A sub-basement contains the scant remains of London's 6,000-seater Roman amphitheatre, built around AD 70.
Guildhall Yard, off Gresham Street, EC2P 2EJ (7332 3700, www.guildhall-art-gallery.org.uk). Bank tube/DLR. Open 10am-5pm Mon-Sat; noon-4pm Sun. Admission free. Temporary exhibitions £5; £3 reductions; free under-16s.

MONUMENT & THE TOWER OF LONDON

From Bank, King William Street runs south-east towards London Bridge, passing the small square containing the **Monument** (*see p27*). South on Lower Thames Street is the moody-looking church of **St Magnus the Martyr** (Lower Thames Street, EC3R 6DN, 7626 4481, www.stmagnusmartyr.org.uk); nearby are several relics from the days when this area was a busy port, including the old Customs House and Billingsgate Market, London's main fish market until 1982 (it was relocated to east London, in the shadow of Canary Wharf).

North of the Monument along Gracechurch Street is the atmospheric **Leadenhall Market**, constructed in 1881 by Horace Jones (who also built the market at Smithfield). The vaulted roof was restored to its original Victorian finery in 1991 and City workers come here in droves to lunch at the pubs, cafés and restaurants, including the historic Lamb Tavern. Fantasy fans may recognise the market as Diagon Alley in *Harry Potter & the Philosopher's Stone*.

Behind the market is Lord Rogers's high-tech **Lloyd's of London** building, constructed in 1986, with all its ducts, vents, stairwells and lift shafts on the outside, like an oil rig dumped in the heart of the City. Rogers has a lofty new building – 122 Leadenhall (the **Cheesegrater**) – directly opposite. The original **Lloyd's Register of Shipping**, decorated with evocative bas-reliefs of sea monsters and nautical scenes, is on Fenchurch Street, where the next

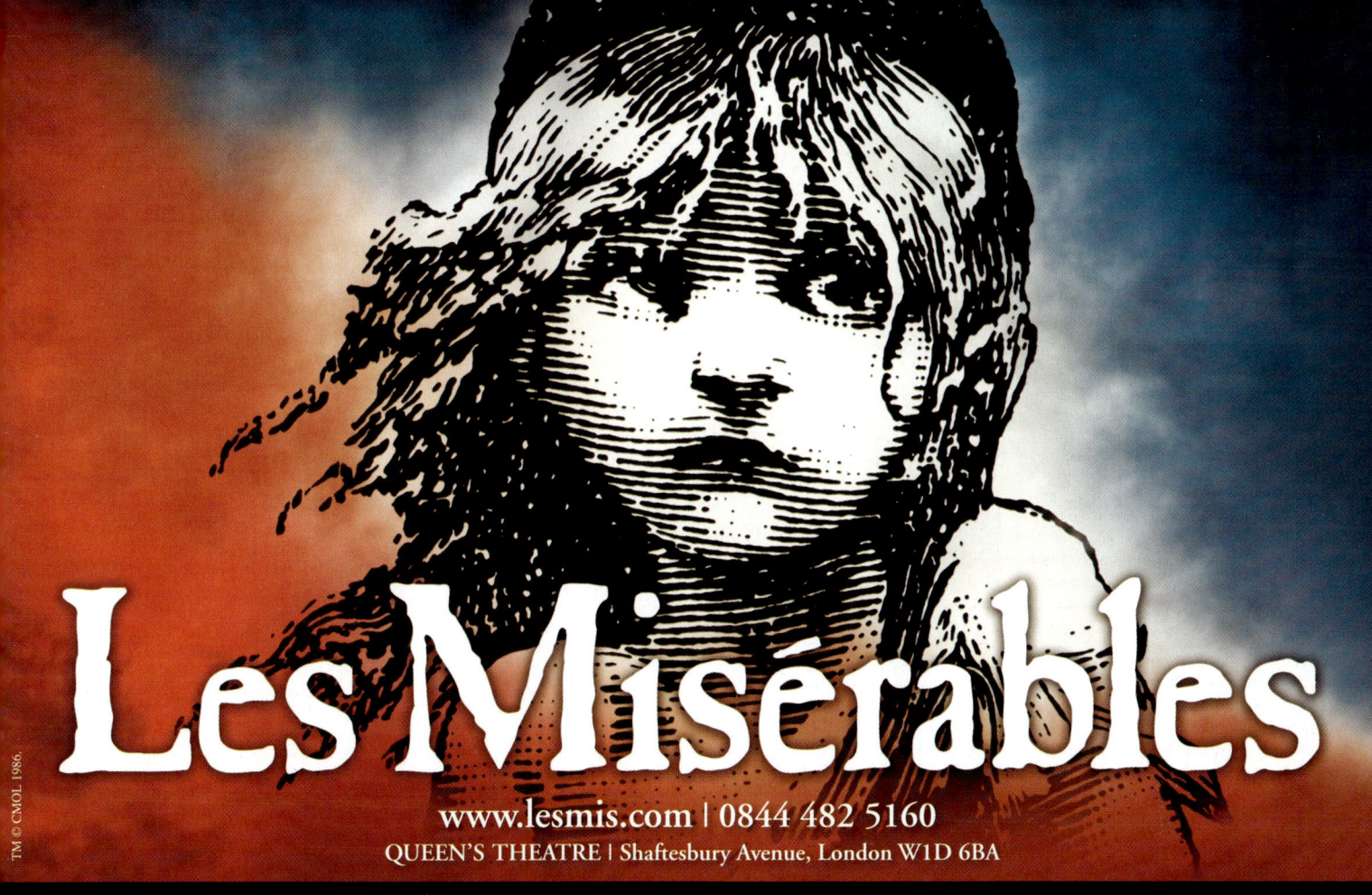

EXPERIENCE
THE GREATEST SPORTS STADIUM
IN THE UNITED KINGDOM

From England's World Cup victory in 1966, the Live Aid concert in 1985, Barcelona's UEFA Champion's League triumph in 2011 or the tradition of the FA Cup Final, the Wembley Stadium Tour gives you the chance to relive your greatest moments, and create some new ones, as you go behind-the-scenes at the most famous stadium in the world.

- Sense the history in the England Changing Rooms
- Take Roy Hodgson's hot-seat in the Press Room
- Take photographs from some of the best views in the stadium
- Experience the tension of the Players Tunnel
- Climb the 107 sacred Trophy Winner's steps
- Visit the Royal Box and get your hands on the FA Cup

Your guided tour will include access to Wembley's treasures such as the 1966 World Cup crossbar, the Jules Rimet Trophy, the original flag from London's 1948 Olympic Games & The FA 150 Exhibition.

TO FIND OUT MORE LOG ONTO wembleystadium.com/tours

18 STAFFORD TERRACE
THE SAMBOURNE FAMILY HOME

Remarkably well-preserved and complete with its original interior decoration and contents, 18 Stafford Terrace is one of London's best kept secrets.

VISITS ARE BY GUIDED TOURS ONLY
Tickets: Adult £8, Concessions £6 and Under 16s £3.

Public Tours:
Wednesdays 11.15am and 2.15pm, Saturdays and Sundays at 11.15am, 1.00pm, 2.15pm and 3.30pm. Weekend afternoon tours are led by costumed actors.

Private Group Tours:
For adults and schools groups, different rates apply,
Please call 020 7471 9158 for more information.

Address: 18 Stafford Terrace, London W8 7BH

LEIGHTON HOUSE MUSEUM
EAST MEETS WEST

One of the most extraordinary houses in the country. Built as a studio-house by the eminent artist Frederic, Lord Leighton from 1864, it grew to become a 'Private Palace of Art', famous for its exotic interiors and the collections of one and decorative art that were displayed through its rooms.

Open daily from 10am-5.30pm, except Tuesdays.
Tickets: £6 Adult and Concessions £3.

Public Tours:
One-hour tours of the house are available every Wednesday and Sunday at 3.00pm.

Address: 12 Holland Park Road, London W14 8LZ

CONTACT BOTH HOUSES ON:

Tel: 020 7602 3316
Email: museums@rbkc.gov.uk

www.rbkc.gov.uk/museums

 Leighton House

 @RBKCLeightonH

THE ROYAL BOROUGH OF
KENSINGTON AND CHELSEA

in the sequence of distinctive new City skyscrapers has emerged: Rafael Viñoly's **20 Fenchurch Street** (www.20fenchurchstreet.co.uk), nicknamed the Walkie Talkie due to its distinctive top-heavy shape. South of Fenchurch Street, on Eastcheap (derived from the Old English *ceap* meaning 'barter'), is Wren's **St Margaret Pattens**, with an original 17th-century interior.

Several more of the City's tallest buildings are nearby. To the north, the ugly and rather dated **Tower 42** (25 Old Broad Street) was the tallest building in Britain until the construction of One Canada Square in Docklands in 1990. And topped out at 755 feet (including a radio mast), **Heron Tower** (110 Bishopsgate, www.herontower.com) became the City's tallest building at the end of 2009. Its 46 storeys include bar-restaurants, complete with outdoor terraces, and reached by an external, glass-sided lift. A rival, 945-foot monster called the **Pinnacle** has been begun on Bishopsgate – but is currently stalled. Also on Bishopsgate, behind Tower 42, is **Gibson Hall**, ostentatious former offices of the National Provincial Bank of England.

A block south, St Mary Axe is an insignificant street named after a vanished church that is said to have contained an axe used by Attila the Hun to behead English virgins. It is now known for Lord Foster's **30 St Mary Axe**, arguably London's finest modern building. The building is known as 'the **Gherkin**', for reasons that are obvious. On curved stone benches either side of 30 St Mary Axe are inscribed the 20 lines of Scottish poet Ian Hamilton Finlay's 'Arcadian Dream Garden', a curious counterpart to Lord Foster's building. Nearby are two medieval churches that survived the Great Fire: **St Helen's Bishopsgate** (Great St Helen's, EC3A 6AT, 7283 2231, www.st-helens.org.uk) and, just off Leadenhall, St Andrew Undershaft.

The north end of St Mary Axe intersects with two interesting streets. The more northerly, Houndsditch, is where Londoners threw dead dogs and other rubbish in medieval times – the ditch ran outside the London Wall, dividing the City from the East End. The southerly one is Bevis Marks, home to the superbly preserved **Bevis Marks Synagogue** (7626 1274; open 10.30am-2pm Mon, Wed, Thur; 10.30am-1pm Tue, Fri; 10.30am-12.30pm Sun), founded in 1701 by Sephardic Jews fleeing the Spanish Inquisition. Services are still held in Portuguese as well as Hebrew. There's a kosher restaurant here too – **Restaurant 1701** (7621 1701, www.restaurant1701.co.uk).

South along Bevis Marks are **St Botolph's-without-Aldgate** (Aldgate High Street, EC3N 1AB, 7283 1670, www.stbotolphs.org.uk) and the tiny stone church of **St Katharine Cree** (7488 4318; open 9am-5pm Mon-Fri) on Leadenhall Street, one of only eight churches to survive the Great

Fire. Inside is a memorial to Sir Nicholas Throckmorton, Queen Elizabeth I's ambassador to France, who was imprisoned for treason on numerous occasions, despite – or perhaps because of – his friendship with the temperamental queen.

Further south, towards the Tower of London, streets and alleys have evocative names: Crutched Friars, Savage Gardens, Pepys Street and the like. The famous diarist lived in nearby Seething Lane and observed the Great Fire of London from All Hallows by the Tower (Byward Street, EC3R 5BJ, 7481 2928, www.ahbtt.org.uk). Pepys is buried in the church of St Olave (8 Hart Street, 7488 4318, www.sanctuaryinthecity.net), nicknamed 'St Ghastly Grim' by Dickens due to the skulls above the entrance.

Marking the eastern edge of the City, the **Tower of London** was the palace of the medieval kings and queens of England. Home to the Crown Jewels and the Royal Armoury, it is mobbed by visitors seven days a week. Overlooking the Tower from the north, beside the tube station, **Trinity Square Gardens** is a humbling memorial to the tens of thousands of merchant seamen killed in the two World Wars, and across the road is a small square in which London's druids celebrate each spring equinox with an elaborate ceremony. Just beyond is one of the City's finest Edwardian buildings: the former **Port of London HQ** at 10 Trinity Square, with a huge neoclassical façade and gigantic statues symbolising Commerce, Navigation, Export, Produce and Father Thames. Long-term plans are afoot to make this into a superluxury hotel. Next door is **Trinity House**, the home of the General Lighthouse Authority, founded by Henry VIII for the upkeep of shipping beacons along the river.

At the south-east corner of the Tower is **Tower Bridge**, built in 1894 and still London's most distinctive bridge. Used as a navigation aid by German bombers, it escaped the firestorm of the Blitz. East across Bridge Approach is **St Katharine Docks**, the first London docks to be formally closed. Today it's a marina, with pubs and restaurants.

Monument

One of 17th-century London's most important landmarks, the Monument is a magnificent Portland stone column, topped by a landmark golden orb with more than 30,000 fiery leaves of gold. The Monument was designed by Sir Christopher Wren and his (often overlooked) associate Robert Hooke as a memorial to the Great Fire. The world's tallest free-standing stone column, it measures 202ft from the ground to the tip of its golden flames, exactly the distance east to Farriner's bakery in Pudding Lane, where the fire is supposed to have begun on 2 September 1666. The viewing platform is surrounded by a lightweight mesh cage, but the views

are great – you have to walk 311 steps up the internal spiral staircase to enjoy them, though.
Monument Street, EC3R 8AH (7626 2717, www.themonument.info). Monument tube. Open Oct-Mar 9.30am-5pm daily; Apr-Sept 9.30am-5.30pm daily. Admission £3; £1.50-£2 reductions; free under-5s. No credit cards.

Tower Bridge Exhibition

Opened in 1894, this is the 'London Bridge' that wasn't sold to America. Originally powered by steam, the drawbridge is now opened by electric rams when big ships need to venture upstream (check when the bridge is next due to be raised on the bridge's website or follow the feed on Twitter). The bridge is looking resplendent after a three-year restoration, completed in 2011. An entertaining exhibition on its history is displayed in the old steamrooms and the west walkway.
Tower Bridge, SE1 2UP (7403 3761, www.towerbridge.org.uk). Tower Hill tube or Tower Gateway DLR. Open Apr-Sept 10am-6pm daily. Oct-Mar 9.30am-5.30pm daily. Admission £8; £3.40-£5.60 reductions; £12.50-£18 family; free under-5s.

Tower of London

Despite the exhausting crowds and long climbs up barely accessible, narrow stairways, this is one of Britain's finest historical attractions. Who would not be fascinated by a close-up look at the crown of Queen Victoria or the armour (and prodigious codpiece) of King Henry VIII? The buildings of the Tower span 900 years of – mostly violent – history, and the bastions and battlements house a series of interactive displays on the lives of British monarchs, and the often painful deaths of traitors. There's easily enough to do here to fill a whole day, which makes the steep entry price pretty good value, and it's worth joining one of the highly recommended and entertaining free tours led by the Yeoman Warders (or Beefeaters).

Make the Crown Jewels your first stop, and as early in the day as you can: if you wait until you've pottered around a few other things the queues are usually immense. Beyond satisfyingly solid vault doors, you get to glide along a set of travelators past such treasures of state as the Monarch's Sceptre and the Imperial State Crown, worn by the Queen for the opening of Parliament.

The other big draw is the Royal Armoury in the central White Tower, with its swords, armour, poleaxes, halberds, morning stars (spiky maces) and other gruesome tools for separating human beings from their body parts. Kids are entertained by swordsmanship games, coin-minting activities and even a child-sized longbow. The garderobes (medieval toilets) also seem to appeal.

Back outside, Tower Green – where executions of prisoners of noble birth were carried out, continuing until 1941

– is marked by a poem and a stiff glass pillow, sculpted by poet and artist Brian Catling. Overlooking the green, Beauchamp Tower, dating to 1280, has an upper floor full of intriguing graffiti by the prisoners (including Anne Boleyn, Rudolf Hess and the Krays).

Towards the entrance, the 13th-century Bloody Tower is another must-see that gets overwhelmed by numbers later in the day. The ground floor is a reconstruction of Sir Walter Raleigh's study, the upper floor details the fate of the Princes in the Tower. In the riverside wall is the unexpectedly beautiful Medieval Palace, with its reconstructed bedroom and throne room, and spectacularly complex stained glass in the private chapel.
Tower Hill, EC3N 4AB (0844 482 7777, www.hrp.org.uk). Tower Hill tube or Tower Gateway DLR. Open Mar-Oct 10am-5.30pm Mon, Sun; 9am-5.30pm Tue-Sat. Nov-Feb 10am-4.30pm Mon, Sun; 9am-4.30pm Tue-Sat. Admission £21.45; £10.75-£18.15; £57.20 family; free under-5s.

A sharp left turn out of Holborn tube and then another left leads into the unexpectedly lovely Lincoln's Inn Fields. Surely London's largest square (indeed, it's more of a park), it's blessed with gnarled oaks casting dappled shade over a tired bandstand. On the south side, the neoclassical façade of the Royal College of Surgeons hides the **Hunterian Museum** (Royal College of Surgeons, 35-43 Lincoln's Inn Fields, WC2A 3PE (7869 6560, www.rcseng.ac.uk/museums), full of grisly anatomical remains; facing it from the north is the magical **Sir John Soane's Museum** (*see p28*).

East of the square lies **Lincoln's Inn** (7405 1393, www.lincolnsinn.org.uk), one of the city's four Inns of Court. Its grounds are open to the public and offer an odd mix of Gothic, Tudor and Palladian buildings. On nearby Portsmouth Street lies the Old Curiosity Shop (nos.13-14, WC2A 2ES, 7405 9891, www.curiosityuk.com), its timbers apparently known to Charles Dickens, but now selling fashion shoes. Nearby, Gray's Inn Road runs north alongside the second Inn of Court. The sculpted gardens at **Gray's Inn** (7458 7800, www.graysinn.org.uk), dating to 1606, are open weekdays, noon-2.30pm.

There are glittering displays on **Hatton Garden**, the city's jewellery and diamond centre. It's no distance to walk but a million miles in nature from the Cockney fruit stalls and sock merchants of the market on **Leather Lane** (10am-2.30pm Mon-Fri). Further on is **Ely Place**, its postcode absent from the street sign as a result of it technically falling under the jurisdiction of Cambridgeshire. The church garden of ancient **St Etheldreda** (14 Ely Place, EC1N 6RY, 7405 1061, www.stetheldreda.com) produced strawberries so delicious that they made the pages of Shakespeare's *Richard III*. The 16th-century **Ye Olde Mitre** (*see p70*) is an atmospheric pub, hidden down a barely marked alley.

Few places encapsulate London's capacity for reinvention quite like Clerkenwell, to the north of Smithfield, an erstwhile religious centre that takes its name from the parish clerks who once performed Biblical mystery plays on its streets. The most lasting holy legacy is that of the 11th-century knights of the Order of St John; the remains of their priory can still be seen at St John's Gate, a crenellated gatehouse that dates from 1504 and is home to the **Museum & Library of the Order of St John** (St John's Gate, St John's Lane, EC1M 4DA, 7324 4005, www.museumstjohn.org.uk). Industrial dereliction and decay were the theme until property development in the 1980s and '90s turned Clerkenwell into a desirable area. Check out the colourful strip of **Exmouth Market**, with its food stalls, restaurants, bars and shops.

Sir John Soane's Museum
When he wasn't designing notable buildings (among them the original Bank of England), Sir John Soane (1753-1837) obsessively collected art, furniture and architectural ornamentation. In the 19th century, he turned his house into a museum to which, he said, 'amateurs and students' should have access. The result is this perfectly amazing place. Much of the museum's appeal derives from the domestic setting. The modest rooms were modified by Soane with ingenious devices to channel and direct daylight, and to expand space, including walls that open out like cabinets to display some of his many paintings (Turner, Hogarth, Canaletto). The Breakfast Room has a beautiful domed ceiling, inset with convex mirrors. The extraordinary Monument Court contains a sarcophagus of alabaster, so fine that it's almost translucent, that was carved for the pharaoh Seti I (1291-78 BC) and discovered in his tomb in Egypt's Valley of the Kings. There are also numerous examples of Soane's eccentricity, not least the cell for his imaginary monk 'Padre Giovanni'.
13 Lincoln's Inn Fields, WC2A 3BP (7405 2107, www.soane.org). Holborn tube. Open 10am-5pm Tue-Sat; 10am-5pm, 6-9pm 1st Tue of mth. Tours 11am Sat. Admission free; donations appreciated. Tours £15.

The West End

The 'West End' is a catch-all term for the area of London that any visitor would consider the centre – Covent Garden and the plays and musicals of Theatreland, Leicester Square and its movie palaces, louche Soho, Bloomsbury's marvellous British Museum, the shopping on Oxford Street and Regent Street, the statue of Eros in Piccadilly Circus and sedately wealthy Mayfair. That curious name, the West End, is easily explained: the original London was what is now still called the City; outside the city walls, lay the East and West Ends.

BLOOMSBURY

Bloomsbury's name is, prosaically, taken from 'Blemondisberi' – the manor ('bury') of William Blemond, who acquired the area in the 13th century. It remained rural until the 1660s, when the fourth Earl of Southampton built Bloomsbury Square around his house. The Southamptons intermarried with the Russells, the Dukes of Bedford; together, they developed the area as one of London's first planned suburbs.

Over the next two centuries, the group built a series of grand squares. **Bedford Square** (1775-80) is London's only complete Georgian square (regrettably, its central garden is usually closed to the public); huge **Russell Square** has been restored as a public park with a popular café. To the east, the cantilevered postwar **Brunswick Centre** is full of shops, flats, restaurants and a cinema. Nearby streets, particularly **Marchmont Street**, are some of the more characterful in the West End.

Bloomsbury's charm is the sum of its parts, best experienced on a meander through its bookshops (many on **Great Russell Street**) and pubs. The blue plaques are a *Who's Who* of literary modernists – TS Eliot, Virginia Woolf, WB Yeats – with a few interlopers from more distant history: Anthony Trollope (6 Store Street), Edgar Allan Poe (83 Southampton Row),and, of course, Dickens (48 Doughty Street; *see p29* **Charles Dickens Museum**).

On Bloomsbury's western border, Malet Street, Gordon Street and Gower Street are dominated by the **University of London**. The most notable building is Gower Street's University College, founded in 1826. Inside is the 'autoicon' of utilitarian philosopher and founder of the university Jeremy Bentham: his preserved cadaver, fully clothed, sits in a glass-fronted cabinet. The university's main library is housed in towering **Senate House** on Malet Street, one of the city's most imposing examples of monumental art deco.

South of the university sprawls the **British Museum**, the must-see of all London must-sees. Running off Great Russell Street, where you'll find the museum's main entrance, are three attractive parallel streets (Coptic, Museum and Bury) and, nearby, the **Cartoon Museum**; also close by, Bloomsbury Way is home to Hawksmoor's **St George's**

TOP TIP!
TV tours
There are daily tours of the BBC's HQ, but you'll need to book ahead on www.bbc.co.uk/shows andtours/tours – and under-9s are not admitted.

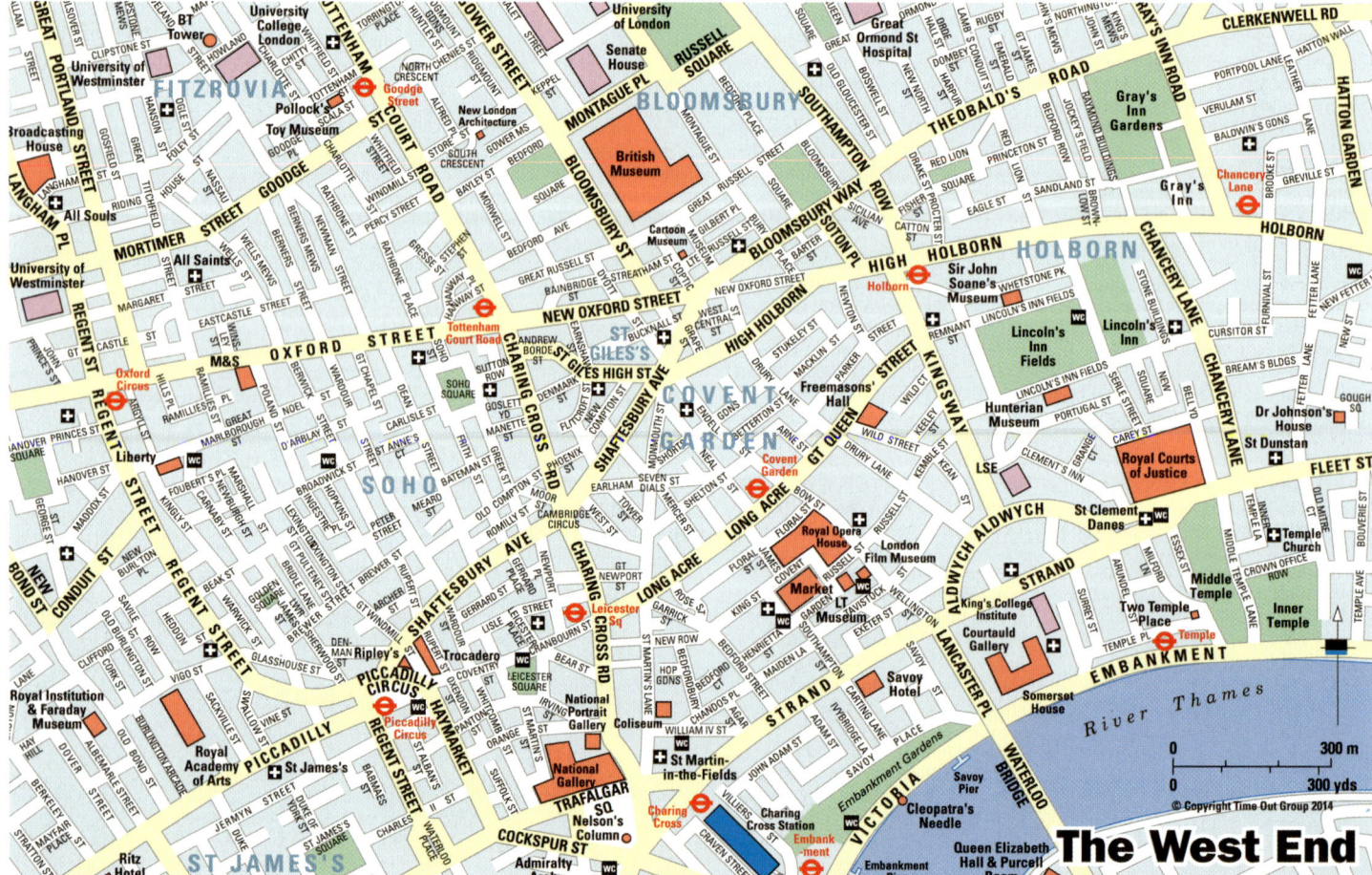

The West End

PETERBOROUGH

Read all about who's running the country

READERS OF NATIONAL NEWSPAPERS 1965-1995

The Times: Read by the people who run the country.

Daily Mirror: Read by the people who think they run the country.

The Guardian: Read by the people who think they should run the country.

Morning Star: Read by the people who think we should be run by another country.

Daily Mail: Read by the wives of the people who run the country.

Financial Times: Read by the people who own the country.

Daily Express: Read by the people who think the country should be run as it used to be run.

Daily Telegraph: Read by the people who think it still is.

The Sun: Read by the people who don't care who runs the country as long as she's got big breasts.

READERS OF NATIONAL NEWSPAPERS 1995-PRESENT

The Times: Read by the people who think Rupert Murdoch should run the country.

Daily Mirror: Read by the people who think they should run the country.

The Guardian: Read by the neo-socialists who actually do run the country.

Morning Star: Read by the people who think we should be run by any country other than America.

Daily Mail: Read by the people who pay for the country.

Financial Times: Read by the people who *should* pay but keep their wealth out of the country.

Daily Express: Read by the people who think the country should be run by pressure groups and think-tanks.

Daily Telegraph: Read by the people who know that it is.

The Sun: Read by the people who still don't care who runs the country, as long as she's got big breasts.

Submitted by Stephen Green, Great Missenden, Bucks.

Picture that!

of sorrow

ery, the earliest traces of humans in Europe north of the Alps were dated to about 500,000 years ago. They included flint artefacts and even human remains discovered in Bosgrove, West Sussex.

The flints show humans lived in Northern Europe 200,000 years earlier than was previously thought. Britain was connected to the European mainland and the climate was warm enough to be the home of lions, elephants and tigers.

Dr Mark Edmonds, Southsea, Hants.

QUESTION My father-in-law, a navigator/bomb aimer in World War II, says he went a bit astray on a training exercise and dropped a dummy bomb on a church in Burton-on-Trent. Was he pulling my leg?

FURTHER to the earlier answer, we didn't drop dummy bombs but we did 'sandbag' the Scottish village of Rhu, near Helensburgh, in 1942.

as an AC1 Flight Mechanic ned at Rhu, the RAF Marine aft Experimental Establish-. The un. was responsible ssessing and testing new boats.

t of the assessment was ing the take-off weight for aircraft — the weight being e up with sandbags. But these e the aircraft too heavy to , so the sandbags had to be wn overboard, which is where umble dogsbodies came into wn. Two of us were taken up

The hen night is *'l'enterrement de vie de jeune fille'*.

Julia Houston, Manchester.

IN CANADA, where packaging is marked in English and French, I came across this French alternative on a packet of what they call Flushable Wipes, and we call Moists: *'Serviettes rafraichissantes jetables dans la toilette.'* C'est la vie!

Nigel Power, Exeter.

QUESTION In a Christian cemetery in the old part of Tehran, Iran, there are the graves of more than 2,000 Polish men, women and children, who died at the same time in 1942. What happened?

FURTHER to the earlier answers, I was in Tehran from Christmas 1942 until April 1944. I was part of a cleansing and decontamination unit working for the hospitals.

The Polish General Anders visited our unit and paid us a compliment, remarking on what a good job we were doing, and said he hoped we could carry on, which we did until being disbanded in mid-1944.

As I was one of the youngest in our unit, I often wonder whether anyone else is still around. I would particularly like to hear from Basia Andgneska, a Polish girl from Krakow, who acted as our interpreter for her family.

Vic Laight, ex-Royal Army Ordnance Corp, Solihull.

Bloomsbury (7242 1979, www.st georgesbloomsbury.org.uk). Across from here, **Sicilian Avenue** is an Italianate, pedestrian precinct of colonnaded shops – take it in over a fine ale at the Holborn Whippet (3137 9937, www.holbornwhippet.com).

North-east of the British Museum, **Lamb's Conduit Street** is a convivial neighbourhood lined with interesting shops. At the north end of the street is **Coram's Fields** (see p93), a delightful children's park on the grounds of the former Foundling Hospital, now the beautiful **Foundling Museum**.

British Museum

Officially the country's most popular tourist attraction, the British Museum opened to the public in 1759 in Montagu House, which then occupied this site. The current building is a neoclassical marvel built in 1847 by Robert Smirke, one of the pioneers of the Greek Revival style. The most high-profile addition since then was Lord Foster's popular glass-roofed Great Court, open since 2000 and claimed to be 'the largest covered public square in Europe'. This £100m landmark surrounds the domed Reading Room, where Marx, Dickens, Darwin and Yeats once worked. In 2014, the museum added a new building to the east of the original premises, containing research and conservation labs, and the Sainsbury Exhibitions Gallery, which will host more of the fabulous, sell-out blockbuster shows (currently the Vikings) that have propelled the museum to the top of the visitor-number charts.

In the museum proper, star exhibits include ancient Egyptian artefacts – the Rosetta Stone on the ground floor (with a barely noticed, perfect replica in the King's Library), mummies upstairs – and Greek antiquities, including the marble friezes from the Parthenon known as the Elgin Marbles. Room 41 has just reopened, with a display of early medieval artefacts, including the famous Sutton Hoo treasure. Also upstairs, the Celts gallery has Lindow Man, killed in 300 BC and so well preserved in peat you can see his beard, while the Wellcome Gallery of Ethnography holds an Easter Island statue and regalia collected during Captain Cook's travels. The King's Library provides a calming home to the permanent exhibition 'Enlightenment: Discovering the World in the 18th Century', a 5,000-piece collection devoted to the extraordinary formative period of the museum. The remit covers science, archaeology and the natural world; the objects include a beautiful orrery.

You won't be able to see everything in one day, so buy a souvenir guide and pick out the showstoppers, or plan several visits. Highlights tours focus on specific aspects of the huge collection; Eye Opener tours offer specific introductions to world cultures.

Great Russell Street, WC1B 3DG (7323 8299, www.britishmuseum.org). Russell Square or Tottenham Court Road tube. Open Galleries 10am-5.30pm Mon-Thur, Sat, Sun; 10am-8.30pm Fri. Great Court 9am-6pm Mon-Thur, Sat; Sun; 9am-8.30pm Fri. Multimedia guides 10am-4.30pm Thur, Sat, Sun; 10am-7.30pm Fri. Eye Opener tours (40mins) phone for details. Admission free; donations appreciated. Temporary exhibitions prices vary. Multimedia guides £5; £3.50-£4.50 reductions.

Cartoon Museum

The best of British cartoon art is displayed on the ground floor of this former dairy. The displays start in the early 18th century, when high-society types back from the Grand Tour introduced the Italian practice of *caricatura* to polite company. From Hogarth, it moves through Britain's cartooning 'golden age' (1770-1830) to examples of wartime cartoons, ending up with modern satirists such as Gerald Scarfe and the wonderfully loopy Ralph Steadman. Upstairs is a celebration of UK comic art, with original 1921 *Rupert the Bear* artwork by Mary Tourtel and Leo Baxendale's Bash Street Kids.
35 Little Russell Street, WC1A 2HH (7580 8155, www.cartoonmuseum. org). Tottenham Court Road tube. Open 10.30am-5.30pm Mon-Sat; noon-5.30pm Sun. Admission £7; free-£5 reductions.

Charles Dickens Museum

London is scattered with plaques marking addresses where Dickens lived, but this is the only one to have been preserved as a museum. He lived here from 1837 to 1840, writing *Nicholas Nickleby* and *Oliver Twist* while in residence. Ring the doorbell to gain access to four floors of Dickensiana, collected over the years from various former residences. Some rooms are arranged as they might have been when he lived here; others deal with different aspects of his life, from struggling hack to famous performer. Recent refurbishment has created a pleasant downstairs café and good little shop.
48 Doughty Street, WC1N 2LX (7405 2127, www.dickensmuseum.com). Chancery Lane or Russell Square tube. Open 10am-5pm daily. Tours by arrangement. Admission £8; £4-£6 reductions; free under-6s.

Foundling Museum

The Foundling Museum recalls the social history of the Foundling Hospital, set up in 1739 by shipwright and sailor Thomas Coram. Securing royal patronage, he persuaded Hogarth and Handel to become governors; it was Hogarth who made the building Britain's first public art gallery; works by artists as notable as Gainsborough and Reynolds are on display. The most heart-rending display is a tiny case of mementoes that were all mothers could leave the children they abandoned.

GUIDED TOURS
You choose the mode of transport, we suggest a tour to suit.

London Kayak Tours

BY BICYCLE

London Bicycle Tour Company (1A Gabriel's Wharf, 56 Upper Ground, South Bank, SE1 9PP, 3318 3088, www.londonbicycle.com) runs a range of tours in central London, while **Capital Sport** (01296 631671, www.capital-sport.co.uk) offers gentle tours by the Thames.

BY BOAT

City Cruises: Red River Rover 7740 0400, www.citycruises.com. Rates from £15.30. Hop-on, hop-off river journeys.
Jason's Trip Canal Boats www.jasons.co.uk. Rates £14 return; £13 reductions. Narrow-boat tours from Little Venice to Camden.
London Kayak Tours 0845 453 2002, www.londonkayaktours. co.uk. Rates from £19.99. Guided tours from Tower Bridge or Hampton Court Palace, or on the Regent's Canal, from March to October.
Thames RIB Experience 7930 5746, www.thamesribexperience. com. Rates £34-£48; £20-£29 reductions. One of several speedboat tour companies: zoom from the Embankment to Canary Wharf (50mins) or the Thames Barrier (80mins), and back.

BY BUS

Big Bus Company 7233 9533, www.bigbustours.com. Rates from £29; £12 reductions; free under-5s.
Original London Sightseeing Tour 8877 1722, www.theoriginaltour. com. Rates £26; £13 reductions; £91 family; free under-5s. Both offer hop-on hop-off stops near the central London sights; tickets include a river cruise.

BY AIR

Adventure Balloons 01252 844222, www.adventureballoons. co.uk. Rates from £189. Flights run at dawn on weekdays from late April to mid August.

London Helicopter Tour 7887 2626, www.thelondonhelicopter. com. Rates from £150. Half-hour flights from Redhill in Surrey along the Thames and back.

BY CAR

Black Taxi Tours of London 7935 9363, www.blacktaxitours.co.uk. Rates £140-£150. Tailored 2hr tours for up to five.
Small Car Big City 7585 0399, www.smallcarbigcity.com. Rates £54-£549. Themed tours in a classic Mini Cooper – for half an hour or the entire day.

ON FOOT

For free, self-guided walking tours head to **www.walklondon.org.uk** or the **Royal Geographical Society**'s www.discoveringbritain. org/walks/region/greater-london, and try the themed audio walks from the **Guardian** newspaper (www.guardian.co.uk/travel/serie s/london-walks). Good choices for paid group tours include **And Did Those Feet** (8806 4325, www.chr. org.uk), **Performing London** (01234 404774, www.performing london.co.uk), **Silver Cane Tours** (07720 715295, www.silvercane tours.com) and **Urban Gentry** (8149 6253, www.urbangentry. com). **Original London Walks** (7624 3978, www.walks.com) provides an astonishing 140 different walks on a variety of themes. **Idiosyncratic outings** follow old London maps (www. londontrails.wordpress.com), trace a pun-ishing route through the city's history via its public conveniences (www.lootours.com), look at the vanished docks (www. tiht.org.uk) or journey through the art scene (www.foxandsquirrel. com and streetartlondon.co.uk/ tours). Finally, **Unseen Tours** (www.sockmobevents.org.uk) are a terrific initiative: they are led by homeless guides, who bring their own stories and perspectives to the city walks.

Work is currently under way on a new introductory gallery and café. *40 Brunswick Square, WC1N 1AZ (7841 3600, www.foundlingmuseum. org.uk). Russell Square tube. Open 10am-5pm Tue-Sat; 11am-5pm Sun. Admission £8.25; £5.50 reductions; free under-16s.*

Wellcome Collection

Sir Henry Wellcome, a pioneering 19th-century pharmacist, amassed a vast and idiosyncratic collection of implements and curios relating to the medical trade, now displayed here. In addition to these fascinating and often grisly items – ivory carvings of pregnant women, used guillotine blades, Napoleon's toothbrush – there are several serious works of modern art, most on display in a smaller room to one side of the main chamber of curiosities. Downstairs, the temporary exhibitions are often brilliant and come with all manner of associated events, from talks to walks. The Wellcome remains open while undergoing a £17.5m redevelopment, which will open up even more areas of the building to the public: in autumn 2014, it should reopen fully with a new second gallery and the 'Reading Room', which will be a combination of library, gallery and event space. *183 Euston Road, NW1 2BE (7611 2222, www.wellcomecollection.org). Euston Square tube or Euston tube/rail. Open 10am-6pm Tue, Wed, Fri, Sat; 10am-10pm Thur; 11am-6pm Sun. Library 10am-6pm Mon-Wed, Fri; 10am-8pm Thur; 10am-4pm Sat. Admission free.*

KING'S CROSS & ST PANCRAS

North-east of Bloomsbury, King's Cross is now a major European transport hub, thanks to a £500m makeover. The renovated and restored **St Pancras International** was the key arrival, but neighbouring King's Cross station has now been transformed too; 2013 saw the completion in front of the 1851 façade of a new public square. What were once gaping badlands to the north have been transformed into a mixed-use nucleus called **King's Cross Central**, with the University of the Arts London the key new resident, on the beautiful **Granary Square**, which steps down to the canal and is connected to the station by a street of funky food stalls. There were already a couple of places to explore – the **London Canal Museum** (12-13 New Wharf Road, off Wharfdale Road, N1 9RT, 7713 0836, www.canalmuseum. org.uk) and **Kings Place** (*see p105*) – now supported by some excellent restaurants. They are due to be joined in summer 2014 by the **House of Illustration** (2 Granary Square, N1C 4BH, www.houseofillustration.org.uk), the world's first gallery dedicated to the art of illustration.

British Library

'One of the ugliest buildings in the world,' opined a Parliamentary committee on the opening of the new British Library in 1997. But don't judge a book by its cover: the interior is a model of cool, spacious functionality, the collection is unmatched (150 million items and counting), and the reading rooms (open only to cardholders) are very popular. The focal point of the building is the King's Library, a six-storey glass-walled tower housing George III's collection, but the library's main treasures are on permanent display in the John Ritblat Gallery: Magna Carta, the Lindisfarne Gospels, original Beatles lyrics. There is also a great programme of temporary exhibitions and associated events: the Folio Society Gallery (upstairs from the foyer) is free and hosts focused little shows based around key artefacts (such as Kerouac's *On the Road* scroll manuscript) or themes ('Beautiful Science: Picturing Data, Inspiring Insight'), while the engaging blockbuster shows are ticketed but cover meaty themes such as propaganda, the Georgians and the English language itself. *96 Euston Road, NW1 2DB (0843 208 1114, www.bl.uk). Euston or King's Cross tube/rail. Open 9.30am-6pm Mon, Wed-Fri; 9.30am-8pm Tue; 9.30am-5pm Sat; 11am-5pm Sun. Admission free.*

St Pancras International

The redeveloped St Pancras station has become a destination in more ways than the obvious, now containing large sculptures, the self-proclaimed 'longest champagne bar in Europe', high-end boutiques – even a gastropub and farmers' market. But the new additions are mere window-dressing for the stunning original structures: famously George Gilbert Scott's grandiloquent red-brick exterior (much of which is now the St Pancras Renaissance hotel), but perhaps more impressively William Barlow's gorgeous Victorian glass-and-iron roof to the train shed, a single span airy and light as some kind of cathedral to 19th-century industry.

British Library

Pancras Road, N1C 4QP (7843 7688, www.stpancras.com). King's Cross tube/rail. Open 24hrs daily. Admission free. No credit cards.

FITZROVIA

Squeezed in between Tottenham Court Road, Oxford Street, Great Portland Street and Euston Road, Fitzrovia isn't as famous as Bloomsbury, but its history is just as rich. The origins of the name are hazy: some believe it comes from **Fitzroy Square**, named after Henry Fitzroy (son of Charles II); others insist it's due to the famous **Fitzroy Tavern** (16 Charlotte Street, 7580 3714), focal venue for London bohemia of the 1930s and '40s and a favourite with the likes of Dylan Thomas and George Orwell. Fitzrovia also had its share of artists: James McNeill Whistler lived at 8 Fitzroy Square, later taken over by British Impressionist Walter Sickert. Fitzrovia's raffish image is largely a thing of the past (media offices are in the ascendance these days) but the steady arrival of new galleries – Pilar Corrias heads the pack scattered along Eastcastle Street – have given the district back some of its artiness. **Charlotte Street** and neighbouring byways have plenty of good options for food and drink. The district's icon is the **BT Tower**, completed in 1964 as the Post Office Tower.

COVENT GARDEN

Covent Garden was once the property of the medieval Abbey ('convent') of Westminster. When Henry VIII dissolved the monasteries, it passed to John Russell, first Earl of Bedford, in 1552; his family still owns land hereabouts. During the 16th and 17th centuries, they developed the area: the fourth Earl employed Inigo Jones to create the Italianate open square that remains the area's centrepiece.

A market was first documented here in 1640 and grew into London's pre-eminent fruit and vegetable wholesaler, employing over 1,000 porters. Its success led to the opening of coffeehouses, theatres, gambling dens and brothels. A flower market was added (where the **London Transport Museum** now stands).

In the second half of the 20th century, it became obvious that the congested streets of central London were unsuitable for such market traffic and the decision was taken to move the traders out. In 1974, with the market gone, the threat of property development loomed for the empty stalls and offices. It was only through demonstrations that the area was saved. It's now a pleasant place for a stroll, especially if you catch it early before the crowds descend.

Centred on Covent Garden Piazza, the area now offers a combination of gentrified shops, restaurants and cafés, supplemented by street artists and busking musicians in the lower courtyard. The majority of the entertainment takes place under the portico of **St Paul's Covent Garden** (Bedford Street, WC2E 9ED, 7836 5221, www.actorschurch.org), which is itself known as the Actors' Church for its long association with Covent Garden's theatre. Pop in to see the memorial plaques: many thespians are commemorated here, among them Vivien Leigh and Charlie Chaplin.

Tourists favour the 180-year-old **covered market**, which combines upmarket chain stores with a collection of small, sometimes quirky but often rather twee independent shops. Its handsome architecture is best viewed from the Amphitheatre Café Bar's terrace loggia at the **Royal Opera House**. The whole area has benefited from a major, ongoing revamp, with much classier shops being drawn in. There's also been an improvement in the sightseeing, with the always excellent **London Transport Museum** joined by a new outpost of the South Bank's London Film Museum, in the building opposite the Opera House that used to be the Theatre Museum.

Change is barely evident elsewhere. The **Apple Market**, in the North Hall, still has arts and crafts stalls from Tuesday to Sunday, and antiques on Monday. Across the road, the tackier **Jubilee Market** deals mostly in novelty T-shirts and other tat.

Outside Covent Garden Piazza, the area offers a mixed bag of entertainment, eateries and shops. Nearest the markets, most of the more unusual shops have been superseded by a homogeneous mass of cafés, while big fashion chains – and the **St Martin's Courtyard** mall (www.stmartins courtyard.co.uk) – have all but domesticated Long Acre. There are more interesting stores north of here on Neal Street and Monmouth Street; Earlham Street is also home to the **Donmar Warehouse** (*see p108*), a former banana-ripening depot that's now an intimate and groundbreaking theatre. On tiny Shorts Gardens next door is the Neal's Yard Dairy (*see p79*), purveyor of exceptional UK cheeses;

Somerset House & the Embankment Galleries

down a passageway is **Neal's Yard** itself, known for its co-operative cafés, herbalists and head shops.

South of Long Acre and east of the Piazza, historical depravity is called to account at the former **Bow Street Magistrates Court.** Once home to the Bow Street Runners, the precursors of the Metropolitan Police, this was also where Oscar Wilde entered his plea when arrested for 'indecent acts' in 1895. Plans to convert it into a hotel have not yet come to fruition. To the south, Wellington and Catherine streets mix restaurants and theatres, including the grand Theatre Royal. Other diversions in and around Covent Garden include the museum at **Freemasons' Hall** (7395 9257, www.freemasonry.london.museum; call for details of tours), the eye-catchingly bombastic white stone building where Long Acre becomes Great Queen Street. The **Coliseum** (see p106) on St Martin's Lane is home to the English National Opera.

London Film Museum
Having left its former home on the South Bank, the LFM relaunched its collection of Brit film memorabilia in spring 2014 with 'Bond in Motion' – a display of 50 of 007's most covetable high-end motors.
45 Wellington Street, WC2E 7BN (7202 7043, www.londonfilm museum.com). Covent Garden tube. Open 10am-6pm Mon-Fri, Sun; 10am-7pm Sat. Admission £14.50; £9.50 5-15s, reductions; £38 family.

London Transport Museum
The London Transport Museum traces the city's transport history from the horse age to the present day. It does so in an engaging and inspiring fashion, with a focus on social history and design, illustrated by a superb array of preserved buses, trams and trains, and backed up by some brilliant temporary exhibitions. The collections are in broadly chronological order, beginning with the Victorian gallery,

where a replica of Shillibeer's first horse-drawn bus service in 1829 takes pride of place. Another gallery is dedicated to the museum's truly impressive collection of poster art. Under the leadership of Frank Pick, in the early 20th century London Transport developed one of the most coherent brand identities in the world. The new museum also raises some interesting and important questions about the future of public transport in the city, with a display on ideas that are 'coming soon'.
Covent Garden Piazza, WC2E 7BB (7379 6344, www.ltmuseum.co.uk). Covent Garden tube. Open 10am-6pm Mon-Thur, Sat, Sun; 11am-6pm Fri. Admission £15; £11.50 reductions; free under-17s.

Royal Opera House
The Royal Opera House was founded in 1732 by John Rich on the profits of his production of John Gay's *Beggar's Opera;* the current building, constructed roughly 150 years ago but extensively remodelled since, is the third on the site. Visitors can explore the eight floors as part of an organised tour, including the main auditorium, the costume workshops and sometimes even a rehearsal. Certain parts of the building are also open to the general public, including the glass-roofed Paul Hamlyn Hall, the Crush Bar (so named because in Victorian times the only thing served during intermissions was orange and lemon crush) and the Amphitheatre Café Bar. For performances, see p106.
Bow Street, WC2E 9DD (7304 4000, www.roh.org.uk). Covent Garden tube. Open 10am-3.30pm Mon-Sat. Admission free. Stage tours £12; £9-£11 reductions.

THE STRAND & ALDWYCH

Until as recently as the 1860s, the **Strand** ran beside the Thames; indeed, it was originally the river's bridlepath. In the 14th century, it was lined with grand residences

with gardens that ran down to the water. It wasn't until the 1870s that the Thames was pushed back with the creation of the Embankment and its adjacent gardens. By the time George Newnes's famed *Strand* magazine was introducing its readership to Sherlock Holmes (1891), the street boasted the Cecil Hotel (long since demolished), Simpson's, King's College and **Somerset House**. Prime Minister Benjamin Disraeli described it as 'perhaps the finest street in Europe'. Nobody would make such a claim today – but there's still plenty to interest visitors.

In 1292, the body of Eleanor of Castile, consort to King Edward I, completed its funerary procession from Lincoln in the small hamlet of Charing, at the western end of what is now the Strand. The occasion was marked by the erection of the last of 12 elaborate crosses. A replica of the Eleanor Cross (originally set just south of nearby Trafalgar Square) was placed in 1865 on the forecourt of **Charing Cross Station**; it remains there today, looking like the spire of a sunken cathedral. Across the road, behind **St Martin-in-the-Fields** (see p106), is Maggie Hambling's memorial to a more recent queen, *A Conversation with Oscar Wilde.*

The Embankment itself can be reached down Villiers Street. Pass through the tube station to the point at which boat tours with on-board entertainment depart. Just to the east stands **Cleopatra's Needle**, an obelisk presented to the British nation by the viceroy of Egypt, Mohammed Ali, in 1820 but not set in place by the river for a further 59 years. The obelisk was originally erected around 1500 BC by the pharaoh Tuthmosis III at a site near modern-day Cairo, before being moved to Alexandria, Cleopatra's capital, in 10 BC. By this time, however, the great queen was 20 years dead.

Back on the Strand, the majestic **Savoy** hotel (see p113) is back to its august best after a tortuously long and thorough refurbishment. The hotel first opened in 1889, financed by profits from Richard D'Oyly Carte's productions of Gilbert and Sullivan's light operas at the neighbouring **Savoy Theatre**. The theatre, which pre-dates the hotel by eight years, was the first to use electric lights. At the eastern end of the Strand is the Aldwych, guarded by two grand hotels: One Aldwych and, directly opposite, the hip new ME by Meliá London (see p113). This grand crescent dates only from 1905, but the name 'ald wic' (old settlement or market) has its origins in the 14th century. To the south is **Somerset House**; even if you're not interested in the galleries, it's worth visiting the regal fountain courtyard.

Courtauld Gallery
Located for the last two decades in the north wing of Somerset House, the Courtauld has one of Britain's greatest collections of paintings, and contains

several works of world importance. Although there are some outstanding early works (Cranach's *Adam & Eve*, for one), the collection's strongest suit is in Impressionist and Post-Impressionist paintings. Popular masterpieces include Manet's *A Bar at the Folies-Bergère*, alongside plenty of superb Monets and Cézannes, important Gauguins, and some Van Goghs and Seurats. On the top floor, there's a selection of gorgeous Fauvist works, a lovely room of Kandinskys and plenty more besides. Hidden downstairs, the sweet little gallery café is delightful.
The Strand, WC2R 1LA (7848 2526, www.courtauld.ac.uk/gallery). Temple tube or Charing Cross tube/rail. Open 10am-6pm daily. Tours phone for details. Admission £6; £5 reductions. Free 10am-2pm Mon; students & under-18s daily.

Somerset House & the Embankment Galleries
The original Somerset House was a Tudor palace commissioned by the Duke of Somerset. In 1775, it was demolished to make way for the first purpose-built office block in the world. Architect Sir William Chambers spent the last 20 years of his life working on the neoclassical edifice overlooking the Thames, built to accommodate learned societies such as the Royal Academy and government departments. The taxmen are still here, but the rest of the building is open to the public. Attractions include the Courtauld, the handsome fountain court and cafés (one with a broad riverview terrace). The Embankment Galleries explore connections between art, architecture and design in temporary exhibitions. In summer, children never tire of running through the choreographed fountains while parents watch from café tables; in winter, an ice rink takes over.
The Strand, WC2R 1LA (7845 4600, www.somersethouse.org.uk). Temple tube or Charing Cross tube/rail. Open 10am-6pm (last entry to galleries 5.15pm) daily. Tours phone for details. Admission Courtyard & terrace free. Embankment Galleries prices vary; check website for details. Tours phone for details.

SOHO

Forming the area's northern gateway, **Soho Square** was laid out in 1681. It was initially called King's Square; a weather-beaten statue of Charles II stands just north of the centre. On warmer days, the grassy spaces are filled with courting couples as snacking workers occupy its benches; one of these benches is dedicated to singer Kirsty MacColl, in honour of her song named after the square. The denominations of the two churches on the square testify to the area's long-standing European credentials: as well as the French Protestant church, you'll find St Patrick's, one of the first Catholic churches built in England after the Reformation.

Two classic Soho streets run south from the square. **Greek Street**, its name a nod to a church that once stood here, is lined with restaurants and bars, among them 50-year-old Hungarian eaterie the **Gay Hussar** (no.2, 7437 0973, http://gayhussar. co.uk) and the nearby **Pillars of Hercules** pub (no.7, 7437 1179), where the literati once enjoyed long liquid lunches. Just by the Pillars, an arch leads to Manette Street and Charing Cross Road, where you'll find **Foyles** (see p79). Back on Greek Street, no.49 was once Les Cousins, a folk venue; Casanova lived briefly at no.46.

Parallel to Greek Street is **Frith Street**, once home to Mozart (1764-65, no.20) and painter John Constable (1810-11, no.49). Humanist essayist William Hazlitt died in 1830 at no.6, now a discreet hotel named in his memory (see p113 **Hazlitt's**). Further down the street are **Ronnie Scott's** (see p103), Britain's best-known jazz club, and, across from Ronnie's, the similarly mythologised **Bar Italia** (no.22, 7437 4520).

This area has been suffering from major disruption caused by works on the Crossrail link. It's tedious and unsightly, but you can usually find your way around it down one of the area's characteristic backstreets.

Linking Charing Cross Road to Wardour Street and crossed by Greek, Frith and Dean streets, **Old Compton Street** is London's gay catwalk. Tight T-shirts congregate around **Balans** (see p96), **Compton's** (nos.51-53) and the **Admiral Duncan** (no.54). The street has an interesting history that dates back long before rainbow flags were hung above its doors: no.59 was formerly the 2i's Coffee Bar, the skiffle venue where stars and svengalis mingled in the late 1950s and early '60s.

Visit Old Compton Street in the morning for a sense of the mostly vanished immigrant Soho of old. Cheeses and cooked meats from **Camisa** (no.61, 7437 7610, www.icamisa.co.uk) and roasting beans from the **Algerian Coffee Stores** (see p79) scent the air, as **Pâtisserie Valerie** (no.44, 7437 3466, www.patisserie-valerie.co.uk), first of a now significant national chain, does a brisk trade in croissants and cakes.

Valerie's traditional rival is the older **Maison Bertaux** (7437 6007, www.maisonbertaux.com), an atmospheric holdover from the 19th century that sits near the southern end of Greek Street. At the corner of Greek and Romilly streets sits the **Coach & Horses** (no.29, 7437 5920, www. coachandhorsessoho.co.uk), where Soho flâneur Jeffrey Bernard held court for decades. Two streets along, Dean Street holds the **French House** (see p72); formerly the York Minster pub, it was de Gaulle's London base in World War II and in later years became a favourite of painters Francis Bacon and Lucian Freud.

North of Old Compton Street on Dean Street sits the **Groucho Club**

(no.45), a members-only media hangout that was founded in the mid 1980s and named in honour of the Groucho Marx quote about not wanting to join any club that would have him as a member. A few doors along, at no.28, the other famous Marx lived in a garret from 1850 to 1856; he would probably not have approved of the high-class, high-cost dinners served there now – at **Quo Vadis** (nos.26-29). To the north is the **Soho Theatre** (see p108).

Parallel to Dean Street, **Wardour Street** provides offices for film and TV production companies, but is also known for its rock history. No.100 was, for nearly three decades, the Marquee, where Led Zeppelin played their first London gig and Hendrix appeared four times. The latter's favourite Soho haunt was the nearby **Ship** pub (no.116), still with a sprinkling of music-themed knick-knacks. There's more music history at Trident Studios on nearby St Anne's Court: Lou Reed recorded *Transformer* here, and David Bowie cut both *Hunky Dory* and *The Rise and Fall of Ziggy Stardust* on the site.

Back when he was still known as David Jones, Bowie played a gig at the Jack of Clubs on Brewer Street, now **Madame JoJo's** (see p104). But this corner of Soho is most famous not for music but for its position at the heart of Soho's dwindling but still notorious sex trade.

North of here, **Berwick Street** is a lovely mix of old-school London raffishness and new-Soho style. West of Berwick Street was rebranded 'West Soho' in a misplaced bid to give it some kind of upmarket identity. **Brewer Street** does have some interesting places; among them is the **Vintage Magazine Store** (nos.39-43, 7439 8525), offering everything from retro robots to pre-war issues of *Vogue*. On Great Windmill Street is the **Windmill Theatre** (nos.17-19), which gained fame in the 1930s and '40s for its 'revuedeville' shows with erotic 'tableaux' – naked girls who remained stationary in order to stay within the law. The place is now a lap-dancing joint. North of Brewer Street is **Golden Square**. Developed in the 1670s, it became the political and ambassadorial district of the late 17th and early 18th centuries, and remains home to some of the area's grandest buildings (many now bases for media firms) and a purveyor of cinnamon buns: the **Nordic Bakery** (no.14A, 3230 1077, www.nordicbakery.com).

Just north of Golden Square is **Carnaby Street**, which became a fashion mecca shortly after John Stephen opened His Clothes here in 1956; Stephen, who went on to own more than a dozen fashion shops on the street, is now commemorated with a plaque at the corner with Beak Street. After thriving during the Swinging Sixties, Carnaby Street became a rather seamy commercialised backwater. However, along with nearby **Newburgh Street** and

Kingly Court, it's undergone a revival, with the tourist traps and chain stores joined by a wealth of independent stores. A little further north, near Oxford Street, is the new **Photographers' Gallery**.

Photographers' Gallery

Given a handsome refit by Irish architects O'Donnell+Tuomey, this old brick corner building reopened in 2012 as the new home for London's only gallery dedicated solely to the photographic arts. The upper floors have two airy new exhibition spaces, while a bookshop, print sales room and café (open the same hours as the gallery) are tucked into the ground floor and basement. The exhibitions are varied, and enhanced by quirky details such as the camera obscura in the third-floor Eranda Studio and a projection wall in the café. *16-18 Ramillies Street, W1F 7LW (0845 262 1618, www.the photographersgallery.org.uk). Oxford Circus tube. Open 10am-6pm Mon-Wed, Fri, Sat; 10am-8pm Thur; 11.30am-6pm Sun. Admission free. Temporary exhibitions vary.*

CHINATOWN & LEICESTER SQUARE

Shaftesbury Avenue is the very heart of Theatreland. The Victorians built seven grand theatres here, six of which still stand. The most impressive is the gorgeous **Palace Theatre** on Cambridge Circus, which opened in 1891 as the Royal English Opera House; when grand opera flopped, the theatre reopened as a music hall two years later. *The Sound of Music* (1961) and *Jesus Christ Superstar* (1972) had their London premières here, and *Les Misérables* racked up 7,602 performances between 1985 and 2004.

West of Charing Cross Road and south of Shaftesbury Avenue, and officially just outside Soho, is the city's **Chinatown**. The ersatz oriental gates, stone lions and pagoda-topped phone boxes around **Gerrard Street** suggest a Chinese theme park, but this remains a close-knit residential and working enclave, a genuine focal point for London's Chinese community. The area is crammed with restaurants, bakeries and Asian grocery stores.

South of Chinatown, **Leicester Square** was one of London's most exclusive addresses in the 17th century; in the 18th, it became home to the royal court of Prince George (later George II). Satirical painter William Hogarth had a studio here (1733-64), as did 18th-century artist Sir Joshua Reynolds – busts of both once resided in the small gardens at the heart of the square, along with a vanished statue of Charlie Chaplin. They've now been swept away in the fine refurbishment of the square. Film premières are still regularly held in the monolithic **Odeon Leicester Square** (see p95), which once boasted the UK's largest screen and probably still has the UK's highest ticket prices; this is where the London Film Festival kicks off.

OXFORD STREET & AROUND

Few Londoners love **Oxford Street**, yet official estimates put the annual footfall at somewhere near 200 million people per year. It's unbearable on weekends and in the run-up to Christmas, and never pretty outside these times, lined with over-familiar chain stores and choked with buses. The New West End Company (www.newwestend.com) has been charged with changing all that, and Oxford Circus, Marble Arch and Regent Street are beginning to feel the benefits.

The street gets smarter as you walk from east to west. The eastern end around Tottenham Court Road station is under major redevelopment for Crossrail, but its lack of destination shops was solved in 2012 by the opening of bargain-basement fashion flagship **Primark** (nos.14-28). The string of department stores – **John Lewis** (nos.278-306), **Debenhams** (nos.334-348) and **Selfridges** (no.400) – begins west of chaotic **Oxford Circus**, where there are more Crossrail works at Bond Street station. Apart from the art deco splendour of Selfridges, architectural interest along the street is largely limited to Oxford Circus's four identical convex corners, constructed between 1913 and 1928.

Close by, at the western end of Oxford Street, stands **Marble Arch**, with its Carrara marble cladding and sculptures celebrating Nelson and Wellington. It was designed by John Nash in 1827 as the entrance to a rebuilt Buckingham Palace, but the arch was moved here in 1851. Now given a £2m revamp, it's been joined by renovated water fountains and gardens that contain an ongoing series of public sculpture commissions.

North of Oxford Circus runs **Langham Place**, notable for the Bath stone façade of John Nash's **All Souls Church** (Langham Place, 2 All Souls Place, 7580 3522, www.allsouls.org), with its bold combination of a Gothic spire and classical rotunda. Opposite is the BBC's art deco **Broadcasting House**, joined next door in 2013 by New Broadcasting House. Over the road is the **Langham Hotel** (7636 1000, http://london.langhamhotels. co.uk), which opened in 1865 as Britain's first grand hotel and has been home at various points to Mark Twain, Napoleon III and Oscar Wilde.

North, Langham Place turns into **Portland Place**, designed by Robert and James Adam as the glory of 18th-century London. At no.66 is the Royal Institute of British Architects. Parallel to Portland Place are **Harley Street**, famous for its high-cost dentists and doctors, and **Wimpole Street**, erstwhile residence to the poet Elizabeth Barrett Browning, Sir Arthur Conan Doyle and Sir Paul McCartney.

MARYLEBONE

North of Oxford Street, the district known to its boosters as 'Marylebone Village' has become a magnet for

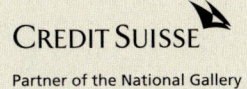

moneyed Londoners. Many visitors to the area head directly for **Madame Tussauds**, but the area's beating heart is **Marylebone High Street**, with its interesting shops.

More lovely boutiques can be found on **Marylebone Lane**, along with the **Golden Eagle** (no.59, 7935 3228), which hosts regular singalongs around its piano. There's fine food, too, with smart, upmarket eateries snuggling alongside delis such as **La Fromagerie** (2-6 Moxon Street, 7935 0341, www.lafromagerie.co.uk) and century-old lunchroom **Paul Rothe & Son** (35 Marylebone Lane, 7935 6783). Cultural diversions include the **Wallace** and **Wigmore** (see p106).

Madame Tussauds

Streams of humanity jostle excitedly here for the chance to take pictures of each other planting a smacker on the waxen visage of fame and fortune. Madame Tussaud brought her show to London in 1802, 32 years after it was founded in Paris, and it's been expanding ever since. There are now some 300 figures in the collection: current movie A-listers who require no more than a first name (Brad, Keira, Arnie), as well as their illustrious forebears for whom the surname seems more fitting (Monroe, Chaplin); a bevy of Royals (not least Wills and Kate), and sundry sportsmen and -women – Nadal, Tendulkar, Messi, Muhammad Ali, Jessica Ennis and Usain Bolt. If you're not already overheating, your palms will be sweating by the time you descend to the Chamber of Horrors in 'Scream', where only teens claim to enjoy the floor drops and scary special effects. Much more pleasant is the kitsch 'Spirit of London' ride, whisking you through 400 years of London life.

Tussauds also hosts Marvel Super Heroes 4D. Interactives and waxworks of Iron Man, Spiderman and an 18ft Hulk provide further photo ops, but the highlight is the nine-minute film in '4D' (as well as 3D projections, there are 'real' effects such as a shaking floor and smoke in the auditorium). *Marylebone Road, NW1 5LR (0870 400 3000, www.madametussauds. com/london). Baker Street tube. Open times vary; check website for details. Admission £30; £25.80 reductions; £111.60 family; free under-4s.*

Wallace Collection

Built in 1776, this handsome house on a quiet square contains an exceptional collection of 18th-century French furniture, painting and objets d'art, as well as medieval armour and weaponry. It all belonged to Sir Richard Wallace, the illegitimate offspring of the fourth Marquess of Hertford, who in 1870 inherited the treasures his father had amassed. Room after grand room contains Louis XIV and XV furnishings and Sèvres porcelain; the galleries are hung with paintings by Titian, Gainsborough and Reynolds, as well as Fragonard's *The Swing*. The refurbished West Galleries display 19th-century and Venetian works, including paintings by Canaletto; the East Galleries are dedicated to Dutch paintings; miniatures and gold boxes are on show in the Boudoir Cabinet. To see the Wallace at its best, though, you'll have to wait until work on the Great Gallery is complete in late 2014. Following painstaking improvements to lighting and decor, there you'll see Franz Hals's *Laughing Cavalier*, Poussin's *A Dance to the Music of Time* and Velázquez's *The Lady with a Fan* in their full glory. *Hertford House, Manchester Square, W1U 3BN (7935 0687, www.wallacecollection.org). Bond Street tube. Open 10am-5pm daily. Admission free.*

REGENT'S PARK

Regent's Park (open 5am-dusk daily) is one of London's most delightful open spaces. Originally a hunting ground for Henry VIII, it remained a royals-only retreat long after it was formally designed by John Nash in 1811; only in 1845 did it open to the public. Attractions run from **ZSL London Zoo** to the **Open Air Theatre** (see p107); rowing boat hire, beautiful rose gardens, ice-cream stands and the **Garden Café** (7935 5729, www.company ofcooks.com) complete the picture.

West of Regent's Park rises the golden dome of the **London Central Mosque** (www.iccuk. org), while the northern end of **Baker Street** is unsurprisingly heavy on nods of respect to the world's favourite freelance detective. At the **Sherlock Holmes Museum** (no.221B, 7224 3688, www.sherlock-holmes.co.uk), Holmes stories are earnestly re-enacted using mannequins, but studious fans may find more of interest among the books and photos of the **Sherlock Holmes Collection** at Marylebone Library (7641 1206, by appointment only).

ZSL London Zoo

London Zoo has been open in one form or another since 1826. Spread over 36 acres and containing more than 600 species, it cares for many of the endangered variety – part of the entry price goes towards the ZSL's projects around the world. Regular events include 'animals in action' and keeper talks. The exhibits are entertaining: look out, for example, for the re-creation of a kitchen overrun with large cockroaches. Tiger Territory, where Sumatran tigers can be watched through floor-to-ceiling windows, brought new baby tigers to the zoo in 2014, while the relaunched 'Rainforest Life' biodome and the 'Meet the Monkeys' attractions allow visitors to walk through the natural habitat of, respectively, tree anteaters and sloths, and black-capped Bolivian squirrel monkeys. 'Gorilla Kingdom' is another highlight, and personal encounters of the avian kind can be had in the Victorian Blackburn Pavilion – as well as at Penguin Beach, where you can watch the black-and-white favourites swim underwater. *Regent's Park, NW1 4RY (0844 225 1826, www.zsl.org/london-zoo). Baker Street or Camden Town tube then bus 274, C2. Open times vary; check website for details. Admission £21-£26; £15.50-£23.40 reductions; free under-3s.*

PICCADILLY CIRCUS & REGENT STREET

Frantic **Piccadilly Circus** is an uneasy mix of the tawdry and the grand, a mix with little to do with the vision of its architect. John Nash's 1820s design for the intersection of Regent Street and Piccadilly, two of the West End's most elegant streets, was a harmonious circle of curved frontages. But 60 years later, Shaftesbury Avenue muscled in, creating the lopsided traffic junction still in place today.

Alfred Gilbert's memorial fountain in honour of child-labour abolitionist Earl Shaftesbury was erected in 1893. It's properly known as the **Shaftesbury Memorial,** with the statue on top intended to show the Angel of Christian Charity, but critics and public alike recognised **Eros**. The illuminated advertising panels around the intersection appeared late in the 19th century and have been present ever since: a Coca-Cola ad has been here since 1955, making it the world's longest-running ad. Running Sky News broadcasts indicate the likely media-saturated future for the illuminations. Opposite is **Ripley's Believe It or Not!**.

Connecting Piccadilly Circus to Oxford Circus to the north and Pall Mall to the south, the broad curve of **Regent Street** was designed by Nash in the early 1800s with the aims of improving access to Regent's Park and bumping up property values in Haymarket and Pall Mall. Much of Nash's architecture was destroyed in the early 20th century, but the street is still grand. Among the highlights are the mammoth children's emporium **Hamleys** (nos.188-196, 0871 704 1977, www.hamleys.com) and landmark department store **Liberty** (see p83).

Ripley's Believe It or Not!

This 'odditorium' follows a formula unchanged since Robert Ripley opened his first display at the Chicago World Fair in 1933: an assortment of 800 curiosities is displayed, ranging from the world's smallest road-safe car to da Vinci's *Last Supper* painted on a grain of rice – via the company's signature shrunken heads. *1 Piccadilly Circus, W1J 0DA (3238 0022, www.ripleyslondon.com). Piccadilly Circus tube. Open 10am-midnight daily (last entry 10.30pm). Admission £26.95; £21.95-£24.95 reductions; £87.95 family; free under-4s.*

MAYFAIR

On Mayfair's busy shopping streets, you may feel out of place without the reassuring heft of a platinum card, but there are many pleasures to enjoy if you fancy a stroll. In the 1700s, the Grosvenor and Berkeley families developed Mayfair into a posh new neighbourhood, focused on a series of landmark squares. The most famous of these, **Grosvenor Square** (1725-31), is dominated by the supremely inelegant US Embassy, due to close in 2017 for its move to Vauxhall. Its only decorative touches a fierce eagle and a mass of post-9/11 barricades. Out front, pride of place is taken by a statue of President Dwight Eisenhower; Roosevelt is in the park nearby.

Brook Street has impressive musical credentials: GF Handel lived and died at no.25, and Jimi Hendrix roomed briefly next door at no.23, adjacent buildings that have been combined into the **Handel House Museum** (25 Brook Street, entrance in Lancashire Court, W1K 4HB, 7399 1953, www.handelhouse.org). For most visitors, however, this part of town is all about shopping. Connecting Brook Street with Oxford Street to the north, **South Molton Street** is home to the fabulous boutique-emporium **Browns** (see p82) and the excellent **Grays Antique Market** (see p83), while **New Bond Street** is an A-Z of top-end, mainstream fashion houses.

Beyond New Bond Street, **Hanover Square** is another of the area's big squares, now a busy traffic chicane. Just to the south is **St George's Church**, built in the 1720s and once everyone's favourite place to be seen and to get married. Handel, who married nobody, attended services here. South of St George's, salubrious **Conduit Street** is where fashion shocker **Vivienne Westwood** (no.44) faces staid **Rigby & Peller** (no.22A), corsetière to the Queen.

Running south off Conduit Street is the most famous Mayfair shopping street of all, **Savile Row**. Gieves & Hawkes (no.1) is a must-visit for anyone interested in the history of British menswear; at no.15, Henry Poole & Co has cut suits for clients including Napoleon III, Charles Dickens and 'Buffalo' Bill Cody. No.3 was the home of the Beatles' Apple Records and their rooftop farewell.

Two streets west, **Cork Street** was long the heart of the West End art scene, but these days major US dealers seem to be driving the Mayfair art scene: notably **David Zwirner**'s 10,000sq ft space at 24 Grafton Street (3538 3165, www.davidzwirner.com). A couple of streets over is Albemarle Street, where you'll find the rejuvenated **Royal Institution** (21 Albemarle Street, W1S 4BS, 7409 2992, www.rigb.org), founded in 1799, and now home to the Faraday Museum, a reconstruction of the pioneering scientist's laboratory.

TOP TIP!
Routemaster rides
London's classic 1950s double-decker runs only one route nowadays: Heritage Route 15 from Trafalgar Square (stop F) to Tower Hill via St Paul's.

Explore

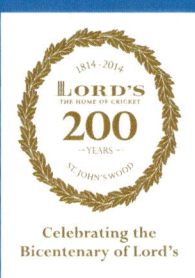

At the renovated **Burlington Arcade** (*see p82*), London's oldest and most famous arcade, top-hatted security staff known as 'beadles' ensure there's no singing, whistling or hurrying in the arcade. Formerly Burlington House (1665), the **Royal Academy of Arts** is next door to the arcade's entrance.

On Piccadilly are further representatives of high-end retail. **Fortnum & Mason** (*see p83*), London's most prestigious food store, was founded in 1707. Look for the fine clock: a 1964 articulated effort, it features 18th-century effigies of Mr Fortnum and Mr Mason, who bow to each other on the hour.

To the west along Piccadilly, smartly uniformed doormen mark the **Wolseley** (*see p65*) restaurant, and the expensive, exclusive **Ritz** (*see p116*). The flat green expanse just beyond the Ritz is **Green Park**; it's a bit dull in itself, but makes a very pleasant middle section of walk through three Royal Parks, connecting St James's Park to Hyde Park. Work your way along Piccadilly, following the northern edge of Green Park past the queue outside the **Hard Rock**

Café (where the Vault's displays of memorabilia are free to visit and open every day; www.hardrock.com) to the Duke of Wellington's old home, **Apsley House**. This is hectic **Hyde Park Corner**; **Buckingham Palace** is just a short walk south-east, while **Hyde Park** is to the west, but it also has a collection of memorials worth lingering over in themselves.

Apsley House

Called No.1 London because it was the first London building encountered on the road to the city from the village of Kensington, Apsley House was built by Robert Adam in the 1770s. The Duke of Wellington kept it as his London home for 35 years. Although his descendants still live here, several rooms are open to the public, providing a superb feel for the man and his era. Admire the porcelain dinnerware and plates or ask for a demonstration of the crafty mirrors in the scarlet and gilt picture gallery, where a fine Velázquez and a Correggio hang near Goya's portrait of the Iron Duke in 1812. *149 Piccadilly, W1J 7NT (7499 5676, www.english-heritage.org.uk). Hyde Park Corner tube. Open Nov-Mar*

11am-4pm Sat, Sun. Apr-Oct 11am-5pm Wed-Sun. Tours by arrangement. Admission £6.90; £4.60-£6.20 reductions; £21.10 family; free under-5s. Tours phone in advance. Joint ticket with Wellington Arch £8.90; £5.30-£8 reductions; £23 family.

Royal Academy of Arts

Britain's first art school was founded in 1768 and moved to the Palladian Burlington House a century later, but it's now best known not for education but exhibitions. Ticketed blockbusters are generally held in the Sackler Wing or the main galleries; shows in the John Madejski Fine Rooms are drawn from the RA's holdings, which range from Constable to Hockney, and are free. The Academy's biggest event is the Summer Exhibition, which for more than two centuries has drawn from works entered by the public. There are also exhibitions in the lofty rooms of 6 Burlington Gardens, just through the Burlington Arcade. *Burlington House, W1J 0BD (7300 8000, www. royalacademy.org.uk). Green Park or Piccadilly Circus tube. Open 10am-6pm Mon-Thur, Sat, Sun; 10am-10pm Fri. Admission free. Exhibitions vary.*

Wellington Arch

Built in the late 1820s to mark Britain's triumph over Napoleonic France, Decimus Burton's Wellington Arch was initially topped by an equestrian statue of Wellington. However, Captain Adrian Jones's 38-ton bronze *Peace Descending on the Quadriga of War* has finished it with a flourish since 1912. The Arch has three floors, with a bookshop and various displays, covering the history of the arch and the Blue Plaques scheme. *Hyde Park Corner, W1J 7JZ (7930 2726, www. english-heritage.org.uk). Hyde Park Corner tube. Open Apr-Oct 10am-5pm daily. Nov-Mar 10am-4pm daily. Admission £4.20; £2.50-£3.80 reductions; free under-5s. Joint ticket with Apsley House £8.90; £5.30-£8 reductions; £23 family.*

Westminster & St James's

England is ruled from **Westminster**. The monarchy has been in residence here since the 11th century, when Edward the Confessor moved west from the City, and the government of

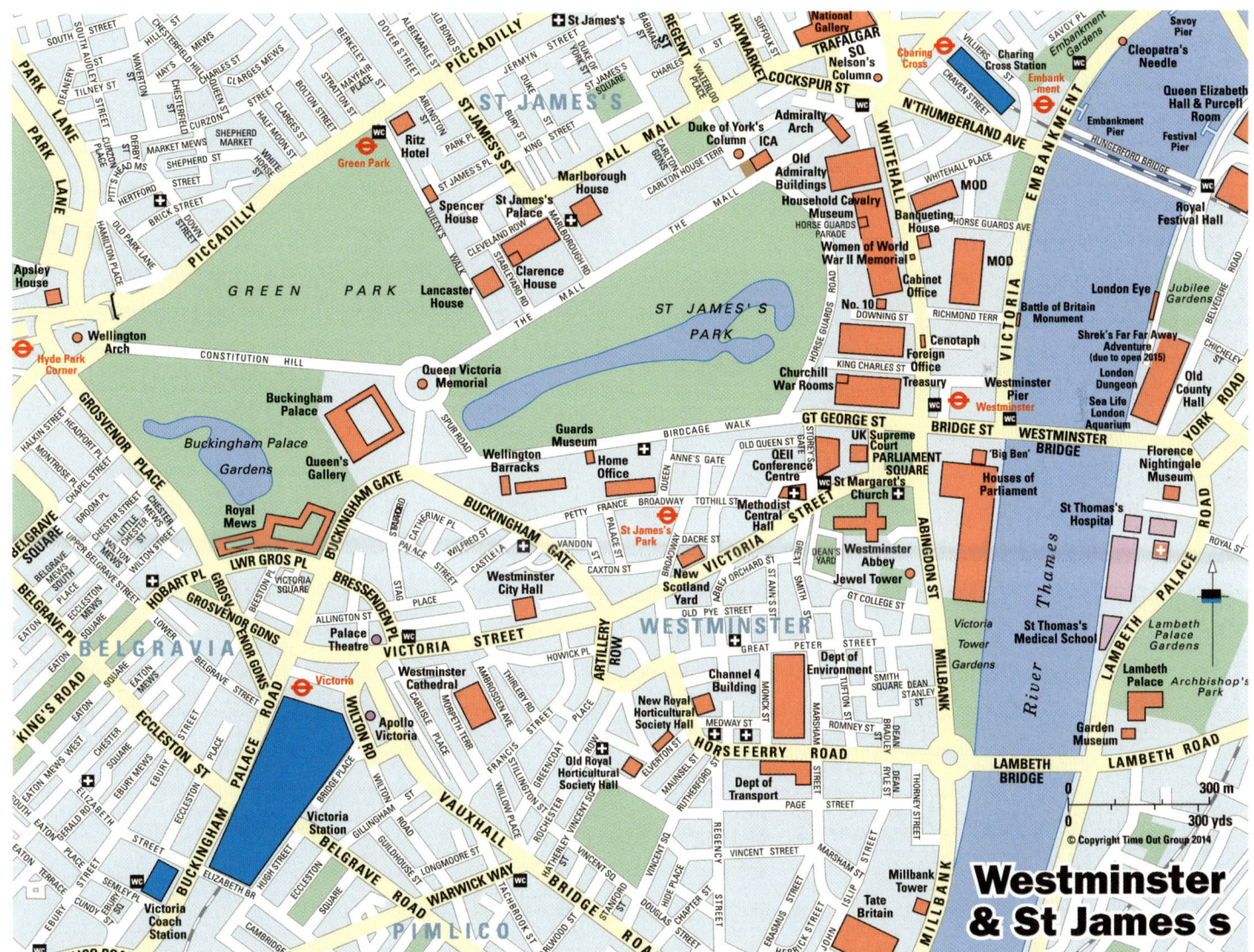

Westminster & St James's

the day also calls it home. It's a key destination for visitors as well, with the most significant area designated a UNESCO World Heritage Site back in 1987. For such an important part of London, it's surprisingly spacious. **St James's Park** is one of London's finest green spaces, **Trafalgar Square** (overlooked by the National Gallery) is a tourist hotspot, and the **Mall** offers a properly regal route to Buckingham Palace.

TRAFALGAR SQUARE

Laid out in the 1820s by John Nash, Trafalgar Square is the heart of modern London. Tourists come in their thousands to pose for photographs in front of **Nelson's Column**. It was erected in 1840 to honour Vice Admiral Horatio Nelson, who died at the point of victory at the Battle of Trafalgar in 1805. The statue atop the 150-foot Corinthian column is foreshortened to appear in perfect proportion from the ground. The granite fountains were added in 1845; Sir Edwin Landseer's bronze lions joined them in 1867.

Once surrounded on all sides by busy roads, the square was improved markedly by pedestrianisation in 2003 of the North Terrace, right in front of the **National Gallery**. The square feels more like public space now, a focus for performance and celebration.

Around the perimeter are three plinths bearing statues of George IV and two Victorian military heroes, Henry Havelock and Sir Charles James Napier. The long-empty **fourth plinth** has been used since 1998 to display temporary, contemporary art. Until spring 2015, Katharina Fritsch's *Hahn/Cock*, a larger-than-life cockerel in bright blue, will stand there, to be replaced by an equine skeleton – *Gift Horse* by Hans Haacke – and then David Shrigley's huge thumbs-up *Really Good*. Other points of interest around the square include an equestrian statue of Charles I, dating from the 1630s, with a plaque behind it that marks the original site of Edward I's Eleanor Cross, the official centre of London. (A recently renovated Victorian replica of the cross stands outside Charing Cross Station.) At the square's north-east corner is the refurbished **St Martin-in-the-Fields** (Trafalgar Square, WC2N 4JJ, 7766 1100, www.smitf.org). It's the parish church for Buckingham Palace (note the royal box to the left of the gallery). In the crypt are a café and the London Brass Rubbing Centre.

National Gallery

Founded in 1824 to display 36 paintings, the National Gallery is now one of the world's great repositories for art. There are masterpieces from virtually every European school of art, from austere 13th-century religious paintings to the sensual delights of Caravaggio and Van Gogh.

Furthest to the left of the main entrance, the modern Sainsbury Wing extension contains the gallery's earliest works: Italian paintings by masters

National Portrait Gallery

such as Giotto and Piero della Francesca, as well as the Wilton Diptych, the finest medieval English picture in the collection, showing Richard II with the Virgin and Child. The basement is the setting for important temporary exhibitions.

In the West Wing (left of the main entrance) are Italian Renaissance masterpieces by Correggio, Titian and Raphael. Straight ahead on entry, in the North Wing, are 17th-century Dutch, Flemish, Italian and Spanish Old Masters, including works such as Rembrandt's *A Woman Bathing in a Stream* and Caravaggio's *Supper at Emmaus*. Velázquez's *Rokeby Venus* is one of the artist's most famous paintings. Also in this wing are works by the great landscape artists Claude and Poussin. Turner insisted that his *Dido Building Carthage* and *Sun Rising through Vapour* should hang alongside two Claudes here.

In the East Wing (to the right of the main entrance) are some of the gallery's most popular paintings: works by the French Impressionists and Post-Impressionists, including Monet's *Water-Lilies*, one of Van Gogh's *Sunflowers* and Seurat's *Bathers at Asnières*. Don't miss Renoir's astonishingly lovely *Les Parapluies*. You shouldn't plan to see everything in one visit, but free guided tours, audio guides and the superb Art Start computer (which allows you to tailor your own itinerary of must-sees) help you make the best of your time. *Trafalgar Square, WC2N 5DN (7747 2885, www.nationalgallery.org.uk). Leicester Square tube or Charing Cross tube/rail. Open 10am-6pm Mon-Thur, Sat, Sun; 10am-9pm Fri. Tours 11.30am, 2.30pm Mon-Thur, Sat, Sun; 11.30am, 2pm, 7pm Fri. Admission free. Special exhibitions vary.*

National Portrait Gallery

Portraits don't have to be stuffy. The excellent National Portrait Gallery has everything from oil paintings of stiff-backed royals to photographs of soccer stars and gloriously unflattering political caricatures. The portraits of musicians, scientists, artists, philanthropists and celebrities are arranged in chronological order from the top to the bottom of the building, with the oldest at the top. At the top of the escalator up from the main foyer, on the second floor, are portraits of Tudor and Stuart royals and notables, including Holbein's 'cartoon' of Henry VIII and the 'Ditchley Portrait' of his daughter, Elizabeth I, her pearly slippers placed firmly on a map of England. On the same floor, the 18th-century collection features Georgian writers and artists, with one room devoted to the influential Kit-Cat Club of bewigged Whig intellectuals, Congreve and Dryden among them. More famous names include Wren and Swift. The second floor also shows Regency greats, military men such as Nelson and Wellington, plus Byron, Wordsworth and other Romantics. The first floor is devoted to the Victorians and to 20th-century luminaries. *St Martin's Place, WC2H 0HE (7306 0055, www.npg.org.uk). Leicester Square tube or Charing Cross tube/rail. Open 10am-6pm Mon-Wed, Sat, Sun; 10am-9pm Thur, Fri. Admission free. Special exhibitions vary.*

WHITEHALL TO PARLIAMENT SQUARE

The offices of the British government are lined along **Whitehall**, itself named after Henry VIII's magnificent palace, which burned to the ground in 1698. Walking south from Trafalgar

Square, you pass the old **Admiralty Offices** and **War Office**, the **Ministry of Defence**, the **Foreign Office** and the **Treasury**, as well as the **Banqueting House**, one of the few buildings to survive the blaze. Also here is **Horse Guards**, headquarters of the Household Cavalry, the army unit that protects the Queen.

Either side of **Downing Street** – home to the prime minister (no.10) and chancellor (no.11), but closed to the public after IRA attacks in the 1980s – are significant war memorials. The millions who died in World Wars I and II are commemorated by Sir Edwin Lutyens's dignified **Cenotaph**, focal point of Remembrance Day (see *p14 Diary*), while a separate memorial to the women of World War II, by sculptor John Mills, recalls the seven million women who contributed to the war effort. Just past the Cenotaph and hidden beneath government offices at the St James's Park end of King Charles Street, the claustrophobic **Churchill War Rooms** (see *p40*) are where Britain's wartime PM delivered his fiery speeches.

The broad sweep of Whitehall is an apt introduction to the monuments of **Parliament Square**. Laid out in 1868, this tiny green space is flanked by the extravagant **Houses of Parliament**, the neo-Gothic Middlesex Guildhall (now the **Supreme Court**) and the twin, square spires of **Westminster Abbey** (see *p40*). Like a pre-pedestrianised Trafalgar Square, Parliament Square can seem little more than a glorified traffic island, despite all the statues of British politicians (Disraeli, Churchill) and foreign dignitaries (Lincoln, Mandela).

Parliament itself simply dazzles. An outrageous neo-Gothic fantasy, the seat of the British government is still formally known as the Palace of Westminster, though the only remaining parts of the medieval palace are **Westminster Hall** and the **Jewel Tower** (see *p40*). At the north end of the palace is the clocktower housing the huge '**Big Ben**' bell that gives the clocktower its popular name; more than seven feet tall, the bell (itself formally known as the 'Great Bell') weighs over 13 tons. The clocktower was, in fact, renamed in 2012 – it became the Elizabeth Tower – in honour of the Queen's Diamond Jubilee.

Banqueting House

This handsome Italianate mansion, which was designed by Inigo Jones and constructed in 1620, was the first true Renaissance building in London. The sole surviving part of the Tudor and Stuart kings' Whitehall Palace, the Banqueting House features a lavish painted ceiling by Rubens, glorifying James I, 'the wisest fool in Christendom'. Regrettably, James's successor, Charles I, did not rule so wisely. After losing the English Civil War, he was executed in front of Banqueting House in 1649 – subject of a new set of displays here.

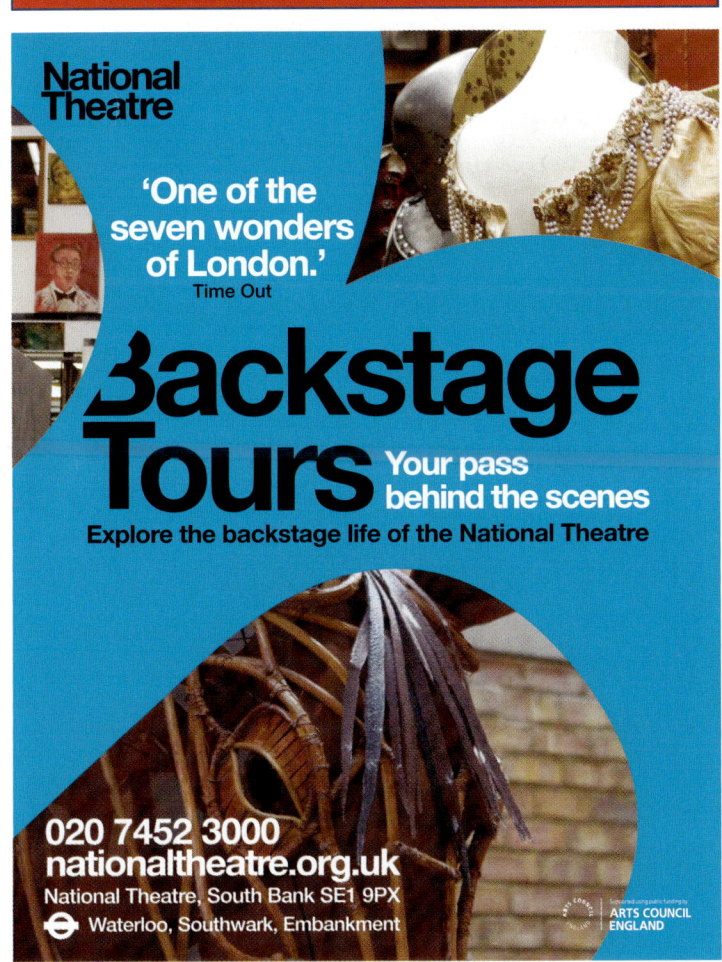

Whitehall, SW1A 2ER (0844 482 7777, www.hrp.org.uk). Westminster tube or Charing Cross tube/rail. Open 10am-5pm Mon-Sat. Admission £6; £5 reductions; free under-16s.

Churchill War Rooms

Out of harm's way beneath Whitehall, this cramped and spartan bunker was where Winston Churchill planned the Allied victory in World War II. The cabinet rooms powerfully bring to life the reality of a nation at war, having been sealed on 16 August 1945, keeping the complex in a state of suspended animation: every pin stuck into the vast charts was placed there in the final days of the conflict. The humble quarters occupied by Churchill and his deputies give a tangible sense of wartime hardship, an effect reinforced by the wailing sirens and wartime speeches on the audio guide.
Clive Steps, King Charles Street, SW1A 2AQ (7930 6961, www.iwm.org.uk). St James's Park tube. Open 9.30am-6pm daily. Admission £17.50; £14 reductions; free under-16s.

Houses of Parliament

The British parliament has an extremely long history, with the first parliamentary session held in St Stephen's Chapel in 1275. The Palace of Westminster, however, only became the permanent seat of Parliament in 1532, when Henry VIII moved to a new des-res in Whitehall. The current Palace is a wonderful mish-mash of styles, dominated by Gothic buttresses, towers and arches. It looks much older than it is: the Parliament buildings were designed in 1860 by Charles Barry (ably assisted by Augustus Welby Northmore Pugin) to replace the original building, which had been destroyed by fire in 1834. Now the compound contains 1,000 rooms, 11 courtyards, eight bars and six restaurants, plus a small cafeteria for visitors. Of the original palace, only the Jewel Tower and the ancient Westminster Hall remain.

Visitors are welcome (subject to stringent security checks at St Stephen's Gate, the only public access point) to observe the political debates in the House of Lords and House of Commons, but tickets must be arranged through your embassy or MP, who can also arrange tours – even trips up the 334 spiral steps of the Elizabeth Tower to hear 'Big Ben'.
Parliament Square, SW1A 0AA (Commons information 7219 4272, Lords information 7219 3107, www.parliament.uk). Westminster tube. Open (when in session) House of Commons Visitors' Gallery 2.30-10.30pm Mon; 11.30am-7.30pm Tue-Wed; 9.30am-5.30pm Thur; 9.30am-3pm Fri. House of Lords Visitors' Gallery 2.30-10pm Mon, Tue; 3pm-10pm Wed; 11am-7.30pm Thur; from 10am Fri. Tours 9.15am-4.30pm Sat & summer recess; check website for details. Admission Visitors' Galleries free. Tours £16.50; £7-£14 reductions; free under-15s (accompanied by adult).

Jewel Tower

This easy-to-overlook little stone tower opposite Parliament was built in 1365 to house Edward III's treasure. It is, with Westminster Hall, all that remains of the medieval Palace of Westminster. It contains a small exhibition on Parliament's history.
Abingdon Street, SW1P 3JY (7222 2219, www. english-heritage.org.uk). Westminster tube. Open Apr-Oct 10am-5pm daily. Nov-Mar 10am-4pm Sat, Sun. Admission £3.90; £2.30-£3.50 reductions; free under-5s.

Westminster Abbey

The cultural, historic and religious significance of Westminster Abbey is impossible to overstate, but also hard to remember as you're shepherded around, forced to elbow fellow tourists out of the way to read a plaque or see a tomb. The best plan is to get here as early in the day as you can. Edward the Confessor commissioned a church to St Peter on the site of a 7th-century version, but it was only consecrated on 28 December 1065, eight days before he died. William the Conqueror had himself crowned here on Christmas Day 1066 and, with just two exceptions, every English coronation since has taken place in the abbey.

Many royal, military and cultural notables are interred here. The most haunting memorial is the Grave of the Unknown Warrior, in the nave. Elaborate resting places in side chapels are taken up by the tombs of Elizabeth I and Mary Queen of Scots. In Innocents Corner lie the remains of two lads believed to be Edward V and his brother Richard (their bodies

were found at the Tower of London), as well as two of James I's children. Poets' Corner is the final resting place of Chaucer, the first to be buried here. Few of the other writers who have stones here are buried in the abbey, but the remains of Dryden, Johnson, Browning and Tennyson are all present.

In the vaulted area under the former monks' dormitory, one of the abbey's oldest parts, the Abbey Museum celebrated its centenary in 2008. You'll find effigies and waxworks of British monarchs, among them Edward II and Henry VII, wearing the robes they donned in life. The 900-year-old College Garden is one of the oldest cultivated spaces in Britain and a useful place to escape the crowds. For snacks, there is a new refectory-style restaurant – the Cellarium Café & Terrace (www.cellariumcafe.com).
20 Dean's Yard, SW1P 3PA (7222 5152 information, 7654 4834 tours, www.westminster-abbey.org). St James's Park or Westminster tube. Open May-Aug 9.30am-3.30pm Mon, Tue, Thur-Sat; 9.30am-6pm Wed. Sept-Apr 9.30am-3.30pm Mon, Tue, Thur, Fri; 9.30am-6pm Wed; 9.30am-1.30pm Sat. Abbey Museum, Chapter House & College Gardens times vary, phone for details. Tours May-Aug 10am, 10.30am, 11am, 2pm, 2.30pm Mon-Fri; 10am, 10.30am, 11am Sat. Sept-Apr 10.30am, 11am, 2pm, 2.30pm Mon-Fri; 10.30am, 11pm Sat. Admission £18; £8-£15 reductions; £44 family; free under-10s with adult. Tours £3.

MILLBANK

Running south from Parliament along the river, Millbank leads eventually to **Tate Britain**, built on the site of an extraordinary pentagonal prison that held criminals destined for

Westminster Abbey

transportation to Botany Bay. If you're walking south from the Palace of Westminster, look out on the left for **Victoria Tower Gardens**, which contain a statue of suffragette leader Emmeline Pankhurst and the rather colourful Buxton Drinking Fountain, commemorating the emancipation of slaves. There's also a version of Rodin's sombre *Burghers of Calais*.

On the other side of the road, Dean Stanley Street leads to Smith Square, home to the architecturally striking **St John's Smith Square** (*see p106 Diary*), now a popular venue for classical music.

Across the river from Millbank is **Vauxhall Cross**, the oddly conspicuous HQ of the Secret Intelligence Service (SIS), commonly referred to by its old name MI6.

Tate Britain

Tate Modern (*see p18*) gets the attention, but the original Tate Gallery, founded by sugar magnate Sir Henry Tate, has a broader brief. Housed in a stately building on the riverside, Tate Britain is second only to the National Gallery when it comes to British art. It's also looking to steal back a bit of the limelight with a 20-year redevelopment plan.

In 2013, a comprehensive rehang was revealed. Covering British art from Holbein in the 1540s up to the present, the major holdings are now shown largely in chronological order – allowing you to trace the development of British art through history – and with a minimum of hectoring curatorial captions. A few key artists are given more substantial treatment: the Turners remain together in their own galleries, and works by Henry Moore and William Blake are grouped rather than being separated by date.

Caruso St John architects have also improved the fabric of the oldest part of the building: sturdier floors mean more sculpture can be displayed, and the amount of natural light allowed in has been increased. At the Millbank entrance, there's a stained-glass window by Turner Prize-winner Richard Wright; inside, you'll find a spiral staircase; and downstairs in the restaurant, a new ceiling mural has been designed by Alan Johnston to complement the restored 1926-27 Rex Whistler wall mural *Pursuit of Rare Meats*. There is also a space for temporary exhibits, including an exploration of the site's fascinating early history as the ill-fated Millbank prison. Alongside the headline-hungry blockbuster temporary shows, Art Now installations showcase up-and-coming or little-known British artists.
Millbank, SW1P 4RG (7887 8888, www.tate.org.uk). Pimlico tube. Open 10am-6pm daily. Tours 11am, noon, 2pm, 3pm daily. Admission free. Special exhibitions vary.

VICTORIA

As you might expect from London's main backpacker hangout, Victoria is busy and chaotic. The rail station is a major hub for trains to southern

Tate Britain

England, while the nearby coach station is served by buses from all over Europe. Catering to new arrivals, Belgrave Road provides an almost unbroken line of cheap and often shabby B&Bs, hotels and hostels. The theatres dotted around form a western outpost of the West End's Theatreland.

Westminster Cathedral is the headquarters of the Roman Catholic Church in England. South of Victoria station are the Georgian terraces of **Pimlico**. Antique stores and restaurants line Pimlico Road; the intriguing independent shops of Tachbrook Street are worth a look.

North of Victoria Street towards Parliament Square is **Christchurch Gardens**, burial site of Thomas ('Colonel') Blood, who stole the Crown Jewels in 1671. He was apprehended making his getaway but managed to talk his way into a full pardon. Also in the area are **New Scotland Yard**, with its famous revolving sign, and the art deco headquarters of **London Underground** at 55 Broadway.

Westminster Cathedral

With its domes, arches and soaring tower, the most important Catholic church in England looks surprisingly Byzantine. There's a reason: architect John Francis Bentley, who built it between 1895 and 1903, was heavily influenced by Hagia Sophia in Istanbul. Compared to the candy-cane exterior, the interior is surprisingly restrained (in fact, it's unfinished), but there are still more impressive marble columns and mosaics. Eric Gill's sculptures of the Stations of the Cross (1914-18) were dismissed as 'Babylonian' when they were first installed, but worshippers have come to love them. An upper gallery holds the 'Treasures of the Cathedral' exhibition, where you can see an impressive coronet, holy relics and Bentley's amazing architectural model of his cathedral.

42 Francis Street, SW1P 1QW (7798 9055, www.westminster cathedral.org.uk). Victoria tube/rail. Open 7am-7pm Mon-Fri; 8am-8pm Sat, Sun. Exhibition & Bell tower 9.30am-4.45pm Mon-Sat; 9.30am-5.30pm Sun. Admission free; donations appreciated. Exhibition £5; free-£2.50 reductions; £11 family. Bell tower & exhibition £8; free-£4 reductions; £17.50 family.

ST JAMES'S

Handsome **St James's Park** was founded as a deer park for the royal occupants of St James's Palace, and remodelled by John Nash on the orders of George IV. The central lake is home to various species of wildfowl; pelicans have been kept here since the 17th century. The bridge over the lake offers good views of **Buckingham Palace**. Along the north side of the park, the **Mall** connects Buckingham Palace with Trafalgar Square. It looks like a processional route, but the Mall was actually laid out as a pitch for Charles II to play 'pallemaille' (an early version of croquet) after the one at Pall Mall became too crowded. On the south side of the park, Wellington Barracks holds the **Guards Museum**; to the east, Horse Guards contains the **Household Cavalry Museum**.

Carlton House Terrace, on the north flank of the Mall, was the last project completed by John Nash before his death in 1835. Part of the terrace now houses the **ICA**. Just behind is the **Duke of York column**, commemorating Prince Frederick, Duke of York. He's the nursery rhyme's 'Grand old Duke of York'.

Nestling between the Mall and the park is one of London's most refined residential areas. St James's was laid out in the 1660s for royal and aristocratic families. Bordered by Piccadilly, Haymarket, the Mall and Green Park, the district is centred on

St James's Square. Just south of the square, Pall Mall is lined with exclusive, members-only gentlemen's clubs (in the old-fashioned sense of the word). Polished nameplates reveal such prestigious establishments as the **Institute of Directors** (no.116) and the **Reform Club** (nos.104-105), site of Phileas Fogg's famous bet in *Around the World in Eighty Days*. Around the corner on St James's Street, the **Carlton Club** (no.69) is the official club of the Conservative Party; Lady Thatcher remains the only woman to be granted full membership. Nearby on King Street is **Christie's** (7839 9060, www.christies.com), the world's oldest fine-art auctioneers.

At the south end of St James's Street, **St James's Palace** was built for Henry VIII in the 1530s. Extensively remodelled over the centuries, the red-brick palace is still the official address of the Royal Court, even though every monarch since 1837 has lived at Buckingham Palace. From here, Mary Tudor surrendered Calais and Elizabeth I led the campaign against the Spanish Armada; this is also where Charles I was confined before his 1649 execution. The palace is home to the Princess Royal (the title given to the monarch's eldest daughter, currently Princess Anne); it's closed to the public, but you can attend Sunday services at its historic **Chapel Royal** (1st Sun of mth, Oct-Easter Sunday; 8.30am, 11.15am).

Adjacent to St James's Palace is **Clarence House** (The Mall, SW1A 1AA, 7766 7303, www.royalcollection. org.uk), former residence of the Queen Mother; a few streets north, delightful **Spencer House** (27 St James's Place, SW1A 1NR, 7499 8620, www.spencer house.co.uk) is the ancestral home of the family of the late Princess Diana.

Buckingham Palace & Royal Mews

Although nearby St James's Palace remains the official seat of the British court, every monarch since Victoria has used Buckingham Palace as their primary home. Originally known as Buckingham House, the present home of the British royals was constructed as a private house for the Duke of Buckingham in 1703, but George III liked it so much he purchased it for his bride Charlotte in 1761. George IV decided to occupy the mansion himself and John Nash was hired to convert it into a palace. Construction was beset with problems, and Nash was dismissed in 1830. When Victoria came to the throne in 1837, the building was barely habitable. The job of finishing the palace fell to the unimaginative Edward Blore ('Blore the Bore'). The neoclassical frontage now in place was the work of Aston Webb in 1913.

As the home of the Queen, the palace is usually closed to visitors, but you can view the interior for a brief period each year while the Windsors are on holiday; you'll be able to see the State Rooms, and part of the garden. There's even a café – paper cups, sadly, but coloured a pretty blue-green and clearly marked

with the palace crest. At any time of year, you can visit the Queen's Gallery to see her personal collection of treasures, including paintings by Rubens and Rembrandt, Sèvres porcelain and the Diamond Diadem crown. Further along Buckingham Palace Road, the Royal Mews is a grand garage for the royal fleet of Rolls-Royces and home to the splendid royal carriages and the horses that pull them. *The Mall, SW1A 1AA (Palace 7766 7300, Royal Mews 7766 7302, Queen's Gallery 7766 7301, www. royalcollection.org.uk). Green Park tube or Victoria tube/rail. Open times vary; check website for details. Admission prices vary; check website for details.*

Guards Museum

This small museum tells the 350-year story of the Foot Guards, using flamboyant uniforms, period paintings, medals and intriguing memorabilia, such as the stuffed body of Jacob the Goose, the Guard's Victorian mascot, who was regrettably run over by a van in barracks. *Wellington Barracks, Birdcage Walk, SW1E 6HQ (7414 3428, www.theguardsmuseum.com). St James's Park tube. Open 10am-4pm daily. Admission £5; £1-£2.50 reductions; free under-16s.*

Household Cavalry Museum

Troopers of the Household Cavalry get to tell their stories through video diaries at this small but entertaining museum, which also offers the chance to see medals, uniforms and shiny cuirasses (breastplates). You'll also get a peek – and sniff – of the magnificent horses that parade just outside every day: the stables are only separated from the main museum a glass screen. *Horse Guards, Whitehall, SW1A 2AX (7930 3070, www.householdcavalry museum.co.uk). Westminster tube or Charing Cross tube/rail. Open Mar-Sept 10am-6pm daily. Oct-Feb 10am-5pm daily. Admission £7; £5 reductions; £18 family ticket; free under-5s.*

ICA (Institute of Contemporary Arts)

Founded in 1947 by a collective of poets, artists and critics, the ICA has recently found itself somewhat adrift. It's a venue for arthouse cinema, performance art, philosophical debates, exhibitions and club nights. New director Gregor Muir is pursuing some interesting ideas for its rebirth. *The Mall, SW1Y 5AH (7930 0493, tickets 7930 3647, www.ica.org.uk). Piccadilly Circus tube or Charing Cross tube/rail. Open (during exhibitions) 11am-6pm Tue, Wed, Fri-Sun; 11am-9pm Thur. Admission free.*

Chelsea

Chelsea was a 'village of palaces' by the 16th century, home to the likes of Sir Thomas More. Artists and poets (Whistler, Carlyle, Wilde)

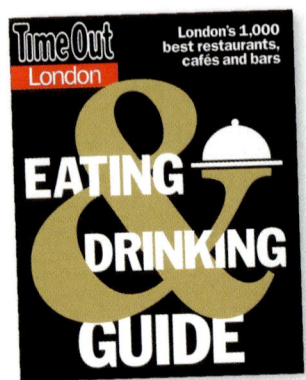

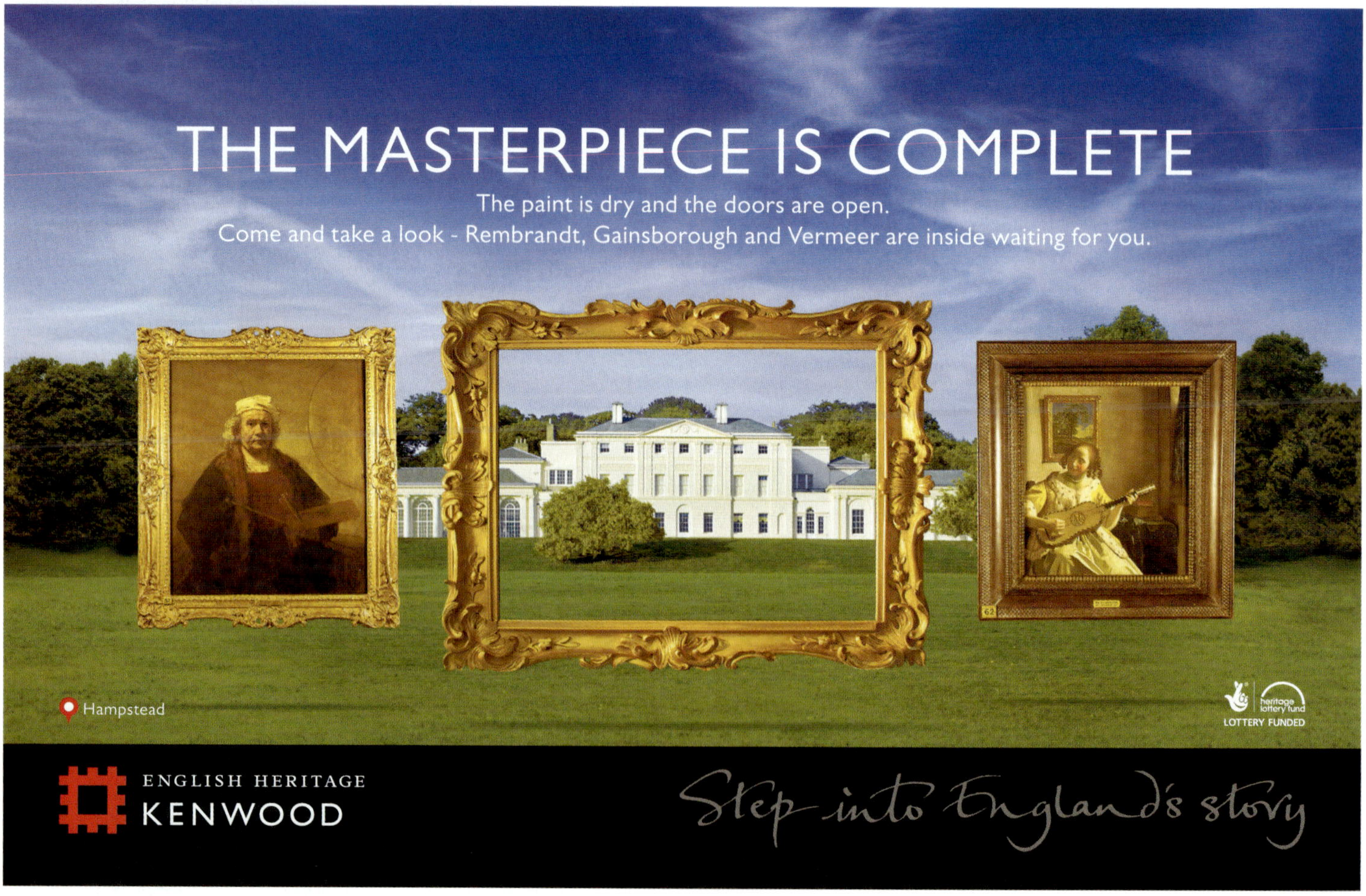

followed from the 1880s, before the fashionistas arrived with the opening of Mary Quant's Bazaar in 1955. Soon after, Chelsea had acquired a raffish reputation and was at the forefront of successive youth culture revolutions. Those days are long gone. Now there are smart shops and streets of immaculate terraced housing, but – with the exceptions of the **Saatchi Gallery** and the **Chelsea Physic Garden** – cultural pleasures are few.

SLOANE SQUARE & THE KING'S ROAD

Synonymous with the Swinging Sixties and immortalised by punk, the dissipated phase of the **King's Road** is now a matter for historians as the street teems with upmarket chain stores. Yet on a sunny day, it does make a vivid stroll, full of expensive red-brick houses that slumber down leafy mews and cobbled sidestreets.

At the top (east end) of the King's Road is **Sloane Square**. It's named after Sir Hans Sloane, who provided the land for the **Chelsea Physic Garden**, invented milk chocolate in the early 18th century and was instrumental in the founding of the British Museum. A certain edginess is lent to proceedings by the **Royal Court Theatre** (see p107).

To escape the bustle and fumes, head to the **Duke of York Square**, a pedestrianised enclave of boutiques and restaurants presided over by a statue of Sir Hans. In the summer, the cooling fountains attract hordes of children, their parents watching from the outdoor café tables. It's also home to Saturday food market, and the **Saatchi Gallery**.

Saatchi Gallery

Charles Saatchi's gallery offers 50,000sq ft of space for temporary exhibitions. Given his fame as a promoter in the 1990s of what became known as the Young British Artists – Damien Hirst, Tracey Emin, Gavin Turk, Sarah Lucas et al – it will surprise many that the opening exhibition a few years back was devoted to new Chinese art. More recent shows have continued the international feel.
Duke of York's HQ, King's Road, SW3 4SQ (7811 3070, www.saatchi-gallery.co.uk). Sloane Square tube. Open 10am-6pm daily. Admission free.

CHEYNE WALK & CHELSEA

Chelsea's riverside has long been noted for its nurseries and gardens, lending a village air that befits a place of retirement for soldiers; in summer, the Chelsea Pensioners regularly don red coats and tricorn hats when venturing beyond the gates of **Royal Hospital Chelsea** (7881 5200, www.chelsea-pensioners.org.uk). The Royal Hospital's lovely gardens host the Chelsea Flower Show (see p11) each May. Next door is the **National Army Museum**. West from the river end of Royal Hospital Road is **Cheyne Walk**, its river-view benches good spots for a sit-down, but the tranquil **Chelsea Physic Garden** is the real treat.

Chelsea Physic Garden

The capacious grounds of this gorgeous botanic garden are filled with healing herbs and vegetables, rare trees and dye plants. The garden was founded in 1673 by Sir Hans Sloane with the purpose of cultivating and studying plants for medicine. The first plant specimens were brought to England and planted here in 1676, and the garden eventually opened to the public in 1893. In April 2014, a new Garden of Medicinal Plants will open here, tracing the chronology of plant remedies over almost an acre, from ancient Greek herbs to plants that are likely to be used in future medicine.
66 Royal Hospital Road, SW3 4HS (7352 5646, www.chelseaphysicgarden.co.uk). Sloane Square tube or bus 11, 19, 22. Open Apr-June, Oct 11am-6pm Tue-Fri, Sun. July, Aug 11am-6pm Mon, Tue, Thur, Fri, Sun; 11am-10pm Wed. Tours times vary; phone to check. Admission £9.90; £6.60 reductions; free under-5s. Tours free.

National Army Museum

More entertaining than its modern exterior might suggest, this museum dedicated to the history of the British Army runs chronologically, running from the wars of Empire ('Changing the World, 1784-1904'), through two World Wars and into contemporary conflicts including the Falklands, Northern Ireland and Afghanistan ('Conflicts of Interest, 1969- present'). Key artefacts include a French eagle standard from the Napoleonic Wars and a model of Waterloo with 70,000 soldiers. There's also a gallery of military art since the 17th century.

Royal Hospital Road, SW3 4HT (7730 0717, www.nam.ac.uk). Sloane Square tube or bus 11, 137, 170. Open 10am-5.30pm daily. Admission free.

Knightsbridge & South Kensington

A certain type of Londoner goes to **Knightsbridge** to spend, spend, spend. Many of the key designer labels have major shops in the area, which gets plenty of foot traffic thanks to its world-famous department stores and high-end restaurants. Nearby, **South Kensington**'s footprint is cultural rather than commercial: three of the world's greatest museums are there.

TOP TIP!
Planning is all
The South Ken museums are ace, but, boy, they get busy. Arrive early and avoid school hols, if you can, and grown-ups – check out the monthly late openings.

KNIGHTSBRIDGE

Knightsbridge is all about credit-card abuse. Voguish **Harvey Nichols** holds court at the top of **Sloane Street**, which leads down to Sloane Square. Expensive brands – Gucci, Prada, Chanel – dominate. East of Sloane Street, **Belgravia** is characterised by a cluster of embassies around **Belgrave Square**. Hidden behind the stucco-clad parades fronting the square are numerous mews, worth exploring for the pubs they conceal, notably the **Nag's Head** (53 Kinnerton Street, 7235 1135).

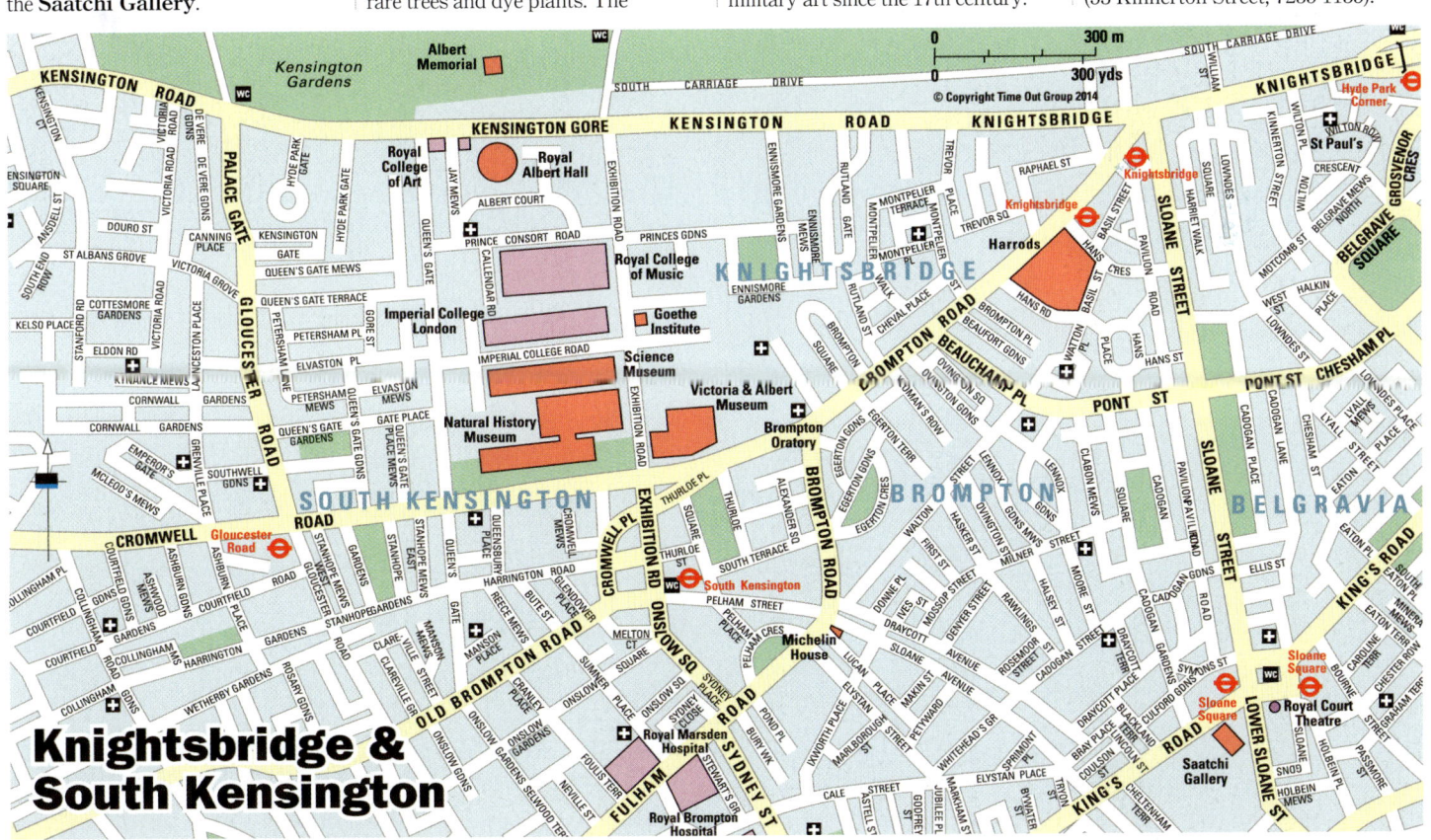

Knightsbridge & South Kensington

The Swinging 1760s
Romantic Rococo Revelations

THE WALLACE COLLECTION

A serene oasis just minutes from Oxford Street
Free & Open Daily 10am – 5pm
www.wallacecollection.org

Jean-Honoré Fragonard, *The Swing*, 1767, detail

Experience wonderful art from around the world
in one beautiful, central London setting

Don't miss out! 19 September – the refurbished Great Gallery opens after two years

The Wallace Collection, Manchester Square, London W1U 3BN (nearest tube Bond Street)

A FAMILY COLLECTION | A NATIONAL MUSEUM | AN INTERNATIONAL TREASURE HOUSE

For many tourists, Knightsbridge means one thing: **Harrods** (*see p84*). Further along is the second-biggest Catholic church in the country: the imposing **Brompton Oratory** (Thurloe Place, Brompton Road, SW7 2RP, 7808 0900, www.brompton oratory.com).

SOUTH KENSINGTON

It was Prince Albert who oversaw the inception of this area's world-class museums, colleges and concert hall, using the profits of the 1851 Great Exhibition; the area was nicknamed 'Albertopolis' in his honour. You'll find the **Natural History Museum**, the **Science Museum** and the **Victoria & Albert Museum**, **Imperial College**, the **Royal College of Art** and the **Royal College of Music** (Prince Consort Road, 7589 3643), which forms a unity with the **Royal Albert Hall** (*see p106*). Opposite is the **Albert Memorial**.

Albert Memorial

'I would rather not be made the prominent feature of such a monument' was Prince Albert's reported response when the subject of his commemoration arose. Hard, then, to imagine what he would have made of this extraordinary thing, unveiled 15 years after his death. Created by Sir George Gilbert Scott, it centres around a gilded Albert holding a catalogue of the 1851 Great Exhibition. The pillars are crowned with bronze statues of the sciences, and a frieze depicts major artists, architects and musicians. *Kensington Gardens (7936 2568, www.royalparks.org.uk). South Kensington tube. Tours Mar-Dec 2pm, 3pm 1st Sun of mth. Admission Tours £7; £6 reductions. No credit cards.*

Natural History Museum

Both a research institution and a fabulous museum, the NHM opened in Alfred Waterhouse's purpose-built, Romanesque palazzo on the Cromwell Road in 1881. Now joined by the splendid Darwin Centre extension, the original building looks magnificent. The pale blue and terracotta façade just about prepares you for the natural wonders within. Taking up the full length of the vast entrance hall is the cast of a *Diplodocus* skeleton. A left turn leads into the west wing or Blue Zone, where long queues form to see animatronic dinosaurs – especially the endlessly popular *T rex*. A display on biology features an illuminated, man-sized model of a foetus in the womb along with graphic diagrams of how it might have got there. A right turn from the central hall leads past the 'Creepy Crawlies' exhibition to the Green Zone. Stars include a cross-section through a Giant Sequoia tree and an amazing array of stuffed birds, including the chance to compare the tiny egg of a hummingbird with the football-sized egg of an elephant bird (now extinct). Beyond is the Red Zone: 'Earth's Treasury' is a mine of information on a variety of precious metals, gems and crystals; 'From the Beginning' is a brave attempt to give the expanse of geological time a human perspective.

Many of the museum's 22 million insect and plant specimens are housed in the new Darwin Centre, where they take up nearly 17 miles of shelving. With its eight-storey Cocoon, this is also home to research scientists, who can be watched at work. *Cromwell Road, SW7 5BD (7942 5000, www.nhm.ac.uk). South Kensington tube. Open 10am-5.50pm daily. Admission free; charges apply for special exhibitions. Tours free.*

Science Museum

The Science Museum is a celebration of the wonders of technology in the service of our daily lives. On the ground floor, the shop – selling brilliant toys – is part of the 'Energy Hall', which introduces the museum's collections with impressive 18th-century steam engines. In 'Exploring Space', rocket science and the lunar landings are illustrated by dramatically lit mock-ups and models, before the museum gears up for its core collection in 'Making the Modern World'. Introduced by Puffing Billy, the world's oldest steam locomotive (1815), the gallery also contains Stephenson's Rocket. Also here are the Apollo 10 command module, classic cars and an absorbing collection of everyday technological marvels from 1750 right up to the present.

In the main body of the museum, the second floor holds displays on computing, marine engineering and mathematics; the third floor is dedicated to flight, among other things, including the hands-on Launchpad gallery, which has levers, pulleys, explosions and all manner of experiments for children. On the fifth floor, you'll find an old-fashioned display on medicine.

Beyond 'Making the Modern World', the three floors of the Wellcome Wing are where the museum makes sure it stays on the cutting edge of science. On the ground floor, 'Antenna' is a web-savvy look at breaking science stories. Upstairs is the enjoyable and troubling 'Who Am I?' gallery. A dozen silver pods surround brightly lit cases of objects with engaging interactive displays – from a cartoon of ethical dilemmas that introduces you to your dorsolateral prefrontal cortex to a chance to find out what gender your brain is. Compelling objects include a jellyfish that's 'technically immortal', the statistically average British man (he's called Jose) and a pound of human fat. There's also the new Media Space on the second floor, for exhibitions drawn from the museum's impressive photographic archive. *Exhibition Road, SW7 2DD (7942 4000, information 0870 870 4868, www.sciencemuseum.org.uk). South Kensington tube. Open 10am-6pm daily. Admission free; charges apply for special exhibitions.*

Victoria & Albert Museum

The V&A is one of the world's – let alone London's – most magnificent museums, its foundation stone laid on this site by Queen Victoria in her last official public engagement in 1899. It is a superb showcase for applied arts from around the world, appreciably calmer than its tearaway cousins on the other side of Exhibition Road. Some 150 grand galleries on seven floors contain countless pieces of furniture, ceramics, sculpture, paintings, jewellery, metalwork, glass, textiles and dress, spanning several centuries.

Highlights include the seven Raphael Cartoons painted in 1515 as tapestry designs for the Sistine Chapel; the finest collection of Italian Renaissance sculpture outside Italy; the Ardabil carpet, the world's oldest and arguably most splendid floor covering, in the Jameel Gallery of Islamic Art; and the Luck of Edenhall, a 13th-century glass beaker from Syria. The fashion galleries run from 18th-century court dress right up to contemporary chiffon numbers; the architecture gallery has videos, models, plans and descriptions of various styles; and the famous photography collection holds over 500,000 images.

Over more than a decade, the V&A's ongoing FuturePlan transformation has been a revelation. The completely refurbished Medieval & Renaissance Galleries are stunning, but there are many other eye-catching new or redisplayed exhibits: the Furniture Galleries, for instance, which were an immediate hit on opening in 2012. On a smaller scale, the Gilbert Collection of silver, gold and gemmed ornaments arrived from Somerset House; the Ceramics Galleries have been renovated and supplemented with an eye-catching bridge; and the Theatre & Performance Galleries took over from Covent Garden's defunct Theatre Museum.

There's more to come. In December 2014, the latest grand opening will be the ambitious Europe 1600-1800 galleries, which cost £12.5m. A stunning 13ft-long table fountain is due to form the centrepiece of seven new galleries, taking a chronological and thematic approach to European clothes, furnishings and other artefacts. We're also looking forward to seeing what's been done with the magnificent Cast Courts – the public should be allowed back to ogle the 18ft-high plaster David and other monumental sculptures in these double-height Victorian galleries in November 2014. *Cromwell Road, SW7 2RL (7942 2000, www.vam.ac.uk). South Kensington tube. Open 10am-5.45pm*

Victoria & Albert Museum

V&A: VICTORIA AND ALBERT MUSEUM

Mon-Thur, Sat, Sun; 10am-10pm Fri. Tours 10.30am, 12.30pm, 1.30pm, 3.30pm daily. Admission free; charges for special exhibitions.

HYDE PARK & KENSINGTON GARDENS

At one and a half miles long and about a mile wide, **Hyde Park** (7298 2000, www.royalparks. gov.uk) is one of the largest of London's Royal Parks. The land was appropriated in 1536 from the monks of Westminster Abbey by Henry VIII for hunting deer. At the end of the 17th century, William III, averse to the dank air of Whitehall Palace, relocated to **Kensington Palace**. A corner of Hyde Park was sectioned off to make grounds for the palace and closed to the public, until King George II opened it on Sundays – to those wearing formal dress. Now, **Kensington Gardens** is delineated from Hyde Park only by the line of the Serpentine and the Long Water. Beside the Long Water is a bronze statue of **Peter Pan**: it was in Kensington Gardens that playwright JM Barrie met Jack Llewelyn Davies, the boy who was the inspiration for Peter. **The Diana, Princess of Wales Memorial Playground** (*see p93*) is a kids' favourite, as is Kathryn Gustafson's ring-shaped **Princess Diana Memorial Fountain**. There is contemporary art at the **Serpentine & Serpentine Sackler Galleries**, which are at either end of a bridge acrss the **Serpentine**, London's oldest boating lake.

Hyde Park isn't an especially beautiful park, but is of historic interest. The legalisation of public assembly in the park led to the establishment of Speakers' Corner in 1872 (close to Marble Arch tube), where political and religious ranters – sane and otherwise – still have the floor every Sunday. Marx, Orwell and the Pankhursts all spoke here. It has made the park a traditional destination for protest marches: notably the million opponents of the Iraq War in 2003, more recently trades union protests against government austerity measures in 2012.

The park perimeter is popular with skaters, as well as cyclists and horse-riders. Look out too for the Liberty Drives (May-Oct). Driven by volunteers, these buggies pick up sightseers and ferry them around; there's no fare, but offer a donation if you can.

Kensington Palace

Sir Christopher Wren extended this Jacobean mansion to palatial proportions on the instructions of William III. The palace has been recently refurbished, with visitors now able to follow a whimsical trail focused on four 'stories' of former royal residents (as well as Princess Diana, it features Queens Mary, Anne and Victoria).
Kensington Gardens, W8 4PX (0844 482 7777, reservations 0844 482 7799, www.hrp.org.uk). High Street Kensington or Queensway tube. Open

Serpentine Sackler Gallery

Apr-Oct 10am-6pm daily. Nov-Mar 10am-5pm daily. Admission £16.50; £13.75 reductions; free under-16s.

Serpentine & Serpentine Sackler Galleries

The secluded location south-west of the Long Water and Serpentine makes the original Serpentine Gallery – in the 1930s a small tea house – an attractive destination for lovers of contemporary art. The two-monthly programme of exhibitions features a mix of up-to-the-minute artists and edgy retrospectives. Every spring, a renowned architect, who's never before built in the UK, is commissioned to build a new pavilion. It then opens to the public, with cultural events from June to September.

In 2013, the gallery underwent a massive expansion – by dint of opening a second location, the Serpentine Sackler, just across the bridge. Devoted to emerging art in all forms, the Sackler is a Grade II-listed, Palladian former gunpowder store, over the restaurant area of which starchitect Zaha Hadid has cast a billowing white cape of roof.
Kensington Gardens, nr Albert Memorial, W2 3XA (7402 6075, www.serpentinegallery.org). Lancaster Gate or South Kensington tube. Open 10am-6pm daily. Admission free; donations appreciated.

North London

The list of famous residents gives an idea of the scope of north London: rich popstrel Amy Winehouse, émigré psychoanalyst Sigmund Freud, brainy leftie Karl Marx and frilly shirted young poet John Keats have all lived here, whether in the area's pretty, sleepy retreats or its buzzing, creative party zones. First stop for most is **Camden Town**, with its markets, indie pubs and alternative vibe, but

there's fun to be found in the squares of **Islington** or lapping up the genteel atmosphere in **Hampstead** and **Highgate**.

CAMDEN & ST JOHN'S WOOD

Despite the pressures of gentrification, Camden refuses to leave behind its grungy history as the cradle of British rock music. The music still plays at Camden icon the **Roundhouse** (*see p101*) in the north, **Koko** (*see p101*) to the south, and any number of pubs and clubs between: try the **Underworld** (*see p103*) and the **Dublin Castle** (94 Parkway, 7485 1773), where Madness and, later, Blur were launched. The **Jazz Café** and the **Blues Kitchen** (for both, *see p102*) offer a different vibe. Tourists travel here in their thousands for the sprawling mayhem of **Camden Market** (*see p86*).

Cutting through the market is **Regent's Canal**, which opened in 1820 to provide a link between east and west London for narrowboats loaded with coal. Today, the canal is used by the jolly tour boats, which run between Camden Lock and **Little Venice**.

Camden's one avowed 'sight' is the excellent **Jewish Museum** – but, on the far side of Regent's Park in posh St John's Wood, a major tourist attraction is **Lord's** cricket ground. Music fans pay tribute to the Beatles by walking over the zebra crossing near **Abbey Road Studios** (3 Abbey Road).

Jewish Museum

A brilliant exploration of Jewish life in Britain since 1066, combining fun interactives with serious history. There's a powerful Holocaust section, using the testimony of a single survivor, Leon Greenman, to bring tight focus to the horror of it all. Opposite, a beautiful room of religious artefacts does an elegant job of introducing Jewish ritual.

Raymond Burton House, 129-131 Albert Street, NW1 7NB (7284 7384, www.jewishmuseum.org.uk). Camden Town tube. Open 10am-5pm Mon-Thur, Sun; 10am-2pm Fri. Admission £7.50; £3.50-£6.50 reductions; free under-5s; £18 family.

Lord's Tour & MCC Museum

Lord's is more than just a famous cricket ground. As the headquarters of the Marylebone Cricket Club (MCC), it is official guardian of the rules – and self-appointed guardian of the elusive 'spirit' – of cricket. As well as staging Test matches and internationals, the ground is home to the Middlesex County Cricket Club (MCCC). Visitors can take an organised tour round the futuristic, pod-like JP Morgan Media Centre and the august, portrait-bedecked Long Room. A museum highlight is the tiny urn containing the Ashes (this coveted trophy never leaves Lord's, even though the Australians won it back in formidable style in 2013/14).
St John's Wood Road, NW8 8QN (7616 8500, www.lords.org). St John's Wood tube. Open Tours phone or check website for details. Admission £15; £9 reductions; free under-5s; £40 family.

HAMPSTEAD & HIGHGATE

Hilltop Hampstead has long been a favoured roost for literary and artistic types: Keats and Constable lived here in the 19th century, and sculptors Barbara Hepworth and Henry Moore took up residence in the 1930s. However, the area is now popular with City workers. The undisputed highlight is **Hampstead Heath**, the vast and in places wonderfully overgrown tract of land between Hampstead village and Highgate. The heath covers 791 acres of woodland, playing fields, swimming ponds and meadows of tall grass.

At the south end of the heath, dinky Hampstead village is all genteel shops and cafés, restaurants and lovely pubs such as the **Holly Bush** (see p73). At the top of Hampstead, North End Way divides the main heath from the wooded West Heath, one of London's oldest gay cruising areas (but perfectly family-friendly by day).

East of Hampstead tube, a maze of postcard-pretty residential streets shelters **Burgh House** (New End Square, 7431 0144, www.burgh house.org.uk), a Queen Anne house with a small local history museum and gallery. Also in the area is **40 Well Walk**, Constable's home for the last ten years of his life. Downhill towards Hampstead Heath Overground station is **Keats House**. Further west, and marginally closer to Finchley Road tube, is the **Freud Museum**.

North of Hampstead, Highgate is inexorably linked with London's medieval mayor, Richard 'Dick' Whittington. As the story goes, the disheartened Whittington, having failed to make his fortune, fled the City as far as Highgate Hill, but turned back when he heard the Bow Bells peal out 'Turn again, Whittington, thrice Mayor of London'. Today, the area is best known for the atmospheric grounds of **Highgate Cemetery**. North of Highgate tube, **Highgate Woods** is a conservation area, with an adventure playground and a café.

Freud Museum

Driven from Vienna by the Nazis, Sigmund Freud lived in this quiet suburban house with his wife Martha and daughter Anna until his death in 1939. Now a museum with imaginative temporary exhibitions, the house displays Freud's antiques, art and therapy tools, including his famous couch. Unusually, the building has two blue plaques, one for Sigmund and one for Anna, a pioneer in child psychiatry. *20 Maresfield Gardens, NW3 5SX (7435 2002, www.freud.org.uk). Finchley Road tube. Open noon-5pm Wed-Sun. Admission £6; £3-£4.50 reductions; free under-12s.*

Highgate Cemetery

Highgate Cemetery is a wonderfully overgrown maze of ivy-cloaked Victorian tombs and time-shattered urns. Visitors can wander at their own pace through the East Cemetery, with its memorials to Karl Marx, George Eliot and Douglas Adams, but the most atmospheric part of the cemetery is the foliage-shrouded West Cemetery, laid out in 1839. Only accessible on an organised tour (book ahead, dress respectfully and arrive 30mins early), the shady paths wind past gloomy catacombs, grand Victorian pharaonic tombs, and the graves of notables such as poet Christina Rossetti, scientist Michael Faraday and poisoned Russian dissident Alexander Litvinenko. *Swains Lane, N6 6PJ (8340 1834, www.highgate-cemetery.org). Archway tube. Open East Cemetery Mar-Oct 10am-5pm Mon-Fri; 11am-5pm Sat,*

Sun. Nov-Feb 10am-4pm Mon-Fri; 11am-4pm Sat, Sun. West Cemetery by tour only. Admission £4; free under 18s. Tours £12; £6 reductions.

Keats House

Keats House was the Romantic poet's last British home before tuberculosis forced him to Italy and death at the age of 25. The garden, in which he wrote 'Ode to a Nightingale', is lovely. *Keats Grove, NW3 2RR (7332 3868, www.cityoflondon.gov.uk/keatshouse hampstead). Hampstead tube or Hampstead Heath rail, or bus 24, 46, 168. Open Mar-Oct 1-5pm Tue-Sun. Nov-Feb 1-5pm Fri-Sun. Admission £5; £3 reductions; free under-18s.*

Kenwood House/Iveagh Bequest

Set in lovely grounds at the top of Hampstead Heath, Kenwood House is every inch the country manor house. Built in 1616, the mansion was remodelled in the 18th century for William Murray, who made the pivotal court ruling in 1772 that made it illegal to own slaves in England. The house was purchased by brewing magnate Edward Guinness, who was kind enough to donate his art collection to the nation in 1927. It reopened in 2014 after extensive, splendid renovations, returning the interiors to a state that enhances such highlights as Vermeer's The Guitar Player, Gainsborough's Countess Howe, and one of Rembrandt's finest self-portraits (dating to c1663). *Hampstead Lane, NW3 7JR (8348 1286, www.english-heritage.org.uk). Hampstead tube, or Golders Green tube then bus 210. Open 9am-4pm daily. Admission free.*

ISLINGTON

For visitors to Islington, the cafés, restaurants and boutiques around Upper Street and Essex Road are the real draw. Close to the station, the **Camden Passage** antique market

bustles with browsers on Wednesdays and Saturdays. There's also culture: celluloid offerings at the **Screen on the Green** (see p95) and the stage productions at the **Almeida** (see p108). East of Angel, Regency-era **Canonbury Square** was once home to George Orwell (no.27) and Evelyn Waugh (no.17A). One of the handsome townhouses now contains the **Estorick Collection of Modern Italian Art**. Just beyond the end of Upper Street is **Highbury Fields**, where 200,000 Londoners fled in 1666 to escape the Great Fire. The surrounding district is best known as the home of Arsenal Football Club, the gleaming 60,000-seater Emirates Stadium.

Estorick Collection of Modern Italian Art

This is a wonderful depository of early 20th-century Italian art. It is one of the world's foremost collections of futurism, Italy's confrontational contribution to modernism. *39A Canonbury Square, N1 2AN (7704 9522, www.estorickcollection. com). Highbury & Islington tube/rail or bus 271. Open 11am-6pm Wed-Sat; noon-5pm Sun. Admission £5; £3.50 reductions; free under-16s & students.*

East London

The planners of the London 2012 Games chose well. For years, east London has been on the cultural cutting-edge. Read the fashion blogs, and it's hard to believe how recently the East End was notorious for its slums, petty gangsters and urban blight. It was also cursed with the smelliest and most unpleasant of London's dock-side industries.

How things change. East London now has some of London's most vital areas. Alongside the City,

Spitalfields and **Brick Lane** are tourist must-visits, with markets, boutiques, restaurants and – as they shade beyond increasingly upmarket **Shoreditch** into **Hackney & Dalston** – art-student trendy nightlife. To the north, **London Fields** drives the arts and fashion zeitgeist; eastwards, **Docklands** rivals the City for blue-chip institutions. And, beyond it all, eyes are drawn to the **Queen Elizabeth Olympic Park**: can those heady promises of a 'legacy' for east London be delivered?

SPITALFIELDS & BRICK LANE

The magnificent spike spire of **Christ Church Spitalfields** (Commercial Street, E1 6QE, 7859 3035, www.christ churchspitalfields.org), built in 1729 by architect Nicholas Hawksmoor, dominates Spitalfields. The area's other signature sight, the redeveloped **Spitalfields Market**, has market stalls under an original vaulted Victorian roof. Settle any anxieties about the area's gentrification by heading a few streets south: on Sundays, **Petticoat Lane Market** hawks knickers and cheap electronics around Middlesex Street.

You're now on the Whitechapel Road – busy but anonymous. One bright spot is **Whitechapel Gallery** (see p48), west from the foot of Brick Lane, while a little to the east, the **Whitechapel Bell Foundry** (nos.32 & 34, 7247 2599, www.whitechapel bellfoundry.co.uk) continues to make bells, as it has since 1420, among them 'Big Ben'. To join one of the Saturday tours, book a place well in advance.

A block north of Spitalfields Market is **Dennis Severs' House** (see p48), while across from the market, in the shadow of Christ Church, the **Ten Bells** (84 Commercial Street, 07530 492986) is where one of Jack the Ripper's victims drank her last gin. On the next corner, Sandra Esqulant's **Golden Heart** pub (no.110, 7247 2158) has hosted every Young British Artist of note, ever since Gilbert & George decided to pop in on their new local. The streets between here and Brick Lane to the east are lined with tall, shuttered Huguenot houses; **19 Princelet Street** (www.19princelet street.org.uk) opens to the public a few times a year. This unrestored 18th-century house was home to French silk merchants and later Polish Jews who built a synagogue in the garden.

Join the crowds flowing east from Spitalfields Market along Hanbury Street during the weekend, and you're on **Brick Lane**. Turn south and you'll know you're in 'Banglatown', the name adopted by the ward back in 2002: until you hit the bland modern offices beside the kitsch Banglatown arch, it's almost all Bangladeshi cafés, curry houses, grocery stores, money transfer services and sari shops – plus the **Pride of Spitalfields** (3 Heneage Street, 7247 8933), an old-style East End boozer. Despite the street's reputation for Indian food, most of the restaurants on the street

Highgate Cemetery

are disappointing: try **Tayyabs** (*see p68*) or **Needoo Grill** (*see p67*) instead, or opt for Bengali sweets from **Madhubon Sweet Centre** (no.42).

Between Fournier Street and Princelet Street, **Jamme Masjid Mosque** is a key symbol of Brick Lane's hybridity: it began as a Huguenot chapel, became a synagogue and was converted, in 1976, into a mosque. After that, it's all boho gentrification. On Sunday, there's the lively street market, complemented by the trendier UpMarket – superior, clothes-wise, to Spitalfields Market – and Backyard Market (for arts and crafts), both held in the **Old Truman Brewery** (nos.91-95). Pedestrianised Dray Walk, full of hip independent businesses, is crowded every day. Heading north, you'll find bars, cafés and vintage fashion. At the top of Brick Lane, **Redchurch Street** has several of the area's best boutiques.

Dennis Severs' House

The ten rooms of this Huguenot house have been decked out to recreate vivid snapshots of daily life in Spitalfields between 1724 and 1914. A tour through the compelling 'still-life drama', as American creator Dennis Severs dubbed it, takes you through the cellar, kitchen, dining room, smoking room and upstairs to the bedrooms. With hearth and candles burning, smells lingering and objects scattered about, it feels as though the inhabitants have deserted the building only moments before. *18 Folgate Street, E1 6BX (7247 4013, www.dennissevershouse.co.uk). Liverpool Street tube/rail or Shoreditch High Street rail. Open 6-9pm Mon, Wed; noon-4pm Sun; noon-2pm 1st & 3rd Mon of the mth. Admission £10 Sun; £7 noon-2pm Mon; £14 Mon evenings.*

Whitechapel Gallery

This East End stalwart reopened in 2009, following a major redesign that saw the Grade II-listed building expand into the similarly historic former library next door. As well as nearly tripling its exhibition space, the Whitechapel gave itself a research centre and archives, plus a proper restaurant and good café. With no permanent collection, there's a rolling programme of temporary shows. *77-82 Whitechapel High Street, E1 7QX (7522 7888, www.whitechapel gallery.org). Aldgate East tube. Open 11am-6pm Tue-Sun. Admission free. Temporary exhibitions vary.*

SHOREDITCH TO BETHNAL GREEN

The story is familiar: in the 1980s, impecunious artists moved into the derelict warehouses in the triangle formed by Old Street, Shoreditch High Street and Great Eastern Street, and turned it into the place to be. Forced out by rocketing rents, they've been replaced by the tech-hip denizens of 'silicon roundabout'. The area around Old Street roundabout has become a focus for digital start-ups, the beginning of Prime Minister David Cameron's **Tech City** (www.east londontechcity.com). Nightlife still permeates the area, but the nature of the scene has changed: scuzzy is making way for smart.

Apart from countless galleries – White Cube left focal Hoxton Square in December 2012, but the Wharf Road neighbours (**Parasol Unit**, no.14, N1 7RW, 7490 7373, www.parasol-unit.org; **Victoria Miro**, no.16, N1 7RW, 7336 8109, www.victoria-miro.com) and not-for-profit pioneer **Raven Row** (56 Artillery Lane, E1 7LS, 7377 4300, www.ravenrow.org) are notable – the area's sole bona fide tourist attraction is the exquisite **Geffrye Museum**.

Heading east, you'll find more artists in Bethnal Green: the longstanding **Maureen Paley** gallery (no.21) in Herald Street remains the key venue, but the new vibe is typified by **Herald Street** (no.2), just down the road, and the ambitious **Town Hall Hotel** (*see p118*). Take a seat at **E Pellicci** (*see p67*), the exemplary trad London caff, for a taste of the old Bethnal Green. A visit to the weekly **Columbia Road flower market** (*see p87*) is a lovely way to fritter away a sunny Sunday morning, while the **V&A Museum of Childhood** is perfect for a rainy Tuesday.

Geffrye Museum

Housed in a set of 18th-century almshouses, the Geffrye Museum offers a vivid physical history of the English interior. Displaying original furniture, paintings, textiles and decorative arts, the museum recreates a fascinating sequence of typical middle-class living rooms from 1600 to the present. An airy café overlooks lovely gardens. In 2014 the museum celebrates a special anniversary – or rather two. It is 300 years since these charming brick buildings were founded as almshouses, and 100 years since those almshouses reopened as the Geffrye. Check the website for celebratory events. *136 Kingsland Road, E2 8EA (7739 9893, www.geffrye-museum.org.uk). Hoxton rail. Open 10am-5pm Tue-Sun. Almshouse tours 1st Sat, 1st & 3rd Tue, Wed of mth. Admission free; donations appreciated. Almshouse tours £2.50; free under-16s.*

V&A Museum of Childhood

Home to one of the world's finest collections of children's toys, dolls' houses, games and costumes, the Museum of Childhood shines brighter than ever after refurbishment. The museum has been amassing objects since 1872 and continues to do so, with *Incredibles* figures complementing bonkers 1970s puppets, Barbie Dolls and Victorian praxinoscopes. *Cambridge Heath Road, E2 9PA (8983 5235, www.museumof childhood.org.uk). Bethnal Green tube/rail. Open 10am-5.45pm daily. Admission free; donations appreciated.*

DOCKLANDS

London's docks were fundamental to the prosperity of the British Empire. Between 1802 and 1921, ten docks were built between Tower Bridge and Woolwich, employing tens of thousands of people. Yet by the 1960s, the shipping industry was changing irrevocably. The new 'container' system of cargo demanded deep-draught ships, as a result of which the work moved out to Tilbury. By 1980, the London docks had closed.

The London Docklands Development Corporation (LDDC), founded in 1981, spent £790m of public money on redevelopment during the following decade, only for a country-wide property slump in the early 1990s to leave the shiny new buildings unoccupied. Nowadays, though, Docklands is a booming rival to the City, with an estimated 90,000 workers commuting to the area daily.

Almost all of the interest for visitors is at the north end of the **Isle of Dogs** peninsula, where stands Cesar Pelli's **One Canada Square**, the country's tallest habitable building from 1991 to 2012, when it was topped by the Shard. The only slightly shorter HSBC and Citigroup towers joined it in the noughties, and clones are springing up thick and fast. Shopping options are limited to the mall beneath the towers (www.mycanarywharf.com). Across a floating bridge over the dock to the north, there's the **Museum of London Docklands**.

Further east (get off at East India DLR), the Lea River empties into the Thames at **Bow Creek**, almost directly opposite the O2 Arena. Here, **Trinity Buoy Wharf** (64 Orchard Place, E14 0JW, www.trinitybuoy wharf.com) has London's only lighthouse, now the perfect setting for the *Longplayer* sound installation (http://longplayer.org).

A couple more stops east give you access to the **Royal Docks** – get off at Royal Victoria or Royal Albert – as well as the ExCeL conference centre, the dry-docked SS *Robin* steamship (www.ssrobin.org) and a new attraction, the Crystal. But most visitors come here for one reason only: a ride on the **Emirates Air Line cable car**. A footbridge from ExCeL, high above the dock, takes you to the beautiful **Thames Barrier Park**. Opened in 2001, this was London's first new park in half a century. It offers perhaps the best views from land of the Thames Barrier.

Geffrye Museum

Crystal

The slick, enjoyable interactives in this black, pointy building attempt to explain how cities work, and how they might meet the challenges of global warming, population growth, ageing and the shortage of key resources, especially water. Try to beat the computer at face recognition, say, or plan the transport mix for different cities. Good café too.
Royal Victoria Dock, 1 Siemens Brothers Way, E16 1GB (7055 6400, http://the crystal.org). Royal Victoria DLR. Open 10am-5pm Tue-Fri; noon-11pm Sat; noon-10.30 Sun. Admission free.

Emirates Air Line

Arguments for a cable car across the Thames as a solution to any of London's transport problems are, at best, moot, but its value as a tourist thrill is huge. The pods zoom 295 feet up elegant stanchions at a gratifying pace. There are brilliant views of the Royal Docks, the Thames and the Thames Barrier. Good value too – especially if you use a pre-paid Oyster card , which also means you can skip past the ticket window queues.
North terminal *27 Western Gateway, E16 4FA. Royal Victoria DLR.* **South terminal** *Edmund Halley Way, SE10 0FR. North Greenwich tube.* **Both** *Open 7am-9pm Mon-Fri; 8am-9pm Sat; 9am-9pm Sun. Tickets £4.30 single; £2.20 5-15s, free under-5s.*

Museum of London Docklands

Housed in a 19th-century warehouse (itself a Grade I-listed building), this huge museum has been exploring the complex history of London's docklands and the river for a decade. Displays spreading over three storeys take you from the arrival of the Romans all the way to the docks' 1980s closure and the area's subsequent redevelopment. The Docklands at War section is very moving, while a haunting new permanent exhibition explores the slave trade. Temporary exhibitions are set up on the ground floor, where there's a café and a docks-themed play area for kids. Just like its elder brother, the Museum of London, the MoLD has a great programme of events.
No.1 Warehouse, West India Quay, Hertsmere Road, E14 4AL (7001 9844, www.museumindocklands. org.uk). Canary Wharf tube or West India Quay DLR. Open 10am-6pm daily. Admission free. Temporary exhibitions vary; check website for details.

HACKNEY & DALSTON

The opening of the Overground line in 2010 left even bus-averse visitors few excuses to ignore this part of town. Hackney has few blockbuster sights, but is one of London's fastest changing areas. Its admistrative centre is Town Hall Square on Mare Street, where you'll find a century-old music hall, the **Hackney Empire** (291 Mare Street, 8985 2424, www.hackneyempire.co.uk) and the little **Hackney Museum** (1 Reading Lane, 8356 3500,

Emirates Air Line

www.hackney.gov.uk/cm-museum. htm). Opposite is **Hackney Picturehouse** (*see p95*). Within walking distance to the north-east is **Sutton House** (2-4 Homerton High Street, E9 6JQ, 8986 2264, www.nationaltrust.org.uk); built in 1535, it is east London's oldest home.

The area of London Fields, to the west, demonstrates the borough's changing demographics. Once a fruit and veg market, **Broadway Market** is now brimming with young urbanites and trendy families. The food and vintage garb market on Saturdays has been joined by two food and collectibles markets on Westgate Street; the street is lined with browsable boutiques, curiosity shops and modish boho eating and drinking venues. The old days are represented by **F Cooke** (no.9, 7254 6458), a pie and mash place.

From the south end of Broadway Market, you can walk east along the Regent's Canal to **Victoria Park**. Opened in 1845 to give the working classes access to green space, a sprawling, 290-acre oasis, complete with rose garden and waterfowl lake. There's also a cool waterfront café. At the eastern end of the park – opposite the Olympic Park – is Hackney Wick.

West of Hackney, scruffy **Dalston** is clinging on to its reputation as London's hipster quarter, even as the suits descend on the increasingly well-established clubs. All tribes play together happily enough at the appealingly urban Dalston Jazz Bar (4 Bradbury Street, 7254 9728), the brilliant Vortex Jazz Club (*see p104*) and Café Oto (*see p103*); for clubs, *see p101*. Also near the Overground station is an appealing 'micropark', the delightfully urban Dalston Eastern Curve Garden (3 Dalston Lane, E8 3DF, http://dalstongarden.org).

Neighbouring **Stoke Newington** is the richer cousin of Dalston and

poorer cousin of Islington. At weekends, pretty Clissold Park (www.clissoldpark.com) is overrun with picnickers and mums pushing prams. Most visitors head to Stoke Newington for bijou Church Street, lined with second-hand bookshops, cute boutiques and kids' stores, and superior cafés and restaurants – Keralan vegetarian restaurant Rasa (no.55, 7249 0344) is probably the best. Another local highlight is Abney Park Cemetery (www.abney-park.org.uk), a wild, overgrown Victorian boneyard and nature reserve.

OLYMPIC PARK & AROUND

The Lea River wriggles south-east for 50 miles from its source near Luton to join the River Thames. Through history, it has been a working river used for transport, irrigation and industry: the latter turned its lower reaches into neglected industrial land that was taken over as the focal Olympic Park for the 2012 Games. The **Lea Valley Walk** (www.lea valleywalk.org.uk) provides a glimpse of hidden London and its suburbs; a mixture of bucolic greenery, bleak warehouses, moody marshland, wildlife sanctuaries, posh new-build flats – and what has now reopened as the **Queen Elizabeth Olympic Park**. You can also visit the Westfield Stratford City shopping mall, which overlooks the Olympic Park from the east, and a cluster of attractions, including Theatre Royal Stratford East (*see p108*) and the Discover Story Centre (*see p93*).

Unless you fancy walking all the way up from the Thames, get off the tube at Bromley-by-Bow and follow the signs past the thundering roads to the cobbles of **Three Mills Island**. The House Mill (8980 4626, www. housemill.org.uk), built in 1776, is the oldest and largest tidal mill in Britain and, though out of service, is

occasionally opened to the public; it contains a café. The island has walks that can feel quite rural, as well as much improved waterside walkways.

The **Greenway** then provides a pleasant route (apart from when you have to cross the A11) north from Abbey Mills Pumping Station right past the Park. The best vantage point over the Olympic Park as it approaches reopening is the **View Tube** (*see p67*) – easily accessible from Pudding Mill DLR. A little further up the river, at pretty Old Ford Lock, the river splits again into the straighter, artificial Lee Navigation and the windier river proper.

If you turn left (west) off the Lea Navigation, by crossing the bridge just past the Olympic Stadium, you can get on to the towpath of the mile-long Hertford Union Canal, eventually running alongside Victoria Park. North of the Hertford Union in **Hackney Wick**, an enclave of artist-occupied former industrial spaces has begun to breed venues: the pioneer was Hackney Pearl restaurant (11 Prince Edward Road, 8510 3605, www.the hackneypearl.com), but it has now been followed by 90 Mainyard bar-diner-gig space (90 Wallis Road, 8986 0090, http:// 90mainyard.co.uk), Crate microbrewery and pizzeria (White Building, Queen's Yard, www.cratebrewery.com) and even a 130-seat theatre, the Yard (Queen's Yard, www.theyardtheatre. co.uk), made from recycled materials.

Queen Elizabeth Olympic Park

Even in terms of public money, £8.77bn is a lot of moolah. But that's what the UK paid for an expectation-busting Olympic and Paralympic Games in 2012 – and the acres of parkland and handful of venues that now dominate an area significant enough to be granted its own postcode: E20. The immaculately tailored green area of North Park was

launched in 2013, its paths, waterways and public art enhanced by the rather good Unity Kitchen Café. The next tranche of openings came in 2014. First, the Zaha Hadid-designed Aquatics Centre, now offering public swimming and diving sessions (£3.50-£4.50 adults, £2-£2.50 concs), was revealed in its true glory without the ugly Games-time seating stands. Then the VeloPark opened its road, track, BMX and mountain biking. And finally the South Park – all the remaining parkland, including children's play areas, four walking trails, a couple of dozen more public artworks, plus the attraction of ascending the ArcelorMittal Orbit (0333 800 8099, www.arcelormittal orbit.com, open 10am-6pm daily; £15; £12 concs; £7 children; £40 family). Designed by the artist Anish Kapoor and structural engineer Cecil Balmond, this curly-wurly red scaffolding tower stands 114.5m (376ft) tall – with lifts (and a 455-step staircase) up to two platforms from which you take in the interesting but not spectacular view. There are also some of Kapoor's entertaining distorting mirrors inside and some newly installed digital telescopes so that you can get closer to the views. This side of the park you'll find another good café: Moka East (see p67). Now the only public space that remains incomplete is the Olympic Stadium, which is currently being retooled (including the addition of a roof over the seats) to host the Rugby World Cup in 2015, before West Ham Football Club take up permanent residence in 2016.
http://queenelizabetholympicpark.co.uk. Stratford tube/DLR/rail.

Queen Elizabeth Olympic Park

South-east London

Beyond the world-famous sights of **Greenwich**, south-east London used to be ignored by many tourists – largely because the absence of the Underground made it seem remote from the centre. With the development of the London Overground, that's all changing.

Riverside Greenwich is an irresistible mixture of maritime, royal and horological history, a combination that earned it recognition as a UNESCO World Heritage Site – and, in 2012, elevation to the status of a Royal Borough as part of the Queen's Jubilee. A number of local attractions, the reopened **Cutty Sark** included, are now proudly clustered as the **Royal Museums Greenwich**.

In truth, royalty has stalked the area since 1300, when Edward I stayed here. Henry VIII was born in Greenwich Palace; the palace was built on land that later contained Wren's Royal Naval Hospital, now the **Old Royal Naval College**. It is a very handy first port-of-call: its Pepys Building contains the

Greenwich Tourist Information Centre, but is also the home to a great introduction to the area: **Discover Greenwich**. Just opposite, is **Greenwich Market**.

Near the DLR stop, Greenwich Pier offers **Thames Clipper** (*see p121*) boat rides every 15 minutes (peak times), and beside the *Cutty Sark* a domed structure marks the entrance to a Victorian **pedestrian tunnel** that emerges on the far side of the Thames in Island Gardens. The tunnel is rather dingy, but it's still fun to walk beneath the river.

To the north, at the bottom of Greenwich Park, are the **Queen's House** and **National Maritime Museum**, beyond which it's a ten-minute walk (or shorter shuttle-bus trip) up the steep slopes of Greenwich Park to the **Royal Observatory**.

The riverside Thames Path leads past rusting piers and boarded-up factories to the **Greenwich Peninsula**, dominated by the **O2 Arena**, designed by the Richard Rogers Partnership as the Millennium Dome. Alongside concerts and sporting events in the huge arena, attractions include restaurants, movies and the glossy **British Music Experience** (O2 Bubble, Millennium Way, SE10 0BB, 8463 2000, www.britishmusic experience.com) – you can also book **Up at the O2** tickets (www.theo2. co.uk/upattheo2) to walk right over the top of the Dome. The **Emirates Air Line** cable car (*see p49*) runs from the east flank of the peninsula across the Thames to ExCeL.

The Dome and its environs are all something of a contrast with the **Greenwich Peninsula Ecology Park** (www.urbanecology.co.uk), and with the nearby riverside walks that

afford broad, flat, bracing views and artworks; you could hardly miss *Slice of Reality*, a rusting ship cut in half by Richard Wilson, and Antony Gormley's 100-foot *Quantum Cloud*.

Cutty Sark
Built in Scotland in 1869, this tea clipper was the quickest in the business when it was launched in 1870 – renovation was rather slower, especially after the ship went up in flames in May 2007 (fortunately most of the timbers had already been removed for refurbishment), but is now complete, with visitors able to buy timed tickets. Permanently berthed in a dry dock beside the Thames, she's again enjoying a useful retirement as a popular tourist attraction (and, since early 2014, comedy and music venue) after crossing the world's oceans with cargos of tea, wine, spirits, beer, coal, jute, wool and castor oil. The tea trade in particular involved reckless races from China to London. Now she's at rest, raised three metres off the ground, so you can admire the ship's splendid copper bottom – as well as fine collection of 80 figureheads.
King William Walk, SE10 9HT (8858 2698, www.cuttysark.org.uk). Cutty Sark DLR. Open 10am-6pm daily. Admission £13.50; £7-£11 reductions; £24-£35 family; free under-5s.

Discover Greenwich & the Old Royal Naval College
The block of the Old Royal Naval College nearest to the *Cutty Sark*, the pier and Cutty Sark DLR is full of focused, informative exhibits on architecture and building techniques of the surrounding buildings, the life of Greenwich pensioners, Tudor

royalty and so forth, delivered with a real sense of fun: while grown-ups read about coade stone or scagliola (popular fake stone building materials), for example, the nippers can build their own chapel with soft bricks or try on a knight's helmet.

It's a perfect introduction to the superb collection of buildings that make up the Naval College. Designed by Wren in 1694, with Hawksmoor and Vanbrugh helping to complete the project, it was originally a hospital for seamen and their dependants. In 1869, the complex became the Royal Naval College. The Navy left in 1998, and the neoclassical buildings now house part of the University of Greenwich and Trinity College of Music. The public are allowed into the impressive rococo chapel, where there are free organ recitals, and Painted Hall, a tribute to William and Mary that took Sir James Thornhill 19 years to complete.
2 Cutty Sark Gardens, SE10 9LW (8269 4799, www.ornc.org.uk). Cutty Sark DLR or Greenwich DLR/rail. Open 10am-5pm daily. Tours noon daily; other times by arrangement. Admission free. Tours £5.

National Maritime Museum
The world's largest maritime museum is even bigger since the impressive expansion in 2011 into the new Sammy Ofer Wing. Centred on Voyagers: Britons and the Sea – a collection of 200 artefacts, accompanied by an impressive audio-visual installation called the Wave – this extension also has the Compass Lounge (with free Wi-Fi), where you can explore the collection using computers, and a brasserie, café and shop. Downstairs, the temporary gallery is building a reputation for compelling – and varied – exhibitions of historic art.

Ground-level galleries include Explorers, which covers great sea expeditions back to medieval times, and Maritime London, which concentrates on the city as a port. Level two holds the interactives: the Bridge has a ship simulator, and All Hands lets children load cargo, and you can even try your hand as a ship's gunner. The Atlantic: Slavery, Trade, Empires gallery looks at the transport of goods between Britain, Africa and the Americas during the 17th to 19th centuries. More recent additions are the Great Map, a large interactive floor map of the oceans, and a Nelson, Navy, Nation gallery, which recalls the sea-borne battles of the 18th century, and the glamour and gore of life as a Naval Officer at the time. Here you'll find Nelson's Trafalgar uniform, blood-stained and with fatal bullet-hole. *Romney Road, SE10 9NF (8858 4422, information 8312 6565, www.nmm.ac.uk). Cutty Sark DLR or Greenwich DLR/rail. Open 10am-5pm Mon-Wed, Fri-Sun; 10am-8pm Thur. Tours phone for details. Admission free; donations appreciated. Temporary exhibitions vary; check website for details.*

Queen's House
The art collection of the National Maritime Museum is displayed in what was the summer villa of Charles I's queen, Henrietta Maria. Completed in 1638 by Inigo Jones, the house has an interior as impressive as the paintings on the walls. As well as the stunning 1635 marble floor, look for Britain's first centrally unsupported spiral stair, fine painted woodwork and ceilings, and the Great Hall, a perfect cube. The collection includes portraits of famous maritime figures and works by Hogarth, as well as exotic pictures from Captain Cook's explorations. *Romney Road, SE10 9NF (8312 6565, www.nmm.ac.uk). Cutty Sark DLR or Greenwich DLR/rail. Open 10am-5pm daily. Admission free.*

Royal Observatory & Planetarium
The northern section of this two-halved attraction chronicles Greenwich's horological connection. Flamsteed House, the observatory built in 1675 on the orders of Charles II, containing the apartments of Sir John Flamsteed and other Astronomers Royal, as well as the instruments used in timekeeping since the 14th century. John Harrison's four timekeepers, used to crack the problem of longitude, are here, and the onion dome houses the country's largest (28-inch) refracting telescope. Still, most visitors are here to be snapped straddling the Prime Meridian Line in the Meridian Courtyard. To the south are the Weller Astronomy Centre and Peter Harrison Planetarium, screening shows such as 'Sky Tonight Live' and 'The Universe Exposed'. *Greenwich Park, SE10 9NF (8312 6565, www.rmg.co.uk/royal-observatory). Cutty Sark DLR or Greenwich DLR/rail. Open 10am-5pm daily. Tours phone for details. Admission Astronomy Centre free. Flamsteed House & Meridian Courtyard £7, £5.50 reductions,*

£2.50 6-15s, free under-6s, £9.50-£16 family. Planetarium £6.50, £5.50 reductions, £4.50 3-15s, free under-3s, £14.50-£20 family.*

OTHER ATTRACTIONS
Dulwich Picture Gallery
This bijou attraction was designed by Sir John Soane in 1811 as the first purpose-built gallery in the UK. It's a beautiful space that shows off Soane's ingenuity with lighting effects, especially in the quiet mausoleum at the heart of the building where the gallery's founders rest. The gallery displays a small but outstanding collection of work by Old Masters – Rembrandt, Rubens, Poussin, Gainsborough – and some excellent temporary exhibitions. *Gallery Road, Dulwich, SE21 7AD (8693 5254, www.dulwichpicture gallery.org.uk). North Dulwich or West Dulwich rail. Open 10am-5pm Tue-Fri; 11am-5pm Sat, Sun. Admission £6; free-£5 reductions. Special exhibitions £11; free-£10 reductions.*

Horniman Museum
South-east London's premier free family attraction, the Horniman was once the home of tea trader Frederick J Horniman. It's an eccentric-looking art nouveau building (check out the clocktower, which starts as a circle and ends as a square), with a main entrance that gives out on to extensive gardens. The oldest section is the Natural History gallery, dominated by an ancient walrus (mistakenly overstuffed by Victorian taxidermists, who thought they ought to get the wrinkles out) and now ringed by glass cabinets containing pickled animals, stuffed birds and insect models. Other galleries include the Nature Base, African Worlds and the Centenary Gallery, which focuses on world cultures. Downstairs, the Music

Gallery contains hundreds of instruments: their sounds can be unleashed via touch-screen tables, while hardier instruments can be bashed with impunity.

The most popular part of the museum is its Aquarium, where a series of tanks and rockpools cover seven aquatic ecosystems. There are mesmerising moon jellyfish, strangely large British seahorses, starfish, tropical fish and mangrove creatures. It forms a key part of the Evolution 2010 project, which brought together the natural history collection, aquarium and gardens to explore biodiversity and evolution. *100 London Road, Forest Hill, SE23 3PQ (8699 1872, www.horniman. ac.uk). Forest Hill rail. Open 10.30am-5.30pm daily. Admission free; donations appreciated. Temporary exhibitions prices vary. Aquarium £3; £1.10 reductions; £7 family; free under-3s.*

South-west London

Towards the Surrey border, south-west London can start to feel like a collection of villages rather than a single sprawling metropolis. World-class tourist attractions are **Kew Gardens**, **Hampton Court Palace**, and the huge Royal Park in Richmond. Towards the centre, areas such as Brixton are like their south-east London neighbours: diverse, busy and vibrant, despite creeping gentrification.

VAUXHALL & BRIXTON
Vauxhall's heyday was in the 18th century when the infamous Pleasure Gardens, built back in 1661, reached the height of their popularity. All that remains is **Spring Garden**, behind

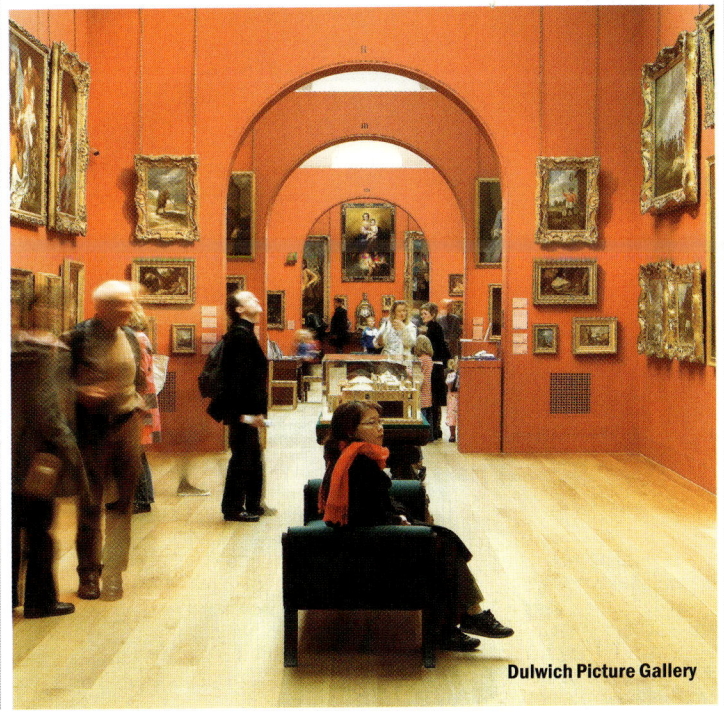
Dulwich Picture Gallery

popular gay haunt the Royal Vauxhall Tavern (aka **RVT**; *see p97*). To the south, **Brixton** is a lively hub of clubs and music. The town centre has been enjoying significant redevelopment, with Windrush Square completed at the end of Coldharbour Lane in 2010. The square's name is significant: HMS *Windrush* was the boat that brought West Indian immigrants from Jamaica in 1948. They were hardly welcomed, but managed to make Brixton a thriving community. As late as the 1980s, tensions were still strong: the riots of 1981 and 1985 around Railton Road and Coldharbour Lane left the district scarred for years. Now, most visitors come to Brixton for **Brixton Village Market** (*see p88*), with its Grade II-listed covered arcades.

BATTERSEA
Battersea started life as an island in the Thames, but it was reclaimed when the surrounding marshes were drained. The river is now dominated by Sir Giles Gilbert Scott's magnificent four-chimneyed **Battersea Power Station** (www.batterseapower station.co.uk). Work started – including the temporary removal of those landmark chimneys – on what was to become the largest brick-built structure in Europe in 1929, and the power station was in operation through to the early 1980s.

Overlooking the river further west, **Battersea Park** (www.battersea park.org) has pretty lakes and gardens, and a Peace Pagoda, built by a Buddhist sect in 1985 to commemorate Hiroshima Day. The park extends to the Thames; from the wide and lovely riverside walk you can see both the elaborate Albert Bridge and the simpler Battersea Bridge.

FURTHER AFIELD
Central London is, of course, rich with unmissable tourist destinations, but there are several attractions in south-west London that make a journey there appealing. **Kew Gardens** and **Hampton Court Palace** could easily fill a day by themselves, no tennis fan will want to miss **Wimbledon**, and nature-lovers adore **WWT Wetland Centre** (*see p93*).

Hampton Court Palace
This spectacular palace, once owned by Henry VIII, is just a half-hour journey from central London. It was built in 1514 by Cardinal Wolsey, the high-flying Lord Chancellor, but Henry liked it so much he seized it for himself in 1528. For the next 200 years it was a focal point of English history: Elizabeth I was imprisoned in a tower by her jealous and fearful elder sister Mary I; Shakespeare gave his first performance to James I in 1604; and, after the Civil War, Oliver Cromwell was so besotted with the building he ditched his puritanical principles and moved in to enjoy its luxuries.

Centuries later, the rosy walls of the palace still dazzle. Its vast size can be daunting, so it's a good idea to take advantage of the guided tours. If you

DULWICH PICTURE GALLERY; ANTHONY WEBB

do decide to go it alone, start with Henry VIII's State Apartments, which include the Great Hall, noted for its beautiful stained-glass windows and elaborate religious tapestries; in the Haunted Gallery, the ghost of Catherine Howard – Henry's fifth wife, executed for adultery in 1542 – can reputedly be heard shrieking. The King's Apartments, added in 1689 by Wren, are notable for a splendid mural of Alexander the Great, painted by Antonio Verrio. The Queen's Apartments and Georgian Rooms feature similarly elaborate paintings, chandeliers and tapestries. The Tudor Kitchens are great fun, with their giant cauldrons, fake pies and blood-spattered walls.

More extraordinary sights await outside, where the exquisitely landscaped gardens contain topiary, Thames views, a reconstruction of a 16th-century heraldic garden and the famous Hampton Court maze. *East Molesey, Surrey KT8 9AU (0844 482 7777, www.hrp.org.uk). Hampton Court rail, or riverboat from Westminster or Richmond to Hampton Court Pier (Apr-Oct). Open Palace Apr-Oct 10am-6pm daily; Nov-Mar 10am-4.30pm daily. Park dawn-dusk daily. Admission Palace, courtyard, cloister & maze £18.15; £9.08-£15.40 reductions; £46.75 family; free under-5s. Maze only £4.40; £2.75 reductions. Gardens only Apr-Oct £5.72; £4.84 reductions; free under-15s. Nov-Mar free to all.*

Royal Botanic Gardens (Kew Gardens)

Kew's lush, landscaped beauty represents the pinnacle of our national gardening obsession. From the early 1700s until 1840, when the gardens were given to the nation, these were the grounds for two fine royal residences – the White House and Richmond Lodge. Early resident Queen Caroline, who was wife of George II, was very fond of exotic plants brought back by botanists voyaging to far-flung parts of the world. In 1759, the renowned 'Capability' Brown was employed by George III to improve on the work of his predecessors here, William Kent and Charles Bridgeman. Thus began the shape of the extraordinary garden that today attracts hundreds of thousands of visitors each year.

Covering half a square mile, Kew feels surprisingly big – pick up a map at the ticket office and follow the handy signs. Head straight for the 19th-century greenhouses, filled to the roof with plants – some of which have been here as long as the enormous glass structures themselves. The sultry Palm House holds tropical plants: palms, bamboo, tamarind, fig and mango trees, and fragrant hibiscus and frangipani. The Temperate House is closed for 2014.

Also worth seeking out are the Princess of Wales Conservatory, divided into ten climate zones; the Marine Display, downstairs from the Palm House (it isn't always open, but

when it is you can see the delightful seahorses); the lovely, quiet indoor pond of the Waterlily House (closed in winter); and the exquisite Victorian botanical drawings found in the fabulous Marianne North Gallery. The Xstrata Treetop Walkway has been a popular addition to the gardens, giving a completely different woodland walk up in the leaf canopy. *Kew, Richmond, Surrey TW9 3AB (8332 5655, www.kew.org). Kew Gardens tube/rail, Kew Bridge rail or riverboat to Kew Pier. Open times vary; check website for details. Admission £16; £14 reductions; free under-17s.*

Wimbledon Lawn Tennis Museum

Wimbledon is little but a wealthy and genteel suburb, except for one thing: its world-famous summer tennis tournament. At other times of year, you can always visit the popular museum on the history of tennis. Highlights include a 200° cinema screen that allows you to find out what it's like to play on Centre Court, a re-creation of a 1980s men's dressing room, complete with a 'ghost' of John McEnroe, and a behind-the-scenes tour. *Museum Building, All England Lawn Tennis Club, Church Road, SW19 5AE (8946 6131, www.wimbledon. org/museum). Southfields tube. Open 10am-5pm daily; ticket holders only during championships. Admission (incl tour) £22; £13-£19 reductions; free under-5s.*

West London

It's fitting that west London still has a distinct air of aristocash. This was the first of the city's frontiers to be developed, outside the political hub

of the City of Westminster and out of the way of the westerly smog-carrying winds. Even today, the elegant Georgian townhouses of **Holland Park** and **Kensington** retain their high status. Unlike London's north, east and south, where the posher neighbourhoods are in more remote, leafier suburbs, the smartest parts of the west – chiefly **Kensington** and **Notting Hill** – are conveniently central.

NOTTING HILL

Sprawled beneath the Westway flyover, with its railway terminus and branch of the Grand Union Canal, **Paddington** is where central London meets the west of England. It's not an attractive area, but it holds appeal thanks to the goodies hidden away in **Alfie's Antique Market** (*see p81*). There's nothing hidden away about Notting Hill, where Portobello Market is surrounded by some of the most desirable addresses in west London, one of which houses the inimitable **Museum of Brands, Packaging & Advertising** (Colville Mews, Lonsdale Road, W11 2AR, 7908 0880, www.museumofbrands.com), Robert Opie's collection of anything – from milk bottles to vacuum cleaners – that reflects the last century of British consumerism, design and domestic life.

Head north up Queensway from Kensington Gardens and turn west along Westbourne Grove. The road starts humble but gets posher the further west you go; cross Chepstow Road and you're in upmarket **Notting Hill**. A host of fashionable restaurants and bars exploit the lingering street cred of the fast-disappearing black and working-class communities; posh shops are a better reflection of the area's current character. Notting Hill Gate isn't a

pretty street, but the leafy avenues to the south are; so is Pembridge Road, to the north, leading to the boutique-filled streets of Westbourne Grove and Ledbury Road, and to **Portobello Road** and its renowned **market** (*see p86*).

North of the Westway, that elevated section of the M40 motorway linking London with Oxford, Portobello's vitality fizzles out. It sparks back to life at Golborne Road, the heartland of London's North African community. Here, too, is a fine Portuguese café-deli, the Lisboa Pâtisserie (no.57, 8968 5242). At its western end, Golborne Road connects with Ladbroke Grove, which can be followed north to the neo-classical gates of **Kensal Green Cemetery** (Harrow Road, W10 4RA, 8969 0152, www.kensalgreen.co.uk).

KENSINGTON & HOLLAND PARK

There are more millionaires per square mile in this corner of London than in any other part of Europe. Just off **Kensington High Street**, a smart but rarely intoxicating shopping drag, an array of handsome squares are lined with grand 19th-century houses. The **Design Museum** (*see p18*) is due to move into the Grade II*-listed former Commonwealth Institute on the street in 2015. Opened in 1962, but closed since 2002, the Institute building is very distinctive: built to look like a tent, it has a remarkable hyperbolic paraboloid copper roof. The new museum will be designed by John Pawson, at a cost of £80m. Linking with Notting Hill to the north, **Kensington Church Street** has many chi-chi antique shops, while **St Mary Abbots** (7937 6032/5136, http://smanews.weebly.com) is a Victorian neo-Gothic church, built by Sir George Gilbert Scott between 1869 and 1872. It has London's tallest spire (278 feet).

South down Derry Street, is Kensington Square, which has a concentration of blue plaques. The writer William Thackeray lived at no.16 and the painter Edward Burne-Jones at no.41; at no.18, John Stuart Mill's maid used Carlyle's sole manuscript of *The French Revolution* to start the fire.

Further west is one of London's finest green spaces: **Holland Park**. Along its eastern edge, Holland Walk is one of the most pleasant paths in central London, but the heart of the park is the Jacobean Holland House. Also here is the Japanese-style Kyoto Garden. To the south of the park is an extraordinary historic house: **Leighton House** (12 Holland Park Road, W14 8LZ, 7602 3316, www.rbkc.gov.uk), commissioned as a showpiece house by artist Frederic Leighton in the 1860s. Behind the sternly Victorian façade, every inch of the house is decorated in high style: above all, the 'Arab Hall', which showcases Leighton's huge collection of 16th-century Middle Eastern tiles.

Royal Botanic Gardens (Kew Gardens)

Consume

The city's top restaurants, cafés, bars and shops

Restaurants & Cafés

Tramshed. See p68.

A world of food in a single city

London's restaurants and cafés get better, sassier and ever more diverse.

Whether it's an haute cuisine extravaganza or a barbecue blow-out, the capital's multi-faceted dining scene can provide a quality restaurant to match your needs, including any number of excellent British options, from **St John** (responsible for rebooting British dining in 1995) to **Poppies** (new wave fish and chips). Gastropubs continue to be a big factor, with some – **Harwood Arms**, say, or the **Bull & Last** – offering stellar food; for them, and further drinking options, look at our **Pubs & Bars** chapter (see pp69-74).

While you're here, do make sure you sample the culinary riches from London's many immigrants. Fine Indian, Turkish, Moroccan, Korean and Vietnamese restaurants are listed in this chapter, as are top-notch exponents of the cuisines of France, Italy, Japan, Spain, China and Thailand. And welcome the coffee revolution: finally, some genuine conoisseurship is going into selecting and serving the bean.

Essential information
Try to book a table in advance. At many establishments, booking is vital; at a select few restaurants, you may need to book far in advance. Smoking is banned in all cafés and restaurants. Tipping is standard practice: ten to 15 per cent is usual.

We've included a range of meal prices for each establishment that we've listed. However, restaurants often change their menus, so treat these prices only as guidelines.

The South Bank & Bankside

Around the Royal Festival Hall you'll find plenty of chain restaurants (including Canteen, Feng Sushi, Giraffe, Pizza Express, Wahaca and Wagamama), as well as crêpe and pizza options in Gabriel's Wharf. There are some more chain restaurants (Pizza Express, The Real Greek, Tas Pide) on the river near the Globe Theatre, and yet more (Tsuru, Leon) behind Tate Modern on Canvey Street.

Albion Neo Bankside British
This glass-walled eatery just behind Tate Modern is the second of Terence Conran's poshed-up British cafés (the first is in the Boundary Hotel, see p118). A secluded outdoor terrace overlooks a beautifully landscaped garden of mature silver birches – perfect for summer dining. Breakfast runs from toast and Marmite to a full English or kedgeree. Later on, the menu expands to include fish and chips, pies, bread and butter pudding and afternoon teas. *Pavilion B, Holland Street, SE1 9FU (7827 4343, www.albioncafes.com). Southwark tube. Open 8am-11pm Mon-Sat; 9am-10.30pm Sun. Main courses £5.50-£13.50.*

Baltic Eastern European
A modern take on Polish/central European classics is served in surroundings of understated glamour, with pared-down monochrome decor punctuated by a supersized chandelier dripping shards of golden amber. Home-style pleasures abound, such as rabbit braised in a fragrant broth flavoured with sweet prune and smoky bacon, served with little knobbly spaetzle dumplings. Start with a classy clear vodka like Zytnia (rye), then move on to one of Baltic's own ginger or spicy orange varieties. *74 Blackfriars Road, SE1 8HA (7928 1111, www.balticrestaurant.co.uk). Southwark tube. Open 5.30-11.15pm Mon; noon-3pm, 5.30-11.15pm Tue-Sat; noon-4.30pm, 5.30-10pm Sun. Main courses £9-£18.50.*

Elliot's
Light and airy, with stripped brick walls and a contemporary feel, Elliot's is a busy little spot. Sit out front and watch the world go by, perch at the bar or take a seat in the bright back area. The seasonal menu is small but innovative, and carefully sourced. Smaller plates such as crab on toast or mozzarella and polenta are listed alongside larger plates such as lemon sole, wild garlic and fino. Drinks include a selection of natural wines (orange wines are listed alongside the expected white, red and rosé). *12 Stoney Street, SE1 9AD (7403 7436, www.elliotscafe.com). London Bridge tube/rail. Open 8am-10pm Mon-Sat. Main courses £12-£23.*

Gelateria 3bis Ice-cream
The menu at one of our favourite gelaterias encompasses frozen yoghurt, ice-cream cakes, brioches and crêpes, plus speciality coffees – but the real star is the gelato. It's made on the premises and includes Italian classics as well as creative English innovations (eton mess, anyone?). The bright, spacious dining room has full-length windows opening on to the pavement in summer. *4 Park Street, SE1 9AB (7378 1977, www.gelateria3bis.it). London Bridge tube/rail. Open Summer 8am-10pm Mon-Sat; 10am-6pm Sun. Winter 8am-8pm Mon-Sat; 11am-6pm Sun.*

Hutong Chinese
The original Hutong in Hong Kong is a glitzy restaurant with magnificent views. This branch, halfway up the Shard, is exactly the same. The same Sichuanese and northern Chinese menu, the same mix of plate glass and ersatz Old Beijing decor. Prices are high: but then this is the Shard, not Chinatown. A great place to impress a date. *Level 33, The Shard, 31 St Thomas Street, SE1 9RY (7478 0540, www.hutong.co.uk). London Bridge tube/rail. Open noon-3pm, 6-11pm daily. Dishes £8-£58.*

Delaunay

Critic's choice

1 **Delaunay** The London benchmark for treat eats with no snobbishness. *See p58.*

2 **Restaurant Story** Book far ahead for a table at one of London's finest arrivals. *See p55.*

3 **Polpetto** More brilliant Venetian bar snacks from Russell Norman. *See p60.*

4 **E Pellicci** Squeeze yourself in for some proper East End café culture. *See p67.*

5 **Hoi Polloi** A funky new arrival from the United States, serving food all day. *See p67.*

M Manze Pie & mash
One of the few remaining purveyors of the dirt-cheap traditional foodstuff of London's working classes. It's the oldest pie shop in town, established in 1902, with tiles, marble-topped tables and wooden benches – and is almost as beautiful as L Manze's on Walthamstow High Street, now Grade II listed. Orders are simple: minced beef pies or, stewed eels with mashed potato and liquor (a thin parsley sauce). *87 Tower Bridge Road, SE1 4TW (7407 2985, www.manze.co.uk). Bus 1, 42, 188. Open 11am-2pm Mon; 10.30am-2pm Tue-Thur; 10am-2.30pm Fri; 10am-2.45pm Sat. Main courses £2.75-£5.20.*

Pizarro Spanish
José Pizarro's restaurant continues in the style set in his tapas bar, José, up the street (no.104, SE1 3UB, 7403 4902, http://joserestaurant.co.uk). Menus are a selection of mostly traditional dishes prepared with care and skill, and fine ingredients, including an expertly slow-braised beef stew. The space artfully combines old-Spanish touches – tiles, warm wood, exposed brick – with a stripped-down New Bermondsey look. *194 Bermondsey Street, SE1 3TQ (7378 9455, www.pizarrorestaurant. com). Borough tube or London Bridge tube/rail. Open noon-3pm, 6-11pm Mon-Fri; noon-11pm Sat; 10am-10pm Sun. Main courses £12-£18.*

Restaurant Story British
Story, from starry young chef Tom Sellers, continues this area's rise to foodie haven, securing a Michelin star within months of opening. It's set in a sparse room – all the better to emphasise the view of the Shard through floor-to-ceiling windows, and, of course, the food: an enjoyable procession of modernist dishes layered with culinary puns (bread and dripping, for instance, features a lit candle made from dripping) and tastebud challenges (mackerel versus green strawberries). As with many of London's coolest restaurants, you'll need to book ahead: a month's notice at time of writing. *201 Tooley Street, SE1 2UE (7183 2117, www.restaurantstory.co.uk). London Bridge tube/rail. Open noon-2pm, 6.30-9.30pm Tue-Sat. Set meal £55 6 courses, £75 10 courses.*

Roast British
This formal operation (pianist, precise service, gleaming tableware on white cloths) contrasts with the jolly mayhem of Borough Market below. It's a very pleasant place for a long lunch or luxurious breakfast, and the roasts themselves are among the city's best. Free-range pork belly with apple sauce, Goosnargh chicken with bread sauce, or Blackface lamb with mint relish all appear. These are bracketed by sophisticated starters and grown-up versions of British puds. *Floral Hall, Borough Market, Stoney Street, SE1 1TL (3641 7958, www.roast-restaurant.com). London Bridge tube/rail. Open 7-11am, noon-3.45pm, 5.30-10.45pm Mon-Fri; 8.30-11.30am, noon-3.45pm, 5.30-10.45pm Sat; 11.30am-6.30pm Sun. Main courses £10-£37*

Zucca Italian
The sleek interior and light streaming in through the floor-to-ceiling windows lend a sophisticated Sydney vibe to Zucca. Own-made breads might be followed by burrata with broad beans in a garlicky dressing, or spider crab served prettily in its shell. The own-made pasta is superb, served with sauces such as a sweetly earthy combination of lentils, walnuts and basil. *184 Bermondsey Street, SE1 3TQ (7378 6809, www.zuccalondon.com). Bermondsey tube or London Bridge tube/rail. Open noon-3pm, 6-10pm Tue-Fri; noon-3.30pm, 6-10pm Sat; noon-4pm Sun. Main courses £14-£18.*

The City

Dining options in the Barbican Centre aren't inspiring, although the café-bar in the new Beech Street screens (*see p94*) is appealing. Otherwise, the **Jugged Hare** (49 Chiswell Street, EC1Y 4SA, 7614 013456, www.thejugged hare.com) is an upscale gastropub across from the main entrance, or there are some cheap-and-cheerful places on Whitecross Street.

Bread Street Kitchen Brasserie
Part of the Gordon Ramsay Holdings stable, Bread Street Kitchen is set in the glitzy One New Change shopping centre, on the doorstep of St Paul's Cathedral. The space is vast, with floor-to-ceiling windows on one side, and a long open kitchen on the other. The menu is pretty huge too, with influences from Britain, Italy, the States and beyond. It's a fun place to eat, with friendly and focused staff, and mostly excellent cooking. *One New Change, 10 Bread Street, EC4M 9AB (3030 4050, www.bread streetkitchen.com). St Paul's tube. Open 7am-11pm Mon-Fri; 11.30am-11pm Sat; 11am-8pm Sun. Main courses £12.50-£35.*

Fish Central Fish & chips
This long-standing, family-run restaurant still has fish and chips at its centre – despite serving treats such as oysters and lobster at smartly clothed tables in a bright, modern room. The quality is outstanding. Fish Central is slightly off the beaten track, in a shopping precinct, but it's handy not only for the Barbican but also LSO St Luke's. *149-155 Central Street, EC1V 8AP (7253 4970, www.fishcentral.co.uk). Old Street tube/rail or bus 55. Open 11.30am-2.30pm, 5-10.30pm Mon-Thur; 11.30am-2.30pm, 5-11pm Fri; noon-10pm Sat. Main courses £5.95-£19.95.*

Perkin Reveller Brasserie
This white, minimal dining room is named after the cook's apprentice in Chaucer's Canterbury Tales, who preferred revelry to hard work. The reason? The location, on Tower Wharf, had its construction overseen by Chaucer. Food is a seasonal mix of classic British and Modern European dishes, plus breakfast and afternoon tea. *The Wharf at the Tower of London, EC3N 4AB (3166 6949, www.perkin reveller.co.uk). Tower Hill tube or Tower Gateway tube/DLR. Open 10am-11pm Tue-Sat; 10am-5pm Sun. Main courses £13.50-£28.*

Sushisamba Japanese/Brazilian/Peruvian
Take the glass elevator that clings to the side of Heron Tower, shoot up 38 floors in a few stomach-flipping seconds, then walk into a bar (close views of the Gherkin) and through to the double-height glasshouse of a restaurant. Here your table will likely face north across Spitalfields towards Alexandra Palace or east over Stepney and out to Essex. It's tough visual competition for the food, but the sushi does its damnedest to catch the eye with cloaks of red or green yuba (soybean curd skin). On the 40th floor is Duck & Waffle (3640 7310, www.duckandwaffle.com), serving a menu of small plates. It's open 24 hours, every day. *Floors 38 & 39, Heron Tower, 110 Bishopsgate, EC2N 4AY (3640 7330, www.sushisamba.com). Liverpool Street tube/rail. Open 11.30am-midnight Mon-Fri; 11.30am-11pm Sun. Dishes £8-£42.*

Sweetings Fish & seafood
Things don't change much at this enduring City classic, and that's the way everyone likes it. The walls remain covered with photos of old sports teams, and many of the staff have been here for years. Lobster and crab bisques preface a choice of fish and seafood dishes that read and taste like upmarket versions of a pub-side stall – smoked fish, whitebait, smoked trout and so forth. Top-quality fish are then served fried, grilled or poached to order. The handful of more elaborate dishes includes a fish pie that bears witness to its well-practised makers.

Bread Street Kitchen

39 Queen Victoria Street, EC4N 4SA (7248 3062, www.sweetings restaurant.com). Mansion House tube. Open 11.30am-3pm Mon-Fri. Main courses £12.50-£35.

Holborn & Clerkenwell

Leather Lane, EC4, is a good place to grab a bite, as it's lined with street food stalls (during market hours), caffs and two great coffee bars, **Department of Coffee & Social Affairs** (nos.14-16, EC1N 7SU, no phone, www.departmentof coffee.co.uk) and **Prufrock Coffee** (nos.23-25 EC1N 7TE, 7242 0467, www.prufrockcoffee.com).

Comptoir Gascon French
This bistro/deli specialises in the cuisine of Gascony. Pork and duck appear in various dishes – grilled duck hearts, crackling with duck egg, duck confit – while starters include the must-order 'piggy treats', a charcuterie board with saucisson, pâté, rillettes and slivers of cured tongue. Rustic, yes, but sophisticated too, and every dish comes with a bold whack of flavour. The oddly shaped space is stripped back to brick, but manages to be cosy and welcoming. The smarter, similarly excellent Club Gascon (57 West Smithfield, EC1A 9DS, 7600 6144, www.clubgascon.com) is across the meat market.
61-63 Charterhouse Street, EC1M 6HJ (7608 0851, www.comptoir gascon.com). Farringdon tube/rail. Open noon-2.30pm, 6-10pm Tue-Sat. Main courses £9-£14.50.

Foxlow International
Will Beckett and Huw Gott, the duo behind the popular Hawksmoor steakhouses, have scored again with this newcomer. It has a cosily masculine vibe (warm woods, low lighting and comfortable retro-themed furniture) and a compact menu of meaty dishes, plus impeccably sourced steaks. 'Smokehouse rillettes' sees a smoky mound of beef, turkey, pork and lardo knocked into shape by a tart jumble of cucumber, pickles and capers. The youthful staff are a marvel, with a nothing-too-much-trouble attitude.
69-73 St John Street, EC1M 4AN (7014 8070, www.foxlow.co.uk). Farringdon tube/rail. Open noon-3pm, 5.30-10.30pm Mon-Sat; noon-5.30pm Sun. Main courses £10-£19.50.

Modern Pantry International
Chef Anna Hansen creates enticing fusion dishes that make the most of unusual ingredients sourced from around the globe. Antipodean and Asian flavours (yuzu, tamarind) pop up frequently, alongside plenty of seasonal British fare (wild garlic, purple sprouting broccoli); the combinations can seem bewildering on the page, but rarely falter in execution, and the signature dish

of sugar-cured prawn omelette with chilli, coriander and spring onion is still a winner. There's a stylish, light ground-floor café and a more formal restaurant upstairs.
47-48 St John's Square, EC1V 4JJ (7250 0833, www.themodernpantry. co.uk). Farringdon tube/rail. Open Café 8am-10pm Mon; 8am-10.30pm Tue-Fri; 9am-4pm, 6-10.30pm Sat; 10am-4pm, 6-10pm Sun. Restaurant noon-3pm, 6-11pm Tue-Fri; 9am-5pm, 6-11pm Sat; 10am-4pm Sun. Main courses £8.50-£20.50.

Moro North African/Spanish
Sam(antha) and Sam Clark's Exmouth Market restaurant and cookbooks set the benchmark for a distinctly British style of Iberian-with-a-North-African-twist Mediterranean cooking, and they're still in the front rank 17 years later. Moro provides a spectacular showcase of modern Spanish and Portuguese wines, and vibrantly fresh food, such as chargrilled trout cleverly balanced by lemon, capers and a bitter note from hispi cabbage. Next door, Morito (no.32, 7278 7007, closed Sun) is a fine no-booking tapas bar offshoot.
34-36 Exmouth Market, EC1R 4QE (7833 8336, www.moro.co.uk). Farringdon tube/rail. Open Bar noon-10.30pm Mon-Sat; 12.30-2.45pm Sun. Restaurant noon-2.30pm, 6-10.30pm Mon-Sat; 12.30-2.45pm Sun. Main courses £18.50-£21. Tapas £3.50-£14.50.

St John British
Fergus Henderson and Trevor Gulliver's restaurant has been praised to the skies for reacquainting the British with the full possibilities of native produce, and especially anything gutsy and offal-ish. Delicate dishes such as as in black cuttlefish and onions, with a deep-flavoured ink-based sauce with a hint of mint appear too. Perhaps as influential, however, has been its almost defiantly casual style. The mezzanine dining room in the former Smithfield smokehouse has bare white walls, battered floorboards and tables lined up canteen-style. The airy bar here is a great place for a drink and a no-fuss snack. The more bistro-like St John Bread & Wine (94-96 Commercial Street, Spitalfields, E1 6LZ, 7251 0848) is also a well-loved venue.
26 St John Street, EC1M 4AY (7251 0848, www.stjohnrestaurant. com). Barbican tube or Farringdon tube/rail. Open noon-2.45pm, 6-10.45pm Mon-Fri; 6-10.45pm Sat; 1-2.30pm Sun. Main courses £13.50-£23.80.

Bloomsbury & King's Cross

The newly-developed area behind King's Cross station – focused on Granary Square – is shaping some excellent restaurants and a healthy street food scene.

Caravan King's Cross Global
This offshoot of Caravan is an altogether bigger, more urbane operation than the original in Clerkenwell (11-13 Exmouth Market, EC1R 4QD, 7833 115). The ethos is the same in both branches: welcoming staff and a menu of what they call 'well-travelled food'. Most are small plates – deep-fried duck egg with baba ganoush, chorizo oil and crispy shallots, say – plus a few large plates and (at King's Cross only) a handful of first-class pizzas. The setting, overlooking the fountains of Granary Square, is another plus.
Granary Building, 1 Granary Square, N1C 4AA (7101 7661, www.caravan kingscross.co.uk). King's Cross St Pancras tube/rail. Meals served 8am-10.30pm Mon-Fri; 10am-10.30pm Sat; 10am-4pm Sun. Main courses £7-£15.50.

Grain Store Modern European
Grain Store occupies just one part of a vast former Victorian warehouse, next to Caravan (see left). Most of the rest of the building has been imaginatively transformed into Central Saint Martins arts college. The restaurant is run by Bruno Loubet, the man behind Bistrot Bruno Loubet (86-88 Clerkenwell Road, EC1M 5RJ, 7324 4455). His cooking is grounded in the classical traditions of south-west France, but not bound by them. The menu is a pick 'n' mix of ingredients and cuisines: a dish such as sticky pork belly with a corn and quinoa tamale is typical.
Granary Square, 1-3 Stable Street, N1C 4AB (7324 4466, www.grain store.com). King's Cross St Pancras tube/rail. Open noon-2.30pm, 6-10.30pm Mon-Fri; 11am-3pm, 6-10.30pm Sat; 11am-4pm Sun. Main courses £9.50-£16. Set dinner £35 5 courses.

Fitzrovia

Berners Tavern Modern European
The huge lobby bar of the London Edition hotel (see p112) looks fabulous, but the vast dining room, with its ornate plasterwork ceiling and lively bar area, looks even better. Food is playful and appealing: tender pork belly with capers, golden raisins and apple coleslaw, and cod with fennel and cider sauce, are sublime. Any caveats? Sometimes dizzy service; frequent upselling of extras; and lighting so low it's hard to read the menu. But Berners Tavern is glamtastic. Wear your best threads, and book ahead for a preliminary cocktail in the adjoining Punch Room bar to steel yourself for the bill.
10 Berners Street, W1T 3NP (7908 7979, www.bernerstavern.com). Oxford Circus or Tottenham Court Road tube. Open Bar 11am-11pm daily. Restaurant 7-10.30am, noon-2.30pm, 6-10.30pm Mon-Fri; 7-10.30am, 11am-4pm, 6-10.30pm Sat, Sun. Main courses £15-£26.

Bonnie Gull Fish
After starting as a pop-up in Hackney in 2011, Bonnie Gull landed here in 2012. The premises do a good job of evoking a seaside shack. The menu changes daily, but super-fresh crab, with the brown meat mixed with mayo in the shell and the white meat ready to be cracked out, is often featured. More complex dishes are beautifully presented, and equally good – hake with courgette purée, beer-battered courgette flower and courgette ribbons is an assured plateful. A branch opened on Exmouth Market in April 2014 .
21A Foley Street, W1W 6DS (7436 0921, www.bonniegull.com). Goodge Street tube. Open noon-2.45pm, 6-9.45pm Mon-Fri; noon-3.45pm, 6-9.45pm Sat; noon-3.45pm, 6.30-8.45pm Sun. Main courses £13-£23.

Dabbous International
The hype surrounding Dabbous' 2012 opening has not entirely diminished and securing a booking can be tricky, so it's a pleasure to arrive and find a relaxed, friendly restaurant. Even at £59 per person for seven dishes the tasting menu is great value. The kitchen majors in plant foods, setting a light, contemporary culinary tone concisely expressed in dishes such as mixed alliums with chilled pine infusion. Meats are skilfully cooked too; we love the barbecued ibérico pork with almond praline. There's a great bar, Oskar's (see p71), in the basement.
39 Whitfield Street, W1T 2SF (7323 1544, www.dabbous.co.uk). Goodge Street or Warren Street tube. Open noon-2.30pm, 6.30-9.30pm Tue-Fri; 6.15-9.30pm Sat. Set lunch £28 4 courses. Set dinner £45 4 courses. Tasting menu £59 7 courses.

Hakkasan Chinese
More than a decade after it started wowing London's big spenders with its classy Cantonese cooking, this Michelin-starred trendsetter remains a benchmark against which high-end Chinese restaurants should be judged. The basement's stylish interior (all dark wood lattice screens and moody lighting) still attracts beautiful people, who come for signature dishes such as silver cod roasted in champagne, and jasmine tea-smoked organic pork ribs. Drinks run from cocktails via high-priced wines to specialist teas. There's also a branch in Mayfair – 17 Bruton Street, W1J 6QB (7907 1888).
8 Hanway Place, W1T 1HD (7927 7000, www.hakkasan.com). Tottenham Court Road tube. Open Restaurant noon-3pm, 6-11pm Mon-Wed; noon-3pm, 5.45-11.45pm Thur, Fri; noon-4pm, 5.45-11.45pm Sat; noon-5.45pm, 6-11pm Sun. Main courses £17-£61.

Honey & Co Middle Eastern
A bijou delight, with small tables and chairs packed closely together. The kitchen is run by an accomplished Israeli husband-and-wife team. This pedigree shines in a daily-changing

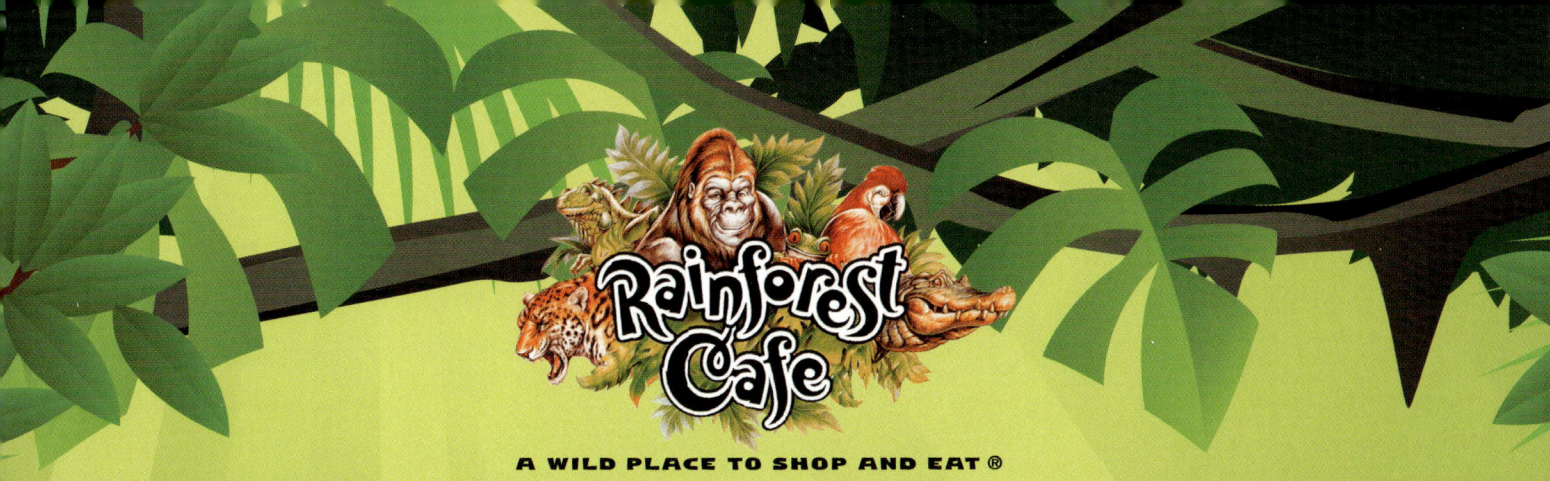

A WILD PLACE TO SHOP AND EAT ®

HOW ABOUT A WILD DAY OUT?

Located in Piccadilly Circus, Rainforest Cafe is a unique and vibrant restaurant and bar bringing together the sights and sounds of the jungle.

15% DISCOUNT
off your final food bill*

PERFECT FOR KIDS & BIG KIDS
GREAT FOR GROUPS &
BIRTHDAY CELEBRATIONS

Book online: www.therainforestcafe.co.uk
Tel: 020 7434 3111
Email: sales@therainforestcafe.co.uk

*Offer valid seven days a week. Maximum party size of 6. Please present to your safari guide when seated. Cannot be used in conjunction with any other offer.

menu that draws influences from across the Middle East. The meze selection includes fabulously spongy, oily bread, sumac-spiked tahini, smoky taramasalata, crisp courgette croquettes with labneh, pan-fried feta and a bright salad with lemon and radishes. A main might be a whole baby chicken with lemon and a chilli and walnut muhamara paste. It's imaginative home-style cooking, and service is charming.

25A Warren Street, W1T 5LZ (7388 6175, www.honeyandco.co.uk). Warren Street tube. Open 8am-10.30pm Mon-Fri; 9.30am-10.30pm Sat. Main courses £8.50-£12.50. Set dinner (Mon-Sat) £26.50 2 courses; £29.50 3 courses.

Koba Korean

Koba is one of the strongest players on the West End Korean scene. Barbecue meats such as beef kalbi or bulgogi are well marinated, and grilled at the table by efficient staff. Stews make a sound choice too, with umami-rich stocks and accompanying bowls of pearly rice. Service is polished but not too formal, and the dark, modern-East-Asian-meets-industrial interior is slick. Drinks include Korean beers, soju and a short wine list.

11 Rathbone Street, W1T 1NA (7580 8825). Goodge Street tube. Lunch served noon-2.30pm, 6-10.30pm Mon-Sat; 6-10.30pm Sun. Main courses £8.50-£12. Set lunch £6.50-£11.50. Set meal £25-£35.

Lantana Café

Lantana is a lively spot. Its look – wooden tables, mismatched chairs, small pieces of art on white walls – is now commonplace, but the staff pride themselves on their coffee-making and baking skills, and rightly so. The flat whites are super-smooth and go well with a moist raspberry friand. The breakfast and brunch menu includes the likes of maple french toast with streaky bacon, grilled banana and candied pecans. Savoury dishes can be ordered with a glass of wine. The kiosk next door offers takeaways.

13 Charlotte Place, W1T 1SN (7637 3347, www.lantanacafe.co.uk). Goodge Street tube. Meals served 8-11.30am, noon-3pm Mon-Fri; 9am-3pm Sat, Sun. Main courses £5.50-£11.50.

Lima London Peruvian

Part of the 'Peruvian wave' of restaurants to hit the capital in 2012, Lima London pitched itself squarely at the high end. The modish rear dining room mixes the hum of low-level beats with polite chatter; only the occasional Inca-patterned cushion adds colour. Well-drilled staff bring out a medley of carefully crafted small plates, the likes of sea bream ceviche flecked with hot aji limo chilli and pieces of roasted corn, and thick wedges of suckling pig – part dense meat, part salty, crispy crackling, matched by a rough corn mash spiked with two kinds of peppers.

31 Rathbone Place, W1T 1JH (3002 2640, www.limalondon.com).

Caravan King's Cross. *See p56.*

Tottenham Court Road tube. Open noon-2.30pm, 5.30-10.30pm Mon-Sat. Main courses £16-£29. Set meal noon-2.30pm, 5.30-6pm Mon-Fri £20 2 courses, £23 3 courses.

Covent Garden & the Strand

Balthazar Brasserie

NYC import Balthazar presents a Manhattan interpretation of a French brasserie, with signature dishes such as the onion soup (grilled gruyère lid on thick country bread, immersed in a rich and sweet chicken stock); duck shepherd's pie is another powerfully flavoured treat. Bread, from master baker Jon Rolfe, is a must-try – and is sold at the Boulangerie next door. Balthazar London mimics the New York original, with red awnings, red leather banquettes, giant antique-mirrored walls and mosaic floors.

4-6 Russell Street, WC2E 7BN (3301 1155, www.balthazarlondon.com). Covent Garden tube. Open 7.30am-midnight Mon-Fri; 10am-midnight Sat; 10am-11pm Sun. Main courses £13-£37.

Delaunay Brasserie

European grand cafés are the inspiration here, resulting in a striking interior of green leather banquette seating, dark wood, antique mirrors and a black and white marble floor. The menu runs from breakfast to dinner, taking in afternoon tea (try the Austrian-biased cakes, all made in-house). There's a dish of the day (goulash, say), soups, sandwiches, salads and egg dishes, plus savouries (welsh and buck rarebits) and crustacea. In short, there's something for everyone. If the Delaunay is full, try their no-bookings Counter café next door for cakes and light meals.

55 Aldwych, WC2B 4BB (7499 8558, www.thedelaunay.com). Covent Garden or Temple tube. Open 7am-midnight Mon-Fri; 8am-midnight Sat; 9am-11pm Sun. Main courses £6.50-£27.50. Cover £2.

Dishoom Pan-Indian

A swish, self-styled 'Bombay café', Dishoom is filled with retro features: whirring ceiling fans, low-level lighting and vintage Bollywood posters. The place is crowded all day, from breakfast (for sausage naan rolls with chilli jam) to dinner (for the usual curries and tandoori grills). Bookings are only taken for groups at dinner.

12 Upper St Martin's Lane, WC2H 9FB (7420 9320, www.dishoom.com). Leicester Square tube. Open 8am-11pm Mon-Thur; 8am-midnight Fri; 9am-midnight Sat; 9am-10pm Sun. Main courses £5.50-£16.50.

Fernandez & Wells Café

Four impressive rooms in the east wing of Somerset House, set up for all-day grazing. Meat is central: the 'ham room' is set up for carving slices of lomito ibérico, jamón de lampiño, or wild fennel Tuscan salami. Breakfasts are simple but good, and feature dishes such as fried eggs sprinkled with za'atar, miniature morcilla sausages and toasted sourdough.

East Wing, Somerset House, the Strand, WC2R 1LA (7420 9408, www.fernandezandwells.com). Temple tube. Open 10am-10pm Mon-Sat; 10am-8pm Sun. Sharing plates £4.50-£15.

Flesh & Buns Japanese

Flesh & Buns is hidden in a capacious basement, with industrial-chic decor and young, pierced and tattooed staff setting the tone. It serves hirata buns – a US take on Taiwanese street food – with a side order of rock music. Sweet, fluffy dough is folded, then steamed and brought to table. Diners then stuff these pockets with their choice of 'flesh'. Mustard miso and a few slices of subtly pickled apple make a foil for tender pulled pork.

41 Earlham Street, WC2H 9LX (7632 9500, www.fleshandbuns.com). Covent Garden tube. Open noon-3pm, 5-10.30pm Mon, Tue; noon-3pm, 5-11.30pm Wed-Fri; noon-11.30pm Sat; noon-9.30pm Sun. Main courses £13.50-£19.50.

La Giaconda Modern European

Here the front café area covers breakfast fry-ups, porridge, and toasted banana bread at very fair prices, while lunch might be takeaway sandwiches or a dish of the day or two: maybe polenta with chicken leg and a red pepper ragout. But slip through to the more formal rear dining room, and you have a very different menu to choose from, with starters from around £7 and mains at £17. Game, veal and offal always feature, showcasing Paul Merrony's elegantly butch cooking. The owners' Australian heritage gets a nod on the idiosyncratic wine list.

9 Denmark Street, WC2H 8LS (7240 3334, www.giacondadining.com). Tottenham Court Road tube. Open 8am-10pm Mon-Fri; 9am-6pm Sat. Main courses £10.50-£32. Cover £1.50.

Great Queen Street British

The location, steps away from central Covent Garden, ensures Great Queen Street's perennial popularity (walk-ins may find space at the bar, where the full menu is served). The menu changes daily. There's minimal fussing with ingredients in dishes such as a plump piece of bone-in smoked mackerel with a dollop each of cooked gooseberries and horseradish.

32 Great Queen Street, WC2B 5AA (7242 0622). Covent Garden or Holborn tube. Open Bar 5.30-11.30pm Tue-Sat. Restaurant noon-2.30pm, 6-10.30pm Mon-Sat; 1-3pm Sun. Main courses £10.80-£22.

Hawksmoor Seven Dials Steakhouse

The short main menu centres on steak (ribeye, T-bone, porterhouse, fillet, sirloin and more), at serious prices, plus the likes of grilled chicken, lobster with garlic butter, monkfish grilled over charcoal, and a meat-free choice for the odd misplaced vegetarian. A good kick-off is one of Hawksmoor's renowned cocktails.

11 Langley Street, WC2H 9JJ (7856 2154, www.thehawksmoor.co.uk). Covent Garden tube. Open noon-3pm, 5-10.30pm Mon-Thur; noon-3pm, 5-11pm Fri, Sat; noon-9.30pm Sun. Main courses £14.50-£49.50.

Homeslice Pizza

Served fresh from the wood-fired oven, most of the thin-crust pizzas here are available by the slice. Or you can order a 20-incher: enough to feed you and two pals. A well-constructed margherita can be a little slice of heaven – there are a couple of ingredient combos that wouldn't get

the green light in Naples, but taste pretty good. On one, slivers of bone marrow are melted over the tomato base, imparting a meaty savouring, then it's scattered with watercress and roasted spring onions. Service is attentive and chummy. To drink, there are craft beers, and prosecco on tap.
13 Neal's Yard, WC2H 9DP (7836 4604, www.homeslicepizza.co.uk). Covent Garden tube. Open noon-10.30pm Mon-Sat; noon-8pm Sun. Pizza £4 slice, £20 whole.

J Sheekey Fish & seafood
After well over a century of service, Sheekey's status as a West End institution is assured. With its monochrome photos of stars of stage and screen, wooden panelling and cream crackle walls, and array of silver dishes atop thick white tablecloths, it oozes old-fashioned glamour. The menu runs from oysters and shellfish via old-fashioned snacks (herring roe on toast) to upmarket classics (dover sole, lobster thermidor). The fish pie is deservedly acclaimed. The adjoining Oyster Bar serves a similar menu to customers sitting casually at the counter, and with an expanded choice of oysters.
28-32 St Martin's Court, Leicester Square, WC2N 4AL (7240 2565, www.j-sheekey.co.uk). Leicester Square tube. Open noon-3pm, 5.30pm-midnight Mon-Sat; noon-3.30pm, 6-11pm Sun. Main courses £13.50-£48.50.

Kopapa Fusion
The exciting and well-executed menu at this handily located all-dayer includes Turkish eggs (poached eggs with yoghurt, hot chilli butter and flatbread) for breakfast and brunch. Lunch features weighty sandwiches (steak on focaccia with caramelised onion, mustard cream cheese, roast tomatoes and pickles) and burgers (soft-shell crab burger with Asian salad, spicy peanut mayonnaise and avocado), alongside salads and a selection of more inventive dishes, many of which also appear on the evening menu. Quality produce, imaginatively teamed, served by smiling, clued-up staff.
32-34 Monmouth Street, WC2H 9HA (7240 6076, www.kopapa.co.uk). Covent Garden tube. Open 8.30-11am, noon-11pm Mon-Fri; 9.30am-4pm, 4.30-11pm Sat; 9.30am-4pm, 4.30-9.45pm Sun. Main courses £18-£23.

Mishkin's American
Mishkin's calls itself 'a kind-of Jewish deli with cocktails', which is a pretty good description. We're partial to the reuben (pastrami, sauerkraut, swiss cheese and russian dressing on toasted rye bread), though it's no bargain at £11. Sides such as chips, fried onion rings and coleslaw are hard to resist too. The menu is an attractive selection, mixing tradition (chicken matzo ball soup) and innovation (cod cheek popcorn), sometimes in the same dish (smoked mackerel latkes). The small, shabby-chic, NYC-style interior is low-lit, and staff mix a mean cocktail.
25 Catherine Street, WC2B 5JS (7240 2078, www.mishkins.co.uk). Covent Garden tube. Open noon-11.30pm Mon-Sat; noon-10.30pm Sun. Main courses £6-£12.

Opera Tavern Spanish/Italian tapas
The Opera Tavern, split into an upstairs restaurant and a cosy, mirror-backed bar, is one of London's top tapas restaurants. The signature burger of juicy ibérico pork and foie gras is deservedly popular, though more inventive combinations better showcase the kitchen's delicate touch and careful sourcing of ingredients. Chargrilled venison, for example, is enlivened by jerusalem artichoke, pickled walnuts and truffle.
3 Catherine Street, WC2B 5JS (7836 3680, www.operatavern.co.uk). Covent Garden tube. Open noon-3pm, 5-11.30pm Mon-Fri; noon-11.30pm Sat; noon-5pm Sun. Tapas £3.75-£12.

Paramount Modern European
On the 33rd floor of the Centre Point building, with spectacular views on every side across central London, Paramount bar and restaurant is a glam spot, especially by night. Cooking is competent; prices are high, though set meals offer better value. Afternoon tea is popular too.
32nd floor, Centre Point, 101-103 New Oxford Street, WC1A 1DD (7420 2900, www.paramount.uk.net). Tottenham Court Road tube. Open Bar 8am-1.30am Mon-Wed; 8am-2.30am Thur, Fri; noon-2.30am Sat; noon-10pm Sun. Restaurant 8-10.30am, noon-2.45pm, 3-5pm (tea), 5.30-11pm Mon-Fri; noon-2.45pm, 3-5pm (tea), 5.30-11pm Sat; noon-2.45pm, 3-5pm (tea), 5-9.45pm Sun. Main courses £10.50-£28.

Wahaca Mexican
Thomasina Miers's Mexican 'market food' concept is a successful mini-chain, with a dozen branches across London. The restaurants share a cheery vibe, with young, efficient staff buzzing round bright interiors. Tortillas loom large – in soft, crisp, toasted and chip variations, and in flour and corn versions – though there are also a few grills (fish, steak or chicken served with green rice). Favourites include steak burrito with a zingy chipotle salsa.
66 Chandos Place, WC2N 4HG (7240 1883, www.wahaca.co.uk). Covent Garden or Leicester Square tube. Open noon-11pm Mon-Sat; noon-10.30pm Sun. Main courses £5-£14.45.

Soho & Chinatown

Chinatown stalwarts such as **Mr Kong** (21 Lisle Street, 7437 7341) and **Wong Kei** (41-43 Wardour Street, 7437 8408) still ply their reliable Anglo-Cantonese trade, but there's more gastronomic excitement offered by newcomers such as **Barshu** (*see below*).

10 Greek Street Modern European
This small, unshowy restaurant has made a name for itself with a short but perfectly formed menu and an easy-going conviviality. Dishes are seasonal and the kitchen produces lots of interesting but ungimmicky combos – like a special of halibut fillet with yellow beans, chilli and garlic, on a vivid romesco sauce. It's good value, too. Tables are closely packed, and in the evening it can get noisy; bookings are taken for lunch but not dinner.
10 Greek Street, W1D 4DH (7734 4677, www.10greekstreet.com). Tottenham Court Road tube. Open noon-2.30pm, 5.30pm-10.45pm Mon-Sat. Main courses £12-£19.

Arbutus Modern European
This smart modern eaterie is successfully creative with unusual and less-used ingredients: saddle of rabbit, prettily presented with small root vegetables and stuffed with liver, accompanied by shepherd's pie, for example. We like the good-value set lunch and pre-theatre menus, the posh but proper puds and the fact that every wine is available by 250ml carafe.
63-64 Frith Street, W1D 3JW (7734 4545, www.arbutusrestaurant.co.uk). Tottenham Court Road tube. Open noon-2.30pm, 5-11pm Mon-Thur; noon-2.30pm, 5-11.30pm Fri, Sat; noon-3pm, 5.30-10.30pm Sun. Main courses £8-£19.

Barrafina Spanish
If proof is needed that tapas is fashionable, the queues at Barrafina are it. (Bookings aren't taken for the 20 or so stools around the L-shaped bar.) Nibbles and drinks are served as you wait – service is excellent. Meanwhile, chefs shout out orders, grill, fry and plate up their creations. Barrafina's menu is studded with Mallorcan and Catalan tapas dishes, such as juicy, crisp-skinned grilled chicken thighs served with exemplary romesco sauce.
54 Frith Street, W1D 4SL (7813 8010, www.barrafina.co.uk). Leicester Square tube. Open noon-3pm, 5-11pm Mon-Sat; 1-3.30pm, 5.30-10.30pm Sun. Tapas £4-£18.50.

Barshu Chinese
Barshu is distinct from Chinatown's mostly Cantonese restaurants in looks and pricing, as well as its Sichuanese cuisine. The dark wooden ground floor is brightened by red lanterns and partitioned by a beautifully carved screen; upstairs is similarly woody. Sichuan cooking is characterised by fiery, sour flavours, and the menu holds much interest, listing the likes of pea jelly, prairie tripe, and stir-fried chicken gizzards with pickled chilli. Many dishes are hot and oily, so order steamed rice and plain vegetables for balance. We also like Barshu's siblings Ba Shan (24 Romilly Street, W1D 5AH, 7287 3266) and Baozi Inn (25 Newport Court, WC2H 7JS, 7287 6877).
28 Frith Street, W1D 5LF (7287 6688, www.bar-shu.co.uk). Leicester Square tube. Open noon-11pm Mon-Thur, Sun; noon-11.30pm Fri, Sat. Main courses £9.90-£30.90.

Bocca di Lupo Italian
The buzz is as important as the food at this popular restaurant. The menu is a slightly confusing mix of small and large plates to share: buttery brown shrimp on soft, silky white polenta, say, and a deep-fried mix of calamari, soft-shell crab and lemon. The radish, celeriac, pomegranate and pecorino salad with truffle dressing is a much-imitated Bocca di Lupo signature. The same team runs the fine gelateria, Gelupo, at no.7 (7287 5555, www.gelupo.com).
12 Archer Street, W1D 7BB (7734 2223, www.boccadilupo.com). Piccadilly Circus tube. Open 12.15-2.45pm, 5.15-11pm Mon-Sat; 12.15-3.15pm, 5.15-11pm Sun. Dishes £6-£26.50.

Dishoom

La Bodega Negra Mexican

It's so dark and loud in this nightclub-like basement restaurant that you'll need a moment to adjust. The cooking is perhaps the least thrilling aspect of the place, though effort is put into presentation. Soft flour tacos with a tender beef filling are beautifully arranged on a wooden board. Factor in the small portions and two-hour table limits and you might wonder what the fuss is all about. But that would be missing the point. You come here to see and be seen, and for a thrilling atmosphere.
16 Moor Street, W1D 5NH (7758 4100, www.labodeganegra.com). Leicester Square tube. Open Café noon-midnight Mon-Wed; noon-1am Thur-Sat; noon-11pm Sun. Restaurant 6pm-1am Mon-Sat; 6-midnight Sun. Main courses £12-£26.

Cây Tre Vietnamese

Cây Tre is chic, with minimal decor, impeccably smart and efficient black-clad staff, and beautifully served food. The chain prides itself on using fresh ingredients with impeccable provenance – witness the barbecued Somerset ribs with lemongrass, Sriracha chilli sauce and galangal. The original is in Shoreditch, at 301 Old Street, EC1V 9LA (7729 8662).
42-43 Dean Street, W1D 4PZ (7317 9118, www.caytresoho.co.uk). Leicester Square tube. Open noon-11pm Mon-Thur; noon-11.30pm Fri, Sat; noon-10pm Sun. Main courses £8-£13.`

Ceviche Peruvian

Ceviche showcases the country's most sexy and metropolitan export: ceviche. Here, citrus-cured fish is available in half a dozen different forms, though the menu also includes everything from terrific chargrilled meat and fish skewers (anticuchos) to a simple but perfectly executed corn cake. Factor in the charismatic, attentive staff and the party atmosphere, and it's no wonder this place has been such a hit.
17 Frith Street, W1D 4RG (7292 2040, www.cevicheuk.com). Leicester Square tube. Open noon-11.30pm Mon-Sat; noon-10.15pm Sun. Tapas £4.50-£11.

Herman Ze German German

A purveyor of German sausages with a playfully utilitarian interior. The sausages are imported from the Schwarzwald (the Black Forest), and are sehr gut: high-quality pork; juicy, springy middles; and a proper 'knack' when you bite. More bonus points for serving them in chewy baguettes.
33 Old Compton Street, W1D 5JU (no phone, www.herman-ze-german.co.uk). Leicester Square tube. Open 11am-11.30pm Mon-Thur; 11am-midnight Fri, Sat; 11am-10.30pm Sun. Main courses £4.45-£9.95.

Hummus Bros Café

The humble chickpea paste is elevated to something altogether more delicious here. Though the wraps aren't bad, go for the bowls of silky-smooth houmous sprinkled

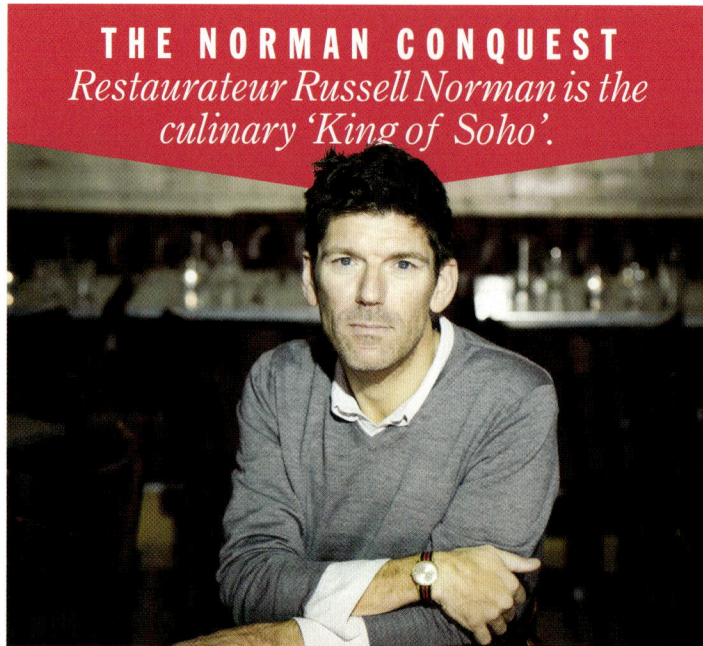

THE NORMAN CONQUEST
Restaurateur Russell Norman is the culinary 'King of Soho'.

In the days when exotic dancers still gyrated around the Raymond Revuebar in Walker's Court, it would have been inconceivable that a restaurateur could become the 'King of Soho'. But today the area is a hotspot for culinary rather than carnal pleasures. From the latest small-plates places to rock 'n' roll ramen joints, Soho has become a magnet for diners. And when it comes to successful ventures in the area, restaurateur Russell Norman takes the crown.

There's no denying Norman's credentials as a trendsetting restaurateur. After he and business partner Richard Beatty opened **Polpo** (41 Beak Street, W1F 9SB, 7734 4479, www.polpo.co.uk) in 2009, there was a ripple of me-too establishments – focused on small plates (in Polpo's case, Venetian bar snacks) served in a relaxed setting – and there's no shortage of pared-down New York-style diners in the style of their Rupert Street establishment **Spuntino** (*see below*). Nor did Beatty and Norman sit on their laurels: there are two further branches of Polpo now – one in Covent Garden, the other in Smithfield. And these days Norman even presents a BBC TV series (*The Restaurant Man*) in which he shares his wisdom with variously deluded start-up restaurateurs.

Then, in 2014, there were two new openings. We were a little disappointed by Norman's first gastropub **Ape & Bird** (142 Shaftesbury Avenue, WC2H 8HJ, 7836 3119), but the second coming of **Polpetto** (*see right*) – under the capable hands of Florence Knight, a star chef of the future – confirmed his golden touch.

with paprika and olive oil. Mashed, cumin-scented fava beans is a good choice of topping, but our favourite is the chunky slow-cooked beef. Side dishes are heartily recommended, with smoky barbecued aubergine and zingy tabouleh particular highlights
88 Wardour Street, W1F 0TH (7734 1311, www.hbros.co.uk). Tottenham Court Road tube. Open noon-10pm Mon-Wed; noon-11pm Thur-Sat; noon-4pm Sun. Dishes £3.20-£8.45.

Koya Japanese

With blond-wood sharing tables, white walls and a generally fresh-faced crowd of diners, the venue feels more like a friendly caff than a slick West End eaterie. The handmade udon noodles produced here are top notch, which explains why expectant diners often queue out of the door (no bookings are taken). Service is snappy, so you won't have to wait too long.
49 Frith Street, W1D 4SG (7434 4463, www.koya.co.uk). Tottenham Court Road tube. Open noon-3pm;

5.30-10.30pm Mon-Sat; 5.30-10pm Sun. Main courses £6.90-£14.90.*

Pitt Cue Co North American

Come to this trailblazing 30-seater rib joint on a Friday or Saturday night and there's one certainty: a painfully long queue. For rib-lovers, it'll be worth it. The Pitt Cue-ers's cooking rarely misses a beat. The gargantuan signature ribs arrive with blistered, blackened skin, revealing ruby fall-off-the-bone meat that is both smoky and dangerously rich. A fine 'slaw, with two kinds of cabbage, coriander seeds and a zingy vinaigrette, is a must-try.
1 Newburgh Street, W1F 7RB (www.pittcue.co.uk). Oxford Circus tube. Open noon-3pm, 6-10.30pm Mon-Sat; noon-4pm Sun. Main courses £9.50-£16.

Pizza Pilgrims Pizza

The main basement dining area is intimate, with wipe-clean green checked tablecloths and 1960s Italian film posters helping to create the feel

of a retro Soho trattoria. The friendly, slightly trendy mood is helped by an alcove for table football. Pizzas are chewy and soft in the Neapolitan style, the appealing, thick bases layered with on-trend toppings: 'nduja, a spicy Calabrian sausage, is paired with a simple marinara sauce, for example. No bookings.
11 Dean Street, W1D 3RP (7287 8964, http://pizzapilgrims.co.uk). Tottenham Court Road tube. Meals served noon-10.30pm daily. Main courses £7-£11.

Polpetto Italian

The long, low-lit dining room buzzes with attentive staff serving small plates to the appreciative crowd who don't seem to mind being seated on tightly packed tables. In the basement dining room, there's the bonus of a view of chef Florence Knight and her team in a glass-fronted kitchen. As well as more familiar assemblies such as fork-tender veal cheeks in an earthy fennel, white wine and bean stew, there are many options on the menu which will have you reaching for your encyclopaedia. Small, green 'cuckoo flower' leaves added a fiery horseradish-like hit to a plate of boiled pink fir potatoes.
11 Berwick Street, W1F 0PL (7439 8627, www.polpo.co.uk). Oxford Circus tube. Open noon-11pm Mon-Sat; noon-4pm Sun.

Princi Bakery-café

This smart outpost of a Milanese bakery chain remains a popular all-day option. It's an airy, good-looking room, and the food is varied: as well as cakes, pastries and breads, there's a choice of filled focaccia (parma ham, say, or mortadella), hot dishes (lasagne, aubergine parmigiana), slices of pizza and lots of attractive salads. It's all quality, seasonal stuff. Finding a seat at the communal counters can be something of a trial. Opt out by dining in the pizzeria, which offers table service and a calmer atmosphere in which to enjoy a short but classy range of pizzas.
135 Wardour Street, W1F 0UF (7478 8888, www.princi.co.uk). Leicester Square tube. Open 8am-midnight Mon-Sat; 8.30am-10pm Sun. Main courses £7.50-£12.50.

Spuntino North American

A challenge to find (look for 'number 61'), the venue is laid out as a bar – and a tiny one at that, with a smattering of fixed, backless seats allowing diners to perch along the counter. This is no wholesome 1950s-style diner, but a dark, grungy space where dim lights dangle in cages, the walls are cracked and battered, and the staff sport daring tattoos under flimsy vests. The menu is Italian-American, featuring bold flavours packed into tiny portions. No bookings are taken.
61 Rupert Street, W1D 7PW (no phone, www.spuntino.co.uk). Piccadilly Circus tube. Open noon-midnight Mon-Wed; noon-1am Thur-Sat; noon-11pm Sun. Main courses £5-£10.

Mimmo La Bufala
Healthy Food. Healthy Life.

45a Southend Road
London NW3 2QB
www.mimmolabufala.co.uk
Telephone: 020 7435 7814

This authentic Italian restaurant, owned by Mimmo Rimoli, will soon be celebrating 10 years in Hampstead.

The Pizzas here continue to make awards and Mimmo has introduced the novelty 'Pizza Metro' (one metre long pizza base) for parties and groups. The selection of fresh fish which Mimmo gets from the markets in the early hours of the morning continue to satisfy the best pallet. Other favourites include the prime Scottish fillet, veal al limone and the tasty veal Milanese prepared by the Italian chefs.

Mimmo says it has been a real pleasure to serve his many loyal friends in the area but he is always happy to welcome new friends from all over to enjoy and evening meal during the week or lunch and dinner at weekends.

"Ciao – welcome and buon appetito" – Mimmo

Mimmo La Bufala is highly recommended by:

Yalla Yalla Lebanese

The 'Beirut street food' resonates with the upbeat informality of these dinky Soho premises. Diners cram on to faux-rustic tables, while others nip in for takeaway wraps – filled with everything from falafel to spicy sujuk sausage. A concise list of classic meze dishes includes a chunky, smoky baba ganoush and a flavour-packed fattoush salad. There's also a selection of grills. Cocktails are served in the evening.
1 Green's Court, W1F 0HA (7287 7663, www.yalla-yalla.co.uk). Piccadilly Circus tube. Open 10am-11pm daily. Main courses £9.75-£14.50.

Oxford Street & Marylebone

Busaba Eathai Thai

Busaba is a ten-strong chain, but it's not your average Thai joint. The handsome interior combines dark wood, incense and dimly lit lanterns. With spacious shared tables, no reservervations and brisk service, it remains a great spot for a casual meal with friends. Among the Thai classics you'll find a few dishes that aren't often seen in London, such as sen chan pad thai (a pimped pad thai with crab originating from the Chanthaburi province of eastern Thailand).
8-13 Bird Street, W1U 1BU (7518 8080, www.busaba.com). Bond Street tube. Open noon-11pm Mon-Thur; noon-11.30pm Fri, Sat; noon-10pm Sun. Main courses £7.30-£12.50.

La Fromagerie Café

There are cheeseboards and then there are La Fromagerie cheeseboards: carefully sourced, themed by nation (with suggested wines to match) and prettily arranged on a wooden slab at the back of an enticing deli and cheese shop. The café doesn't take bookings, so time your visit with care – a late-afternoon table (the cakes are delicious) offers prime people-watching potential.
2-6 Moxon Street, W1U 4EW (7935 0341, www.lafromagerie.co.uk). Baker Street tube. Open 8am-7.30pm Mon-Fri; 9am-7pm Sat; 10am-6pm Sun. Main courses £6.95-£18.50.

Meat Liquor North American

Inside, this cult destination is dark and loud: more hell-raising nightclub than restaurant. Signs point out the rules ('No suits', 'No ballet pumps'). The graffiti murals are occult-themed, and the staff heavily tattooed. The Deep South cooking is gutsy stuff, with the likes of crunchy-coated 'bingo wings' served not only with a terrific Louisiana-style hot sauce but also a feisty blue cheese dip. There are cheese steaks and dogs, though the real show-stoppers are the burgers. Staff make a mean cocktail.
74 Welbeck Street, W1G 0BA (7224 4239, www.meatliquor.com). Bond Street tube. Meals served noon-4pm, 6-10.30pm Mon-Sat; noon-4pm, 6-8.30pm Sun. Main courses £6.50-£8.50.

Patty & Bun Burgers

P&B has carved out a reputation for serving some of London's finest burgers. All-day queues are testament to the fact that it's tiny (with space for only 30 diners) and that the amiable staff have the format spot-on. The signature Ari Gold burger is a generous patty slathered in ketchup and smoky mayo, inside a glazed brioche bun. More original is the Lambshank Redemption, a firm lamb burger strongly flavoured with coriander, chilli and cumin aïoli. Don't miss the skin-on rosemary salt chips.
4 James Street, W1U 1HE (7487 3188, www.pattyandbun.co.uk). Bond Street tube. Open noon-10.15pm Tue-Sat; noon-9.15pm Sun. Main courses £7.50-£8.50.

Roti Chai Pan-Indian

The ground-floor 'street kitchen', with its utilitarian furniture and canteen vibe, is ideal for a swift midday feed – and the alert young staff keep things pacy. The menu is modelled on those of urban India's snack shacks, so you'll find bhel pooris, samosas and moist, light Gujarati dhokra sponge, topped with two relishes: tangy tamarind and spicy coconut. Larger dishes include 'railway lamb curry' (meat and potato in a rich gravy spiced with star anise and cinnamon bark). In the basement, the evening-only 'dining room' is a darker, sexier (and pricier) space.
3-4 Portman Mews South, W1H 6HS (7408 0101, www.rotichai.com). Marble Arch tube. Meals served noon-10.30pm Mon-Sat; 12.30-9pm Sun. Main courses £4.80-£8.50.

Piccadilly Circus & Mayfair

Set in a grand art-deco basement just off Piccadilly Circus, Brasserie Zédel is a huge, all-day French eaterie run by the team behind the **Wolseley** (*see p65*); good on its own terms, it's also home to **Bar Américain** (*see p72*).

Bentley's Oyster Bar & Grill

Richard Corrigan overhauled this grande dame of the restaurant scene (established 1916) in 2005. The interior remains as polished as ever, with art deco windows, the original marble oyster bar and wood panelling. Week-nights in the more formal first-floor Grill restaurant have a restrained business-dinner vibe, but the downstairs oyster bar is pleasingly laid-back. Theatrics at the gleaming marble counter (part staff speedily shucking, part competitive knocking 'em back) provide entertaining distraction as you decide between menu classics and imaginative daily specials.
11-15 Swallow Street, W1B 4DG (7734 4756, www.bentleys.org). Piccadilly Circus tube. Open Oyster Bar noon-midnight Mon-Sat; noon-

Yalla Yalla

10pm Sun. Restaurant noon-3pm, 5.30-10.45pm Mon-Fri; 5.30-10.45pm Sat. Main courses Oyster Bar £12.50-£50. Restaurant £19-£50.

Galvin at Windows
Modern European

There's suddenly no shortage of rooftop venues in London, but the location of Windows is still superb. It offers remarkable panoramic views from the 28th floor of the Park Lane Hilton. Add a sleek interior that mixes art deco glamour with a hint of 1970s petrodollar kitsch, and you can't go wrong. The wine and cocktails don't come cheap, but the drinks are assembled with care, and the service is attentive without being obsequious.
London Hilton, Park Lane, W1K 1BE (7208 4021). Hyde Park Corner tube. Open 11am-1am Mon-Wed; 11am-2.30am Thur, Fri; 3pm-2.30am Sat; 11am-10.30pm Sun. Food served noon-midnight Mon-Fri; 3pm-2.30am Sat; noon-10.30pm Sun.

Gymkhana Indian

Much-lauded Gymkhana looks and feels like an Indian colonial club, with its retro ceiling fans, marble-topped tables and yesteryear photos of polo and cricket team triumphs. It serves a splendid spread of modern Indian dishes based on regional masalas and marinades: a starter of South Indian fried chicken wings, steeped in chilli batter, perhaps, followed by Goan pork vindaloo – slow-cooked chunks of suckling pig cheek, with a red chilli and garlic masala, spiced with sweet cinnamon and pounded coriander.
42 Albemarle Street, W1S 4JH (3011 5900, www.gymkhanalondon.com). Green Park tube. Open noon-2.45pm, 5.30-10.30pm Mon-Sat. Main courses £7.50-£40.

Momo North African

Always fun and glamorous, the kasbah-like Momo rocks. Though serious enough about its food not to be a themed restaurant, the staff's end-of-evening ululating and dancing to Maghrebi beats can send confusing signals. Seductive lighting, plush seating, and heavy crystal glasses indicate the kind of bill to expect. Meze are pastries and dips of the highest calibre; tagines, such as lamb tagine with whole almonds in a rich sauce with prune and pear, have a good balance of flavours. Tables on the street terrace for shisha smoking add to the authenticity.
25 Heddon Street, W1B 4BH (7434 4040, www.momoresto.com). Piccadilly Circus tube. Open Restauraunt noon-2.15pm, 6.30pm-1am Mon-Sat; 6.30pm-midnight Sun. Café/Bar noon-1am Mon-Sat; noon-midnight Sun. Main courses £13-£28. Meze Café/bar only £4.50-£9.75.

Pollen Street Social
Modern European

Pollen Street Social's philosophy is 'deformalised fine dining', and to this end the decor is smart but approachable – white-walled, linen-draped and wood-panelled. Dishes are grounded in French and English tradition and embellished with occasionally esoteric side notes of texture and taste. The delicious subtlety and artistry of Cornish sea bass and red mullet with bouillabaisse sauce, fennel, cuttlefish and saffron potato (self-served from the pan) revealed real skill in the kitchen.
8 Pollen Street, W1S 1NQ (7290 7600, www.pollenstreetsocial.com). Oxford Circus tube. Open Bar noon-midnight Mon-Sat. Restaurant noon-2.30pm, 6-10.30pm Mon-Sat. Main courses £29.50-£38.

Shoryu Ramen Japanese

Shoryu pips its West End tonkotsu rivals when it comes to the texture and stock of its broth. As well as Hakata-style ramen (noodles in a rich, boiled-down, pork-bone broth), the other notable feature is speed. Both help to ease the hassle of no-bookings dining. Dracula tonkotsu – with caramelised garlic oil, balsamic vinegar and garlic chips – packs

a flavoursome punch. Extra toppings such as bamboo shoots and boiled egg are to be expected, but kaedama (plain refill noodles) are a godsend for anyone sharing soup stock between small children. There's a varied choice of sides, sakés and sweets.
9 Regent Street, SW1Y 4LR (no phone, www.shoryuramen.com). Piccadilly Circus tube. Open 11am-3.30pm, 5-11.30pm Mon-Sat; 11am-3.30pm, 5-10.30pm Sun. Main courses £9-£12.50.

Theo Randall at the InterContinental Italian
This colourful, spacious dining room is high on comfort, if a little corporate, service is caring and warm-hearted and the cooking is joyous. The carte is not cheap, but the lunchtime and off-peak hours set menu (around £30) shows the kitchen's quality output. Follow a subtle combination of smoked eel, golden and red beetroots, and horseradish with a wood-roasted guinea fowl, stuffed with parma ham and mascarpone, and served with porcini and portobello mushrooms.
1 Hamilton Place, Park Lane, W1J 7QY (7409 3131, www.theorandall.com). Hyde Park Corner tube. Open noon-3pm, 5.45-11pm Mon-Fri; 5.45-11pm Sat. Main courses £30-£50.

Westminster & St James's

Boulestin French
Named after Marcel Boulestin – a pioneer of pre-war London cooking – this new Boulestin is no relation, though it does pay homage to the era of the great chef. The menu lists oeufs en gelée – a dish which, much like old-school St James's, is preserved in aspic. Classic French cooking at its best shines in dishes such as daube of beef or boudin noir. The adjoining all-day Café Marcel is cheaper and less formal, and serves good-value pre- and post-theatre menus.
5 St James's Street, SW1A 1EF (7930 2030, www.boulestin.com). Green Park tube. Open 7am-3pm, 5-11pm Mon-Wed; 7am-3pm, 5-11.30pm Thur, Fri; 11.30am-4pm, 5-11.30pm Sat. Main courses £12.50-£37. Set dinner (5.30-6.45pm) £19.50 2 courses; £24.50 3 courses.

Inn the Park British
It's all about the location at this beautifully appointed and designed café-restaurant. The seasonal British cooking isn't always up to expectations, especially given the prices, but there is plenty on the plus side: staff are lovely, and the setting (overlooking the duck lake, with trees all around and the London Eye in the distance) is really wonderful.
St James's Park, SW1A 2BJ (7451 9999, www.innthepark.com). St James's Park tube. Open Summer 8am-10pm Mon-Fri, 9am-10pm Sat, Sun. Winter 8am-5pm Mon-Fri; 9am-5pm Sat, Sun. Main courses £14-£23.50.

National Dining Rooms British
Ascend the stairs to Oliver Peyton's first-floor dining room and enter a professionally run and peaceful place, where the views (over the Square in one direction, of a vast Paula Rego mural in the other) are matched by the superb food. Dishes make the most of in-season ingredients: an early spring vegetable salad featured delicately braised chunks of squash, golden beetroot and carrot, a line of vivid beetroot 'dust' and horseradish popcorn. The bakery side of the operation ably fulfils the cakes-and-a-cuppa role of the traditional museum café. Also check out the National Café, on the east side of the gallery.
Sainsbury Wing, National Gallery, Trafalgar Square, WC2N 5DN (7747 2525, www.peyton andbyrne.co.uk). Charing Cross tube/rail. Open Bakery 10am-5pm Mon-Thur, Sat, Sun; 10am-8pm Fri. Restaurant noon-3pm Mon-Thur, Sat, Sun; noon-3pm, 5-7.30pm Fri. Main courses Bakery £6.50-£11.50. Restaurant £16.50-£32.50.

Regency Café Café
Behind its black-tiled art deco exterior, this classic caff has been here since 1946. Customers sit on brown plastic chairs at Formica-topped tables, watched over by photos of muscular boxers and Spurs stars of yore. Lasagne, omelettes, salads, every conceivable cooked breakfast and mugs of tannin-rich tea are meat and drink to the Regency. Stodgetastic own-made specials include steak pie.
17-19 Regency Street, SW1P 4BY (7821 6596). St James's Park tube or Victoria tube/rail. Meals served 7am-2.30pm, 4-7.15pm Mon-Fri; 7am-noon Sat. Main courses £2.70-£6.55.

Wolseley Brasserie
A self-proclaimed 'café-restaurant in the grand European tradition', the Wolseley combines London heritage and Viennese grandeur. The kitchen is much-celebrated for its breakfasts, and the scope of the main menu is admirable. From oysters, steak tartare or soufflé suisse, via wiener schnitzel or grilled halibut with wilted spinach and béarnaise, to tarte au citron or apple strudel, there's something for everyone. On Sunday afternoons, three-tiered afternoon tea stands are in abundance.
160 Piccadilly, W1J 9EB (7499 6996, www.thewolseley.com). Green Park tube. Open 7am-midnight Mon-Fri; 8am-midnight Sat; 8am-11pm Sun. Main courses £11.25-£34.75. Cover £2.

Chelsea

Colbert Brasserie
Paying homage to Continental grand cafés with marble, linen napkins and mirrors aplenty, Colbert feels more casual and local than its siblings – (such as the Wolseley, see above) – and the posters in the booth-lined bar area advertising performances by Olivier and Vivien Leigh next door

at the Royal Court Theatre lend a sense of history. It also trumps the others with pavement tables from which to admire the beautiful people of SW3. More importantly, it serves the best lunch in the area: perhaps a deliciously decadent smoked haddock florentine served on spinach, under a perfectly poached egg, in a buttery cream sauce, or a croque grand'mère – perfectly fried brioche filled with melted comté cheese, bayonne ham and béchamel sauce, topped with a fried egg.
51 Sloane Square, SW1W 8AX (7730 2804, www.colbertchelsea.com). Sloane Square tube. Open 8am-11pm Mon-Thur; 8am-11.30pm Fri, Sat; 8am-10.30pm Sun. Main courses £6.95-£30.

Gallery Mess Brasserie
As befits its Chelsea location, this welcoming brasserie at the Saatchi art gallery is smarter than most, with white linen tablecloths, exposed brickwork and impressive bar all somewhat in thrall to the vaulted ceiling and expansive curtain of floor-to-ceiling arched windows. There's also a large outdoor terrace. Service is disarmingly friendly and mains offer comforting flavours and proportions. So you'll find cod and chips, steak sandwich, charcuterie and smoked fish platters, caesar salad and afternoon tea.
Saatchi Gallery, Duke of York's HQ, King's Road, SW3 4LY (7730 8135, www.saatchigallery.com/gallerymess). Sloane Square tube. Open Bar 10am-11pm Mon-Sat; 10am-7pm Sun. Restaurant noon-9.30pm Mon-Sat; noon-6.30pm Sun. Main courses £13.50-£22.

Mona Lisa Café
Not much to look at, either inside or out, the Mona Lisa is hidden away at the 'wrong' end of the King's Road, just beyond World's End. But the bonhomie is infectious, and if you order the right thing, such as the meltingly tender calf's liver alla salvia (with butter and sage), served with old-school potatoes and veg, you won't care about the homely decor. The menu ranges across breakfasts, sandwiches, burgers, omelettes, jacket potatoes and pastas to three-course blow-outs (at lunch, he latter is just £8.95).
417 King's Road, SW10 0LR (7376 5447). Fulham Broadway tube or bus 11, 22. Meals served 6.30am-11pm Mon-Sat; 8.30am-5.30pm Sun. Main courses £6-£18.95.

Knightsbridge & South Kensington

Bar Boulud French
Overseen by renowned chef Daniel Boulud, the restaurant has an eye-catching view of the open-plan kitchen where chefs work in zen-like calm.

Charcuterie from Gilles Verot is a big draw, as are the elegant French brasserie options and finger-licking American staples. We've had burgers here and loved every bite – try a beef patty topped with pulled pork and green chilli mayonnaise. On our latest visit, we enjoyed such culinary gems as a robust french onion soup, resplendent with caramelised onions and topped with molten gruyère.
Mandarin Oriental Hyde Park, 66 Knightsbridge, SW1X 7LA (7201 3899, www.barboulud.com). Knightsbridge tube. Open noon-11pm Mon-Sat; noon-10pm Sun. Main courses £13-£32.

Daquise Polish
In May 2013 regulars were distressed at news that this much-loved grande dame of London Polish restaurants (established 1947) was to close – but staff and the restaurant's previous owners rallied round to save it. In the shabby-chic, light and airy interior, enlivened with fresh flowers, robust, flavourful, no-nonsense traditional dishes are served with great charm. Classic cold starters of meltingly tender herring with cream, apple, onion and flax oil, or beetroot with subtly warming horseradish, are ladled directly from capacious earthenware bowls, while mains are assembled directly at the table from well-worn saucepans, borne by the chefs who prepared the dishes.
20 Thurloe Street, SW7 2LT (7589 6117, www.daquise.co.uk). South Kensington tube. Open noon-11pm daily. Main courses £15-£22. Set lunch (noon-4pm Mon-Fri) £9 2 courses.

Zuma Japanese
Out of simplicity can come excellence, and the food at Zuma is a case in point. The venue may be swish but when it comes to the food, much of the wow factor is down to high-class ingredients that haven't been messed around with too much. Own-made silken tofu, presented in a cedar saké cup, is rich, creamy and light. More indulgent dishes like spicy miso with lobster have a clarity of flavour. Give the saké list a proper look too: there are more than 40 to choose from.
5 Raphael Street, SW7 1DL (7584 1010, www.zumarestaurant.com). Knightsbridge tube. Open Restaurant noon-2.45pm, 6-10.45pm Mon-Fri; 12.30-3.15pm, 6-10.45pm Sat, Sun. Bar noon-11pm Mon-Fri; 12.30-11pm Sat, Sun. Main courses £14.80-£70.

Paddington & Notting Hill

Assaggi Italian
The look is low-key and the style is relaxed and informal, but there's nothing frivolous about the cooking at Assaggi: the likes of chargrilled cuttlefish and artichoke salad with a dressing of squid ink, or soft gnocchi served with an intensely

flavoured venison and tomato ragù. Don't miss the classic Assaggi dessert, a fluffy baverese (vanilla cream) doused with espresso.
1st floor, 39 Chepstow Place, W2 4TS (7792 5501). Bayswater, Notting Hill Gate or Queensway tube. Open 12.30-2.30pm, 7.30-11pm Mon-Fri; 1-2.30pm, 7.30-11pm Sat. Main courses £19.80-£29.99.

Le Café Anglais Modern European
Rowley Leigh's celebrated brasserie looks as good as when it opened in 2008, with its art deco lines, tall leaded windows and graceful grey-green banquettes. At one end, beneath a stunning chandelier, is the café/oyster bar; at the other, the open kitchen. The appealing menu is nicely varied, from raw, cured and smoked seafood and meat (oysters, pickled herrings, rabbit rillettes) via assorted appetisers (the famous parmesan custard with anchovy toast) to straightforward bistro fare (omelette, burger, fish pie) and dishes such as roast chicken leg with oregano and skordalia.
8 Porchester Gardens, W2 4DB (7221 1415, www.lecafeanglais.co.uk). Bayswater tube. Open noon-3.30pm, 6.30-10.30pm Mon-Thur; noon-3.30pm, 6.30-11pm Fri; 11am-3.30pm, 6.30-11pm Sat; noon-3.30pm, 6.30-10pm Sun. Main courses £9.50-£27.50.

Electric Diner Americas
The unfinished brick and concrete walls, low lighting, french grey-painted plank ceiling, red leather banquettes and lively open kitchen evoke a sort of chic US railway car diner. The hip vibe extends to the menu, which features artery-unfriendly American classics: cheeseburgers; hot dogs; milkshakes. Each dish is well-thought-out and composed of good ingredients: french fries are thin and crispy, and even a simple bibb lettuce and avocado salad was enlivened with finely chopped chives and tarragon.
191 Portobello Road, W11 2ED (7908 9696, www.electricdiner.com). Ladbroke Grove tube. Open 8am-11pm Mon-Wed; 8am-midnight Thur-Sat; 8am-10pm Sun. Main courses £7-£19.

Hereford Road British
This restaurant makes its intentions clear: the first thing you see upon entering the long, narrow space is the kitchen; if it were any more open you'd be eating off the chefs' laps. Sit and wonder how the restaurant can manage to serve two marvellous courses for £13 at lunch as you tuck into hearty dishes such as devilled duck livers with shallots, brill with roasted cauliflower, or onglet and chips. The slightly fancier à la carte menu includes the likes of lamb rump with purple sprouting broccoli.

3 Hereford Road, W2 4AB (7727 1144, www.herefordroad.org). Bayswater tube. Open noon-3pm, 6-10.30pm Mon-Sat; noon-4pm, 6-10pm Sun. Main courses £10-£16.50.

Ledbury French
Few haute establishments have the hospitable hum of the Ledbury; this former pub remains top-tier for gustatory good times. British ingredients – smoked eel, Cumbrian lamb – line up alongside delicacies such as Tokyo turnips, Bresse chicken and black truffle, but it's chef Brett Graham's clever contemporary treatment of them that sets the place apart. Ledbury signatures are consistently thrilling – particularly the flame-grilled mackerel with pickled cucumber, celtic mustard and shiso; and, well, all the desserts.
127 Ledbury Road, W11 2AQ (7792 9090, www.theledbury.com). Westbourne Park tube. Open 6.30-10.15pm Mon; noon-2.15pm, 6.30-10.15pm Tue-Sat; noon-2.30pm, 7-10pm Sun. Main courses (lunch) £32-£34. Set dinner £90 4 courses.

Mazi Greek
Purists might be troubled by the progressive presentation – mezédes are served in Kilner jars – but the Greek flavours are reassuringly authentic. A jar of creamy white taramá hits just the right note of tangy, savoury deliciousness; another of fava (spilt-pea purée), accompanied by tender octopus, is so light it could have been whipped. Hot dishes are better still: slabs of feta encased in black-sesame tempura with punchy lemon marmalade might well consign the humble saganáki to history.
12-14 Hillgate Street, W8 7SR (7229 3794, www.mazi.co.uk). Notting Hill tube. Open 6.30-10.30pm Mon, Tue; noon-3pm, 6.30-10.30pm Wed-Sat; noon-3pm, 6.30-10pm Sun. Main courses £8-£28.

Shed British
From a distance, with its white wooden cladding and high pitched roof, this restaurant does look suspiciously like a shed. Close up, it's as much barnyard as back-garden, with piggy portraits, bits of tractor, and charming staff in check shirts. Plates are small, meant for sharing. Many ingredients are sourced from in or around the family farm in Nutbourne, West Sussex. From the meaty goodness of the Nutbourne banger with own-made mustard to hake with samphire, capers and a slick of red pepper sauce, it's all delicious, and inventive without being tricksy.
122 Palace Gardens Terrace, W8 4RT (7229 4024, www.theshed-restaurant.com). Notting Hill Gate tube. Open 6-10pm Mon; noon-3pm, 6-11pm Tue-Fri; noon-4pm, 6-11pm Sat. Dishes £4-£9.50.

TOP TIP!
Treat Eats
Chris Corbin and Jeremy King, owners of the **Wolseley** (*see p65*), also run the **Delaunay** (*p58*), **Colbert** (*p65*) and **Brasserie Zédel** (*p63*).

Taqueria Mexican
The word 'taqueria' is traditionally associated with street stands churning out endless tacos. They do that here too, but in rather more salubrious surroundings. It's a charming, independent-feeling little place of two rooms, with dark wood floors and pristine white walls decorated with a few Mexican film posters. The food is equally unfussy: a dozen or so tacos (using corn tortillas made in-house daily), a handful of tostadas and a few monthly changing specials.
139-143 Westbourne Grove, W11 2RS (7229 4734, www.taqueria.co.uk). Notting Hill Gate tube. Open noon-11pm Mon-Thur; noon-11.30pm Fri; 10am-11.30pm Sat; noon-10.30pm Sun. Main courses £5-£8.20.

North London

Haché Burgers
If you can imagine a girly burger joint, Haché would be it. It's full of feminine French touches: from pretty vintage chandeliers to the creamy walls with ornate, oversized mirrors. In the open kitchen at the back, classic 'man food' is prettied up wherever possible. Thick-cut slices of onions are encased in huge balloons of batter, while frites are thin-cut, seasoned and skinny – and the upmarket burgers are decent too. If you want to be really metrosexual, ditch the bun entirely: staff will happily replace it with a green salad. Who said burger joints have to be butch?
24 Inverness Street, NW1 7HJ (7485 9100, www.hacheburgers.com). Camden Town tube. Open noon-10.30pm Mon-Wed; noon-11pm Thur-Sat; noon-10pm Sun. Main courses £6.95-£17.95.

Made in Camden Modern European
This bar and restaurant in the Roundhouse concert venue has won much applause. The kitchen is capable of excellent fusion cooking,

with memorable plates such as fennel with feta, pistachios, salted caramel, lemon zest and dill. Once the concert-goers have taken their seats, noise diminishes and the red and wood-toned room transforms into a chilled spot well worth considering as an alternative to standalone restaurants.
Roundhouse, Chalk Farm Road, NW1 8EH (7424 8495, www.madein camden.com). Chalk Farm tube. Open noon-2.30pm, 6-10.30pm Mon-Fri; 10.30am-3pm, 6-10.30pm Sat; 10.30am-3pm Sun. Main courses £8-£16.50. Set lunch (noon-3pm Tue-Sun) £11.95 3 courses.

Market British
One of the best venues to eat in the area. 'Simple things, done well' is a phrase that could apply to the whole operation. The narrow space has been denuded back to its structural brick; specials are chalked on a blackboard. The proudly British and mainly meaty food is straightforward and effective too, like a spring starter of golden and mauve beetroot adorned simply with goat's cheese and pickled walnuts. You might move on to a signature pie – chicken and leek, say – or the 'modern British' modish standard of onglet and chips.
43 Parkway, NW1 7PN (7267 9700, www.marketrestaurant.co.uk). Camden Town tube. Open noon-2.30pm, 6-10.30pm Mon-Sat; noon-3pm Sun. Main courses £13-£17. Set lunch (Mon-Sat) £10 2 courses. Set dinner (6-7pm) £17.50 2 courses.

Ottolenghi Café
Hit cookbooks have made this flagship branch of the burgeoning Ottolenghi empire a point of pilgrimage for foodies the world over. French toast made from brioche and served with crème fraîche and a thin berry and muscat compote makes a heady start to the day. Or there's welsh rarebit, scrambled eggs with smoked salmon or a lively chorizo-spiked take on baked beans served

Bar Boulud. *See p65.*

with sourdough, fried egg and black pudding. In the evening (when bookings are taken), the cool white interior works a double shift as a smart and comparatively pricey restaurant serving elegant fusion dishes for sharing. Expect the likes of grilled quail with smoked chilli chocolate sauce, potato, pak choi and sesame – and expect to have trouble snaring a table.
287 Upper Street, N1 2TZ (7288 1454, www.ottolenghi.co.uk). Angel tube . Open 8am-10.30pm Mon-Sat; 9am-7pm Sun. Main courses £11.50-£16.70.

Porky's Brasserie
From Carolina 'cue' joints to rough-and-ready pop-ups, southern barbecue is all over London now. The vibe here is low-key and the service friendly, providing massive, full-flavoured portions at reasonable prices. Hog is the main attraction: tender, perfectly seasoned, 18-hour slow-cooked pulled pork, and plump, juicy wet ribs are the most popular dishes, but you'll also find spit-roast barbecue chicken, fried catfish and quinoa chilli, a polite nod to vegetarians. The corn and cheese hush puppies were the most sublime we've encountered outside the US, and the British and American craft beer menu is extensive.
18 Chalk Farm Road, NW1 8AG (7428 0998, www.porkys.co.uk). Camden Town tube. Open 5-10pm Mon-Thur; noon-11pm Fri; 9am-11pm Sat; 9am-10pm Sun. Main courses £5.95-£9.80.

Smokehouse Barbecue
In the Big Smoke, chef Neil Rankin has become a high priest of barbecue. Trendy though the menu seems – it includes French bistro dishes, carefully sourced British produce and even Korean flavours – the mutton chops come from the grill, not the barman's cheeks, and they come fatty and full-flavoured. Mullet is smoked, cut into translucent slivers and served with white pickled clams, radishes and sea purslane. Pit-roasted corn on the cob, slathered with buttery smoked béarnaise sauce, shows that a barbecue expert doesn't just cook flesh.
63-69 Canonbury Road, N1 2DG (7354 1144, www.smokehouse islington.co.uk). Highbury & Islington tube/rail. Open 6-10pm Mon-Fri; 11am-4pm, 6-10pm Sat; noon-9pm Sun. Main courses £12.50-£25.

Trullo Italian
While evenings are still busy-to-frantic in this contemporary two-floor trattoria, lunchtime finds Trullo calm and the cooking relaxed and assured. A bargain £15 set menu gleans two courses (primi plus either antipasti or dessert) from a daily-changing menu. Grills and roasts from the carte might include Black Hampshire pork chop and cod with cannellini beans and mussels, while pappardelle with beef shin ragù has been a staple since Trullo's early days and remains a silky substantial delight.

Electric Diner

300-302 St Paul's Road, Islington, N1 2LH (7226 2733, www.trullo restaurant.com). Highbury & Islington tube/rail. Open 12.30-3pm, 6-10.30pm Mon-Sat; 12.30pm-3pm Sun. Main courses £14-£30.

East London

19 Numara Bos Cirrik Turkish
Benefiting from Dalston's gentrification, 19 Numara Bos Cirrik has firmly established itself as the hipsters' ocakbası of choice, yet standards haven't slipped at this ever-busy joint: starting with bread that's piping-hot, feather-light, smoky and carrying hints of onion and tomato. The pide is every bit as good, while the likes of lamb beyti perfectly balance garlic, chilli and smoky charcoal tones.
34 Stoke Newington Road, N16 7XJ (7249 0400, www.cirrik1.co.uk). Dalston Kingsland rail. Open noon-midnight daily Main courses £9.50-£13.50.

Beagle British
Beagle is a smart café, bar and restaurant in the railway arches below Hoxton station.There's a bar, serving sophisticated cocktails, leading into a dining area with open kitchen. A back-to-basics British ethos governs the food. Grilled cuttlefish comes with new potatoes and a salsa-like coriander pesto. Pigeon terrine, made in-house, is well textured and has a slightly gamey flavour. A worthy addition to the area's famous budget Vietnamese cafés.
397-400 Geffrye Street, E2 8HZ (7613 2967, www.beaglelondon.co.uk). Hoxton rail. Open Bar 4pm-midnight Mon, Tue; noon-midnight Wed-Fri; 11am-midnight Sat; 11am-10.30pm Sun. Restaurant 6-10pm Tue; noon-3pm, 6-10pm Wed-Fri; 11am-3pm, 6-10pm Sat; 11am-5pm Sun. Main courses £13.50-£18.

Brawn Modern European
With its lack of airs and graces and bare-brick decor, Brawn may look unassuming, but the cooking is quietly ambitious, precise and, above all, delicious. The meat dishes that run through the menu might have peasant origins, but they're executed with top-drawer flair, including offal dishes such as the seldom-found tête de veau with sauce ravigote, or pork cheek and trotter pie. Fish, shellfish and vegetable dishes show the same judgement.
49 Columbia Road, E2 7RG (7729 5692, www.brawn.co). Hoxton rail or bus 26, 48, 55. Open 6-10.30pm Mon; noon-3pm, 6-10.30pm Tue-Thur; noon-3pm, 6-11pm Fri, Sat; noon-3pm Sun. Dishes £6-£16.

Brick Lane Beigel Bake Jewish
This little East End institution rolls out perfect bagels (egg, cream cheese, tender salt beef, all at seriously low prices), good bread and moreish cakes. Even at 3am, fresh-baked goods are pulled from the ovens at the back; no wonder the queue for bagels trails out the door when the local bars and clubs close. Note that it's essentially a takeaway operation.
159 Brick Lane, E1 6SB (7729 0616). Shoreditch High Street rail. Open 24hrs daily. Bagels £1.95-£5.95. No credit cards.

Chez Elles Bistro
Chez Elles narrowly misses being a parody of itself, saved by fantastic cooking and an unexpected location – somehow, the cutesy Parisian hipster vibe grates far less on Brick Lane than it would elsewhere. There's coffee and own-made cakes at a counter propping up (French) regulars, and a disarming, heavily accented welcome. The menu is beyond reproach: smoky, spicy, peppery charcuterie with lots of bread; soft, nutty snails swimming in garlic butter; and a seriously good, tearingly tender bavette steak.

45 Brick Lane, E1 6PU (7247 9699, www.chezellesbistroquet.co.uk). Aldgate East tube or Shoreditch High Street rail. Open 6.30-10.30pm Tue; noon-3pm, 6.30-10.30pm Wed-Sat; 11am-5pm Sun. Main courses £12.50-£16.50.

E Pellicci Italian
You go to Pellicci's as much for the atmosphere as for the food. Opened in 1900, and still in the hands of the same family, this Bethnal Green landmark has chrome and Vitrolite outside, wood panelling with deco marquetry, Formica tabletops and stained glass within – it earned the café a Grade II listing in 2005. Fry-ups are first rate, and the fish and chips, daily grills and Italian specials aren't half bad either.
332 Bethnal Green Road, E2 0AG (7739 4873). Bethnal Green tube/rail or bus 8. Open 7am-4pm Mon-Sat. Main courses £5.50-£8.20. No credit cards.

Hoi Polloi Brasserie
You enter this restaurant via the tiny flower shop of the Ace Hotel (see p118), to find yourself amid retro and contemporary styling that wouldn't look out of place on a 1950s Scandinavian cruise ship. The casual and sneaker-clad service is notably smooth and well informed. The music (a mix of retro '80s pop and US alt electronic) isn't too loud, allowing attention to focus on conversation – and the food. Covering breakfast, lunch, snacks, cocktails and dinner, the dishes are British, seasonal and juxtapose flavours in modern but not outlandish ways that leave you craving more. The small bar is a destination in itself, with cocktails that bear obscure names (they're in Polari) but appealing combinations of modish spirits.
Ace Hotel, 100 Shoreditch High Street, E1 6JQ (8880 6100, www. hoi-polloi.co.uk). Shoreditch High Street rail. Open 7am-midnight Mon-Wed, Sun; 7am-1am Thur-Sat. Main courses £14-£18.

Moka East Café
Set up as a viewing point during the construction of the Olympic Park, this café is housed in stacked-up acid-green shipping containers. It's now run by the family behind Mario's Cafe – sung about by St Etienne, and one of London's proper old-fashioned caffs. Breakfast options include standard bacon, sausage and eggs, and also muesli with yoghurt and berries, and even kippers. The café is right in front of the Olympic Stadium – Anish Kapoor's ArcelorMittal Orbit sculpture is directly opposite.
View Tube, Marshgate Lane, E15 2PJ (www.theviewtube.co.uk). Pudding Mill Lane DLR. Open 9am-5pm daily.

Needoo Grill Pakistani
This squashed space doesn't suffer from the same problem of endless queues as its rival Tayyabs (see p68), though you will usually have

a wait, but it is just as gaudy. Bright red walls, leather benches and blaring flatscreen TVs are the order of the day, yet with curries this good, the decor just fades into the background. What you get are succulent karahi dishes and specials that include nihari (lamb on the bone) and a very passable biriani. Service is swift and friendly, and it's hard to argue with the appeal of BYOB and curries of such high standard.
87 New Road, E1 1HH (7247 0648, www.needoo grill.co.uk). Whitechapel tube. Open noon-11.30pm daily. Main courses £5-£14.

Pizza East Pizza

The huge warehouse space features sharing benches, industrial decor and more bare brick and concrete than your average multistorey car park. It's busy, noisy and dark. The regularly changing menu, however, remains inventive and original. Pizza bases are crusty around the outside and thin and gorgeously saturated in the middle, and toppings employ fresh, quality ingredients. Antipasti and salads are also good.
56 Shoreditch High Street, E1 6JJ (7729 1888, www.pizzaeast.com). Shoreditch High Street rail. Open noon-midnight Mon-Wed; noon-1am Thur; noon-2am Fri; 10am-2am Sat; 10am-midnight Sun. Main courses £8-£17.

Poppies Fish & chips

Poppies' pick and mix assortment of shiny British kitsch – including a jukebox, mini red telephone box and a monochrome photo of heart-throb Cliff Richard – makes it look like a simulation of a fish and chip shop. The food on the plate is also better than the real thing, and offered grilled as well as fried. Extending beyond the staples of cod and haddock, the menu encompasses mackerel, seafood platters and jellied eels. The bill, however, gives the game away – Poppies is a cut above. It's spawned a second branch in Camden (30 Hawley Crescent, NW1 8NP, 7267 0440): not suprising, since this is as good as fish and chips gets.
6-8 Hanbury Street, E1 6QR (7247 0892, www.poppiesfishandchips.co.uk). Liverpool Street tube/rail or Shoreditch High Street rail. Meals served 11am-11pm Mon-Sat; 11am-10.30pm Sun. Main courses £10.90-£15.90.

Rosa's Thai

The original branch of Rosa's plays host to a vibrant young crowd of visiting tourists and local hipsters. The dining room is clean and contemporary, and the usual Thai repertoire is executed well: stir-fried slices of European aubergine coated in a sweet, salty soya and yellow bean sauce, and laced with plenty of ginger and black pepper, or a salad of chargrilled beef strips in chilli dressing. Service is mostly quick and efficient.
2 Hanbury Street, E1 6QR (7247 1093, www.rosaslondon.com). Liverpool Street tube/rail. Meals served noon-10.30pm Mon-Thur,

Sun; noon-11pm Fri, Sat. Main courses £7.50-£16.50.

Sông Quê Vietnamese

This is still the undoubted star of the Kingsland Road Vietnamese scene. Big, light, buzzy (if slightly canteen-like), Sông Quê is constantly packed with customers including many families and a good showing of Vietnamese locals. Flavours are full and true, and textures perfect, bringing the best out of each dish. Fans claim the kitchen makes the best pho in London. It's very handy for the Geffrye Museum.
134 Kingsland Road, E2 8DY (7613 3222). Hoxton rail. Open noon-3pm, 5.30-11pm Mon-Fri; noon-11pm Sat; noon-10.30pm Sun. Main courses £4.80-£14.80.

Stories Café

From the people behind Book Club (see p73), Stories is a handsome all-rounder – and heaving at weekends. Large, sail-like lights are adjusted by complex pulleys across the ceiling; on the walls hang local artworks. The comestibles are as cool, from an innovative cocktail list to the likes of beef and chorizo burger with manchego and triple-cooked chips.
30 Broadway Market, E8 4QJ (7254 6898, www.storieson broadway.com). London Fields rail. Open 10am-midnight daily. Main courses £6-£9.

Tayyabs Pakistani

Tayyabs is a full-on, hectic, loud, in-and-out sort of place, and if you come here without booking, expect to wait up to an hour for a table. But we recommend this Punjabi stalwart because of the cheapness and unreserved boldness of the food. Fiery grilled lamb chops are a must. The rest of the menu is all about rich dals and masala channa; unctuous, slow-cooked lamb curries; and good versions of North Indian staples – spice-rubbed tikka, hot, buttery breads and juicy kebabs. The corkage-free BYO policy doesn't do its popularity any harm either.
83 Fieldgate Street, E1 1JU (7247 9543, www.tayyabs.co.uk). Aldgate East or Whitechapel tube. Open noon-11.30pm daily. Main courses £5-£13.

Tina, We Salute You Café

Tina's puts you instantly at ease: the large communal table (sofas and a handful of pavement tables also available for early arrivers) – populated with help-yourself jars of Marmite and jam, and locals helping each other with the *Guardian* crossword – feels like your best friend's kitchen table. A comforting breakfast menu (poached eggs, pancakes with berries, porridge) eases itself into lunch (toasted sandwiches, bagels, ploughman's). Tina's also serves good coffee; expand your tastes beyond the usual latte with a Gibraltar (between a mini latte and a large macchiato).

47 King Henry's Walk, N1 4NH (3119 0047, www.tinawesaluteyou.com). Dalston Kingsland rail. Open 8am-6pm Mon-Fri; 10am-6pm Sat, Sun. Main courses £4-£6. No credit cards.

Towpath Café

This simple operation on Regent's Canal towpath was a novelty when it opened in 2010, but even with a couple of more elaborate restaurants now on the same block, its four shallow units continue to lure passing walkers and cyclists with the originality of its setting and its enticing food and drink. If you manage to grab a table in the sunshine on a summer's day, and you might end up staying for hours. Relaxed entertainment is provided by coots tending their nests and passing bikes whizzing by, as you tuck into delicious grilled cheese sandwiches and decent coffee.
Regent's Canal towpath, between Whitmore Bridge and Kingsland Road Bridge, N1 5SB (no phone). Open Mar-Nov 8am-dusk Tue-Fri; 9am-dusk Sat, Sun. Main courses £3-£8.

Tramshed British

Mark Hix's chicken and steak joint serves steaks, roast chicken for one or to share (it can stretch to three, especially if accompanied by seasonal sides such as wild garlic mushrooms), along with chicken salad and steak salad. All this happens in a turn-of-the-century Grade II-listed industrial building, a vast room with a soaring ceiling. In pride of place is a work by Damien Hirst: a formaldehyde-filled tank containing a bullock and a rooster.
32 Rivington Street, EC2A 3LX (7749 0478, www.chickenandsteak. co.uk). Old Street tube/rail. Open 11.30am-11pm Mon-Tue; 11.30am-midnight Wed-Sat; 11.30am-9.30pm Sun. Main courses £13.50-£32.50.

Les Trois Garçons French

London's most OTT restaurant interior gives the eye no idea where to settle. Inside this former pub is an entire zoo of stuffed, ceramic and other animals, cascading glass, dangling handbags, giant, unearthly purple flowers and more – all to sustain the mood of ironic, decadent opulence. Les Trois Garçons buzzes at night, when hip crowds come to enjoy inventive modern French cuisine. The 3G mini-empire also includes the equally louche Loungelover Bar next door and, most recently, Maison Trois Garçons 'lifestyle café' in nearby Redchurch Street.
1 Club Row, E1 6JX (7613 1924, www.lestrois garcons.com). Shoreditch High Street rail. Open 6-9.30pm Mon-Wed; noon-2.30pm, 6-9.30pm Thur; noon-2.30pm, 6-10.30pm Fri; 6-10.30pm Sat. Main courses £15-£32.50.

TOP TIP!
Upmarket Ottolenghi
For Ottolenghi (see p66) eats in a smart restaurant setting, try **Nopi** (21-22 Warwick Street, Soho, W1B 5NE, 7494 9584).

South-west London

Brunswick House Café Brasserie

This Georgian mansion is a tiny beacon of calm amid the chaos of Vauxhall. Some of the young, high-spending clientele are simply stopping by for a cocktail while perusing the desirable bric-a-brac on offer from architectural salvage company Lassco, but most are here to meet, drink, eat and generally enjoy the appealing combination of boho-chic comfort and minimalist menu presentation.
30 Wandsworth Road, Vauxhall Cross, SW8 2LG (7720 2926, www.brunswickhouse.co). Vauxhall tube/rail. Open 9.30am-10.30pm Mon-Fri; 10am-10.30pm Sat; noon-4pm Sun. Main courses £11.80-£17.

Franco Manca Pizza

With its top-notch ingredients, friendly service, and rapid turnover, the original Brixton branch of Franco Manca remains, for our money, the best pizza joint in London. Both indoor and outdoor seating overlooks the bustling market arcade. Genuine, Neapolitan-style pizza comes with a flavourful slow-rise sourdough crust and both traditional and innovative toppings.
4 Market Row, Electric Lane, Brixton, SW9 8LD (7738 3021, www.franco manca.co.uk). Brixton tube/rail. Open noon-5pm Mon; noon-10.30pm Tue-Thur, Sun; noon-11pm Fri, Sat. Main courses £4.50-£7.50.

West London

Clarke's Modern European

At Clarke's, the overused 'best ingredients, simply prepared' phrase is actually true; a salad of peas, baby broad beans, spinach and grilled courgette looks like spring on a plate, while deep-pink roast salmon is set off by explosively sweet baked tomatoes and olives. Chef-proprietor Sally Clarke has been espousing the 'local and seasonal' ethic since the mid '80s. There's a deli across the road, where goodies include Clarke's bread, at 1 Campden Street, W8 7EP, 7229 2190.
124 Kensington Church Street, W8 4BH (7221 9225, www.sallyclarke. com). Notting Hill Gate tube. Open 8am-10pm Mon-Sat. Main courses £20-£27.50.

Yashin Sushi

Yashin's exterior looks more like a smart French brasserie than a Japanese restaurant. But the centrepiece sushi counter gives the game away as soon as you step inside. Set on the dark green tiles behind the team of itamae (sushi chefs), a neon sign reads 'without soy sauce', and this is how the chefs ask you to eat your artfully crafted sushi.
1A Argyll Road, W8 7DB (7938 1536, www.yashinsushi.com). High Street Kensington tube. Open noon-2.15pm, 6-10pm daily. Dishes £3.50-£24.80.

Pubs & Bar

Happiness Forgets. See p74.

Cock Tavern

HAPPINESS FORGETS; ROB GREIG, COCK TAVERN: ED MARSHALL

Critic's choice

1 **White Lyan** The new cutting-edge of London's cocktail scene. *See p74.*

2 **Cock Tavern** The best of the new breed of beer-loving pubs. *See p73.*

3 **Terroirs** A journey through interesting modern wines – with great food, too. *See p71.*

4 **French House** A proper pub – small, busy and with plenty of history. *See p72.*

5 **Lady Ottoline** Fine dining while you drink – a great new gastropub. *See p71.*

Mixing your drinks

Craft beer and apothecary cocktails rule the booze in the Big Smoke.

The drinking map of London has changed radically over the last few years. The bad news is that the traditional British pub has been in decline for a while, and nowhere more so than in the capital. But the good news is that pubs have adapted to survive – 'wet' pubs, where food is limited to crisps and peanuts, are few and far between these days – and the best ones continue to do a roaring trade. London's surge of interest in craft beer has led to the birth – and frequently rebirth (the **Wenlock**, for example) – of any number of fine venues for connoisseurs of the hop, while the revolutionary notion of serving restaurant-quality nosh in a boozer – the 'gastropub' – has remained a significant presence in town ever since the **Eagle** opened in the 1990s. **Lady Ottoline** is just one of several excellent newcomers.

Meanwhile, the capital's bar scene remains as dynamic as ever. The dominant trends over the last several years have

been to ape Prohibition-era speakeasies and/or or to give liquor a 'steampunk' makeover, Victorian-ising the process with outlandish fizzing, bubbling, steaming confections (**Purl** and **Worship Street Whistling Shop** being prime examples). There is also keen interest in seriously experimental cocktails, pioneered at **69 Colebrooke Row** but reaching its latest fruition at the **White Lyan**, as well as in timeless quality of historic drinks: **Dukes Bar**, perhaps, or the **Booking Office**.

Wine bars, too, continue to flourish, with many brand new ventures springing up. For the past few years, 'natural' wines have been in vogue: fermented grape juice with little added or taken away. **Terroirs** led the way. Some others, such as **28°-50°**, also offer wine flights: groups of taster samples built around a theme, giving an excellent opportunity for getting to know a region or collection of vintages.

The South Bank & Bankside

If top-quality beer is your priority, then you're in luck: there's a superb range at the tiny **Rake** (14A Winchester Walk, SE1 9AG, 7407 0557), while the unflashy **Royal Oak** (44 Tabard Street, SE1 4JU, 7357 7173) is the only London pub run by estimable Sussex brewer Harveys.

Anchor & Hope Gastropub

Open for more than a decade, the Anchor & Hope is still a leading exponent of head-to-tail ingredients in simple but artful combinations, served in a relaxed setting. Bookings aren't taken, so most evenings you join the waiting list for a table (45 minutes midweek is typical) and hover at the crammed bar enjoying a glass of wine or a pint. The food is terrific: venison kofte, say, served on perkily dressed

gem lettuce leaves, or rabbit served savagely red, with salty jus, fat chips and a big pot of béarnaise.
36 The Cut, SE1 8LP (7928 9898). Waterloo tube/rail. Open 5-11pm Mon; 11am-11pm Tue-Sat; 12.30-5pm Sun. Food served 6-10.30pm Mon; noon-2.30pm, 6-10.30pm Tue-Sat.

Bar Topolski Bar

The former Topolski Century, an extensive mural by Polish-born artist Feliks Topolski depicting an extraordinary procession of 20th-century events and faces, has been turned into a bar-café. Occupying two capacious brick arches beneath Hungerford Bridge (some of Topolski's artworks are incorporated into the design), it serves cured meat, fish and cheese and other snacks, both savoury and sweet. There are assorted musical entertainments too.
150-152 Hungerford Arches, Concert Hall Approach, SE1 8XU (7620 0627, www.bartopolski.co.uk). Waterloo tube/rail. Open 11am-11pm Mon-Wed; 11am-midnight Thur; 11am-1am Fri, Sat.

Gladstone Arms Pub
While the Victorian prime minister glares from the massive mural on the outer wall, inside is funky, freaky and candlelit. Gigs (blues, folk, acoustic, five nights a week) take place at one end of a cosy space; opposite is the bar. Pies provide sustenance. Retro touches include an old-fashioned 'On Air' studio sign and a communist-style railway clock.
64 Lant Street, SE1 1QN (7407 3962, www.thegladpub.com). Borough tube. Open noon-11pm Mon-Thur; noon-midnight Fri; 1pm-midnight Sat; 1-10.30pm Sun. Food served noon-10pm Mon-Fri; 1-9pm Sat, Sun.

Skylon Bar
There can't be many better river views in town – certainly for transport geeks. Sit at the cocktail bar (between the two restaurant areas), and gaze at trains trundling out of Charing Cross, cars and buses whizzing across Waterloo Bridge, and boats and cruisers pootling along the Thames. Drinks aren't cheap, but they're well made, and you're nicely insulated from the madness of the riverbank crowds.
Royal Festival Hall, Belvedere Road, SE1 8XX (7654 7800, www.skylon-restaurant.co.uk). Waterloo tube/rail. Open noon-1am Mon-Sat; noon-10.30pm Sun. Food served noon-11pm Mon-Sat; noon-10.30pm Sun.

The City

Artillery Arms Pub
Close to the Barbican and opposite Bunhill Fields, this small tucked-away pub has an agreeably local feel, as post-work City folk mix easily with neighbourhood stalwarts at the bar. It has a slightly austere feel, but is an easy place to lose track of time, aided by the local vibe and the fine Fuller's beers: easygoing Chiswick, toothsome London Pride and potent ESB.
102 Bunhill Row, EC1Y 8ND (7253 4683, www.artillery-arms.co.uk). Moorgate or Old Street tube/rail. Open noon-11pm Mon-Sat; noon-10.30pm Sun. Food served noon-3pm, 5-9pm Mon-Fri; noon-7pm Sat, Sun.

Black Friar Pub
Built in 1875 on the site of a medieval Dominican friary, the Black Friar had its interior completely remodelled in the Arts and Crafts style. It is now a Nicholson's (they run most of the trad pubs in the City: serving moderate food, but decent real ales), but the bright panes, intricate friezes and carved slogans ('Industry is Ale', 'Haste is Slow') of the main saloon make it a stunning work of art. Admittedly, there's a far more prosaic bar adjoining it but this remains one of London's most stunning pub interiors.
174 Queen Victoria Street, EC4V 4EG (7236 5474, www.nicholson-pubs.co.uk). Blackfriars tube/rail or Mansion House tube. Open 10am-11pm Mon-Thur, Sat; 10am-11.30pm Fri; noon-10.30pm Sun.

Draft House Pub
Pretty much the archetypal 'beer bars', the Draft House minichain focuses on serving a brilliant range of superb beers, simple but relaxed surroundings, and eats that don't travel far from the sausage/burger/hot dog booze fodder axis. In addition to its handy location, this branch has a big screen for sporting events – which it shows with considerable verve. Other central locations include 206-208 Tower Bridge Road, Borough, SE1 2UP (7378 9995) and 43 Goodge Street, Fitzrovia, W1T 1TA (7323 9361).
14-15 Seething Lane, EC3N 4AX (7626 3360, www.drafthouse.co.uk). Tower Hill tube or Tower Gateway tube/DLR. Open 11am-11pm Mon-Wed; 11am-midnight Thur, Fri; 10am-midnight Sat.

Vertigo 42 Bar
Stretching out across the City, the views from this 42nd-floor bar are breathtaking. So, too, are the prices (house wine, £9.20 a glass). Food is tapas and small plates, while seating is arranged so everyone can enjoy the 360° panorama; for the privilege, you must book ahead, promise a minimum £10 spend and then undergo airport-style security.
Tower 42, 25 Old Broad Street, EC2N 1HQ (7877 7842, www.vertigo42.co.uk). Bank tube/DLR or Liverpool Street tube/rail. Open noon-4.30pm, 5-11pm Mon-Fri; 5-11pm Sat.

Holborn & Clerkenwell

28°-50° Wine Workshop & Kitchen Wine Bar
The Fetter Lane branch of 28°-50°, in a basement with a French country-kitchen vibe, has a French-inspired menu and a bright, on-the-ball attitude. The wine list is a thing of joy, offering upwards of 30 varied and delicious wines, many of them from small producers, plus a changing themed selection. It's well worth exploring: order 75ml glasses and follow the young staff's enthusiastic advice.
140 Fetter Lane, EC4A 1BT (7242 8877, www.2850.co.uk). Farringdon tube/rail. Open noon-11pm Mon-Fri. Food served noon-2.30pm, 6-9.30pm Mon-Fri.

Café Kick Bar
Clerkenwell's most likeable bar is this table football- themed gem. The soccer paraphernalia is authentic, retro-cool and mainly Latin (you'll find a Zenit St Petersburg scarf amid the St Etienne and Lusitanian gear); bar staff, beers and bites give the impression you could be in Lisbon. A modest open kitchen ('we don't microwave or deep-fry') dishes out tapas, sandwiches and charcuterie. There's an outpost in Shoreditch too – Bar Kick, 127 Shoreditch High Street, E1 6JE (7739 8700).
43 Exmouth Market, EC1R 4QL (7837 8077, www.cafekick.co.uk).

Angel tube. *Open 11am-11pm Mon-Thur; 11am-midnight Fri, Sat; noon-10.30pm Sun. Food served noon-3pm Mon-Fri; noon-10pm Sat, Sun.*

Eagle Gastropub
Widely credited with launching the food-in-pubs revolution when it opened in its current form in 1991, the Eagle has long since passed into both legend and middle age. But this high-ceilinged corner room remains a cut above the competition. Globetrotting mains are chalked twice daily above the bar/open kitchen. You can just drink but few do, aware they're missing the big-flavoured likes of moreish tomato and bread soup; daisy-fresh scallops, pan-fried and served on toast with chorizo; and succulent leg of lamb with jansson's temptation.
159 Farringdon Road, EC1R 3AL (7837 1353). Farringdon tube/rail. Open noon-11pm Mon-Sat; noon-5pm Sun. Food served noon-3pm, 6.30-10.30pm Mon-Fri; 12.30-3.30pm, 6.30-10.30pm Sat; 12.30-4pm Sun.

Fox & Anchor Pub
Pristine mosaic tiling, etched glass and a dark wood front bar lined with pewter tankards help make this refurbished old pub a local treasure. To the back is the Fox's Den, a series of intimate rooms used for both drinking and dining. Local sourcing is a priority and a pleasure: in addition to the own-label ale, cask beers might include Red Poll and Old Growler from Suffolk's fine Nethergate brewery. There are plenty more delights among the bottles.
115 Charterhouse Street, EC1M 6AA (7250 1300, www.foxandanchor.com). Barbican tube or Farringdon tube/rail. Open 7am-11pm Mon-Fri; 8.30am-11am Sat; 8.30am-10pm Sun. Food served 7am-9.30pm Mon-Fri; 8.30am-9.30pm Sat; 8.30am-8.30pm Sun.

Three Kings of Clerkenwell Pub
Rhinoceros heads, Egyptian felines and photos of Dennis Bergkamp provide the decorative backdrop at

this great little boozer. Glug Scrumpy Jack, Beck's Vier, Old Speckled Hen or London Pride, and tap the well-worn tables to the Cramps and other gems from an outstanding jukebox that is crammed with fabulous old platters.
7 Clerkenwell Close, EC1R 0DY (7253 0483). Farringdon tube/rail. Open noon-11pm Mon-Fri; 5.30-11pm Sat. Food served noon-3pm, 6-10pm Mon-Fri.

Vinoteca Wine Bar
Charmingly but sparingly decorated, and with delightfully friendly staff, this bijou spot is the original branch in the small chain. Serious about its commitment to the grape, Vinoteca offers 25 wines by the glass, 300 by the bottle, all available to take away. But even without the fabulous wines, it would still be a great restaurant. Dishes such as mussels, clams and john dory with chorizo, or barnsley chop with greens, are excellent combinations of light, bright flavours – and go perfectly with the recommended wines.
7 St John Street, EC1M 4AA (7253 8786, www.vinoteca.co.uk). Barbican tube or Farringdon tube/ rail. Open noon-11pm Mon-Sat. Food served noon-2.45pm, 5.45-10pm Mon-Fri; noon-4pm, 5.45-10pm Sat.

Ye Olde Mitre Pub
Largely due to its location – down a barely marked alley between Hatton Garden's jewellers and Ely Place – this little traditional pub, the foundation of which dates to 1546, is a favourite of secret London lists. There's always a good range of ales on offer at the tiny central bar, but people come for the atmosphere: lots of cosy dark wood and some overlooked curiosities, such as the tree in the front bar. It's a cherry tree that Good Queen Bess is said to have danced around, but now supports a corner of the front bar.
1 Ely Court, EC1N 6SJ (7405 4751, www.yeoldemitreholborn.co.uk). Farringdon tube/rail. Open/Food served 11am-11pm Mon-Fri.

Vinoteca

VINOTECA: ROGAN MACDONALD

Zetter Townhouse Bar

The decor at Townhouse embodies a 'more is more' philosophy: every square inch of surface area is occupied by something lovely. The result: one of the most beautiful bars in London. The cocktail list is of fittingly high quality and is devised by Tony Conigliaro. Even though Conigliaro is known as a techno-wizard, the original drinks here are fairly simple and restrained. And wonderful. Among the house cocktails, check out the Köln martini, the Somerset sour, and the jasmine tea gimlet. Service is friendly and helpful. *49-50 St John's Square, EC1V 4JJ (7324 4545, www.thezetter townhouse.com). Farringdon tube/rail. Open 7am-midnight Mon-Wed, Sun; 7am-1am Thur-Sat.*

Bloomsbury & King's Cross

Booking Office Bar

Sit indoors at this smart cocktail bar and you gaze at Sir George Gilbert Scott's lofty interior, a stirring example of the Victorian architect's interpretation of Gothic revival. Outside, under spacious canopies, you have a nearly ceiling-level view of St Pancras station. The cocktail list gives a prominent place to traditional punches, served in mugs, but the list is a long one. Martinis are well made, and the gin fix (a variant on gin fizz using fresh berries) is a wonderful and refreshing potion. Warning: the free bar snacks – coated peanuts – are dangerously addictive. *St Pancras Renaissance London Hotel, NW1 2AR (7841 3566, www.bookingofficerestaurant.com). King's Cross St Pancras tube/rail. Open 6.30am-1am Mon-Wed, Sun; 6.30am-3am Thur-Sat.*

Lady Ottoline Gastropub

One of a group of upmarket gastropubs, all of which have a commitment to drink as well as food, with space for drinkers and a selection that runs from cocktails and real ales to a thoughtful wine list. Food is served in the ground-floor bar at the Lady Ottoline, but for a more sedate meal, it's best to dine in the pleasant first-floor room. The menu is a bit more adventurous than at most gastropubs – witness creamy rabbit pie with chicory and pomegranate salad. *11A Northington Street, WC1N 2JF (7831 0008, www.theladyottoline. com). Chancery Lane or Russell Square tube. Open Pub noon-11pm Mon-Sat; noon-9pm Sun. Food served noon-3pm, 6.30-10pm Mon-Fri; noon-4pm, 6.30-10pm Sat; noon-8pm Sun.*

Lamb Pub

The standard range of Young's beers is dispensed from a central horseshoe bar in this 280-year-old pub, around which are ringed original etched-glass snob screens, used to prevent Victorian gentlemen from being seen when liaising with 'women of dubious

Brewdog

A simple statistic: in 2006, when Young's quit their historic brewery in Wandsworth and left the capital, there were just two breweries left: Fuller's in Chiswick and Meantime in Greenwich; now there are at least 60, with exponential growth over the last couple of years. In fact, it is becoming rare to see even quite ordinary pubs without some local beer on tap. Many of these come from microbreweries – boutique operations making small batches of beer with as much imagination and enthusiasm as attentiveness to the bottom line.

There are lots of places to enjoy the new generation of beer pubs. East London is something of a homeland for them, with Hackney's Cock Tavern (*see p73*) a prime example, plus the Wenlock Tavern (*see p74*) on the Islington borders. In Camden, check out the Scottish craft brewery Brewdog (*see p73*), or head further up the Northern line to Highgate and the Bull (*see p73*). In south London, either pay a visit to Meantime's flagship venue the Old Brewery (*see p74*) or head to Brixton and the Crown & Anchor (*see p74*). You'll also drink well at any of the Draft House (*see p70*) minichain.

distinction'. A sunken back area gives access to a small summer patio. *94 Lamb's Conduit Street, WC1N 3LZ (7405 0713, www.youngs.co.uk). Holborn or Russell Square tube. Open noon-11pm Mon-Wed; noon-midnight Thur-Sat; noon-10.30pm Sun. Food served noon-9pm daily.*

Fitzrovia

Newman Arms Pub

There's been a business at this gateway to a cobbled alleyway since 1730 – see the red sign outside and etched writing over the bar – but as a pub it had its heyday in the mid 20th century, when George Orwell was a regular and Michael Powell filmed scenes from Peeping Tom outside. Today, this is the lunchtime and post-work haunt of undemanding chaps laying into decent beer, perhaps accompanying a cheese-and-ham toastie or prefacing a shift upstairs from the tiny and often packed street-level bar to the pie room. *23 Rathbone Street, W1T 1NG (7636 1127, www.newmanarms.co.uk). Goodge Street tube. Open noon-midnight Mon-Fri. Food served noon-3pm, 6-10pm Mon-Fri.*

Oskar's Bar Bar

Dabbous astonishes with its cutting-edge cooking, and its downstairs cocktail bar sets out to do the same. There are plenty of unorthodox ingredients: the Giddy Up contains tequila, bramley and gage slider (traditional sloe-infused cider from Devon), elderflower cordial, lemon juice and camomile-infused acacia honey topped with Sierra Nevada IPA. (Other drinks stay closer to classicism.) The bar has the same stripped-back industrial decor as the restaurant, so it can be noisy. Service is solicitous, and bar snacks are a cut above. *Dabbous, 39 Whitfield Street, W1T 2SF (7323 1544, www.dabbous.co.uk). Goodge Street tube. Open noon-3pm, 5.30-11pm Tue-Fri; 6.15-11pm Sat.*

Covent Garden & the Strand

Gordon's Wine Bar Wine Bar

Gordon's was established in its present form as long ago as 1890, but the exposed brickwork and flickering candlelight make this basement feel older still. Although this is the definitive old-school wine

bar, it gets packed with a young and lively crowd. The wine list is surprisingly modern; still, in such surroundings, it seems a shame not to drink the fortified wines (drawn directly from casks behind the bar). *47 Villiers Street, Strand, WC2N 6NE (7930 1408, www.gordonswine bar.com). Embankment tube or Charing Cross tube/rail. Open 11am-11pm Mon-Sat; noon-10pm Sun.*

Lamb & Flag Pub

This dog-leg alleyway used to be a pit of prostitution and bare-knuckle bashes, the latter hosted at this historic, low-ceilinged Covent Garden tavern back when it was called the Bucket of Blood; poet John Dryden was beaten up here in 1679. The place is popular and space is always at a premium. Two centuries of mounted cuttings and caricatures amplify the sense of character. If it's too busy, try the Benelux-themed beer-café Lowlander (36 Drury Lane, WC2B 5RR, 7379 7446, www.lowlander.com). *33 Rose Street, WC2E 9EB (7497 9504, www.lambandflagcovent garden.co.uk). Covent Garden tube. Open 11am-11pm Mon-Thur; 11am-11.30pm Fri, Sat; noon-10.30pm Sun. Food served noon-8pm Mon-Thur, Sun; noon-5pm Sat, Sun.*

Terroirs Wine Bar

Terroirs – a wine bar with excellent food – is really two places under one roof. The always crowded ground floor has a casual wine bar feel and a menu to match, focused on small plates for sharing. You can sample some of the same dishes in the atmospheric and roomy basement, although the menu here, with a focus on rustic French dishes, seems designed to guide diners more towards a starter-main-dessert tradition. The wine list is an encyclopaedia of organic and biodynamic bottles; order by the glass to give yourself a sense of the astonishing variety offered. *5 William IV Street, WC2N 4DW (7036 0660, www.terroirswine bar.com). Charing Cross tube/rail. Open noon-3pm, 5.30-11pm Mon-Sat.*

Soho & Chinatown

Dog & Duck Pub

This Soho landmark pub is best known for its literary heritage, but the vintage interior (etched mirrors, carved mahogany) and ever-changing selection of good ales – from the familiar London Pride to an altogether rarer range of beers from the Newman Brewery – also appeal. Sausages also feature. The George Orwell room upstairs, where the writer sometimes drank, offers more space. *18 Bateman Street, W1D 3AJ (7494 0697, www.nicholsonspubs.co.uk). Tottenham Court Road tube. Open noon-11pm daily. Food served 10am-10pm daily.*

Experimental Cocktail Club Bar

ECC is hard to find, but once inside all is elegant opulence, arranged over three floors of an old townhouse. Booking isn't essential (half of the capacity is kept for walk-ins), but is recommended (email only, between noon and 5pm). The cocktails are among London's best: sophisticated, complex and strong – try the Havana (cigar-infused bourbon, marsala wine, Bruichladdich Octomore single malt 'wash').
13A Gerrard Street, W1D 5PS (7434 3559, www.chinatownecc.com). Leicester Square tube. Open 6pm-3am Mon-Sat; 6pm-midnight Sun. Admission £5 after 11pm.

French House Pub

Through the door of this venerable establishment have passed many titanic drinkers of the pre- and post-war era. The venue's French heritage also enticed de Gaulle to run a Resistance operation from upstairs – it's now a tiny restaurant. De Gaulle's image survives behind the bar, where beer is served in half-pints and litre bottles of Breton cider are still plonked on the famed back alcove table.
49 Dean Street, W1D 5BG (7437 2799, www.frenchhousesoho.com). Leicester Square tube. Open noon-11pm Mon-Sat; noon-10.30pm Sun. Food served noon-4pm daily.

LAB Bar

LAB was created in 1999, which makes it a granddaddy in London's cool bar scene. But it shows no signs of decline. Most cocktails on the long (90-plus) list are grounded in LAB's core principle: understanding and perfecting cocktail fundamentals. Tables are bookable.
12 Old Compton Street, W1D 4TQ (7437 7820, www.labbaruk.com). Leicester Square tube. Open 4pm-midnight Mon-Sat; 4-10.30pm Sun.

Mark's Bar Bar

The basement cocktail bar at Mark Hix's restaurant is first-rate. The historical drinks are both interesting and good, especially those in the Cocktail Explorer's Club list. Rum drinkers should make a beeline for the Royal Bermuda Yacht Club: Mount Gay Barbados rum with orange curaçao, Mark's own falernum and lime juice. The selection of scotch would take several months to drink through. The bar 'snax' are terrific, and the place looks great, with its big smoked mirrors.
Hix, 66-70 Brewer Street, W1F 9UP (7292 3518, www.marksbar.co.uk). Piccadilly Circus tube. Open noon-1am Mon-Sat; noon-midnight Sun.

Oxford St & Marylebone

Artesian Bar

The Artesian is very nearly a very great bar. Its elegant space on the ground floor of the Langham Hilton

is lovely. Tables are well spaced. Service is friendly and ultra-efficient even when – as so often happens – it's packed out. A free plate of tasty canapés may arrive unbidden. Their own cocktails are well conceived, and the classics are flawlessly rendered and generously poured. One downer: piping in incredibly loud Euro-pop, which is completely at odds with the room – and with the pricing of the drinks, which are among London's most expensive.
Langham Hotel, 1C Portland Place, W1B 1JA (7636 1000, www.artesian-bar.co.uk). Oxford Circus tube. Open 11am-2am Mon-Sat; noon-midnight Sun.

Piccadilly Circus & Mayfair

Bar Américain Bar

We love the simplicity of the cocktail list here: around 20 drinks and most of them tried and tested classics. Martinis, manhattans and daiquiris are all expertly rendered, and you can get the true Vesper, James Bond's own-recipe martini made with gin, vodka and Lillet Blanc. For a quiet drink in the West End, in a beautiful art deco interior with widely spaced tables, and without paying ultra-high prices, you can't do much better than the Américain.
Brasserie Zédel, 20 Sherwood Street, W1F 7ED (7734 4888, www.brasserie zedel.com). Piccadilly Circus tube. Open 4.30pm-midnight Mon-Sat; 4.30-11pm Sun.

Coburg Bar Bar

The Connaught has always had the most country house-like feeling of London's great hotels, and the effect reaches perfection in the Coburg. It seems effortlessly beautiful, from the deep patterned carpet to the moulded ceiling; the wing chairs, a long-time fixture, can induce torpor even if you're drinking a double espresso.

Great champagnes and cognacs feature prominently on the drinks menu, and the cocktail list focuses on classics. Execution is flawless. Bowls of crisps and olives, both outstanding in quality, are replaced when empty. If the Coburg isn't 'scene' enough for you, try the hotel's other, noisier and busier bar, the Connaught. One downer:
The Connaught, Carlos Place, W1K 2AL (7499 7070, www.the-connaught.co.uk). Bond Street or Green Park tube. Open 8am-11pm Mon, Sun; 8am-1am Tue-Sat.

Galvin at Windows Bar

There's suddenly no shortage of rooftop venues in London, but the location of Windows is still superb. It offers remarkable panoramic views from the 28th floor of the Park Lane Hilton. Add a sleek interior that mixes art deco glamour with a hint of 1970s petrodollar kitsch, and you can't go wrong. The wine and cocktails don't come cheap, but the drinks are assembled with care, and the service is attentive without being obsequious.
London Hilton, Park Lane, W1K 1BE (7208 4021). Hyde Park Corner tube. Open 11am-1am Mon-Wed; 11am-2.30am Thur, Fri; 3pm-2.30am Sat; 11am-10.30pm Sun. Food served noon-midnight Mon-Fri; 3pm-2.30am Sat; noon-10.30pm Sun.

Purl Bar

Purl, one of London's first speakeasy-type bars, is popular, which means that booking is advisable – though walk-ins will be seated if there's space. The layout of the bar, over a number of smallish spaces in a vaulted basement, gives the opportunity for genuine seclusion, if that's what you're looking for. And if you're interested in cutting-edge cocktail making, you're also in luck. Novel methods and unusual ingredients are used in many of the unique drinks, but the classics are always sound too.
50 Blandford Street, W1U 7HX (7935 0835, www.purl-london.com). Bond Street tube. Open 5-11.30pm Mon-Thur; 5pm-midnight Fri, Sat.

Westminster & St James's

Boisdale of Belgravia Bar

There's nowhere quite like this posh, Scottish-themed enterprise, and that includes its sister branches in the City and Canary Wharf. If you're here to drink, you'll be drinking single malts from a terrific range. That said, the outstanding wine list is surprisingly affordable, with house selections starting at under £20. Additional appeal comes from jazz musicians (six nights a week) and a heated cigar terrace.
13-15 Eccleston Street, SW1W 9LX (7730 6922, www.boisdale.co.uk). Victoria tube/rail. Open/food served noon-1am Mon-Fri; 6pm-1am Sat. Admission free before 10pm, then £12.

Dukes Bar Bar

If you want to go out for a single cocktail, strong and expensive and very well made, go to Dukes. It's in a luxury hotel, but everyone gets the warmest of welcomes. There are three small rooms, all decorated in discreetly opulent style; you feel cocooned. The bar is famous for the theatre of its martini making – at the table, from a trolley, using vermouth made exclusively for them at the Sacred distillery in Highgate – but other drinks are just as good.
Dukes Hotel, 35 St James's Place, SW1A 1NY (7491 4840, www.dukes hotel.com). Green Park tube. Open 2-11pm Mon-Sat; 4-10.30pm Sun.

St Stephen's Tavern Pub

Done out with dark woods, etched mirrors and Arts and Crafts-style wallpaper, this is a lovely old pub. The food is reasonably priced and the ales are excellent, but drinks can be expensive. Opposite Big Ben, its location is terrific, yet it's neither too touristy nor too busy. If the downstairs bars are full, head upstairs and look for a seat on the mezzanine. St Stephen's nearest rival is the Red Lion (48 Parliament Street, SW1A 2NH, 7930 5826), by tradition the politicians' favourite.
10 Bridge Street, SW1A 2JR (7925 2286, www.hall-woodhouse.co.uk). Westminster tube. Open 10am-11.30pm Mon-Thur, Sat; 10am-midnight Fri; 10.30am-10.30pm Sun. Food served 10am-10pm daily.

Chelsea

Cadogan Arms Gastropub

In 2009, this 19th-century Chelsea pub was given a major rebuild by its new owners, the Martin brothers. It now has a countrified look, complete with stuffed animals and fly-fishing displays, and remains a proper boozer, with top-quality real ales, notwithstanding the snug and smoothly run dining area, where good food is on offer.

298 King's Road, SW3 5UG (7352 6500, www.thecadoganarmschelsea. com). Sloane Square tube then bus 19, 22, 319. Open 11am-11pm Mon-Sat; 11am-10pm Sun. Food served noon-3.30pm, 6-10.30pm Mon-Fri; noon-10.30pm Sat; noon-9pm Sun.

South Kensington

Anglesea Arms Pub
The local of both Charles Dickens and DH Lawrence, this old boozer is packed on summer evenings, the front terrace and main bar filled with professional blokes chugging ale, and their female equivalents putting bottles of Sancerre on expenses. But the Anglesea has always had more aura than the average South Kensington hostelry; perhaps it's the link with the Great Train Robbery, reputedly planned here.
15 Selwood Terrace, SW7 3QG (7373 7960, www.capitalpubcompany.com). South Kensington tube. Open 11am-11pm Mon-Sat; 11am-10.30pm Sun. Food served noon-3pm, 6-10pm Mon-Fri; noon-5pm, 6-10pm Sat; noon-5pm, 6-9.30pm Sun.

Mandarin Bar Bar
The Mandarin Oriental is in part famous as the location of Heston Blumenthal's Dinner, so some customers at the bar are praying for a walk-in space in the restaurant. If you're going to choose a waiting room, you can't do much better than this. The room is dazzling, with a central bar and an array of glass, wood and marble. The drinks are done expertly. House cocktails are devised with good sense, and classics are well handled – and with serving sizes to match the high prices. They're matched with polished service and good bar snacks.
Mandarin Oriental Hyde Park, 66 Knightsbridge, SW1X 7LA (7235 2000, www.mandarinoriental.com/ london). Knightsbridge tube. Open 10.30am-1.30am Mon-Sat; 10.30am-12.30am Sun.

Notting Hill

Lonsdale Bar
The scholarliness of the cocktail list here breeds confidence. Nearly every drink is given a time and place of creation and, in most cases, the bartender responsible is named. This makes for informative, sometimes amusing reading, and anything you order will be first rate. Classics like martinis are always very proper. Sitting at the incredibly long and atmospherically lit bar, and watching the bartenders work is entertainment in itself. There's a restaurant too, specialising in top-quality meat.
48 Lonsdale Road, W11 2DE (7727 4080, www.thelonsdale.co.uk). Ladbroke Grove or Notting Hill Gate tube. Open 6pm-midnight Tue-Thur; 6pm-1am Fri, Sat.

Portobello Star Bar
This 'cocktail tavern' deftly blends discerning bar and traditional boozer. The well-stocked bar is manned by friendly staff thoroughly educated in the art of adult refreshment. Mixologist Jake Burger's impeccable, approachable directory of discerning drinks is the last word on sophisticated intoxication. Ginger Pig pies are on hand to soak up the alcohol.
171 Portobello Road, W11 2DY (7229 8016, www.portobellostarbar.co.uk). Ladbroke Grove or Notting Hill Gate tube. Open 11am-11.30pm Mon-Thur, Sun; 11am-12.30am Fri, Sat.

North London

The **Lock Tavern** and **Proud** (for both, *see p98*) are excellent Camden DJ bars, while the **Blues Kitchen** (*see p102*) and scuzzy indie-den the **Dublin Castle** (94 Parkway, NW1 7AN, 7485 1773) supply live music.

69 Colebrooke Row Bar
69 Colebrooke Row, Islington, N1 8AA (07540 528593, www.69 colebrookerow.com). Angel tube. Open 5pm-midnight Mon-Wed, Sun; 5pm-1am Thur; 5pm-2am Fri, Sat. It's not easy to get a seat in this flagship of bar supremo Tony Conigliaro without booking. Punters come for the outstanding cocktails; some of them may push the boundaries of what can be put in a glass, but they always maintain the drinkability of the classics. Take the Terroir, for instance, which lists as its ingredients 'distilled clay, flint and lichen', and tastes wonderfully like a chilled, earthy, minerally vodka. It's made in Conigliaro's upstairs laboratory, which also produces bespoke cocktail ingredients such as Guinness reduction, paprika bitters, rhubarb cordial and pine-infused gin. There's a subtle jazz-age vibe and – on certain nights – a pianist belts out swinging standards.

BrewDog Pub
The Scottish craft brewery's Camden outpost is an initiation into the exciting and groundbreaking world of craft beer, but never feels intimidating. The list features BrewDog's beers on keg draught (with occasional guests). Fridges hold a selection from other microbreweries, mainly from the US.
113 Bayham Street, Camden, NW1 0AG (7284 4626, www.brewdog.com). Camden Town tube or Camden Road rail. Open noon-11.30pm Mon-Thur; noon-midnight Fri, Sat; noon-10.30pm Sun.

Bull Pub
First impressions would suggest the Bull is just another suburban gastropub, but note the enamelled beer memorabilia on the walls and garlands of hop flowers: this pub holds beer in extremely high esteem. You might catch a glimpse of the Willy Wonka tubing and brass vats of the brewing equipment, and the beer taps reveal almost nothing recognisable from the average high-street chain pub. Five of the pumps dispense the fine products of the London Brewing Company, made on the premises, and keg fonts advertise the likes of Sierra Nevada Torpedo and Veltins Pils.
13 North Hill, N6 4AB (8341 0510, www.thebullhighgate.co.uk). Highgate tube. Open noon-11.30pm Mon-Thur; noon-midnight Fri, Sat; noon-10.30pm Sun. Food served noon-10pm Mon-Sat; noon-9pm Sun.

Bull & Last Gastropub
For a place with such a good reputation for its food, the Bull & Last is refreshingly pubby: heavy wooden furniture, velvet drapes, stuffed animals and old prints decorate both the bar and the upstairs dining room. The latter is a calmer and cooler place to eat than the ground-floor bar, and allows diners to focus on dishes such as king scallop carpaccio with pink grapefruit, crème fraîche, coriander and vinaigrette, or pig's cheek with

watermelon pickle, basil and sesame. There are (big) roasts at weekends, a changing selection of beers and ciders from small breweries and a decent wine list.
168 Highgate Road, NW5 1QS (7267 3641, www.thebullandlast.co.uk). Kentish Town tube/rail then bus 214, C2, or Gospel Oak rail then bus C11. Open noon-11pm Mon-Thur; 9am-midnight Fri, Sat; 9am-10.30pm Sun.

Holly Bush Pub
As the trend for gutting old pubs claims yet more Hampstead boozers, this place's cachet increases. Located on a quiet hilltop backstreet, it was built as a house in the 1790s and used as the Assembly Rooms in the 1800s, before becoming a pub in 1928. A higgledy-piggledy air remains, with three low-ceilinged bar areas and one bar counter at which are poured decent pints. Sound food and a good choice of wines by the glass are further draws.
22 Holly Mount, NW3 6SG (7435 2892, www.hollybushhampstead. co.uk). Hampstead tube or Hampstead Heath rail. Open noon-11pm Mon-Sat; noon-10.30pm Sun. Food served noon-3pm, 6-10pm Mon-Fri; noon-4pm, 6-10pm Sat; noon-8pm Sun.

East London

Book Club Bar
Behind the sedate name is one of the most consistently creative cocktail bars in London. You could visit for the drinks alone: cocktails come with names like Don't Go To Dalston. Or – and this is what sets Book Club apart – you could visit for the packed timetable of events, which includes bands, DJs, ping-pong tournaments, life drawing and classic video-game nights. The young and laid-back crowd that packs into the spacious artwork-dotted space are here for a bit of everything.
100-106 Leonard Street, EC2A 4RH (7684 8618, www.wearetbc.com). Old Street tube/rail or Shoreditch High Street rail. Open 8am-midnight Mon-Wed; 8am-2am Thur, Fri; 10am-2am Sat; 10am-midnight Sun. Admission Club free-£12.

Cock Tavern Pub
The Cock Tavern is the sort of place you walk into and think: this is a bloody good pub. It's timelessly classic: dark, uncomplicated and resonant with merry conversation. It's usually rammed here, and it's mainly down to the fabulous beer and cider: the pub cellar is now home to the Howling Hops microbrewery, whose output is mostly drunk in the Cock. A few guests pop up too among the 22 taps, but with a home-brewed selection this good, you might not need them. To fill you up there's gloriously simple food. A bartop cabinet displays Scotch eggs and pork pies, and there's a jar of pickled eggs.
315 Mare Street, E8 1EJ (www.the cocktavern.co.uk). Hackney Central rail. Open from noon daily.

Dukes Bar

Pubs & Bars

Commercial Tavern Pub

The inspired chaos of retro-eccentric decor and warm, inclusive atmosphere make this landmark flat-iron corner pub very likeable. It seems to have escaped the attentions of the necking-it-after-work masses, perhaps because of the absence of wall-to-wall lager pumps in favour of some proper real ale. The bar is made up of colourful art deco tiles, and there's a decorative playfulness throughout; it's a great example of how a historic pub can be lit up with new life. Just down the street, the fabulous, ever-busy Golden Heart (no.110, E1 6LZ, 7247 2158) is a famous nursery for East End artists. *142 Commercial Street, E1 6NU (7247 1888). Liverpool Street tube/rail or Shoreditch High Street rail. Open 5-11pm Mon-Thur; 2-11pm Fri; noon-11pm Sat, Sun.*

Empress Gastropub

Everything about this gloriously updated former pub is bang on, from the linen napkins and red leather banquettes to the food, which packs sensational combinations of flavours. You might find gorgeous guinea fowl on puy lentils with salsa verde; or trout with watercress, apple, celeriac and an English mustard sauce; or perhaps half a hollowed-out bone filled with snails, bone marrow, caramelised onions and pork. Very impressive. *130 Lauriston Road, E9 7LH (8533 5123, www.empresse9.co.uk). Mile End tube then bus 277, 425. Open noon-3.30pm, 6-10.15pm Mon-Fri; 10am-midnight Sat; noon-9.30pm Sun.*

Grapes Pub

If you're trying to evoke the feel of the Thames docks before their Disneyfication into Docklands, these narrow, ivy-covered and etched-glass 1720 riverside premises in Limehouse are a good place to start: the downstairs is all wood panels and nautical jetsam; upstairs is plainer, but it's easier to find seats for Sunday lunch. Expect good ales and a half-dozen wines of each colour by glass and bottle, plus jugs of kir royale or strawberry fizz for summer and port for winter. There's a tiny terrace too. *76 Narrow Street, E14 8BP (7987 4396, www.thegrapes.co.uk). Westferry DLR. Open noon-3.30pm, 5.30-11pm Mon-Wed; noon-11.30pm Thur-Sat; noon-10.30pm Sun. Food served noon-2.30pm, 6.30-9.30pm Mon-Fri; noon-9.30pm Sat; noon-3.30pm Sun.*

Happiness Forgets Bar

The short list of original cocktails is unfailingly good: lots of nice twists on classic ideas but never departing from the essential cocktail principles of balance, harmony and drinkability. Star turns: Mr McRae, Perfect Storm and Tokyo Collins. But the classics are brilliantly handled too, and the food is fabulous, as is the service. This very special place is not very large and plenty of people know about it, so booking is a good idea.

CUTS NO ICE
The bar where your cocktails come unadulterated by frozen water.

Any headlines you read about the White Lyan (for listings, *see below*) are likely to proclaim that it doesn't use ice. That shows how extraordinary it actually is to dispense altogether with such a time-honoured way of chilling drinks, but it's not even the most exciting thing about this new Hoxton cocktail bar. It's the first solo venue from single-minded cocktailian Ryan Chetiyawardana, and not only has he chucked out the frozen water, he also employs no citrus, sugar, fruit or other perishables, and next to no branded products. You can't order off menu, and there's only one of each colour of wine and one lager.

The former White Horse pub doesn't give much away from the outside, but once inside it's clear this is no standard operation. It's all-black with a minimalist New York '80s sort of look about it. Instead of a back bar stacked with spirits there are big fridges holding the pre-made products of hours of labour by Ryan and his team – most of the hard work here is done before opening. Spirits are made to order, or refined and 'rebuilt'.

All this, unsurprisingly, results in some pretty unusual drinks. The Moby Dick Sazerac is made with rye, Peychaud's bitters and absinthe-soaked rice paper. The whale reference comes from the addition of ambergris – yes, the sperm whale secretion – which adds body.

Does all this sound a bit pretentious? Think about it like this: comparing White Lyan to your local boozer is like comparing Heston Blumenthal's Fat Duck to a greasy spoon. It's a genuine pioneer in a new cocktail movement – be a part of it yourself and visit.

8-9 Hoxton Square, N1 6NU (7613 0325, www.happinessforgets.com). Old Street tube/rail. Open 5.30-11pm Mon-Sat; 6pm-11pm Sun.

Wenlock Arms Pub

On an unremarkable backstreet, this old pub was the tap for a nearby brewery, and poured its first pint in 1836; it closed with its parent brewery in the 1960s, then reopened in 1994, whereupon it won awards for the quality of its real ale and plaudits for the toastiness of its real fire. In 2010 threats of redevelopment began, but a sympathetic Hackney Council included it in a conservation area and in 2011 new owners stepped in: cue quality paintjob, new furniture and even more beer fonts. Now the Wenlock is again the quintessence of all that is good about pubs – minimal decor, minimal food and a great range of beer. *26 Wenlock Road, N1 7TA (7608 3406, www.wenlockarms.com). Old Street tube/rail. Open noon-midnight Mon-Thur, Sun; noon-1am Fri, Sat.*

White Lyan Bar

See above **Cuts No Ice**. *153 Hoxton Street, N1 6PJ (3011 1153, www.whitelyan.com). Hoxton rail. Open 6pm-1am Mon-Wed, Sun; 6pm-2am Thur; 6am-3am Fri, Sat.*

Worship Street Whistling Shop Bar

This cellar cocktail bar is decked out in what seems to be a speakeasy/Victorian mash-up. It makes much of its experimental techniques; if your curiosity is tickled by the sound of 'enzymes, acids, proteins and hydrocolloids', you're all set. The list is mercifully short, and classics are well handled. There's an extensive selection of spirits, including their own barrel-aged ones. Staff are skilled, friendly and eager to please. *63 Worship Street, EC2A 2DU (7247 0015, www.whistlingshop.com). Old Street tube/rail. Open 5pm-midnight Mon-Wed; 5pm-1am Thur; 5pm-2am Fri, Sat.*

South-east London

Gipsy Moth Pub

The split-level garden and roomy interior at this moderately funky pub are ideal for a sit-down after roaming around Greenwich. The pub offers an impressive number of beers (Früli, Budvar, Paulaner and at least six others), well-priced wines and pretty decent food, from bar snacks to full meals (including breakfasts). *60 Greenwich Church Street, SE10 9BL (8858 0786, www.thegipsymoth greenwich.co.uk). Cutty Sark DLR. Open/meals served 10am-11pm Mon-Thur; 10am-midnight Fri, Sat; 10am-10.30pm Sun.*

Greenwich Union Pub

Decorated with framed covers of the Picture Post, this is the spiritual home of Alistair Hook's mission to bring his Meantime Brewery's German-style beers to the British public. Six tap options complement a couple of dozen bottled international beers; food runs from bacon butties to steaks. Coffee, tea and a small terrace make it a decent option for non-drinkers. *56 Royal Hill, SE10 8RT (8692 6258, www.greenwichunion.com). Greenwich rail/DLR. Open noon-11pm Mon-Fri; 11am-11pm Sat; 11.30am-10.30pm Sun. Food served noon-4pm, 5.30-10pm Mon-Fri; 11am-10pm Sat; noon-9pm Sun.*

Old Brewery Pub

Meantime Brewery's flagship: by day, it's a café; by night, a restaurant. There's a small bar, with tables outside in a large walled courtyard – a lovely spot in which to test the 50-strong beer list – but most of the action is in the vast, high-ceilinged main space. Dishes, such as smoked barbecue pork ribs with chips and spicy coleslaw, come with matching beers. *Pepys Building, Old Royal Naval College, SE10 9LW (3327 1280, www.oldbrewerygreenwichcom). Cutty Sark DLR. Open 11am-11pm Mon-Sat; 10am-10.30pm Sun.*

South-west London

Crown & Anchor Bar

The most exciting feature of this pub after a back-to-basics restoration is the lengthy bar with its endless fonts: seven cask ales, 14 keg beers and ciders. Clued-up staff are keen to recommend and offer tasting notes and samples. It's an unpretentious, friendly place, devoted to great beer. *246 Brixton Road, Brixton, SW9 6AQ (7737 0060, www.crownandanchor brixton.co.uk). Stockwell tube or Brixton tube/rail. Open 4.30-11pm Mon-Thur; 4.30pm-11.30pm Fri; noon-midnight Sat; noon-11pm Sun. Food served 5-10pm Mon-Fri; noon-10pm Sat; noon-8pm Sun.*

Shops & Services

Burberry. *See p82.*

Shop to it

The stores and stalls that have something for all.

London's retail attractions continue to gather pace despite the economic recession, with new fashion boutiques, independent food retailers and home stores offering a winning counterpoint to established standouts like **Liberty**, an imaginative, compelling department store that captures everything that's great about the capital's shopping scene. And it's not all about central London. Over in Stratford, the £1.45 billion retail monster that is **Westfield Stratford City**, which opened in autumn 2011 at the entrance to the Olympic Park, continues to do business with its 300 units, 70 restaurants, bars and cafés, and a 17-screen cinema.

On the indie scene, east London's **Redchurch Street**, at the top of the more-famous Brick Lane, has been particularly lively over the past couple of years, while a few minutes away **Broadway Market** grows ever bigger, drawing winsome young men sporting Lord Kitchener moustaches and fey-looking girls armed with the Saturday style supplements and the odd chocolate éclair. And classics are still going strong too – among them the centuries-old umbrella specialists **James Smith & Sons**.

Between those extremes lies a changing kaleidoscope of places in which to part with your cash: multicultural street markets, deluxe department stores, design-led homewares stores, flashy food shops and, of course, chain-store flagships. You'll also find some of the best places in Europe to buy books, records and second-hand clothes. Despite credit crunches, London is still one of the world's most exciting, exhaustive and exhausting retail centres.

SHOPPING IN LONDON

Our listings focus on British brands and shops that are not only unique to the city, but also relatively centrally located. For the city's key shopping areas, *see p76* **Where to Shop**.

Most goods – with the notable exceptions of books, food and children's clothes – are subject to value added tax (VAT), which is almost always included in the prices advertised by shops. VAT is currently levied at 20 per cent. Some shops, particularly larger stores, operate a scheme allowing visitors from outside the European Union to claim back VAT when leaving the country.

Central London shops stay open late (until 7pm or 8pm) one night a week – it's Thursday in the West End, and Wednesday in Chelsea and Knightsbridge.

The South Bank

Bermondsey Square Antiques Market Antiques

Following the redevelopment of Bermondsey Square, the antiques market – which started in 1855 in north London – continues in an expanded space that now accommodates 200 stalls. Traditionally good for china and silverware, as well as furniture and glassware, there are now also food, fashion and crafts stalls. It's famous for being the spot where, back in the day, thieves could sell their goods with impunity: it's half car boot sale, half chic Parisian fleamarket. Get there early – lunchtime arrivals will be disappointed to find grouchy antiques sellers (well, they did start work at 4am) packing up. *Corner of Bermondsey Street & Long Lane, SE1. Borough tube or London Bridge tube/rail. Open 4am-1pm Fri. No credit cards.*

Borough Market Food & drink

The food hound's favourite market is also London's oldest, dating back to the 13th century. It's the busiest, too, occupying a sprawling site near London Bridge. Gourmet goodies run the gamut, from fresh loaves and rare-breed meats, via fish, game, fruit and veg, to cakes and all manner of preserves, oils and teas; head out hungry to take advantage of the numerous free samples. A rail viaduct, vigorously campaigned against, is now

Rough Trade East

WHERE TO SHOP
London's shopping neighbourhoods

Covent Garden

COVENT GARDEN & SOHO

The famous former flower market is choked with chains and crowds, but Neal Street and the streets off Seven Dials rule for streetwear, while St Martin's Courtyard (www.stmartinscourtyard.co.uk), is good for the likes of Jaeger and Twenty8Twelve. Another urbanwear centre is Soho's pedestrianised Carnaby Street, as well as Newburgh Street and Kingly Street, which run parallel on either side of Carnaby Street. Berwick Street is the new central London hotspot for vintage clothing shops, as well as a few surviving record shops. Charing Cross Road and Cecil Court are prime browsing territory for books.

OXFORD STREET & AROUND

London's commercial backbone, Oxford Street is heaving with department stores and big chains, which spill over on to elegant Regent Street. North-west of Oxford Street, Marylebone has retained some of its villagey atmosphere, with a thinning array of small shops that sell everything from designer jewellery to artisan cheeses. Venture further north to Church Street for antiques.

NOTTING HILL

Best known for its antiques market on Portobello Road, Notting Hill also has an impressive cache of posh boutiques around the intersection of Westbourne Grove and Ledbury Road. It's also good for rare vinyl and vintage clothes.

MAYFAIR & ST JAMES'S

The traditional home of tailors (Savile Row) and shirtmakers (Jermyn Street), this patch also retains venerable specialist hatters, cobblers and perfumers. Bond Street glitters with jewellers and designer stores, while the reinvigorated Mount Street is the place for niche upmarket labels.

CHELSEA & KNIGHTSBRIDGE

King's Road is pretty bland these days, but punctuated with some interesting shops. An up-and-coming sidestreet is Pavilion Road, home to a number of ultra-feminine boutiques. Designer salons line Sloane Street and mix with chains on Knightsbridge, which is anchored by Harrods.

KENSINGTON

Kensington High Street has surrendered to the chains, but it's worth exploring the backstreets leading up to Notting Hill Gate. Rarefied antiques shops and topnotch charity shops gather on Kensington Church Street. In South Kensington, Brompton Cross has glossy contemporary furniture showrooms and designer boutiques.

EAST LONDON

East London is great for quirkier shops and some of the city's best markets; go there on a Sunday for Columbia Road and Spitalfields markets. Head to Brick Lane and its offshoots, especially Redchurch Street, for clothing, accessories and home goods by idiosyncratic young designers, and vintage fashion. From Shoreditch and Hoxton north into Dalston there are hip boutiques, furniture stores and bookshops, while Hackney's Broadway Market is home to a Saturday farmers' market as well as cool indie stores.

NORTH LONDON

Camden's grungy markets are growing up (the new food stalls at the Lock are particularly welcome), but head into Primrose Hill for an exquisite selection of small shops selling, among other things, quirky lingerie and vintage clothes. Antiques dealers have thinned out on Islington's Camden Passage, but there other indies remian, including lifestyle boutique Smug.

in place, which means restored historic features have been returned and works disruption should now be at an end. As if to celebrate, a new Market Hall, facing on to Borough High Street, has been opened: it acts as a kind of greenhouse for growing plants (including hops), as well as hosting workshops, tastings and foodie demonstrations. You can also nip in with your snack if the weather's poor.

Although the market's open on Monday and Tuesday, those days are mainly for tradespeople, with fewer stalls open. Given that weekends are usually mobbed, Wednesday and Thursday are usually the best days to visit.
Southwark Street, SE1 (7407 1002, www.boroughmarket.org.uk). London Bridge tube/rail. Open 10am-5pm Wed, Thur; 10am-6pm Fri; 8am-5pm Sat. No credit cards.

Konditor & Cook Food & drink

Gerhard Jenne caused a stir when he opened this bakery on a South Bank side street in 1993, selling gingerbread people for grown-ups and lavender-flavoured cakes. Success lay in lively ideas such as cakes that spell the recipient's name in a series of individually decorated squares. Quality pre-packed salads and sandwiches are also sold.
22 Cornwall Road, Waterloo, SE1 8TW (7633 3333, www.konditorandcook.com). Waterloo tube/rail. Open 7.30am-6.30pm Mon-Wed; 7.30am-7pm Thur, Fri; 8.30am-7pm Sat; 10am-4.30pm Sun.

Maltby Street Food & drink

Borough Market's trade has been challenged by former stallholders who have set up camp under the railway arches around Maltby Street and further south. Head here for delicious raclette from Kappacasein (Arch 1), craft beer from Kernel Brewery (Arch 12) and the city's finest custard doughnuts, courtesy of St John Bakery (Arch 72). Most producers are open on Saturday mornings (9am-2pm), some on Sundays too – the website www.spa-terminus.co.uk has a useful map showing locations and opening hours.
Maltby Street, Druid Street, Spa Terminus, Ropewalk, SE1 (www.maltby.st). Bermondsey or Southwark tube.

The City

F Flittner Health & beauty

In business since 1904, Flittner seems not to have noticed that the 21st century has begun. Hidden behind beautifully frosted doors (marked 'Saloon') is a simple, handsome room, done out with an array of classic barber's furniture that's older than your gran. Within these hushed confines, up to six black coat-clad barbers deliver straightforward haircuts (dry cuts £18-£20, wet cuts £25-£30) and shaves (£24 with hot towels).

86 Moorgate, EC2M 6SE (7606 4750, www.fflittner.com). Moorgate tube/rail. Open 8am-6pm Mon-Wed, Fri; 8am-6.30pm Thur.

Kate Kanzier Fashion

Adored for great-value directional footwear for women, Kate Kanzier is the place to visit for brogues, ballerinas, sandals and leather boots in a huge range of colours. Sexy high-heeled pumps in patent, suede, leather and animal prints are characterised by vintage designs. Handbags and clutches are also stocked in the spacious shop.
67-69 Leather Lane, EC1N 7TJ (7242 7232, www.katekanzier.com). Chancery Lane tube or Farringdon tube/rail. Open 9.30am-6.30pm Mon-Fri; 11am-4pm Sat.

One New Change Mall

This sprawling Jean Nouvel-designed development is opposite the east end of St Paul's Cathedral, and features a warren of high-street retailers, office buildings and restaurants (Jamie Oliver's Barbecoa, Wahaca and Bread Street Kitchen among the latter). Nicknamed the 'stealth building' due to the structure's resemblance to a stealth bomber, the place is unsurprisingly popular with City workers on their lunchbreaks or on post-work spending sprees, but the cut-above chain stores are less of a pull than the unusual mid-height view of the cathedral and the Thames from the top floor.
New Change Road, EC4M 9AF (7002 8900, www.onenewchange.com). Mansion House or St Paul's tube or Bank tube/DLR. Open varies; check website for opening hours of individual shops.

Clerkenwell

ec one Accessories

Husband-and-wife team Jos and Alison Skeates have a magpie's eye for good design, which makes for delightfully varied browsing at this stylish shop. Over 50 designers are showcased: the choice runs from serious pieces to tempting trinkets such as colourful lucite bangles and sweet little heart necklaces.
41 Exmouth Market, EC1R 4QL (7713 6185, www.econe.co.uk). Farringdon tube/rail. Open 10am-6pm Mon-Wed, Fri; 11am-7pm Thur; 10.30am-6pm Sat.

Hula Nails Health & beauty

Georgiana Amador worked at Mac for many years, in contrast, Hula's boudoir-style beauty rooms are gloriously decked out in Hawaiian wallcoverings, with plush velvet sofas and burlesque flourishes. The salon specialises in luxurious grooming – come for a vintage style pit-stop, with victory rolls and retro make-up all on offer. Nail treatments take place in the window of the parlour, so you can sip on a free grated ginger tea and have a gossip as you watch the media types

go by (waxes and spray tans are in cosily decked-out backrooms). *203-205 Whitecross Street, EC1Y 8QP (7253 4453, www.hulanails.com). Old Street tube/rail. Open 10.30am-7.30pm Mon, Tue, Thur, Fri; 10.30am-9pm Wed; 11am-6pm Sat.*

Bloomsbury & King's Cross

The Brunswick Centre (www.brunswick.co.uk) has a variety of chain shopping and eating options. Lamb's Conduit Street has become known for its fashion outlets and the tiny but delightful **Persephone Books** (no.59, WC1N 3NB, 7242 9292, www.persephonebooks.co.uk).

Aperture Photographic
Electronics & photography
This camera shop-cum-café has a great atmosphere. The photographic side centres on an excellent selection of new and vintage, manual and autofocus Nikons, Leicas, Canons and Hasselblads, along with a sprinkling of other makes, at reasonable prices. The café is frequented by paparazzi and camera enthusiasts. Staff are happy to answer questions. *44 Museum Street, WC1A 1LY (7242 8681, www.apertureuk.com). Holborn or Tottenham Court Road tube. Open 11am-7pm Mon-Fri; noon-7pm Sat.*

Darkroom Fashion
This shop is quite literally dark (with black walls and lampshades), creating a striking backdrop for the carefully chosen selection of unisex fashion, accessories and interiors items for sale. The space doubles up as a gallery, with art displays intermingling with a range of sculptural jewellery. *52 Lamb's Conduit Street, WC1N 3LL (7831 7244, www.darkroom london.com). Holborn tube. Open 11am-7pm Mon-Fri; 11am-6pm Sat; noon-5pm Sun.*

Folk Fashion
While the menswear store at no.49 (7404 6458) concentrates on the stylish own-label (albeit with additional pieces from Scandinavian brands Our Legacy and Han Kjøbenhavn), this branch of Folk is a godsend for women, with Scandinavian labels such as Acne, as well as boutique faves Humanoid and Sessùn. Bags from Ally Capellino provide the finishing touch. *53 Lamb's Conduit Street, WC1N 3NG (8616 4191, www.folkclothing.com). Holborn or Russell Square tube. Open 11am-7pm Mon-Sat; noon-5pm Sun.*

London Review Bookshop
Books & music
From the inviting presentation to the sheer quality of the books selected, this is an inspiring bookshop – no wonder it was able to celebrate its tenth anniversary in 2014. Politics, current affairs and history are well

Darkroom

represented on the ground floor; downstairs, audio books lead on to exciting poetry and philosophy sections, everything you'd expect from a shop owned by the *London Review of Books*. Browse through your purchases in the sweet little adjoining café, and check the website for stimulating events. *14 Bury Place, WC1A 2JL (7269 9030, www.lrbshop.co.uk). Holborn or Tottenham Court Road tube. Open 10am-6.30pm Mon-Sat; noon-6pm Sun.*

Skoob Books & music
A back-to-basics basement beloved of students from the nearby University of London, Skoob showcases some 50,000 titles covering virtually every subject, from philosophy and biography to politics and the occult. Prices are very reasonable. *Unit 66, The Brunswick, WC1N 1AE (7278 8760, www.skoob.com). Russell Square tube. Open 10.30am-8pm Mon-Sat; 10.30am-6pm Sun.*

Fitzrovia

There are lots of electronics shops at the southern end of Tottenham Court Road, with several offering laptop repairs, while toward the north is a clutch of homeware and furniture stores, the most notable of which is **Heals** (196 Tottenham Court Road, W1T 7LQ, 7636 1666, www.heals.co.uk). And of course, you're only minutes from Oxford Street (*see p80*).

Ask Electronics & photography
Four capacious, well-organised floors, with plenty of space to browse. Stock, spanning digital cameras, MP3 players, laptops, hi-fis and TVs, concentrates on the major consumer brands. Prices are competitive.

248 Tottenham Court Road, W1T 7QZ (7637 0353, www.askdirect. co.uk). Tottenham Court Road tube. Open 10am-7pm Mon-Sat; noon-6pm Sun.

Covent Garden & the Strand

Eco pioneer **Neal's Yard Remedies** (15 Neal's Yard, WC2H 9DP, 7379 7222, www.nealsyardremedies.com) offers organic products and a herbal dispensary. It has several central branches, but this is the most charming.

Apple Store
Electronics & photography
A temple to geekery, this is the world's biggest Apple Store, with separate rooms – set out over three storeys – devoted to each product line. The exposed brickwork, big old oak tables and stone floors make it an inviting place, and it's also the world's first Apple Store with a Start Up Room, where staff will help to set up your new iPad, iPhone, iPod or Mac, or transfer files from your old computer to your new one – all for free. *1-7 The Piazza, WC2E 8HA (7447 1400, www.apple.com). Covent Garden tube. Open 9am-9pm Mon-Sat; noon-6pm Sun.*

Benjamin Pollock's Toy Shop
Children
Best known for its toy theatres, Pollock's is also superb for traditional toys, such as knitted animals, china tea sets, masks, glove puppets, cards, spinning tops and fortune-telling fish. *44 The Market, WC2E 8RF (7379 7866, www.pollocks-covent garden.co.uk). Covent Garden tube. Open 10.30am-6pm Mon-Sat; 11am-4pm Sun.*

Camper Fashion
The successful Spanish eco footwear brand – one of Mallorca's best exports – has become more sophisticated in recent seasons, moving away from its funky but sensible image towards a more fashion-oriented aesthetic. However, most of its styles are still distinctively recognisable, with the classic, round-toed and clod-heeled models still featuring. *34 Shelton Street, WC2H 9HP (7836 7973, www.camper.com). Covent Garden tube. Open 10am-7pm Mon-Wed; 10am-8pm Thur-Sat; noon-6pm Sun.*

Coco de Mer Accessories
London's most glamorous erotic emporium sells a variety of tasteful books, toys and lingerie, from glass dildos that double as objets d'art to a Marie Antoinette costume of crotchless culottes and corset. Trying on items can be fun as well: the peepshow-style velvet changing rooms allow your lover to peer through and watch you undress from a 'confession box' next door. *23 Monmouth Street, WC2H 9DD (7836 8882, www.coco-de-mer.com). Covent Garden tube. Open 11am-7pm Mon-Wed, Fri, Sat; 11am-8pm Thur; noon-6pm Sun.*

Ellis Brigham Travel
This is the largest of a clutch of mountain sports and camping equipment shops in the area, so big, in fact, that it is also able to house the city's only ice-climbing wall, a grand 8m (26ft) high. *Tower House, 3-11 Southampton Street, WC2E 7HA (7395 1010, www.ellis-brigham.com). Covent Garden tube. Open 9am-8pm Mon-Fri; 9.30am-6.30pm Sat; 11.30am-5.30pm Sun.*

Fopp Books & music

Three floors of new releases and back-catalogue surprises, plus good selections of books and DVDs, all at competitive prices, make this a great place for bargains. Look out for world cinema, arthouse masterpieces and anime – plus '80s teen classic DVDs on the ground floor and basement, with Fopp's full music selection upstairs.
1 Earlham Street, WC2H 9LL (7845 9770, www.fopp.com). Leicester Square tube. Open 10am-10pm Mon-Wed; 10am-11pm Thur-Sat; noon-6pm Sun.

Hope & Greenwood Food & drink

Confectionary ranging from chocolate gooseberries to sweetheart candies is prettily displayed in plastic beakers, cellophane bags, glass jars, illustrated boxes, porcelain bowls and cake tins. Indulge in a bag of sherbert Flying Saucers or gobstoppers. Gift possibilities include retro gumball machines.
1 Russell Street, WC2B 5JD (7240 3314, www.hopeandgreenwood.co.uk). Covent Garden tube. Open 11am-7.30pm Mon-Fri; 10.30am-7.30pm Sat; noon-6pm Sun.

James Smith & Sons Accessories

More than 175 years after it was established, this charming shop, with Victorian fittings still intact, is holding its own in the niche market of umbrellas and walking sticks. The stock here isn't the throwaway type of brolly that breaks at the first sign of a bit of wind. Lovingly crafted 'brellas, such as a classic City umbrella with a Malacca Cane handle at £120, are built to last. A repair service is also offered.
53 New Oxford Street, WC1A 1BL (7836 4731, www.james-smith.co.uk). Holborn or Tottenham Court Road tube. Open 10am-6pm Mon-Sat.

Miller Harris Health & beauty

Grasse-trained British perfumer Lyn Harris's scents, in lovely floral packaging, are made with natural extracts and oils. Noix de Tubéreuse, a lighter and more palatable tuberose scent than many on the market, is a perennial favourite, while Fleurs de Bois evokes a traditional English garden. This flagship branch has recently been refurbished.
14 Monmouth Street, WC2H 9HB (7836 9378, www.millerharris.com). Covent Garden tube. Open 10.30am-6.30pm Mon-Sat.

Neal's Yard Dairy Food & drink

Neal's Yard buys from small farms and creameries and matures the cheeses in its own cellars until they're ready to sell in peak condition. Names such as Stinking Bishop and Lincolnshire Poacher are as evocative as the aromas in the shop. It's best to walk in and ask what's good today: you'll be given tasters by the well-trained staff. There's a shop in Borough Market too (6 Park Street, SE1 9AB, 7367 0799).

17 Shorts Gardens, WC2H 9AT (7240 5700, www.nealsyarddairy.co.uk). Covent Garden tube. Open 10am-7pm Mon-Sat.

Stanfords Travel

Three floors of travel guides, travel literature, maps, language guides, atlases and magazines. The basement houses the full range of British Ordnance Survey maps; there's a café too.
12-14 Long Acre, WC2E 9LP (7836 1321, www.stanfords.co.uk). Covent Garden or Leicester Square tube. Open 9am-8pm Mon-Fri; 10am-8pm Sat; noon-6pm Sun.

Soho & Chinatown

Off the Charing Cross Road, Denmark Street was in the 1960s the site of the legendary recording studio Regent Sounds; it is now a hub for music shops, especially those selling guitars. For recorded music, though, head across the road to **Foyles**, which is also home to **Ray's Jazz**. Ray's offers a predominantly CD-based stock that covers blues, avant-garde, gospel, folk and world, but is strongest in modern jazz. **Berwick Street** (www.berwickstreetlondon.co.uk) is really the heart of Soho, with its breezy street market (9am-6pm Mon-Sat), one of London's oldest, in an area better known for its lurid, neon-lit trades. Dating back to 1778, it's still great for seasonal produce and cheap fabric. The indie record shops that used to cluster here have taken a pasting over the last few years, but **Revival Records** (no.30) is full of vinyl beans – as is

Sounds of the Universe, round the corner. **Agent Provocateur** is now a glossy chain, but the original outpost of the shop that went on to popularise high-class kink around the world is still in Soho (6 Broadwick Street, W1F 8HL, 7439 0229, www.agentprovocateur.com). Just next door is a big branch of beauty chain **Space NK** (8-10 Broadwick Street, W1F 8HW, 7734 3734, www.spacenk.com).

As famous as the King's Road back when the Sixties swung, **Carnaby Street** was, until a few years ago, more likely to sell you a postcard of the Queen snogging a punk rocker than a fishtail parka. But the noughties have been kind and Carnaby is cool again. **Kingly Court** is the highlight, but classy chains (Lush, Muji) and boutiques have appeared in the nearby alleys, and branches of **Size?** (nos.33-34, 7287 4016, www.size.co.uk) and **Puma** (nos.52-55, 7439 0221, www.puma.com) make this a good place to stalk some rare sneakers.

Algerian Coffee Stores Food & drink

For over 125 years, this unassuming little shop has been trading over the same wooden counter. The range of coffees is broad, with house blends sold alongside single-origin beans, and some serious teas and brewing hardware are also available. Passing? Take away a single or double espresso for £1, or a cappuccino or a latte for £1.20.

52 Old Compton Street, W1V 6PB (7437 2480, www.algcoffee.co.uk). Open 9am-7pm Mon-Wed; 9am-9pm Thur, Fri; 9am-8pm Sat.

Cecil Court Books & music

Quaint Cecil Court is known for its antiquarian book, map and print dealers, housed in premises that haven't changed in a hundred years. Notable residents include children's specialist Marchpane (no.16, 7836 8661), 40-year veteran David Drummond of Pleasures of Past Times (no.11, 7836 1142) with his playbills and Victoriana, and the mystical, spiritual and occult specialist Watkins (nos.19-21, 7836 2182). *Between Charing Cross Road & St Martin's Lane, WC2N (www.cecilcourt.co.uk). Leicester Square tube.*

Chris Kerr Fashion

Chris Kerr, son of legendary 1960s tailor Eddie Kerr, is the man to visit if Savile Row's prices or attitude aren't to your liking. The versatile Kerr has no house style; instead, he makes every suit to each client's exact specifications, and those clients include Johnny Depp and David Walliams. A good place to get started with British tailoring.
31 Berwick Street, W1F 8RJ (7437 3727, www.eddiekerr.co.uk). Oxford Circus tube. Open 8.30am-5.30pm Mon-Fri; 9am-1pm Sat.

Foyles Books & music

Probably the single most impressive independent bookshop in London: 56 specialist subjects are covered in the flagship store, with the music, gay interest, foreign fiction, law and philosophy sections especially strong.

TOP TIP!
Say cheese
As well as **Neal's Dairy** (*see left*) and **La Fromagerie** (*see p63*), for more great cheese, try **Paxton & Whitfield** (93 Jermyn Street, SW1Y 6JE, 7930 0259).

Gosh! See p80.

The shop's five storeys accommodate several concessions, too, including the Grant & Cutler foreign-language bookstore, and, on the third floor, Ray's Jazz. The popular first-floor café hosts readings, as well as occasional gigs and other events. And things promise to get even better when the store moves into larger premises next door at no.107.
113-119 Charing Cross Road, WC2H 0EB (7437 5660, www.foyles.co.uk). Tottenham Court Road tube. Open 9.30am-9pm Mon-Sat; noon-6pm Sun (browsing from 11.30am).

Gosh! Books & music
There's nowhere better to bolster your comics collection. There's a huge selection of Manga, but graphic novels take centre stage, from early classics such as Krazy Kat to Alan Moore's erotic Peter Pan adaptation Lost Girls. Classic children's books, of the This is London vein, are another strong point.
1 Berwick Street, W1F 0DR (7636 1011, www.goshlondon.com). Oxford Circus tube. Open 10.30am-7pm daily.

Harold Moores Records
Books & music
Harold Moores is not your stereotypical classical music store: young, open-minded staff and an expansive stock of new and second-hand music bolster its credentials. This collection sees some great stuff from old masters complemented by a range of eclectic contemporary music. There's a basement dedicated to second-hand classical vinyl, including an excellent selection of jazz music.
2 Great Marlborough Street, W1F 7HQ (7437 1576, www.hmrecords. co.uk). Oxford Circus tube. Open 10am-6.30pm Mon-Sat; noon-6pm Sun.

Kingly Court Mall
If you want to shop modern Carnaby Street, Kingly Court is the place to start – in fact, it's also the place that started the area's revival as a cool shopping destination. It's a three-tiered complex that contains a funky mix of established chains, independents, vintage and vintage-style boutiques, with courtyard cafés in the centre.
Carnaby Street, opposite Broadwick Street, W1B 5PW (7333 8118, www.carnaby.co.uk). Oxford Circus tube. Open 11am-7pm Mon-Sat; noon-6pm Sun.

Lina Stores Food & drink
Behind the 1950s green ceramic Soho frontage is an iconic family-run Italian deli that's been in business for over half a century. A recent modernisation has taken away some of the old-school character, but a new coffee machine goes some way to making up for it. Besides dried pastas, there's a deli counter chock-full of cured meats, hams, salamis, olives, pesto, cheeses, marinated artichokes and fresh pastas. It's also one of the best places to buy truffles in season.

18 Brewer Street, W1F 0SH (7437 6482, www.linastores.co.uk). Leicester Square tube. Open 8.30am-7.30pm Mon, Tue, Sat; 8.30am-8pm Wed-Fri; 11am-5pm Sun.

Lipman & Sons Fashion
A reliable formalwear firm, that can tailor and/or rent out a morning coat or lounge suit.
22 Charing Cross Road, WC2H 0HR (7240 2310, www.lipmanand sons.co.uk). Leicester Square tube. Open 9am-6pm Mon-Wed, Fri, Sat; 9am-8pm Thur.

OTHER/shop
Fashion
The Other shop opened in 2012, but founders Matthew Murphy and Kirk Beattie have more than a decade's experience in running another successful indie boutique – b Store. Other occupies the same site as its (now defunct) predecessor, sells similar stock, even a continuation of the excellent b Clothing brand – now called Other – that the store had become famous for. A sun-lit basement stocks Other's edit of brands such as Peter Jensen, Our Legacy and Sophie Hulme. The store often houses installations and exhibitions by artists, and also stocks a range of mags and coffee-table books.
21 Kingly Street, W1B 5QA (7734 6846, www.other-shop.com). Oxford Circus tube. Open 10.30am-6.30pm Mon-Sat; noon-5pm Sun.

Sounds of the Universe
Books & music
SOTU's affiliation with reissue kings Soul Jazz records means its remit is broad. This is especially true on the ground floor (new vinyl and CDs), where grime and dubstep 12-inches jostle for space alongside new wave cosmic disco, electro-indie re-rubs and Nigerian compilations. The second-hand vinyl basement is big on soul, jazz, Brazilian and alt-rock.
7 Broadwick Street, W1F 0DA (7734 3430, www.sounds oftheuniverse.com). Oxford Circus tube. Open 11am-7.30pm Mon-Sat; 11.30am-5.30pm Sun.

Supreme Fashion
Europe's first Supreme store opened in 2011 to much excitement among the city's skaters and streetwear fans. The standalone Soho store stocks the entire collection of the cool New York brand's clothing, footwear and boards.
2-3 Peter Street, W1F 0AA (7437 0493, www.supremenewyork.com). Oxford Circus or Piccadilly Circus tube. Open 11am-7pm Mon-Sat; noon-6pm Sun.

Tommy Guns Health & beauty
Now over a decade old, Tommy Guns remains a very cool prospect indeed. This original Soho space, complete with retro fittings, is filled with youthful colourists and cutters and there's a friendly, relaxed buzz to the place most days. Men's cuts start from £39.95, and women's cuts can be had from £49.95. Billy and Bo (65 Brewer Street, Soho, W1F 9TQ, 7287 0011, www.billyandbo.com) is part of the group.
65 Beak Street, W1F 9SN (7439 0777, www.tommyguns.com). Oxford Circus or Piccadilly Circus tube. Open 10am-8pm Mon-Fri; 10am-6pm Sat.

Yamaha Music London
Books & music
This vast three-storied space (previously Chappell of Bond Street) is now the leading Yamaha stockist in the UK, but more portable purchases can be found in the collection of sheet music (classical, pop and jazz), reputedly the largest in Europe.
152-160 Wardour Street, W1F 8YA (7432 4400, www.yamaha musiclondon.com). Tottenham Court Road tube. Open 9.30am-6pm Mon-Fri; 10am-5.30pm Sat.

YMC Fashion
Impeccably designed staples are the forte of this London label, which opened its first store in 2010. It's the place to head to for simple vest tops and T-shirts, stylish macs, tasteful knits and chino-style trousers, for both men and women.
11 Poland Street, W1F 8QA (7494 1619, www.youmustcreate.com). Oxford Circus tube. Open 11am-7pm Mon-Sat.

TOP TIP!
Top Tipples
For the widest range of spirits in London (according to staff, at least) head to Gerry's (74 Old Compton Street, Soho, W1D 4UW, 7734 4215, www.gerrys.uk.com).

RECOMMENDED
Selfridges

Whenever we ask people for a list of favourite shops, one name recurs to the point where we have to reword our question: 'Apart from Selfridges (*see p81*), what is the best shop in London?'. Alongside designer labels and luxurious services, it has clip-in hair extensions, cheapo nail bars and a ground floor of fashion well within the reach of a teenager's purse. There is always something happening, whether a shoe-tattooing service or the world's best make-up artist doing your lippy for free. Stunts aside, if you can't find something to buy in Selfridges, you just aren't looking. In 2013 alone, it unveiled the capital's best denim department and boosted the paltry toy offering to add a messy Play-Doh station, a car-racing track and regular events such as a bear-fixing hospital and Makies 3D printing. But should this talk of egalitarian shopping leave the luxe customer yearning for a little exclusivity, take heart: Louis Vuitton recently unveiled a three-storey townhouse within the store – a London first.

Oxford Street & Marylebone

Popular department store **John Lewis** (www.johnlewis.com) has its flagship branch at 300 Oxford Street, while **Marks & Spencer** (www.marksandspencer.com), high-street favourite for undies, sandwiches and ready meals, but also offering several reliable fashion ranges, has two huge branches here. **Urban Outfitters** (200 Oxford Street, W1D 1NU, 7907 0800, www.urbanoutfitters.co.uk) sells a great range of boutique labels, and **Clarks** (260 Oxford Street, W1C 1LD, 0844 499 9032, www.clarks.co.uk) has shed its school-shoe image to be fêted as the inventor of Wallabees. North of Oxford Street, the fashionable district known to its boosters as 'Marylebone Village' has become a magnet for moneyed Londoners.

Marylebone has a farmers' market (Cramer Street car park, corner of Moxton Street; 10am-2pm Sun), while **Church Street** is a major area for vintage homewares, including those at **Alfie's Antique Market**.

Alfie's Antique Market
Homewares
For more than three decades, Alfie's three floors and basement have hosted a hundred dealers in vintage furniture and fashion, art, books, maps and the like. There's a pleasant rooftop café. *13-25 Church Street, NW8 8DT (7723 6066, www.alfiesantiques.com). Edgware Road tube or Marylebone tube/rail. Open 10am-6pm Tue-Sat. No credit cards.*

Cadenhead's Whisky Shop & Tasting Room **Food & drink**
Cadenhead's is a survivor of a rare breed: the independent whisky bottler. And its shop is one of a kind, at least in London. Cadenhead's selects barrels from distilleries all over Scotland and bottles them without filtration or any other intervention. *26 Chiltern Street, W1U 7QF (7935 6999, www.whiskytastingroom.com). Baker Street tube. Open 10.30am-6.30pm Mon-Fri; 10.30am-6pm Sat.*

Daunt Books **Books & music**
This beautiful Edwardian shop's elegant three-level back room – complete with oak balconies, viridian-green walls and stained-glass window – houses a much-praised travel section featuring guidebooks, maps, language reference, travelogues and related fiction. Travel aside, Daunt is also a first-rate stop for literary fiction, biography, gardening and more. *83-84 Marylebone High Street, W1U 4QW (7224 2295, www.dauntbooks. co.uk). Baker Street tube. Open 9am-7.30pm Mon-Sat; 11am-6pm Sun.*

Hale Clinic **Health & beauty**
Around 100 practitioners are affiliated to the Hale Clinic, which was founded with the aim of integrating complementary and conventional medicine. The treatment list is an A-Z of alternative therapies; the shop stocks supplements, skincare products and books. *7 Park Crescent, W1B 1PF (7631 0156, www.haleclinic.com). Great Portland Street tube. Open 8.30am-9pm Mon-Fri; 9am-5pm Sat.*

Margaret Howell **Fashion**
Margaret Howell's wearable clothes are made in Britain with an old-fashioned attitude to quality. These principles combine with her elegant designs to make for the best 'simple' clothes for sale in London. Her pared-down approach means prices seem steep, but these are clothes that last and seem only to get better with time. Some homewares are also sold here. *34 Wigmore Street, W1U 2RS (7009 9009, www.margarethowell.co.uk). Bond Street tube. Open 10am-6pm Mon-Wed, Fri, Sat; 10am-7pm Thur; noon-5pm Sun.*

THE MIRACLE OF MOUNT STREET
For luxury labels, this is the summit.

Its name may not trip off the tongue in the way that Bond Street and Knightsbridge do, but when it comes to London favourites with young ladies who lunch, and shop, Mount Street looks set to usurp its more famous neighbour Bond Street – and it's all thanks to **Marc Jacobs**. The American designer set up shop here (at no.24) seven years ago, selling his main lines alongside a brilliant edit of music, film and art titles, as well as quirky, fun knick-knacks. Other established and up-and-coming designers were quick to follow, and lots more are due to open spaces here for spring 2014. Of the latter, Serbian-born, London-based designer **Roksanda Ilincic** (no.9) is likely to prove a winner with her richly coloured dresses displayed in a David Adjaye-designed store in the former Pyms Gallery. Nearby at no.6, Britain's hottest young designer **Christopher Kane** will offer boyfriends something to browse while their other halves check out his subtly subversive takes on fashion in a shop that he says will 'really express my vision'. Later this year, online-only brand **Gianvito Rossi** (no.108) should get foot fashionistas cooing over the designs of Rossi junior, who's following in the footsteps (ahem) of his more famous papa Sergio with some rather lovely shoes; in this case, elegant stilettos and ankle boots. And to go with said footwear, **Céline** (no.103) is sure to offer something swoonsome. Having closed its London store in 2009, the label is back later this year, with creative director Pheobe Philo sure to have as much clout as ever with fashion fans. At a whimper-inducing £1,000 for a handbag, we might not be buying, but we'll certainly have a lot of fun browsing.

La Pâtisserie des Rêves **Food & drink**
Imported from Paris in 2014, this cake shop is all about exquisite versions of the classics – both French and English – by chef-pâtissier Philippe Conticini. Whether you choose an éclair, tarte au citron, rhubarb tart or humble croissant, you are unlikely to better the version sold here. *43 Marylebone High Street, W1U 4QD (3603 7333, www.lapatisserie desreves.com/uk). Baker Street or Regent's Park tube. Open 8.30am-7.30pm Mon-Sat; 8.30am-6.30pm Sun.*

Primark **Fashion**
With more than 80,000sq ft over four floors, this branch of Primark is even bigger than its sister branch near Marble Arch (and is in the process of getting even bigger). Stock changes rapidly, and prices are low. Many would argue that the concept of throwaway fashion is increasingly wrong and outmoded, but the value of Primark clothing is precisely that – it trades in trend-led pieces that'll get you through a weekend, a party or a summer holiday, all for a few quid. Primark has even flipped a finger at allegations – proven false – about its overseas production by signing up to the Ethical Trading Initiative. The other big London branch is at 499-517 Oxford Street. *14-28 Oxford Street, W1 1BJ (7580 5510, www.primark.co.uk). Tottenham Court Road tube. Open 8am-10pm Mon-Fri; 8am-9pm Sat; 11.30am-6pm Sun.*

Selfridges **Department store**
With its plethora of concession boutiques, store-wide themed events and collections from all the hottest brands, Selfridges is as dynamic as a department store could be. Although the store layout changes regularly, the useful floor plans make navigating the place easy-peasy. While the basement is chock-full of hip home accessories and stylish kitchen equipment, it's Selfridges' fashion floors that really get hearts racing. With a winning combination of new talent, hip and edgy labels, high-street brands and luxury high-end designers, the store stays ahead of the pack. Highlights include the huge denim section, and the extensive Shoe Galleries, the world's biggest women's footwear department. Level 4 hosts the Toy Shop. There are always new draws in the food hall, ranging from great deli and bakery produce to classy packaged goods. Regularly changing pop-ups and special events keep customers on their toes. *400 Oxford Street, Marylebone, W1A 1AB (0800 123400, www.selfridges.com). Bond Street or Marble Arch tube. Open 9.30am-8pm Mon-Wed, Fri, Sat; 9.30am-9pm Thur; noon-6.15pm Sun (browsing from 11.30am).*

Topshop **Fashion**
Topshop has been the queen of the British high street for the past decade, and walking into the busy Oxford Street flagship, it's easy to see why. Spanning three huge floors, the place lays claim to being the world's largest fashion shop, and is always buzzing with fashion-forward teens and twentysomethings keen to get their hands on the next big trends. The store covers a huge range of styles and sizes, and includes free personal shoppers, boutique label concessions, capsule collections, a Metalmorphosis tattoo parlour, a Daniel Hersheson Blow Dry Bar, a café and sweet shop. Topman is as on-the-ball and innovative as its big sister, stocking niche menswear labels such as Garbstore, and housing a trainer boutique, a suit section, and a new personal shopping suite, featuring consultation rooms, Xbox 360s and an exhibition space. Both shops are even more of a hive of activity than normal during London Fashion Week, when a series of special events are held. *36-38 Great Castle Street, W1W 8LG (0844 848 7487, www.topshop.com). Oxford Circus tube. Open 9am-9pm Mon-Sat; 11.30am-6pm Sun.*

Piccadilly Circus & Mayfair

Behind the grand façades of Regent Street, there are many fashion chains, including branches of **Banana Republic** (no.224, W1B 3BR, 7758 3550, www.banana republic.co.uk) and H&M's upmarket sibling **COS** (no.222, W1B 5BD, 7478 0400, www.cosstores.com), as well as a big **Apple Store** (235 Regent Street, W1B 2 EL, 7153 9000, www.apple.com) that offers all the services you'd expect, including the trademark

'Genius Bar' for technical support. This is a focal area for British designer showcases. The key locations are **Vivienne Westwood** (44 Conduit Street, W1S 2YL, 7439 1109, www.viviennewestwood.com), **Stella McCartney** (30 Bruton Street, W1J 6QR, 7518 3100, www.stella mccartney.com) and **Alexander McQueen** (4-5 Old Bond Street, W1S 4PD, 7355 0088, www.alexander mcqueen.com), plus the diffusion line, **McQ** (14 Dover Street, W1S 4LW, 7318 2220). Those after some Parisian style have the luxurious **Louis Vuitton Maison** flagship (17-20 New Bond Street, W1S 2UE, 3214 9200, www.louisvuitton. com), or the more pared-down but equally fashion-forward **Vanessa Bruno** boutique (1A Grafton Street, W1S 4EB, 7499 7838, www.vanessa bruno.com), the designer's first London store. Also in Mayfair are royal corsetière **Rigby & Peller** (22A Conduit Street, W1S 2XT, 0845 076 5545, www.rigbyandpeller.com) and shoe specialist **Russell & Bromley** (24-25 New Bond Street, W1S 2PS, 7629 6903, www.russelland bromley.co.uk). The Royal Arcades in the vicinity of Piccadilly are a throwback to shopping past – the **Burlington Arcade** is both the largest and grandest, but the **Piccadilly Arcade**, opposite it, and the **Royal Arcade**, at 28 Old Bond Street, are also worth a visit.

A bibliophile could happily waste hours in the **Waterstones** flagship (203-206 Piccadilly, SW1Y 6WW, 7851 2400, www.waterstones. co.uk), which has several floors of books, as well as a refurbished bar-café and a Trailfinders travel agency concession.

Anthropologie Fashion
Anthropologie, the romantically inclined elder sister to fellow US brand Urban Outfitters, opened the doors of its first European store here in 2009. Stock is of a feminine bent, with delicate necklaces and soft-knit cardies, while the store's signature large-scale window displays and 1,500sq ft living wall of plants are worth the trip alone.
158 Regent Street, W1B 5SW (7529 9800, www.anthropologie. co.uk). Piccadilly Circus tube. Open 10am-7pm Mon-Wed, Fri, Sat; 10am-8pm Thur; noon-6pm Sun.

Berry Bros & Rudd Food & drink
Britain's oldest wine merchant has been trading on the same premises since 1698, and its heritage is reflected in its panelled sales and tasting rooms. Burgundy- and claret-lovers will drool at the hundreds of wines, but there are also decent selections from elsewhere in Europe and the New World.
3 St James's Street, SW1A 1EG (7396 9600, www.bbr.com). Green Park tube. Open 10am-6pm Mon-Fri; 10am-5pm Sat.

Bosideng Fashion
Set over three floors, Bosideng's first overseas flagship store and honorary European headquarters is looking as plush as its 500-piece collection (and with a £10,000 origami sculpture and a £30 million renovation we'd expect no less). This menswear label is Asia's largest manufacturer of down apparel – every feather is a by-product we might add – jetting straight in from China where it has a whopping 10,000 outlets. Every item in the collection is sourced from the UK and Europe (apart from the down) and rendered in posh fabrics: pure cashmere cardies, wool-blend tweed blazers and Egyptian-cotton tops. The space itself is ultra-glossy and airy.
28 South Molton Street, W1K 5RF (7290 3170, www.bosidenglondon. com). Bond Street tube. Open 10am-8pm Mon-Sat; noon-6pm Sun.

Browns Fashion
Browns has been on the fashion cutting-edge for more than four decades. Among the 100-odd designers jostling for attention in Joan Burstein's five interconnecting shops (menswear is at no.23) are Chloé, Christopher Kane and Balenciaga, with plenty of fashion exclusives. No.24 now also houses Shop 24, selling 'staple items you can't live without'. Browns Focus is younger and more casual; Labels for Less is loaded with last season's leftovers.
24-27 South Molton Street, W1K 5RD (7514 0016, www.brownsfashion.com). Bond Street tube. Open 10am-6.30pm Mon-Wed, Fri, Sat; 10am-7pm Thur.

Burberry Fashion
The flagship store of the Burberry brand melds together the building's near-200 years of history with the attributes of hyper-modern retailing, but the gracious surroundings and an emphasis on natural light create a welcoming atmosphere. There's a beauty room here, as well as fashion and accessories.
121 Regent Street, W1B 4TB (7806 8904, www.burberry.com). Piccadilly Circus tube. Open 10am-9pm Mon-Sat; 12.30-7pm Sun.

Burlington Arcade
Lord Cavendish commissioned Britain's very first shopping arcade in 1819. Nearly two centuries later, the Burlington is still one of London's most prestigious shopping 'streets', patrolled by 'beadles' decked out in top hats and tailcoats. Highlights include collections of classic watches at David Duggan, established British fragrance house Penhaligon's, the British luxury luggage brand Globe-Trotter and Sermoneta, selling Italian leather gloves in a range of bright colours. High-end food shops come in the form of Luponde Tea and Ladurée; head to the latter for exquisite Parisian macaroons. Burlington also houses a proper shoe-shine boy working with waxes and creams for just £4.
Piccadilly, St James's, W1 (7355 8317, www.burlington-arcade.co.uk). Green Park tube. Open 8am-8pm Mon-Fri; 9am-7pm Sat; 11am-6pm Sun.

Daniel Hersheson Health & beauty
Despite its location in the heart of upmarket Mayfair, this modern two-storey salon isn't at all snooty. Prices start at £60 (£40 for men), though you'll pay £300 for a cut with Daniel (£150 for men). There's also a menu of therapies; the swish Harvey Nichols branch has a dedicated spa. Hersheson's Blow Dry Bars are located at Topshop (see p81; 7927 7888 to book), Westfield London (8743 0868) and One New Change (see p76; 7248 6225).
45 Conduit Street, W1F 2YN (7434 1747, www.danielhersheson.com). Oxford Circus tube. Open 9am-7pm Mon, Sat; 9am-6.30pm Tue, Wed; 9am-8pm Thur, Fri.

Dover Street Market Fashion
Comme des Garçons designer Rei Kawakubo's ground-breaking six-storey space combines the edgy energy of London's indoor markets – concrete floors, tills inside corrugated iron shacks, Portaloo dressing rooms – with a fine range of rarefied labels. All 14 of the Comme des Garçons collections are here, alongside exclusive lines from such designers as Lanvin and Azzedine Alaïa.
17-18 Dover Street, W1S 4LT (7518 0680, www.doverstreetmarket.com). Green Park tube. Open 11am-6.30pm Mon-Wed; 11am-7pm Thur-Sat; noon-5pm Sun.

Elemis Day Spa Health & beauty
This leading British spa brand's exotic, unisex retreat is tucked away down a cobbled lane off Bond Street. Treatments, from wraps to facials, take place in elegantly ethnic treatment rooms.
2-3 Lancashire Court, W1S 1EX (7499 4995, www.elemis.com). Bond Street tube. Open 10.30am-9pm Mon-Fri; 9am-9pm Sat; 10am-6pm Sun.

Garrard Accessories
The Crown Jeweller's diamond-studded designs have appealed to a new generation of bling-seekers since

TOP TIP!
Vintage vision
For cool vintage frames and sunglasses, check out Covent Garden's **Opera Opera** (98 Long Acre, WC2E 9NR, 7836 9246, www.operaopera.net).

Burlington Arcade

BURLINGTON ARCADE: BRITTA JASCHINSKI

Liberty

the brand was modernised by Jade Jagger. It's now in the hands of London-based jeweller Stephen Webster, who took over as creative director in 2009.
24 Albemarle Street, W1S 4HT (0870 871 8888, www.garrard.com). Bond Street or Green Park tube. Open 10am-6pm Mon-Fri; 10am-5pm Sat.

Grays Antique Market & Grays in the Mews Homewares
Sibling of Alfie's (*see p81*), Grays gathers more than 200 dealers in a smart covered market building. They sell everything from antique furniture and rare books to vintage fashion and jewellery.
58 Davies Street, W1K 5LP & 1-7 Davies Mews, W1K 5AB (7629 7034, www.graysantiques.com). Bond Street tube. Open 10am-6pm Mon-Fri; 11am-5pm Sat.

Hamleys Children
Visiting Hamleys is certainly an experience – whether a good one or not will depend on your tolerance for noisy, over-excited children. As you doubtless know, Hamleys is a ginormous toy shop, with attractive displays of all that season's must-have toys across five crazed floors, and perky demonstrators ramping up the temptation levels.
188-196 Regent Street, W1B 5BT (0871 704 1977, www.hamleys.com). Oxford Circus tube. Open 10am-8pm Mon-Fri; 9am-8pm Sat; noon-6pm Sun.

Liberty Department store
Charmingly idiosyncratic, Liberty is housed in a 1920s mock Tudor structure. The store was given a major revamp in early 2009, and

was given a further boost as the subject of a TV documentary series in 2013. The expanded beauty hall on the ground floor goes from strength to strength, with a perfumerie selling scents from cult brands such as Le Labo and Byredo, and skincare from the much-celebrated Egyptian Magic; the basement holds a Margaret Dabbs Sole Spa, for pedicures, polishing and shaping. At the main entrance to the store is Wild at Heart's exuberant floral concession, and just off from here you'll find yourself in a room devoted to the store's own label. Fashion brands focus on high-end British designers, such as Vivienne Westwood and Christopher Kane. But despite being up with the latest fashions, Liberty still respects its dressmaking heritage with a range of cottons in the third-floor haberdashery department. Stationery also pays homage to the traditional, with beautiful Liberty of London notebooks, address books and diaries embossed with the art nouveau 'Ianthe' print, while the interiors departments showcase new furniture designs alongside a dazzling collection of 20th-century classics. Artful and arresting window displays, exciting new collections and luxe labels make it an experience to savour.
Regent Street, W1B 5AH (7734 1234, www.liberty.co.uk). Oxford Circus tube. Open 10am-8pm Mon-Sat; noon-6pm Sun.

Paul Smith Sale Shop Fashion
Samples and previous season's stock are sold at a 30-50% discount at this sale shop. The varied stock includes clothes for men, women and children, as well as a range of accessories.

23 Avery Row, W1X 9HB (7493 1287, www.paulsmith.co.uk). Bond Street tube. Open 10.30am-6.30pm Mon-Wed, Fri, Sat; 10.30am-7pm Thur; noon-6pm Sun.

Postcard Teas Food & drink
The range in Timothy d'Offay's exquisite little shop is not huge, but it is selected with great care, and all teas are sourced from small co-operatives. There's a central table for those who want to try a pot; or book in for one of the tasting sessions held on Saturdays between 10am and 11am. Tea-ware and accessories are also sold.
9 Dering Street, W1S 1AG (7629 3654, www.postcardteas.com). Bond Street or Oxford Circus tube. Open 10.30am-6.30pm Mon-Sat.

Timothy Everest Fashion
One-time apprentice to the legendary Tommy Nutter, Everest is a star among the new generation of London tailors, with an international reputation for his relaxed 21st-century definition of style.
35 Bruton Place, W1J 6NS (7629 6236, www.timothyeverest.co.uk). Bond Street tube. Open 10am-6pm Mon-Fri; 11am-5pm Sat.

Westminster & St James's

DR Harris Health & beauty
Founded in 1790, this venerable chemist has a royal warrant. Wood-and-glass cabinets are full of bottles, jars and old-fashioned shaving brushes. The store is at 34 Bury Street while the St James's Street premises get a refurb. They are due to move back in mid 2015.

29 St James's Street, SW1A 1HB (7930 3915, www.drharris.co.uk). Green Park or Piccadilly Circus tube. Open 8.30am-6pm Mon-Fri; 10am-5pm Sat.

Fortnum & Mason Department store
In business for over 300 years, Fortnum & Mason is as historic as it is inspiring. A sweeping spiral staircase soars through the four-storey building, while light floods down from a central glass dome. The iconic eau de nil blue and gold colour scheme with flashes of rose pink abound on both the store design and the packaging of the fabulous ground-floor treats, such as chocolates, biscuits, teas and preserves. A food hall in the basement has a good range of fresh produce; Fortnum's Bees honey comes from beehives on top of the building. There are various eateries, including an ice-cream parlour. The famous hampers start from £40 – but rise to a whopping £5,000 for the most luxurious.
181 Piccadilly, W1A 1ER (7734 8040, wwww.fortnumandmason.co.uk). Green Park or Piccadilly Circus tube. Open 10am-8pm Mon-Sat; noon-6pm Sun.

Run & Become Health & beauty
The experienced staff here, most of them enthusiastic runners, will find the right pair of shoes for your physique and running style. The gamut of running kit, from clothing to speed monitors, is available.
42 Palmer Street, SW1H 0PH (7222 1314, www.runandbecome.com). St James's Park tube. Open 9am-6pm Mon-Wed, Sat; 9am-8pm Thur; 9am-7pm Fri.

Knightsbridge & Kensington

Conran Shop Homewares
Sir Terence Conran's flagship store in the Fulham Road's beautiful 1909 Michelin Building showcases furniture and design for every room in the house as well as the garden. As well as design classics, such as the Eames DAR chair, there are plenty of portable accessories, gadgets, books, stationery and toiletries that make great gifts or souvenirs.
Michelin House, 81 Fulham Road, South Kensington, SW3 6RD (7589 7401, www.conranshop.co.uk). South Kensington tube. Open 10am-6pm Mon, Tue, Fri; 10am-7pm Wed, Thur; 10am-6.30pm Sat; noon-6pm Sun.

Cutler & Gross Accessories
C&G celebrated its 40th anniversary in 2009, and its stock of handmade frames is still at the cutting edge of optical style. Stock runs from Andy Warhol-inspired glasses to naturally light buffalo-horn frames, and recent collaborations have included frames with trend-leaders Comme des Garçons.

Harvey Nichols

16 Knightsbridge Green, Knightsbridge, SW1X 7QL (7581 2250, www.cutlerandgross.com). Knightsbridge tube. Open 9.30am-7pm Mon-Sat; noon-5pm Sun.

Harrods Department store
All the glitz and marble can be a bit much, but in the store that boasts of selling everything, it's hard not to leave with at least one thing. In fact, it even sold itself in 2010: former owner Mohammed Al Fayed received a reported £1.5bn from Qatar Holdings for the place. It's on the fashion floors that Harrods really comes into its own, with a 10,000sq ft Designer Studio on the first floor, featuring well-edited collections from the heavyweights, including a revamped Chanel boutique. There's also an excellent lingerie section and a top-notch sport section. The legendary food halls and restaurants range even have a branch of 18th-century Venetian coffee bar Caffè Florian.
87-135 Brompton Road, Knightsbridge, SW1X 7XL (7730 1234, www.harrods.com). Knightsbridge tube. Open 10am-8pm Mon-Sat; noon-6pm Sun (browsing from 11.30am).

Harvey Nichols Department store
Harvey Nicks is coasting a little these days, but you'll still find a worthy clutch of unique fashion brands over the eight floors of beauty, fashion, food and homeware. The fashion floors showcase emerging British talent, new designers and established favourites. The fifth floor has the well-stocked food market and a branch of the Burger & Lobster minichain.
109-125 Knightsbridge, SW1X 7RJ (7235 5000, www.harveynichols.com). Knightsbridge tube. Open 10am-8pm Mon-Sat; noon-6pm Sun.

Tom Ford Fashion
Just when Sloane Street's reputation for boutiques that are expensive but hardly classy seemed secure, up rocks the coolest man in fashion. No one who knows Ford's suave tailoring will be surprised that his first stand-alone store in Britain is stunning, with an eye-catchingly sci-fi spiral staircase the centrepiece of an impressive 8,000sq ft of retail space. Expect big lapels for gents, hip-hugging skirts and dresses for ladies – and consummate good taste.
201-202 Sloane Street, SW1X 9QX (3141 7800, www.tomford.com). Knightsbridge tube. Open 10am-6pm Mon-Sat; 10am-7pm Sun.

Whole Foods Market Food & drink
The London flagship of the American health-food supermarket chain occupies the handsome deco building that was once Barkers department store. There are several eateries on the premises.
63-97 Kensington High Street, W8 5SE (7368 4500, www.wholefoodmarket.com). High Street Kensington tube. Open 8am-10pm Mon-Sat; 10am-6pm Sun.

Chelsea

The once-adventurous shops on the King's Road are now a mix of trendier-than-thou fashion houses and high-street chains, but there are still a few gems around: **Shop at Bluebird** and London's second branch of **Anthropologie** suggest future directions. Wander **Cale Street** for some pleasing boutiques, or head for the **Chelsea Farmers' Market** on adjoining Sydney Street to find a clutter of artfully distressed rustic sheds housing restaurants and shops selling everything from cigars to garden products.

John Sandoe Books & music
Tucked away on a side street, this 50-year-old independent always looked just as a bookshop should, with stock literally packed to the rafters – they used to say that of the 25,000 books here, 24,000 were a single copy, which is some serious breadth of stock. The shop was undergoing refurbishment in early 2014, but the enthusiasm and knowledge of the staff can be taken as, forgive us, read.
10 Blacklands Terrace, SW3 2SR (7589 9473, www.johnsandoe.com). Sloane Square tube. Open 9.30am-6.30pm Mon-Sat; 11am-5pm Sun.

Liz Earle Naturally Active Skincare Health & beauty
The London flagship of Liz Earle's botanical skincare range is housed in a large, light, fresh space, and stocks the full range of pleasingly gimmick-free and affordable products based on a regime of cleansing, toning and moisturising. Highlights among the products include the Instant Boost Skin Tonic and Superskin Moisturiser. 'Minis' and essentials packs are a great introduction (£14.75 for a starter kit).
38-39 Duke of York Square, SW3 4LY (7881 7750, http://uk.lizearle.com). Sloane Square tube. Open 10am-7pm Mon, Wed-Sat; 10.30am-7pm Tue; 11am-5pm Sun.

Shop at Bluebird Fashion & homewares
Part lifestyle boutique and part design gallery, the Shop at Bluebird offers a shifting showcase of clothing for men, women and children, furniture, accessories, books and gadgets. The shop has a retro feel, with vintage furniture and hand-printed fabrics. The menswear range is particularly strong.
350 King's Road, SW3 5UU (7351 3873, www.theshopatbluebird.com). Sloane Square tube. Open 10am-7pm Mon-Sat; noon-6pm Sun.

Notting Hill

Cowshed Health & beauty
The London branch of Cowshed (from Somerset's renowned hotel-spa Babington House) does its country cousin proud. The chic, white ground floor is buzzy, with a tiny café area on one side, and a manicure/pedicure section on the other. For facials, waxing and massages, head downstairs.
119 Portland Road, W11 4LN (7078 1944, www.cowshedclarendoncross.com). Holland Park tube. Open 9am-8pm Mon-Fri; 9am-7pm Sat; 10am-5pm Sun.

Honest Jon's Books & music
Honest Jon's found its way to Notting Hill in 1979, and the owner helped James Lavelle to set up Mo'Wax records. You'll find jazz, hip hop, soul, broken beat, reggae and Brazilian music, as well as the label's own brilliant compilations – the first volumes of the London is the Place for Me series, detailing calypso, Afro-jazz and highlife in the post-war years, were a revelation.
278 Portobello Road, W10 5TE (8969 9822, www.honestjons.com). Ladbroke Grove tube. Open 10am-6pm Mon-Sat; 11am-5pm Sun.

Idler Academy Books & music
Tom Hodgkinson has made a career out of being idle. He edits The Idler magazine, has written books on the subject and now runs this café/bookshop/centre of learning to spread the word further. It's a lovely place, with a tiny patio garden and ample space for lounging inside. The emphasis is not really on food. Stop in for a Monmouth filter coffee, or tea and a slice of cake, and take some intellectual nourishment from bookshelves packed with Plato, Virgil and ukuleles.
81 Westbourne Park Road, W2 5QH (0845 250 1281, www.idler.co.uk/academy). Royal Oak tube. Open 10am-6pm Wed-Sun.

Lutyens & Rubinstein Books & music
Lutyens & Rubinstein sells a beautifully arranged selection of literary fiction and general non-fiction. The core stock was put together by the owners canvassing hundreds of readers on the books they'd most like to find in a bookshop; thus every book stocked is sold because somebody has recommended it. The result is an appealing alternative to the homogeneous chain bookshops, with some unusual titles available. As well as books, the shop stocks a small range of stationery, greetings cards, paperweights, local honey and literary-inspired scents from CB I Hate Perfume.

Bags packed, milk cancelled, house raised on stilts.

You've packed the suntan lotion, the snorkel set, the stay-pressed shirts. Just one more thing left to do – your bit for climate change. In some of the world's poorest countries, changing weather patterns are destroying lives.

You can help people to deal with the extreme effects of climate change. Raising houses in flood-prone regions is just one life-saving solution.

Climate change costs lives.
Give £5 and let's sort it *Here & Now*

www.oxfam.org.uk/climate-change

Be Humankind  Oxfam

21 Kensington Park Road, W11 2EU (7229 1010, www.lutyens rubinstein.co.uk). Ladbroke Grove tube. Open 10am-6pm Mon, Sat; 10am-6.30pm Tue-Fri; 11am-6pm Sun.

Portobello Road Market Market

Best known for antiques and collectibles, this is actually several markets rolled into one: antiques start at the Notting Hill end; further up are food stalls; under the Westway and along the walkway to Ladbroke Grove are emerging designer and vintage clothes on Fridays (usually marginally less busy) and Saturdays (invariably manic).
Portobello Road, W10 (www.portobello road.co.uk). Ladbroke Grove or Notting Hill Gate tube. Open General 9am-6pm Mon-Wed; 9am-1pm Thur; 7am-7pm Fri, Sat. Antiques 6am-4pm Fri, Sat. No credit cards.

Sasti Children

This affordable children's boutique sells delightfully fun clothes for little girls and boys. Perennial bestsellers include the bunny dresses, flower-covered skirts, bus pyjamas, nursery rhyme blouses and kitten scarves. Apart from its own-label clothes, Sasti also stocks items from Pixie Dixie.
6 Portobello Green Arcade, 281 Portobello Road, Notting Hill, W10 5TZ (8960 1125, www.sasti.co.uk). Ladbroke Grove tube. Open 10am-6pm Mon-Sat; noon-5pm Sun.

North London

Islington isn't the shopping area it once was – many of the boutiques have vanished to be replaced by chainstores – but Upper Street still rewards a stroll, and Camden Market is much improved.

Camden Market Market

Camden Market actually refers to the microcosm of markets that make up the northern Camden Town area – more than 700 shops and stalls in all. The Camden Market is the place for neon sunglasses and pseudo-witty slogan garments. Almost next door, and perennially threatened by proposed tube station expansions, is the listed building the Electric Ballroom, which sells vinyl and CDs on weekends and is also a music venue. The Inverness Street Market opposite sells similar garb to the Camden Market as well as a diminishing supply of fruit and veg. North, next to the railway bridge, is Camden Lock, with stalls selling crafts, home furnishings, jewellery, toys and gifts – head into the West Yard for global food. There are further crafty doodahs, fashion and nibbles in the Camden Lock Village, which runs along the towpath.
Camden Lock Camden Lock Place, off Chalk Farm Road, NW1 8AF (7485 7963, www.camdenlockmarket.com). Open 10am-6pm daily. Note: there are fewer stalls Mon-Fri.

Camden Market

Camden Lock Village east of Chalk Farm Road, NW1 (www.camden lock.net). Open 10am-6pm daily. Camden Market Camden High Street, at Buck Street, NW1 (www.camdenmarkets.org). Open 10am-5.30pm Thur-Sun. Inverness Street Market Inverness Street, NW1 (www.camdenlock.net/ inverness). Open 8.30am-5pm daily. Stables Market off Chalk Farm Road, opposite Hartland Road, NW1 8AH (7485 5511, www.stables market.com). Open 10.30am-6pm Mon-Fri (reduced stalls); 10am-6pm Sat, Sun. All Camden Town or Chalk Farm tube.

Flashback Books & music

Stock is scrupulously organised at this second-hand treasure trove. The ground floor is dedicated to CDs, while the basement is vinyl-only: an ever-expanding jazz collection jostles for space alongside soul, hip hop and a carpal tunnel-compressing selection of library sounds. A range of rarities is pinned in plastic sleeves to the walls. The shop also sells new vinyl.
50 Essex Road, Islington, N1 8LR (7354 9356, www.flashback.co.uk). Angel tube then bus 38, 56, 73, 341. Open 10am-7pm Mon-Sat; 11.30am-6pm Sun.

Smug Homewares

Graphic designer Lizzie Evans has decked out this lovely lifestyle boutique with all her favourite things. You'll be treated to a well-edited selection of home accessories (owl ceramic candlesticks, say), plus vintage homewares (Welsh blankets, 1960s Formica furniture, colourful cushions, Pixie make-up, home-made brooches, old-fashioned notebooks, retro Casio watches and a range of graphic-print men's T-shirts.

13 Camden Passage, Islington, N1 8EA (7354 0253, www.ifeelsmug. com). Angel tube. Open noon-5pm Tue, Sun; 11am-6pm Wed, Fri, Sat; noon-7pm Thur.

East London

Ally Capellino Accessories

This shop stocks the full range of Ally Capellino's stylishly understated unisex leather and waxed cotton bags, satchels, wallets, purses and laptop cases. Prices start at around £40 for a cute leather coin purse, rising to over £600 for larger, more structured models. There's a second branch in Notting Hill (312 Portobello Road, W10 5RU, 8964 1022).
9 Calvert Avenue, E2 7JP (7033 7843, www.allycapellino.co.uk). Shoreditch High Street rail. Open 11am-6pm Tue-Sat; 11am-5pm Sun.

Aquascutum Fashion

The Aquascutum outlet shop is bang opposite Burberry's factory shop (29-31 Chatham Place, E9 6LP, 8328 4287) – meaning it gets a nice cut of the tourist traffic that comes to this unlikely spot in east London. In many ways, the Aquascutum store is superior to its neighbour. For a start, it's cheaper – a perfect cashmere knit is around £70 (down from £230) and a classic Harrington jacket is £150 (from £300). And, unlike other sale shops, this one has the feel of a luxury store. Nearby, the Pringle of Scotland Outlet, (86 Morning Lane, E9 6NA, www.pringlescotland.com), and an Anya Hindmarch (2 Chatham Place, E9 6LL, www.anyahindmarch.com) are turning this area into something of an outlet hub – which it's set to become literally with the go-ahead for a David Adjaye-designed, Bicester Village-style building, called the Hackney Fashion Hub.

7-8 Chatham Place, E9 6LT (3478 0928, www.aquascutum.co.uk). Hackney Central or Homerton rail. Open 10am-6.30pm Mon-Fri; 9am-6pm Sat; 11am-5pm Sun.

Artwords Books & music

Artwords has its finger firmly on the pulse when it comes to contemporary visual arts publications. Stock relating to contemporary fine art dominates, but there are also plenty of architecture, photography, graphic design, fashion, advertising and film titles on display, plus an excellent range of industry and creative magazines.
20-22 Broadway Market, E8 4QJ (7923 7507, www.artwords.co.uk). London Fields rail. Open 10.30am-6.30pm Mon-Fri; 10am-6pm Sat; noon-6pm Sun.

Bernstock Speirs Accessories

Paul Bernstock and Thelma Speirs's unconventional hats for men and women have a loyal following, being both wearable and fashion-forward. Past ranges have included collaborations with Peter Jensen and Emma Cook.
234 Brick Lane, E2 7EB (7739 7385, www.bernstockspeirs.com). Shoreditch High Street rail. Open 10am-6pm Mon-Fri; 11am-5pm Sat, Sun.

Black Truffle Fashion

Quirky, stylish yet wearable footwear for women, men and children. Look out in particular for shoes by Melissa and Falke. The shop also stocks bags from the likes of Abro, a small range of clothing, and tasteful accessories (such as Falke tights, Dents gloves, hats and affordable jewellery).
4 Broadway Market, E8 4QJ (7923 9450, www.blacktruffle.co.uk). London Fields rail or bus 394. Open 11am-6pm Tue-Fri; 10am-6pm Sat; noon-6pm Sun.

Blitz **Fashion**

Blitz puts the other vintage shops in the capital to shame. This is a vintage department store, covering all floors of a glorious old furniture factory. The building itself is jaw-dropping, and has been renovated beautifully by the Blitz team. There's a furniture selection from Broadway Market's the Dog & Wardrobe, an accessories floor, a book collection and rails and rails of neatly presented fashion. Buyers Jan Skinners and John Howlin look to nearby Brick Lane for inspiration, which means the selection is all killer and no filler – and cleaned, steamed and folded before it hits the shop floor.
55-59 Hanbury Street, E1 5JP (7377 0730, www.blitzlondon.co.uk). Shoreditch High Street rail. Open 11am-7pm Mon-Wed; 11am-8pm Thur-Sat; 11am-7pm Sun.

Boxpark **Mall**

Refitted shipping containers plonked underneath the elevated Shoreditch High Street Overground station make up this contemporary 'shopping mall'. Installed in 2011, the units of Boxpark are full of high-street labels (Puma, Nike), but also contain an impressive array of independents, cafés and pop-ups. Food stalls are open from 8am (or 10am on Sundays).
2-4 Bethnal Green Road, E1 6GY (7033 9441, www.boxpark.co.uk). Shoreditch High Street rail. Open 11am-7pm Mon-Wed, Fri, Sat; 11am-8pm Thur; noon-6pm Sun.

Broadway Market **Market**

For a fashion show and farmers' market rolled into one, Hackney's Broadway Market on Saturday far outdoes anything on offer at London's other market sites. Its winning mix of great streetfood, well-edited vintage clothing, quirky homeware and glorous cakes and food stalls draw thousands of hip young things, and the effect is spreading to radiating streets, with indie fashion retailers setting up shop in nearby streets, including Duncan Road. Round the corner on Westgate Street, the schoolyard market offers more of the same on Saturday and a farmers' market on Sunday.
Broadway Market, E8 4PH (www.broadwaymarket.co.uk). London Fields rail. Open 8am-4pm Sat.

Celestine Eleven **Fashion**

This vast fashion store and holistic treatment centre is a dreamy place, with a focus on pure living and elegant style brands that's more the sort of boutique you'd see in West London. Owner and former stylist Tena Strok has sourced interesting labels from Paris, London and Scandinavia, hoping that her own taste chimes with her customers'. It certainly chimes with us – on our visit, the shelves were stocked with London's finest, from techy shoe designer Joanne Stoker to IT designer of the minute JW Anderson. The basement houses pop-up events, treatment rooms and even fashion-focused book groups for those that take good living seriously. Celestine Eleven is an example of independent shopping at its best, at a time when Shoreditch is at risk of being taken over by chain brands keen to cash in on its cool.
4 Holywell Lane, Shoreditch, EC2A 3ET (7729 2987, www.celestine eleven.com). Shoreditch High Street rail. Open 11am-7pm Mon-Sat; noon-5pm Sun.

Columbia Road Market **Market**

On Sunday mornings, this unassuming East End street is transformed into a swathe of fabulous plant life and the air is fragrant with blooms and the shouts of old-school Cockney stallholders (most offering deals for 'a fiver'). But a visit here isn't only about flowers and pot plants: alongside the market is a growing number of shops selling everything from pottery and arty prints to cupcakes and perfume; don't miss Ryantown's delicate paper cut-outs at no.126 (7613 1510). Refuel at Jones Dairy (23 Ezra Street, 7739 5372, www.jonesdairy.co.uk) or at Brawn (*see p67*).
Columbia Road, Hoxton, E2 (www.columbiaroad.info). Hoxton rail or bus 26, 48, 55. Open 8am-3pm Sun.

Comfort Station **Accessories**

Fine art graduate and designer Amy Anderson is the creative talent behind this ladylike Cheshire Street boutique. Offbeat touches, such as birds painted on the door and a piano-turned-display cabinet, provide the ideal environment to showcase her handmade accessories. Alongside the beautiful, ethically made bags and bone-china crockery covered in wonderfully weird collaged prints is her jewellery line. The collection changes each season, with classically elegant but original designs in gold, silver, cord, wood and onyx. Favourites include 'Sliced Poetry' range (delicate leaf-shaped 'books' that fan open to reveal pages of Victorian poetry), and Anderson's 'Globe' pendants – moveable silver rings that form a clever 3D sphere.
22 Cheshire Street, E2 6EH (7033 9099, www.comfort station.co.uk). Liverpool Street tube/rail or Shoreditch High Street rail. Open 11am-6pm Tue-Sun.

Goodhood Store **Fashion**

A first stop for East End trendies, Goodhood is owned by streetwear obsessives Kyle and Jo. Japanese independent labels are well represented, while other covetable brands include Pendleton, Norse Projects and Wood Wood.
41 Coronet Street, N1 6HD (7729 3600, www.goodhood.co.uk). Old Street tube/rail. Open 11am-6.30pm Mon-Sat; noon-5pm Sun.

House of Hackney **Homewares**

House of Hackney has the makings of a new Liberty: buy your future design classics now, we say. This is one of the most gorgeous retail establishments to land in London in years – bedecked in the deliberately over-the-top juxtapositions of print-on-print-on-print that have made the brand's name, and with the entrance full of flowers. Upstairs you'll find rolls of gorgeous paper, fabric, trays, mugs, fashion and collaborative designs with brands such as Puma; downstairs are generously proportioned sofas and plump armchairs in more-is-more combinations of print and texture. *See also p8.*
131 Shoreditch High Street, E1 6JE (7739 3901, www.houseofhackney. com). Old Street tube/rail or Shoreditch High Street rail. Open 10am-7.30pm Mon-Sat; 11am-5pm Sun.

Labour & Wait **Homewares**

This retro-stylish store, on London's ultra-trendy Redchurch Street, sells the sort of things everybody would have had in their kitchen or pantry 60 years ago: functional domestic goods that have a timeless style. For the kitchen there are some great simple classics such as enamel milk pans in retro pastels, and lovely 1950s-inspired Japanese teapots, and you can garden beautifully with ash-handled trowels. Vintage Welsh wool blankets, classic toiletries, and some great old-fashioned gifts, such as a pinhole camera kit and a lovely range of handmade notebooks from Portugal, make it hard to leave empty-handed. Labour & Wait also has a space at concept store Dover Street Market (*see p82*).
85 Redchurch Street, E2 7DJ (7729 6253, www.labourandwait.co.uk). Shoreditch High Street rail. Open 11am-6pm Tue-Sun.

TOP TIP!
Second best?
Now overshadowed by **Blitz** (*see left*), **Beyond Retro** (112 Cheshire Street, E2 6EJ, 7613 3636, www.beyondretro.com) is still worth a rummage.

Goodhood Store

LN-CC Fashion

LN-CC, otherwise known as the Late Night Chameleon Club, is as mysterious as its name suggests. Accessed by appointment via a basement-level door in an unlikely Shacklewell warehouse building, the store is a Tim Burton-like wonderland rendered in natural wood with a secret dancefloor, tree house, listening library and London's most unique edit of super-rare fashion. Ostensibly a showroom for internet boutique LN-CC.com, the space is a gallery for upscale design, selling super-posh brands like Rik Owens, Givenchy, Lanvin and any number of hard-to-pronounce rarities (try saying shoe brand 'Cherevichkiotvichki' after one too many shandies). With vinyl, art books and eyewear, and stock separated into different themed zones, LN-CC is a shop like no other. *18-24 Shacklewell Lane, E8 2EZ (3174 0726, www.ln-cc.com). Dalston Kingsland rail. Open by appointment only.*

Present Menswear

Owners Eddie Prendergast and Steve Davies are founders of men's mega-brand Duffer of St George, but don't hold that against them. Present's bright white, clinical interior houses labels from funky William Fox & Sons jackets to Les Garcons Faciles shirts and Nanamica outerwear. With Eddie and Steve's collection of knits and T-shirts already on the rails, the pair plans to roll out collaborations and limited edition pieces. Good coffee too. *140 Shoreditch High St, E1 6JE (7033 0500, www.present-london. com). Old Street tube/rail. Open 10am-7pm Mon-Sat; 12.30-5.30pm Sun.*

Rough Trade East
Books & music

Indie music label Rough Trade's 5,000sq ft record store, café and gig space offers a dizzying range of vinyl and CDs, spanning punk, indie, dub, soul, electronica and more. With 16 listening posts and a stage for live sets, this is close to musical nirvana. The second, smaller Rough Trade in west London (130 Talbot Road, Notting Hill, W11 1JA, 7229 8541) has been on the same spot since the early 1980s. *Dray Walk, Old Truman Brewery, 91 Brick Lane, E1 6QL (7392 7788, www.roughtrade.com). Shoreditch High Street rail. Open 8am-9pm Mon-Thur; 8am-8pm Fri; 10am-8pm Sat; 11am-7pm Sun.*

Sunspel Fashion

It may look like a trendy east London newcomer, but Sunspel is actually a classic British label, which has been producing quality menswear for over 150 years. It even claims to have introduced boxer shorts to the UK. This corner space showcases the range of underwear, T-shirts, merino wool knitwear and polo shirts, as well as the smaller line of equally pared-down womenswear.

7 Redchurch Street, E2 7DJ (7739 9729, www.sunspel.com). Shoreditch High Street rail. Open 11am-7pm Mon-Sat; noon-5pm Sun.

Two Columbia Road Homewares

Well-selected 20th-century pieces are the order of the day here, whether it's 1970s chrome pendant lights, Danish 1960s rosewood desks, or Charles Eames wooden chairs. The corner site is owned by Tommy Roberts and run by his son Keith. Expect to find well-known names such as Arne Jacobsen and Willy Rizzo among the stock as well as more affordable pieces. *2 Columbia Road, E2 7NN (7729 9933, www.twocolumbiaroad.com). Hoxton or Shoreditch High Street rail. Open noon-7pm Wed-Fri; noon-6pm Sat; 10am-4pm Sun.*

Vintage Emporium Fashion

With a well-edited range of clothing (in the basement) from the Victorian era to the 1950s, this café-shop's vintage time frame is somewhat tighter than that of its nearby rivals, but maybe it's all the better for it. Beautiful lace blouses, 1950s dresses, great hats, and top-notch accessories are all for sale; prices are high, but – considering the age of most of the items – reasonable. *14 Bacon Street, E1 6LF (7739 0799, www.vintageemporiumcafe.com). Shoreditch High Street rail. Open Shop 11am-7pm Mon-Fri; 10am-7pm Sat, Sun. Café 11am-10pm Mon-Fri; 10am-10pm Sat, Sun.*

Westfield Stratford City Mall

This £1.45bn retail behemoth snakes through what was the London Olympic site, with 300 retail units – including gigantic branches of high-street brands John Lewis, Marks & Spencer and Waitrose – 70 restaurants, bars and cafés, and a 17-screen digital cinema. *Great Eastern Road, E20 (8221 7300, www.westfield.com/stratfordcity). Stratford tube/DLR/rail. Open 10am-9pm Mon-Fri; 9am-9pm Sat; noon-6pm Sun.*

South-east London

Greenwich Market Market

Reprieved in late 2012 from the long-running threat of redevelopment, Greenwich Market can trace its origins to 1737 – although the current covered building dates only to the 19th century. Tuesdays, Thursdays and Fridays up to 120 stalls are dominated by antiques (including classic 20th-century pieces); Tuesdays, Wednesdays and weekends are for the craftier end of things. There is also a cluster of shops dedicated to art, fashion and jewellery – even a stall run by Alex Pittas, 'the Urban Magician'. If you're flagging, there is plenty of street food. *King William Walk, SE10 9HZ (8269 5090, www.greenwichmarket london.com). Cutty Sark DLR. Open 10am-5.30pm Tue-Sun.*

South-west London

Brixton Village Mall

Once almost forgotten, Granville Arcade has found a new lease of life. It originally opened in 1937, when it was proclaimed 'London's Largest Emporium', but by the 1960s had become a Caribbean market. But by the 1990s, many of the arcade's units were unoccupied and its old art deco avenues were falling into a dilapidated state. In 2009, Lambeth Council called in urban regeneration agency Space Makers, which launched a competition for local entrepreneurs to apply for a unit. It then awarded the best initiatives a place on site, and renamed the space Brixton Village, in line with its eclectic, locally minded new contents – from bijoux bakeries and vintage boutiques to international eateries and fledgling fashion labels. Highlights here include Margot Waggoner's Leftovers (unit 71), with its Marseille lace and vintage sailor dresses, and Binkie and Tabitha's Circus (unit 70), which juxtaposes retro glassware with an assortment of socialist literature. *Corner of Coldharbour Lane & Brixton Station Road, SW9 8PR (7274 2990, http://brixtonmarket.net). Brixton tube/rail. Open 6am-6pm Mon; 6am-11.30pm Tue-Sun; check website for opening hours of individual shops.*

Brixton Village

BRIXTON VILLAGE: ALYS TOMLINSON

Arts & Entertainment

For live arts, nights on the town and fun for the kids

Children

London Transport Museum

Big fun for little ones

London has all the playdate possibilities and playgrounds you could wish for.

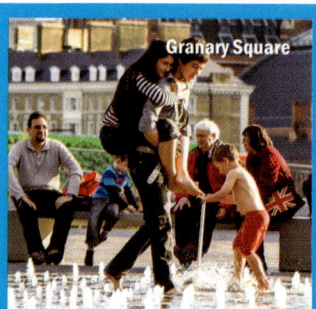

Granary Square

Critic's choice

1 **South Ken museums** Your offspring won't find more fun for free. Arrive early to avoid the queues. See p45.

2 **Emirates Air Line** Useless as public transport, great for the kids. See p49.

3 **Diana, Princess of Wales Memorial Playground** Sand, pirate ship, no unaccompanied grown-ups – the city's best playground. See p93.

4 **British Museum** One word: mummies. Oh, and Romans. And… See p90.

5 **Granary Square** Not just fountains to play in, but neon lights too. See p30.

London has a lot to offer young visitors. Its museums go out of their way to engage the minds of children with enjoyable events, there are gorgeous parks and playgrounds, brilliant theatres with child-oriented productions and world-famous attractions. Many of these, such as the Natural History Museum and the Science Museum, are free; many of those that aren't, such as the Tower of London, give you a lot of fun for your entry fee.

Plan carefully, but don't try to cram too much into one day. Sometimes, the most fun happens in the gaps between the official itinerary – lots of kids get a big kick just from using public transport.

For children's festivals and family-friendly events, see pp10-12 **Diary**.

Where to go

SOUTH BANK & BANKSIDE

This is one of the all-time favourite spots for a family day out in London. Just strolling along the wide riverside promenade will lead you past skateboarders, installations, street artists, book stalls and, often, free performances. The expensive end is around **London Eye** (see p17), **London Aquarium** (see p17) and the **London Dungeon** (see p16). Moving east, visit the **Southbank Centre** (see p106), where free shows and workshops take place in holidays and weekends in the Clore Ballroom. Don't miss Jeppe Hein's *Appearing Rooms* play fountains in summer. Next, the **National Theatre** (see p107) usually offers free entertainment outside through the hotter months.

Keep going along the riverbank, past Gabriel's Wharf, a riverside cluster of restaurants and shops, to reach **Tate Modern** (see p18). Tate Modern is a day out in itself, with its dramatic Turbine Hall, free family trails and a Bloomberg Learning Zone on Level 5. At weekends and in school holidays, age-appropriate activity packs are available from Level 3. (There's a boat service from here to **Tate Britain**; see p40.)

Once you've emerged, pick up the Bankside Walk, ducking under the southern end of Southwark Bridge. Walk down cobbly Clink Street towards the **Golden Hinde** (see p18) and **Southwark Cathedral**, having passed the **Clink Prison Museum**, a cheaper alternative to the London Dungeon. From Tooley Street, march through Hays Galleria to regain the riverside path, which takes you to the excellent warship museum **HMS Belfast** (see p18) and on, past the dancing fountains, to City Hall and **Tower Bridge** (see p27).

THE CITY

It seems pricey, but the **Tower of London** (see p27) is a top day out for all ages. If it is free stuff you're after, though, the **Museum of London** (see p24) is superb. Its Galleries of Modern London put interactivity and drama at the heart of exciting exhibits, but there are dressing-up boxes throughout, and lots of story-telling sessions and workshops. Nearby, in the **Bank of England**

Museum (see p24), kids can try to lift a gold bar – by reaching into an otherwise sealed box, so no bank heist is possible.

KINGS CROSS & BLOOMSBURY

Children are captivated by the mummies at the **British Museum** (see p29). However, the size of the collection can make it overwhelming. The beautifully produced and well-conceived free trails take a theme and lead families around an edited selection (available in the Paul Hamlyn Library). Alternatively, there are regular events and workshops or free backpacks for kids, filled with puzzles and games. For weekends and school holidays, the Ford Centre for Young Visitors provides a picnic-style eating area.

Central London's best playground, **Coram's Fields** (see p93), is close, and the nearby **Foundling Museum** (see p29) is well worth a visit to learn how orphans used to be treated.

Futher play opportunities are to be found a 15-minute walk north at King's Cross, where the lovely illuminated fountains of **Granary Square** (*see p30*) can be frolicked through, and there's the green tranquillity of **Camley Street nature reserve** (*see p93*) just across the canal.

COVENT GARDEN & THE STRAND
At the lively **London Transport Museum** (*see p31*), children can make believe they are driving a bus or riding in a horse-drawn carriage. They love the numbered stamp trail too. The museum also has a programme of school-holiday events. Across the Piazza, the acts in front of **St Paul's Covent Garden** (*see p30*) are worth watching. On the south side of the Strand, **Somerset House** (*see p31*) allows kids to play outside among the fountains in summer and skate on the winter ice rink. There are also regular art workshops.

TRAFALGAR SQUARE
London's central square (www.london.gov.uk/trafalgarsquare) has been a free playground for children since time immemorial – watch out for the imperious, bright-blue cock (on the Fourth Plinth until Feb 2015). Festivals take place most weekends. Even if all is quiet in the square, the **National Gallery** (*see p38*) has paper trails and audio tours, as well as workshops for teens and three- to five-year-olds. For five- to 11-year-olds, the **National Portrait Gallery** (*see p38*) runs Family Art Workshops at weekends and during the school holidays.

Just nearby, **St Martin-in-the-Fields** (*see p38*) has London's only brass-rubbing centre, as well as a fine café that does plenty of the type of food that goes down well with children.

SOUTH KENSINGTON
Top of any Grand Day Out itinerary is this cultural goldmine. The **Science Museum** (*see p45*) offers heaps of excitement, with six play zones for all ages, from the Garden in the basement for under-sixes to the new Atmosphere gallery upstairs, where children can use touchscreens to learn about climate change. Dinosaur fans won't rest until they've visited the **Natural History Museum** (*see p45*), and seen the animatronic beasties in action. An ice rink in winter also draw the crowds. The **Victoria & Albert Museum** (*see p45*) marks interactive displays on its floorplan. Its free weekend and school holiday drop-in family events (featuring trails, activity backpacks, and interactive workshops) provide great ways of focusing on the collection. (Its sister gallery, Bethnal Green's **V&A Museum of Childhood**, *see p48*, has an excellent programme of events for children.) The same rule applies for all of them, but especially the Science Museum and NHM: arrive as early in the day as you can to avoid the screaming throngs.

GREENWICH
Greenwich provides a lovely day out away from the mayhem of the West End. Arrive by boat to appreciate its riverside charms, then take time to check out the restored **Cutty Sark** (*see p50*) and excellent **Discover Greenwich** (*see p50*). Next, head to the very child-friendly **National Maritime Museum** (*see p50*), where there's a boat simulator to pilot and a whole room of interactives. From here it's a pleasant leg-stretch in the Royal Park for views from the top of the hill, crowned by the **Royal Observatory & Planetarium** (*see p51*). When the stars come out, keep an eye out for the luminous green Meridian Line that cuts across the sky towards the city.

Further north, the **Emirates Air Line cable car** (*see p49*) is an exciting way to cross the river. It runs from North Greenwich tube to the Royal Victoria Dock DLR.

Eating & drinking

Other restaurants particularly suitable for children include **Inn the Park** and **Gallery Mess** (for both, *see p65*).

Big Red Bus
Kids love this pizzeria – inside an old double-decker bus. You can either sit inside, or on the pretty decked terrace. It's beside the DLR, so travel is easy, and the nearby Creekside Centre (*see p93*) makes a good excursion. *30 Deptford Church Street, Deptford, SE8 4RZ (3490 8346, www.bigred pizza.co.uk). Deptford Bridge DLR. Open 5-10.30pm Tue, Wed; 5-11pm Fri; noon-1am Sat; noon-6.30pm Sun. Main courses £6.50-£11.*

Frizzante@Hackney City Farm
Trot around the pigs, poultry and sheep outside, then settle down to eat their relatives (or stick to vegetarian options). The oilcloth-covered tables heave with families tucking into healthy nosh, including big breakfasts. *1A Goldsmith's Row, Hackney, E2 8QA (7739 2266, www.frizzanteltd.co.uk). Hoxton rail. Open 10am-4.30pm Tue, Sat, Sun; 10am-10pm Wed, Fri; 10am-4pm, 7-11pm Thur. Main courses £7.50-£14.*

Gracelands
While many places claim to be child-friendly, this café really means it, with its toy-filled play area, a healthy tots-own menu (£3.70 for the likes of pasta bolognese or sausage and mash), and chefs cooing at high-chair diners from the open-plan kitchen. For grown-ups, the burger, made from 21-day matured beef, has proper foodie pedigree and the salads are unfailingly excellent. *118 College Road, Kensal Green, NW10 5HD (8964 9161, www.gracelandscafe.com). Kensal Green tube/rail. Open 8.30am-4.30pm Mon-Fri; 9am-4.30pm Sat; 9.30am-2.30pm Sun. Main courses £7-£13.*

Mudchute Kitchen
A farm fenced in by skyscrapers is an amusing place for anyone to eat lunch, but Mudchute is ideal for families. You can eat at farmhouse kitchen tables in the courtyard, while your babies roll around on a big futon or in the toy corner, or in the spacious interior. Frizzante (*see above*) took over in 2011, which means the food is excellent. *Mudchute Park & Farm, Pier Street, Isle of Dogs, Docklands, E14 3HP (3069 9290, www.mudchute.org). Mudchute DLR. Open 9.30am-4pm Fri-Sun. Main courses £2.50-£9.*

Science Museum

Rainforest Café
This themed restaurant is designed to thrill children with animatronic wildlife, cascading waterfalls and jungle sound-effects. The menu has lots of family-friendly fare, from 'paradise pizza' and 'Bamba's bangers' to amusing dishes for grown-ups. The children's menu costs £12.50 for two courses. *20 Shaftesbury Avenue, Piccadilly, W1D 7EU (7434 3111, www.the rainforestcafe.co.uk). Piccadilly Circus tube. Open noon-10pm Mon-Fri; 11.30am-8pm Sat; 11.30am-10pm Sun. During school holidays the restaurant is open at 11.30am every day. Main courses £12.95-£18.90.*

Tate Modern Café
In addition to views from the windows framing the busy River Thames, there are literacy and art activities on the junior menu, handed out with a pot of crayons. Children can choose haddock fingers with chips, pasta bolognese with parmesan or a ham and cheese bake with focaccia, finished off with ice-cream or a fruit salad; a free children's main is offered when an adult orders a regular main. There is also a 'teen menu' of reduced-price dishes from the adult menu. *Tate Modern, Sumner Street, Bankside, SE1 9TG (7401 5014, www.tate.org.uk). Southwark tube or London Bridge tube/rail. Open 10am-5.30pm Mon-Thur; 10am-8.30pm Fri; 9am-6.30pm Sat; 9am-5.30pm Sun. Main courses £7.50-£13.*

That Place on the Corner
London's only child-friendly café that won't allow unaccompanied grown-ups to enter. Even better, children's needs are provided for by a library, a puppet theatre, two play areas and a dressing-up corner, as well as classes in baking, dance and music. The menu sticks to the trusted formula of pasta, panini and big breakfasts, but also offers some brasserie staples. *1-3 Green Lanes, Stoke Newington, N16 9BS (7704 0079, www.thatplace onthecorner.co.uk). Canonbury rail then bus 73, 141, 341. Open 9.15am-6pm Mon-Fri; 9.30am-3pm Sat. Closes Sat for functions; phone ahead. Main courses £4.50-£8.50.*

Entertainment

CITY FARMS & ZOOS
There's always something new at **ZSL London Zoo** (*see p35*); the admission charge seems high, but it's a guaranteed winner. Easier on the budget is the adorable **Battersea Park Children's Zoo** (www.batterseaparkzoo.co.uk), where ring-tailed lemurs, giant rabbits, inquisitive meerkats and kune kune pigs are among the inhabitants.

City farms all over London charge nothing to get in. Try **Freightliners City Farm** (www.freightlinersfarm.org.uk) and **Kentish Town City Farm** (www.aapi.co.uk/cityfarm) or, in the

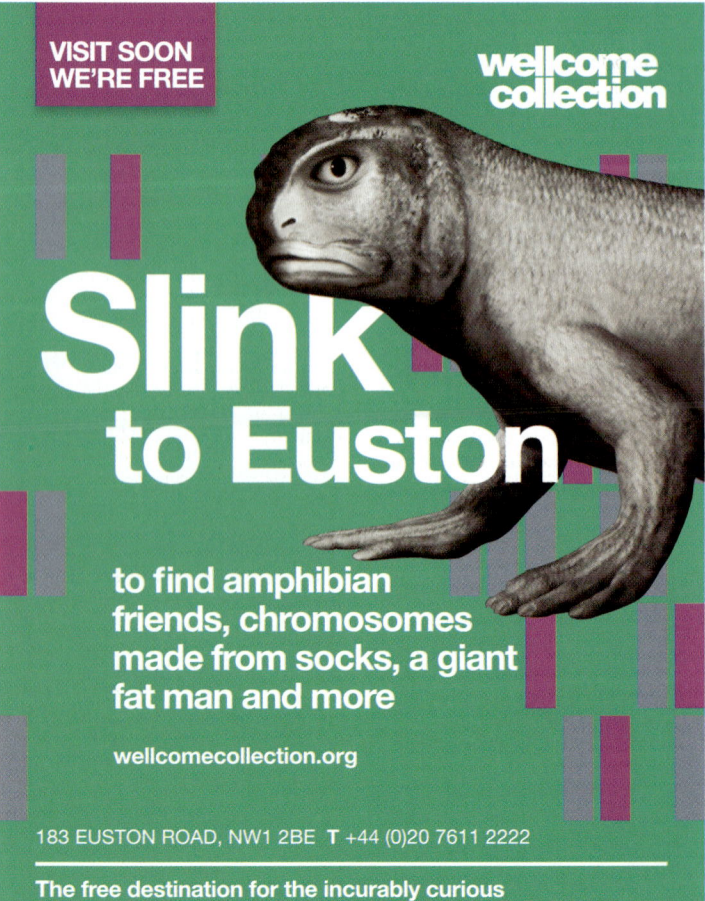

east, **Mudchute City Farm** (www. mudchute.org) and **Hackney City Farm** (www.hackneycityfarm.co.uk), both of which have terrific cafés (for both, *see pp91*).

Little Angel Theatre

London's only permanent puppet theatre is set in a charming old Victorian temperance hall. All aspects of puppetry are covered, with themes, styles and stories drawn from a broad array of traditions. There's a Saturday Puppet Club and a youth puppet theatre. Shows are often for fives and above.
14 Dagmar Passage, off Cross Street, Islington, N1 2DN (7226 1787, www.littleangeltheatre.com). Angel tube or Highbury & Islington tube/rail. Box office 10am-6pm Mon-Fri; 9am-4pm Sat, Sun. Tickets £5-£14.

Puppet Theatre Barge

This intimate waterborne stage is the setting for quality puppet shows that put a modern twist on traditional tales, such as Mr Rabbit meets Brer Santa and The Flight of Babuscha Baboon. The barge is moored here between October and July; shows themselves are held at 3pm on Saturday and Sunday, and daily during school holidays, plus some matinées. During the summer, the barge also holds performances in Richmond.
Opposite 35 Blomfield Road, Little Venice, W9 2PF (07836 202745 summer, 7249 6876 winter, www.puppetbarge.com). Warwick Avenue tube. Box office 10am-6pm daily. Tickets £10; £8.50 reductions.

SCIENCE & NATURE

FREE Camley Street Natural Park

A small but thriving green space on the site of a former coal yard, Camley Street is near the heart of the renovated King's Cross. London Wildlife Trust's flagship reserve, it hosts pond-dipping and nature-watching sessons for children, and its wood-cabin visitor centre is used by the Wildlife Watch Club.
12 Camley Street, King's Cross, N1C 4PW (7833 2311, www.wildlondon. org.uk). King's Cross tube/rail. Open 10am-5pm Mon-Fri, Sun (closes at 4pm in winter). Admission free.

Creekside Centre

Deptford Creek is a tributary of the Thames and this centre allows visitors to explore its surprisingly diverse wildlife and rich heritage. Low-tide walks take place on selected weekend days for accompanied eight-year-olds and above and there's also a programme of puppet theatre. Events vary (and some charge a fee), so phone ahead for the programme.
14 Creekside, Greenwich, SE8 4SA (8692 9922, www.creeksidecentre. org.uk). Deptford Bridge or Greenwich DLR, or bus 53, 177, 188. Open phone for details. Admission free.

WWT Wetland Centre

This wetland reserve is one of London's best-kept secrets. If you can get children past the giant snakes and ladders game (with giant dice), there are 104 acres for them to stretch their legs in, along paths that take them past the main lake, reed beds, ponds and wetland meadows, as well as one of the best playgrounds in London. A series of interactive exhibits exploring the environment was added in 2010.
Queen Elizabeth's Walk, Barnes, SW13 9WT (8409 4400, www.wwt. org.uk/london). Hammersmith tube then bus 33, 72, 209 (alight at Red Lion pub). Open Summer 9.30am-6pm daily. Winter 9.30am-5pm daily. Admission £11.65 (incl donation); £8.70 reductions; £6.50 4-16s; free under-4s; £32.50 family (2+2). Tours free.

THEATRE

Polka Theatre

This children's theatre pioneer has been up and running since 1979. Daily shows are staged by touring companies in the main auditorium, while shorter works for babies and toddlers take over at the Adventure Theatre once a week.
240 Broadway, Merton, SW19 1SB (8543 4888, www.polkatheatre.com). South Wimbledon tube or Wimbledon tube/rail, then bus 57, 93, 219, 493. Box office (by phone and in person) 9.30am-4.30pm Tue-Fri; 10am-4.30pm Sat; noon-4.30pm Sun. Tickets £9-£16.

Unicorn Theatre

This light, bright building, with a huge white unicorn in the foyer, has two performance spaces. Its small ensemble company performs in all shows and focuses on an outreach programme for local children.
147 Tooley Street, Bankside, SE1 2HZ (7645 0560, www.unicorn theatre.com). London Bridge tube/ rail. Box office 9.30am-6pm Mon-Fri; 10am-6pm Sat; noon-5pm Sun. Tickets £9-£22; £7-£13 reductions.

THEME PARKS

There are several theme parks within easy reach of London. Heading out west, **Legoland** (Winkfield Road, Windsor, Berks SL4 4AY, 0871 222 2001, www.legoland.co.uk) has rides including the wet 'n' wild Viking's River Splash, and the extraordinary Miniland London, made of 13 million Lego bricks. **Thorpe Park** (Staines Road, Chertsey, Surrey KT16 8PN, 0871 663 1673, www.thorpe park.com) has the fastest rollercoaster in Europe, called Stealth, and the terrifying horror-movie ride, Saw; it's best for older kids and teens. **Chessington World of Adventures** (Leatherhead Road, Chessington, Surrey KT9 2NE, 0871 663 4477, www.chessington.com) is a gentler option. This theme park is partly a zoo, and children can pay to be zoo keeper for a day.

Diana, Princess of Wales Memorial Playground

Likely to be on any child's visiting wishlist is the new Harry Potter studio tour near Watford, a short journey north of town: **Warner Bros Studio Tour London** (Leavesden Studios, 0845 084 0900, www.wbstudiotour.co.uk). For a day with less of an adrenaline rush, try **Bekonscot Model Village** (Warwick Road, Beaconsfield, Bucks HP9 2PL, 01494 672919, www.bekonscot.com), a haven of vintage miniature villages with a ride-on train. To the north, **Butterfly World** (Miriam Lane, Chiswell Green, Herts AL2 3NY, 01727 869203, www.butterflyworldproject.com) is designed to look like a huge butterfly head from the air with a 330-foot diameter walk-through biome (the butterfly's eye). There's also a walk-through butterfly tunnel and butterfly breeding house.

Spaces to play

London's parks are among the city's greatest treasures, with a ring of green spaces set around the core of the city. **Hyde Park** and **St James's Park** are especially central, but it isn't much further to **Regent's Park** north of Marylebone, and **Greenwich Park** is easily reached by river.

Coram's Fields

This historic site dates to 1747, when Thomas Coram established the Foundling Hospital, but only opened as a park in 1936. It has sandpits, a small petting zoo, ride-on toys and playgrounds for different age groups.
93 Guilford Street, Bloomsbury, WC1N 1DN (7837 6138, www.

coramsfields.org). Russell Square tube. Open Apr-Sept 9am-7pm daily. Oct-Mar 9am-dusk daily. Admission free (adults admitted only if accompanied by child under 16). No credit cards. For the Foundling Hospital's museum, see p29.

Diana, Princess of Wales Memorial Playground

Bring buckets and spades, if you can, to this superb playground: the huge, central pirate ship is moored in a sea of sand. Other attractions include a tepee camp and a treehouse encampment, and excellent provision is made for children with special needs.
Near Black Lion Gate, Broad Walk, Kensington Gardens, South Kensington, W8 2UH (7298 2141, www.royalparks.gov.uk). Bayswater or Queensway tube. Open Summer 10am-6.45pm daily. Winter 10am-dusk daily. Admission free; adults admitted only if accompanied by under-12s.

Discover Children's Story Centre

The UK's first creative learning centre for children is committed to promoting diversity and providing learning opportunities for socially and economically disadvantaged children. The main floor offers all sorts of imaginative exploration, while downstairs houses temporary interactive exhibitions.
383-387 High Street, Stratford, E15 4QZ (8536 5555, www.discover. org.uk). Stratford tube/rail/DLR. Open 10am-5pm Tue-Fri; 11am-5pm Sat, Sun. School holidays 10am-5pm Mon-Fri; 11am 5pm Sat, Sun. Admission £5; £18 family of 4; free under-2s.

Children

Film

Everyman Cinema

BFI Southbank

Films with feeling

Enjoy retrospectives, blockbuster premières and stunning interactive events.

Londoners still seem to have a feel for the romance of film that suburban multiplexes just can't satisfy. Perhaps that's why there's such a lively and varied range of screenings in the capital. Leicester Square underwent a major and much-needed facelift in 2011, and has the biggest first-run cinemas and stages most of the big-budget premières – but it also has the biggest prices. By contrast, the independents provide a cheaper and often more enjoyable night out, and they often show films that wouldn't come within a million miles of a red carpet. For seasonal outdoor screenings, *see p95.*

Among the rep cinemas, the British Film Institute's flagship venue gets top billing. **BFI Southbank** (*see p95*) screens seasons exploring and celebrating various genres of cinema and TV. After the BFI, London's best repertory cinema is found at the **Riverside Studios** (*see p95*).

Unexpected venues for film-viewing include the big museums and galleries. **The British Museum** (*see p29*), **National Gallery** (*see p38*), **Imperial War Museum** (*see p16*) and **Tate Modern** (*see p18*) all have regular screenings themed to their temporary exhibitions. Several luxury hotels open their screening rooms to the public; those at the **Soho Hotel** (*see p113*), **Charlotte Street Hotel** (*see p111*), **Covent Garden Hotel** (*see p113*) and **One Aldwych** (www.onealdwych.com) are favourites. Film shows in these luxe surroundings usually include some sort of refreshment.

Fans of memorabilia can check out the **London Film Museum** (*see p31*), but the latest trend is to mix cinema with other forms of entertainment, and to screen the films in a range of unusual locations (*see p95* **Recommended**).

THE LOWDOWN

Consult *Time Out* magazine's weekly listings or visit www.timeout.com/film for full details of what's on and performance times; note that the programmes change on a Friday. Films released in the UK are classified as follows: U – suitable for all ages; PG – open to all, parental guidance is advised; 12A – under-12s only admitted with an over-18; 15 – no one under 15 is admitted; 18 – no one under 18 is admitted.

First-run cinemas

CENTRAL LONDON

Barbican

Two new (small) screens have been added – at the corner of Beech Street and Whitecross Street – bringing the Barbican Centre's total number of screens back to three (the excellent Cinema 1 remains within the Barbican Centre proper). Expect new releases of quality world and independent films, as well as themed series. *Silk Street, the City, EC2Y 8DS (7638 8891, www.barbican.org.uk). Barbican tube. Tickets £13.50; £7-£8.50 reductions; £6 Mon. Screens 3.*

Curzon Cinemas

Expect a superb range of shorts, rarities, double-bills and seasons alongside new releases across the small Curzon chain. There's 1970s splendour in Mayfair (it's sometimes used for premières) and comfort in Chelsea. But the coolest of the bunch is the Soho outpost, which has a buzzing café, a decent bar and sometimes themes its eating and drinking spaces to tie in with event releases. *Chelsea 206 King's Road, SW3 5XP (0871 703 3990). Sloane Square tube then bus 11, 19, 22, 319. Screens 1. Mayfair 38 Curzon Street, W1J 7TY (0871 703 3989). Green Park or Hyde Park Corner tube. Screens 2. Soho 99 Shaftesbury Avenue, W1D 5DY (0871 703 3988). Leicester Square tube. Screens 3. Map p399 K6. All www.curzoncinemas.com. Tickets £8-£14.50; £6-£11.50 reductions.*

ICA Cinema

London's small contemporary arts centre (*see p41*) has met its brief not only by screening an eclectic range of cinema, but by distributing some of the most noteworthy films of recent years. After an uninspiring few years, there are signs of a renaissance under new leadership. Serious types can often be seen discussing the evening's programme afterwards in the café. *Nash House, the Mall, SW1Y 5AH (7930 0493, 7930 3647 tickets, www.ica.org.uk). Charing Cross tube/rail. Tickets £7-£10; £8 reductions. Screens 2.*

Odeon Leicester Square
You'll often find the red carpets and crush barriers up outside this art deco gem – it's the city's leading site for star-studded premières and hosts the opening and closing nights of the London Film Festival. If you're lucky, you might catch one of the silent film screenings, with accompaniment on a 1937 Compton organ. Otherwise, it's a diet of big-volume mainstream hits. *Leicester Square, WC2H 7LQ (0871 224 4007, www.odeon.co.uk). Leicester Square tube. Tickets £13-£22.50; £7-£17 reductions. Screens 6.*

NEIGHBOURHOOD LONDON

Electric Cinema
The Electric has a handsome restored interior, upgraded sound system and digital projection, and comfortable new seats. *191 Portobello Road, Notting Hill, W11 2ED (7908 9696, www.electric cinema.co.uk). Ladbroke Grove or Notting Hill Gate tube. Tickets £15.50-£18 adult; £10 children. Screens 1.*

Everyman & Screen Cinemas
London's most elegant cinema, the Everyman has a glamorous bar and two-seaters (£30) in its 'screening lounges', complete with foot stools and wine coolers. Everyman now also owns three former Screen cinemas, of which Islington's Screen on the Green is the best. *Everyman 5 Hollybush Vale, Hampstead, NW3 6TX. Hampstead tube. Tickets £11; £9 reductions. Screens 2.
Screen on the Green 83 Upper Street, Islington, N1 0NP. Angel tube. Tickets £10-£12; £9 reductions. Screens 2. Both 0871 906 9060, www.everyman cinema.com.*

Hackney Picturehouse
Opened in autumn 2011, the four-screen Hackney Picturehouse is the newest of the Picturehouse chain, and has become the flagship cinema for a borough woefully served for film. As well as showing the more interesting new releases and hosting festivals and seasons geared towards the diverse local community, the Picturehouse has a café and a performance space. *270 Mare Street, Hackney, E8 1HE (0871 902 5734, www.picturehouses. co.uk). Hackney Central or London Fields rail. Tickets £6-£11.50; £4-£10 reductions. Screens 4.*

Phoenix
Built in 1910 and revamped in the 1930s, the Grade II-listed Phoenix has recently been restored to its copper

and gold, art deco glory. It has real old-fashioned glamour, and is London's oldest cinema to have remained in continuous operation. Owned by a charitable trust, it runs a varied programme including theatre and opera transmissions. The best cinema in north London. *52 High Road, East Finchley, N2 9PJ (8444 6789, www.phoenixcinema. co.uk). East Finchley tube. Tickets £6-£9.50; £6 reductions. Screens 1.*

Rio Cinema
Another great deco survivor, restored to its original sleek lines, the Rio is east London's finest independent. Alongside mainstream releases, the Rio is well known for its Turkish and Kurdish film festivals. *107 Kingsland High Street, Dalston, E8 2PB (7241 9410, www.riocinema. org.uk). Dalston Kingsland rail. Tickets £10; £8 reductions. Screens 1.*

Vue Westfield London
At this Vue multiplex, all the screens are digital, with five 3D-ready and two 18m by 10m whoppers. The main rooms are functional black boxes with good sightlines, but you can also fork out for over-18s 'Scene' screens: you get reclining chairs and access to a private bar and a cloakroom. There's a branch at the Westfield centre in Stratford. *Westfield London, Shepherd's Bush, W12 7GF (0871 224 0240, www.my vue.com). White City or Wood Lane tube, or Shepherd's Bush tube/rail. Tickets check website for details. Screens 14. Other locations throughout the city.*

Repertory cinemas

Several first-run cinemas also offer rep-style fare – check www.timeout.com for locations.

BFI Southbank
The BFI's success is still built on its core function: thought-provoking seasons giving film-fans the chance to enjoy rare and significant British and foreign films. A terrific place to enjoy rare movies. The BFI's Mediatheque gives you free access to its huge film and documentary archive. *South Bank, SE1 8XT (7928 3232 tickets, www.bfi.org.uk). Embankment tube or Waterloo tube/rail. Tickets £12; £8.50 reductions. Screens 4.*

Ciné Lumière
Ciné Lumière reopened in 2009 with better seating and a refreshed art deco interior. No longer screening French films only (there are still, however, regular French previews and classics), the Lumière is a standard-bearer for world cinema in the capital. *Institut Français, 17 Queensberry Place, South Kensington, SW7 2DT (7871 3515, www.institut-francais.org.uk). South Kensington tube. Tickets £8-£10; £6-£8 reductions; £8 Mon. Screens 1.*

Prince Charles
Central and cheap, the Prince Charles is just up an alley from the pricey

RECOMMENDED
Secret Cinema

This mysterious interactive movie happening is so popular it now runs week-long events – including overnight stays for the spring 2014 screenings of Wes Anderson's *Grand Budapest Hotel*. But the basic formula stays the same: register at www.secretcinema.org to receive cryptic emails that set the scene for the next event but keep the location and film's name under wraps. You buy a ticket, dress up accordingly and – having received final instructions on the day – find yourself on set amid hundreds of actors who recreate the film around you. Previous events have included a Halloween *Alien* screening in a warehouse under strict quarantine and a speakeasy-set *Bugsy Malone* in a deco former cinema.

Leicester Square monsters, but even films on the new screen are a bargain. Perfect for catching up on still-fresh films you missed first time round, it is renowned for riotous singalong screenings and cult programming such as The Room, billed as 'the worst film ever made' and shown to a packed house once a month. *7 Leicester Place, off Leicester Square, WC2H 7BY (7494 3654, www.princecharlescinema.com). Leicester Square tube. Tickets £6.50-£10; £4-£6 reductions. Screens 2.*

Riverside Studios
The Riverside offers a superb programme of films and has become well known for inventive double-bills. *Crisp Road, Hammersmith, W6 9RL (8237 1111, www.riverside studios.co.uk). Hammersmith tube. Tickets £8.50; £7.50 reductions. Screens 1.*

IMAX

BFI IMAX
London's biggest screen mixes made-for-IMAX fare and scenery-heavy documentaries with mainstream blockbusters, such as Harry Potter films. *1 Charlie Chaplin Walk, South Bank, SE1 8XR (0330 333 7878, www.bfi.org.uk/imax). Waterloo tube/rail. Tickets £16.60-£20.70; £11.40-£15 reductions. Screens 1.*

Outdoor screenings

The best known open-air screenings are those at Somerset House, but you can find plenty more – some in unusual locations. **Free Film Festivals** (www.freefilmfestivals. org) puts on free outdoor screenings in interesting public spaces in south-east London. **The Scoop** is the location for summer screenings as part of **More London Free Festival** (www.morelondon.com), while **Pop Up Screens** (www.popupscreens. co.uk) shows popular films in parks in west London.

Rooftop Film Club
In summer, the rooftop garden at this bar/club/arts collective screens around five films a week. Tickets are only available online; see the website for details. *Queen of Hoxton, 1-5 Curtain Road, Hoxton, EC2A 3JX (www.rooftopfilm club.com). Tickets £13.*

Somerset House
This summer season takes place in the lovely neoclassical courtyard of Somerset House; tickets sell out way in advance. Bring a picnic and cushions. *The Strand, WC2R 1LA (7845 4600, www.somersethouse.org.uk/film). Tickets vary.*

Film

LGBT

Ku

Proud, loud – and going out

London's multifarious gay scenesters are single-minded in their quest for fun.

In a nightlife scene that runs around the clock and throughout the week, whatever your taste in music, you'll find somewhere that specialises in it. Off the dancefloor, the scene is more varied still, with cabaret nights, literary salons and plays, and a major gay and lesbian film festival.

Roughly speaking, London's gay scene is split into three distinct zones: Soho, Vauxhall and east London. Each of these three districts has its own character.

Centred on Old Compton Street, the **Soho** scene is the most mainstream. Down south, **Vauxhall** is more hedonistic. You could arrive in London on a Friday evening and dance non-stop here for an entire weekend. The most alternative and creative of the capital's queer scenes is in **east London**. You'll be rubbing shoulders with fashion and music's movers and shakers (plus assorted straight folk), to soundtracks built by underground DJs. It can get a little snooty, but a lot of the bars and clubs are also mixed,

which makes the area ideal for a night out with straight mates.

It was a blow for London's **lesbian scene** when the Candy Bar closed in early 2014, but Ku has since opened the basement venue She Soho (23A Old Compton Street, W1D 5LB, http://she-soho.com). Monday or Wednesday at Retro are good choices, and the women-only Glass Bar (www.theglassbar.org.uk), which lost its own premises a few years ago, now runs various events. There's also the glam Bijou Cocktail Club on the second Saturday of the month at Rudds bar in the City (148 Queen Victoria Street, EC4V 4BY, www.elysionevents.co.uk).

Lastly, special mention should go to the **NYC Downlow**, a travelling homo disco straight out of 1970s New York (http://thedownlow radio.com/the-downlow).

RESTAURANTS & CAFÉS

More or less every restaurant in London welcomes gay custom. Certainly nowhere in or around Soho will look twice at you and your other

half having a romantic dinner. For thirtysomething lesbians, there are fun cocktail evenings amid the Italian vintage decor of **Star at Night** (22 Great Chapel Street, Soho, W1F 8FR, 7494 2488, www.thestarat night.com, open 6-11.30pm Tue-Sat) – by day, it's a greasy spoon.

Balans

The gay café-restaurant of choice for many years, Balans is all about location, location, location (plus hot waiters, decent food and long opening hours). The nearby Balans Café (no.34) serves a shorter version of the menu. *60 Old Compton Street, Soho, W1D 4UG (7439 2183, www.balans.co.uk). Piccadilly Circus tube. Open 8am-2am Mon-Thur; 8am-4am Fri, Sat; 7.30am-2am Sun. Admission £2.50 after midnight Mon-Sat.*
Other locations throughout the city.

CLUBS & CLUBNIGHTS

If you want to stay up all night and next day as well, head to Vauxhall. At **Fire** (South Lambeth Road, SW8 1UQ, www.fireclub.co.uk), popular

nights include Orange, a Sunday staple. Still in Vauxhall, on the Albert Embankment, try **Union** (no.66, www.clubunion.co.uk) and **Area** (nos.67-68, www.arealondon.net). If you're near Old Street, keep an eye on **East Bloc** (217 City Road, EC1V 1JN, www.eastbloc.co.uk).

Club Kali

The world's largest LGBT Asian dance club offers Bollywood, bhangra, Arabic tunes, R&B and dance classics spun by DJs Ritu, Riz & Qurra. *Dome, 1 Dartmouth Park Hill, Tufnell Park, N19 5QQ (7272 8153, www.clubkali.com). Tufnell Park tube. Open 10pm-3am 3rd Fri of mth. Admission £8; £5 reductions.*

Exilio Latin Dance Club

London's principal queer Latino club, with girls and guys getting together for merengue, salsa, cumbia and so on. *Venues vary; see website for details (07956 983230, www.exilio.co.uk). Open 9.30pm-2.30am every other Sat. Admission £6-£12. No credit cards.*

Heaven

London's most famous gay club is a bit like *Les Misérables* – it's camp, it's full of history, and tourists love it. Popcorn (Mon) has long been a good bet, but it's really all about G-A-Y (Thur-Sat). *Underneath the Arches, Villiers Street, Covent Garden, WC2N 6NG (7930 2020, www.heaven nightclublondon. com). Charing Cross tube/rail. Open 11pm-5.30am Mon; 11pm-4am Thur, Fri; 10.30pm-5am Sat. Admission prices vary. No credit cards.*

Horse Meat Disco

Not your average gay club. Skinny Soho boys and fashionistas rub shoulders with scally lads and bears in a traditional old boozer. The hip soundtrack is an inspired mix of Studio 54, New York punk and new wave. When Horse Meat isn't in residence, the Eagle is a hub for those wishing to try a bit of leather without a strict dress code. *Eagle London, 349 Kennington Lane, Vauxhall, SE11 5QY (7793 0903, www.eaglelondon.com). Vauxhall tube/rail. Open 8pm-3am Sun. Admission £6. No credit cards.*

Popstarz

What G-A-Y is to cheese, Popstarz is to indie. It's studenty, drunken, attitude-free and popular. There are also occasional PAs from in-demand acts. *Popstarz is currently itinerant. Check the website for the latest venue – and a map. www.popstarz.org. Open 10pm-5am Fri. Admission £3 before 11pm, then £5-£8.*

Dalston Superstore

Critic's choice

1 **Horse Meat Disco** Pioneering disco mash-up. Come to dance. *See p96.*

2 **RVT** Much of London's best alternative cabaret starts here. *See p97.*

3 **Dalston Superstore** Key – and straight-friendly – dance venue. *See p97.*

4 **Heaven** Popstar PAs at G-A-Y, grande dame of queer clubbing. *See p96.*

5 **Ku** Hard-working, multi-tasking pair of venues. *See p97.*

RVT

This pub turned legendary gay cabaret venue, a much-loved stalwart on the scene for years, operates an anything-goes booking policy. Saturday's queer performance night Duckie (www.duckie.co.uk) is the most famous fixture. Punters verge on the bear, but the main dress code is 'no attitude'. *Royal Vauxhall Tavern, 372 Kennington Lane, Vauxhall, SE11 5HY (7820 1222, www.rvt.org.uk). Vauxhall tube/rail. Open 7pm-midnight Mon, Wed, Thur; 6pm-midnight Tue; 7pm-2am Fri; 9pm-2am Sat; 2pm-midnight Sun. Admission £5-£7.*

Vogue Fabrics

Small and sweaty, Vogue Fabrics is the place to come if you like your nights messy and your men of the bear and otter variety. The electro-, disco-, Italo-pumpin' Dirtbox remains a favourite party night. *66 Stoke Newington Road, Dalston, N16 7XB (http://voguefabricsdalston.com/club). Dalston Kingsland rail. Open 10pm-7am Fri, Sat. Admission £3-£5 Fri, Sat. No credit cards.*

XXL

The world's biggest club – naturally! – for bears and their friends, XXL is for chubbier, hairier and blokier gay men and their twinky admirers. *1 Invicta Plaza, South Bank, SE1 9UF (www.xxl-london.com). Southwark tube. Open 10pm-3am Wed; 10pm-6am Sat. Admission £15. No credit cards.*

Unless otherwise stated, these pubs and bars are open to both gay men and lesbians.

Barcode Vauxhall

A massive, lavish venue, which generally attracts a blokey-ish crowd despite its shiny, sparkly surfaces. *Arch 69, Goding Street, Vauxhall, SE11 5AW (7582 4180, www.bar-code.co.uk). Vauxhall tube/rail. Open 8pm-4am Thur; 8pm-8am Fri, Sat; 8pm-3am Sun. Admission £6, £8 after midnight.*

Dalston Superstore

The opening of this gay arts space-cum-bar a few years back cemented Dalston's status as the final frontier of the East End's gay scene. Come during the day for the café grub; at night for an impressive roster of guest DJs spinning anything from garage to pop. The guys also run Trailer Trash (www.club trailertrash.com), a roaming night that pulls in fashion-forward partiers. *117 Kingland High Street, Dalston, E8 2PB (7254 2273, http://dalstonsuperstore.com). Dalston Kingsland rail. Open 11am-2am Mon-Wed; 11am-2.30am Thur; 11am-4am Fri; 10am-4am Sat; 10am-2.30am Sun.*

Freedom Bar

A glitzy cocktail lounge and DJ bar, spread over two floors. The glam ground-floor bar attracts a fashion-conscious crowd. The large basement club and performance space hosts weekday cabaret and gets busy with the gay party crowd over the weekend. *66 Wardour Street, Soho, W1F 0TA (7734 0071, www.freedombarsoho.com). Leicester Square or Piccadilly Circus tube. Open 4pm-3am Mon-Thur; 2pm-3am Fri, Sat; 2-10.30pm Sun. Admission £5 after 10pm Fri, Sat.*

G-A-Y Bar

The G-A-Y night at Heaven (*see p96*) gets the celebrity cameos, but this popular bar is still a shrine to queer pop idols. There's also a women's bar in the basement, called Girls Go Down. G-A-Y bar's plush late-night sibling, G-A-Y Late, is just round the corner at 5 Goslett Yard. *30 Old Compton Street, Soho, W1D 4UR (7494 2756, www.g-a-y.co.uk). Leicester Square or Tottenham Court Road tube. Open noon- midnight daily.*

George & Dragon

The location of this mini-pub ensures a stylish and up-for-it clientele, while the decor (a wall-mounted horse's head, creepy puppets, random garbage) keeps the vibe fun. The music – pop, indie and accessible electronica – is often delivered with a sense of humour. Gay or not, it's one of London's best boozers. Wondering where everyone went at closing time? To the Joiners Arms (116-118 Hackney Road, Bethnal Green, E2 7QL, www.thejoiner shoreditch.com), of course. *2 Hackney Road, Bethnal Green, E2 7NS (7012 1100). Old Street tube/rail or Hoxton rail. Open 6pm-midnight Mon-Thur, Sat, Sun; 5pm-midnight Fri.*

Green Carnation

The Green Carnation had a major refit a few years back, to spectacular effect. Head upstairs for cocktails in posh surroundings, with chandeliers and piano music. There's a bar and a dancefloor downstairs. *4-5 Greek Street, Soho, W1D 4DB (8123 4267, www.greencarnationsoho.co.uk). Tottenham Court Road tube. Open 4pm-2am Mon-Sat; 4pm-12.30am Sun. Admission £5 after 11pm Mon-Sat.*

Hoist

One of only two genuine leather bars in town, this club sits under the arches and makes the most of its underground and industrial setting. The Saturday night event SBN (Stark Bollock Naked) gives you the tone of the place; leather, uniforms, rubber, skinhead or boots are the dress code. *Arches 47B & 47C, South Lambeth Road, Vauxhall, SW8 1RH (7735 9972, www.the hoist.co.uk). Vauxhall tube/rail. Open 9pm-1am Wed; 10pm-3am Fri; 10pm-4am Sat; 2pm-2am Sun. Admission £6 Fri, Sun; £2-£10 Sat. No credit cards.*

Ku

A popular bar and club that offers everything from film nights to comedy. The sheer variety of club nights (which are held in the basement) is impressive. Ku also runs a three-floor bar-club in the heart of the local scene, on the corner of Frith and Old Compton streets. *30 Lisle Street, Chinatown, WC2H 7BA (7437 4303, www.ku-bar.co.uk). Leicester Square tube. Open noon-3am Mon-Sat; noon-midnight Sun.*

KW4

Handy for the heath, this fabulous old local attracts a very Hampstead crowd (read: well-off and ready for fun). On summer weekends, the cute little beer garden tends to fill up with a mix of gay and straight punters. *77 Hampstead High Street, NW3 1RE (7435 5747, www.kingwilliam hampstead. co.uk). Hampstead tube. Open 11am-11pm Mon-Thur; 11am-midnight Fri-Sun.*

Manbar

What was once late-night booze and cruise bar 79CXR now has sexy black and red decor on three levels. Regular nights include Beartrap (Monday), talent show Spotlight (Tuesday), and Sunday School – games, magic, performances and more. *79 Charing Cross Road, Chinatown, WC2H 0NE (7434 2567, www.manbarsoho.com). Leicester Square tube. Open 5pm-3.30am Mon-Thur; 3pm-3.30am Fri, Sat; 3-11pm Sun.*

Retro Bar

Nights here are dedicated to indie rock and 1980s hits. The crowd is mixed in every sense: gay/straight, gay/lesbian and scene queen/true eccentric. Quiz night is Tuesday. *2 George Court, off the Strand, Covent Garden, WC2N 6HH (7839 8760, www.retrobarlondon. co.uk). Charing Cross tube/rail. Open noon-11pm Mon-Fri; 2-11pm Sat; 2-10.30pm Sun.*

Shadow Lounge

For celebrity sightings, suits, cutes and fancy boots, this is your West End venue. Expect a queue at weekends, but a sublime atmosphere inside. *5 Brewer Street, Soho, W1F 0RF (7287 7988, www.theshadowlounge.co.uk). Piccadilly Circus tube. Open 10pm-3am Mon-Sat. Admission free Mon; £5 Tue-Thur; £10 Fri, Sat.*

Yard

Possibly the most reliable gay bar in Soho, the Yard attracts pretty boys, blokes and lesbians in equal measure. *57 Rupert Street, Soho, W1V 7BJ (7437 2652, www.yardbar.co.uk). Leicester Square tube. Open 4-11.30pm Mon-Wed; 3-11.30pm Thur; 2pm-midnight Fri, Sat; 2-10.30pm Sun.*

RVT

Nightlife

Fabric

After dark the city comes alive

From the megaclubs to its many microscenes, London is the place to party.

To say London has a brilliant and diverse nightlife is an understatement, whether clubbing, live music, cabaret or comedy. These days, though, big is rarely best. We have one of the world's largest and most influential nightclubs, Fabric, but as a credible superclub, it still stands alone – albeit with interested eyes drawn to the new Studio 338 in Greenwich.

It's the smaller venues that are really buzzing. In particular, good clubbing is easy to come by along the Kingsland Road strip in Dalston, where you'll find the Nest, Dalston Superstore and a range of party bars. There's more new music from the edge at places such as XOYO and the Shacklewell Arms, the latter proving the London cliché of indie bands in sticky dives endures.

London has more than 250 comedy gigs a week, ranging from pub open-mics to arena shows; the Comedy Store is a good place to start. Meanwhile, the alt cabaret scene rolls on: Bethnal Green Working Men's Club and RVT are key venues.

Clubbing

CENTRAL

Fabric
Fabric is the club that most party people come to see in London, with good reason. Located in a former meatpacking warehouse, it has a well-deserved reputation as the capital's biggest and best club. The line-ups are legendary. Fridays belong to the bass: guaranteed highlights include DJ Hype, with his drum 'n' bass and dubstep night Playaz, plus Andy C's Ram Records takeover and Caspa's Dub Police label nights. Saturdays descend into techy, minimal, deep house territory, with the world's most famous DJs regularly making appearances. Be warned: the queues are also legendary. Blag on to the guestlist or buy tickets in advance to avoid a two-hour wait.
77A Charterhouse Street, Clerkenwell, EC1M 3HJ (7336 8898, www.fabric london.com). Farringdon tube/rail. Open 10pm-6am Fri; 11pm-8am Sat; 11pm-6am Sun. Admission £8-£24.

NORTH LONDON

Better known as gig venues, **Koko** (*see p101*) and **Barfly** (*see p102*) have good reputations for feisty club nights, and the music at the **Blues Kitchen** (*see p102*) can really rock.

Lock Tavern
A favourite of artfully distressed rock urchins, it teems with aesthetic niceties inside (cosy black couches and warm wood panels downstairs; open-air terrace on the first floor), but it's the unpredictable after-party vibe that packs in the punters, with big-name DJs regularly providing the tunes.
35 Chalk Farm Road, Camden, NW1 8AJ (7482 7163, www.lock-tavern. com). Chalk Farm tube. Open noon-midnight Mon-Thur; noon-1am Fri, Sat; noon-11pm Sun. Admission free.

Old Queen's Head
Pulling in fun-seekers since its relaunch way back in 2006, the Old Queen's Head is another place with long queues at the weekends. There are two floors and outside seating front and back, and during the week you can lounge on battered sofas. Weekends are for dancing, minor league celeb-spotting and chatting up the bar staff, or trying out the private karaoke room.
44 Essex Road, Islington, N1 8LN (7354 9993, www.theoldqueens head.com). Angel tube. Open noon-midnight Mon-Wed, Sun; noon-1am Thur; noon-2am Fri, Sat. Admission £4 after 8pm Fri, Sat.

Proud
The north London guitar-slingers have given way to dubstep, rock 'n' rave and drum 'n' bass, but the action at this former equine hospital is still rock 'n' roll. Drape yourself – cocktail in hand – over the luxurious textiles in the individual stable-style booths (you must book in advance), sink into deckchairs on the outdoor terrace, or spin around in the main band room at its naughtily themed nights.
Horse Hospital, Stables Market, Camden, NW1 8AH (7482 3867, www.proudcamden.com). Chalk Farm tube. Open 11am-1.30am Wed; 11am-2.30am Thur-Sat; 11am-12.30am Sun. Admission free-£10.

EAST LONDON

In addition to the venues below, check out gay hangouts the **Dalston Superstore** and **Vogue Fabrics** (for both, *see p97*).

Book Club
The Book Club aims to fuse lively creative events, table tennis (there are regular tournaments) and late-night drinking. Events range from Electro-Swing, the night that started a huge trend in mashing up vintage sounds with electro beats, to arty think-and-drink workshops.
100 Leonard Street, Shoreditch, EC2A 4RH (7684 8618, www.wearetbc.com). Old Street tube/rail. Open 8am-midnight Mon-Wed; 8am-2am Thur, Fri; 10am-2am Sat; noon-midnight Sun. Admission free-£5.

Nest
We love the Nest, one of Dalston's finest. It's kind of like a corridor, but in a good way, with an industrial chic look. Line-ups are usually great, with music on the dancefloor-focused disco, electro and house end of the spectrum.
36 Stoke Newington Road, Dalston, N16 7XJ (7354 9993, www.ilovethe nest.com). Dalston Junction rail. Open 9pm-3am Thur; 9pm-4am Fri, Sat. Admission free-£7.

Oslo
This addition to Hackney's nightlife is a rarity – neither basement dive bar, dilapidated pub nor too-cool-for-school danceteria, Oslo is a proper, real-life

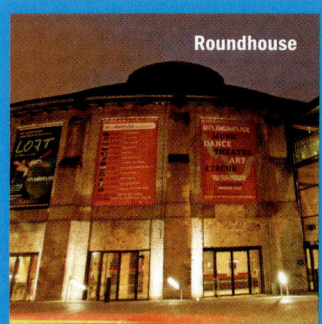

Roundhouse

Critic's choice

1 **O2 Arena** If you want it big, you'll find nowhere better. Stadium gigs a-gogo. *See p101.*

2 **XOYO** Almost single-handedly keeping clubbing real in Shoreditch. *See p99.*

3 **Roundhouse** This historic venue – it hosted hippie happenings – still hosts kicking shows. *See p101.*

4 **Café Oto** If you like your music out-there, open your ears to Oto. *See p103.*

5 **The Invisible Dot** Supercool comedy club. *See p104.*

music venue with a decent-sized stage, proper sound system and light rig. The former railway station next to Hackney Central is London's first venue from Nottingham-based promoters DHP Family, and hosts bands most nights of the week, with an impressive selection of club nights at weekends. Ears ringing? Head downstairs to the fine restaurant (open night and day) and proper bar. *1A Amhurst Road, Hackney, E8 1LL (3553 4831, www.oslohackney.com). Hackney Central rail. Open check website for details.*

Plastic People

The long-established and ever-popular Plastic People subscribes to the old-school line that all you need for a kicking party is a dark basement and a sound system. The programming remains true to form: deep techno to house, all-girl DJ line-ups and many a star DJ squeezing through the doors for a secret gig. *147-149 Curtain Road, Shoreditch, EC2A 3QE (7739 6471, www.plastic people.co.uk). Old Street tube/rail. Open 9.30pm-2am Thur; 10pm-4am Fri, Sat. Admission free-£15.*

Shacklewell Arms

The Shacklewell Arms is a magnet for leftfield music. Bands and DJs come from the electronic, lo-fi, chillwave and post-dubstep arenas, contrasting brilliantly with the shabby interior of this former Afro-Caribbean hotspot.

71 Shacklewell Lane, Dalston, E8 2EB (7249 0810, www.shacklewellarms. com). Dalston Junction rail. Open 5pm-midnight Mon-Wed; 5pm-1am Thur; 5pm-3am Fri; noon-3am Sat; noon-midnight Sun. Admission free-£8.

XOYO

There's live music during the week at this 800-capacity venue, but XOYO is first and foremost a nightclub. This former printworks is a bare concrete cell, defiantly taking the 'chic' out of 'shabby chic'. The open space means the atmosphere is always buzzing, as the only place to escape total immersion in the music is the small smoking courtyard outside. The Victorian loft-style space provides effortlessly cool programming and high-profile DJs, while the return of longer residencies – a 12-week stint for Eats Everything, for instance – is old-school in the best way possible. *32-37 Cowper Street, Shoreditch, EC2A 4AP (7354 9993, www.xoyo.co.uk). Old Street tube/rail. Open/admission varies; check website for details.*

SOUTH LONDON

Building Six

See p102 **All-new Nightlife Nexus**. *Peninsula Square, SE10 0DX (020 8463 2000, www.theO2.co.uk). North Greenwich tube. Open/admission check website for details.*

Corsica Studios

An independent warehouse-styled complex, Corsica aims to breed creativity and culture in areas of regeneration. It's certainly rough around the edges with its makeshift bars and toilets but the club nights are second to none: flagship night Trouble Vision boasts the best of bass, while Sunday sees daytime house and techno events. There's also live music: Silver Apples, Acoustic Ladyland and Lydia Lunch have all gigged here. *4-5 Elephant Road, Elephant & Castle, SE17 1LB (7703 4760, www.corsica studios.com). Elephant & Castle tube/rail. Open times vary Mon-Wed, check website for details; 8pm-3am Thur; 10pm-6am Fri, Sat; 7am-3pm Sun. Admission free-£15.*

Electric Brixton

The Fridge in Brixton was a rave paradise in the early '90s, a stomping ground for the rare groove scene, funky jazz-house and, later, hard dance and psy-trance beats. In 2011, however, it underwent a £1m refit, with new management, and was reborn as Electric Brixton, with a mix of club nights – the likes of Skreamizm with Skream, featuring dubstep with forays into jungle, drum 'n' bass and disco – and live music. *Town Hall Parade, Brixton, SW2 1RJ (7274 2290, www.electricbrixton. com). Brixton tube/rail. Open times vary Thur-Sun; check website for details. Admission £10-£35.*

Ministry of Sound

Ministry of Sound was once the epitome of warehouse cool and is

still possibly the UK's best-known clubbing venue. Laid out across four bars, five rooms and three dancefloors, there's lots to explore. Trance night the Gallery has made its home at Ministry of Sound on Fridays, while Saturday nights boast big-name DJ takeovers from the likes of Connected, Roger Sanchez and Erick Morillo. *103 Gaunt Street, off Newington Causeway, Elephant & Castle, SE1 6DP (7740 8600, www.ministryof sound.com). Elephant & Castle tube/rail. Open 10.30pm-6am Fri; 11pm-7am Sat. Admission £10-£20.*

Plan B

The decor is industrial chic (exposed brickwork, metal pillars, geometric furnishings) and the music programme rampantly eclectic. This, plus a late licence, happy hour every evening and student discount that ensures the place is very often brimming. Watch out for irregular '90s R&B and hip hop night Supa Dupa Fly. *418 Brixton Road, Brixton, SW9 7AY (7733 0926, www.plan-brixton.co.uk). Brixton tube/rail. Open times vary Fri-Sun, check website for details. Admission £5-£12.50.*

Studio 338

See p102 **All-new Nightlife Nexus**. *338 Boord Street, SE10 0PF (www.studio338.co.uk). North Greenwich tube. Open/admission check website for details.*

WEST LONDON

Notting Hill Arts Club

Notting Hill Arts Club almost single-handedly keeps this side of town on the radar thanks to its monthly Death2Disco, plus nights such as Juicebox (electro) and NHAC Presents (DJ sets). *21 Notting Hill Gate, Notting Hill, W11 3JQ (7460 4459, www.nottinghill artsclub.com). Notting Hill Gate tube.*

Open hours vary, but around 7pm-2am Wed-Thur; 6pm-2am Fri; 4pm-2am Sat; 6pm-1am Sun. Admission free-£8.

Paradise

A star among the legion of pub-clubs, thanks to its alternative programme of art auctions, burlesque life drawing and late-night club nights, making it more than just a good local hangout. *19 Kilburn Lane, Kensal Green, W10 4AE (8969 0098, www.theparadise. co.uk). Kensal Green tube or Kensal Rise rail. Open noon-midnight Mon-Wed; noon-1am Thur; noon-2am Fri, Sat; noon-11.30pm Sun. Admission free-£8.*

Music venues

Rock, pop & roots

TICKETS & INFORMATION

Your first stop should be www.timeout.com, which lists hundreds of gigs every week. Most venues' websites detail future shows. Check ticket availability before setting out: venues large and small can sell out weeks in advance. The main exceptions are pub venues, which sell tickets only on the day. Many venues offer tickets online via their websites, but beware: most online box offices are operated by ticket agencies, which add booking fees that can raise the ticket price by as much as 30 per cent. Try to pay cash in person if possible; for details of London's ticket agencies, *see p107*.

There's often a huge disparity between door times and stage times; doors may open at 7pm, for instance, but the gigs often don't start until after 9pm. If in doubt, call ahead.

Koko. *See p101.*

ROUNDHOUSE: JONATHAN PERUGIA; KOKO: MICHELLE GRANT

Nightlife

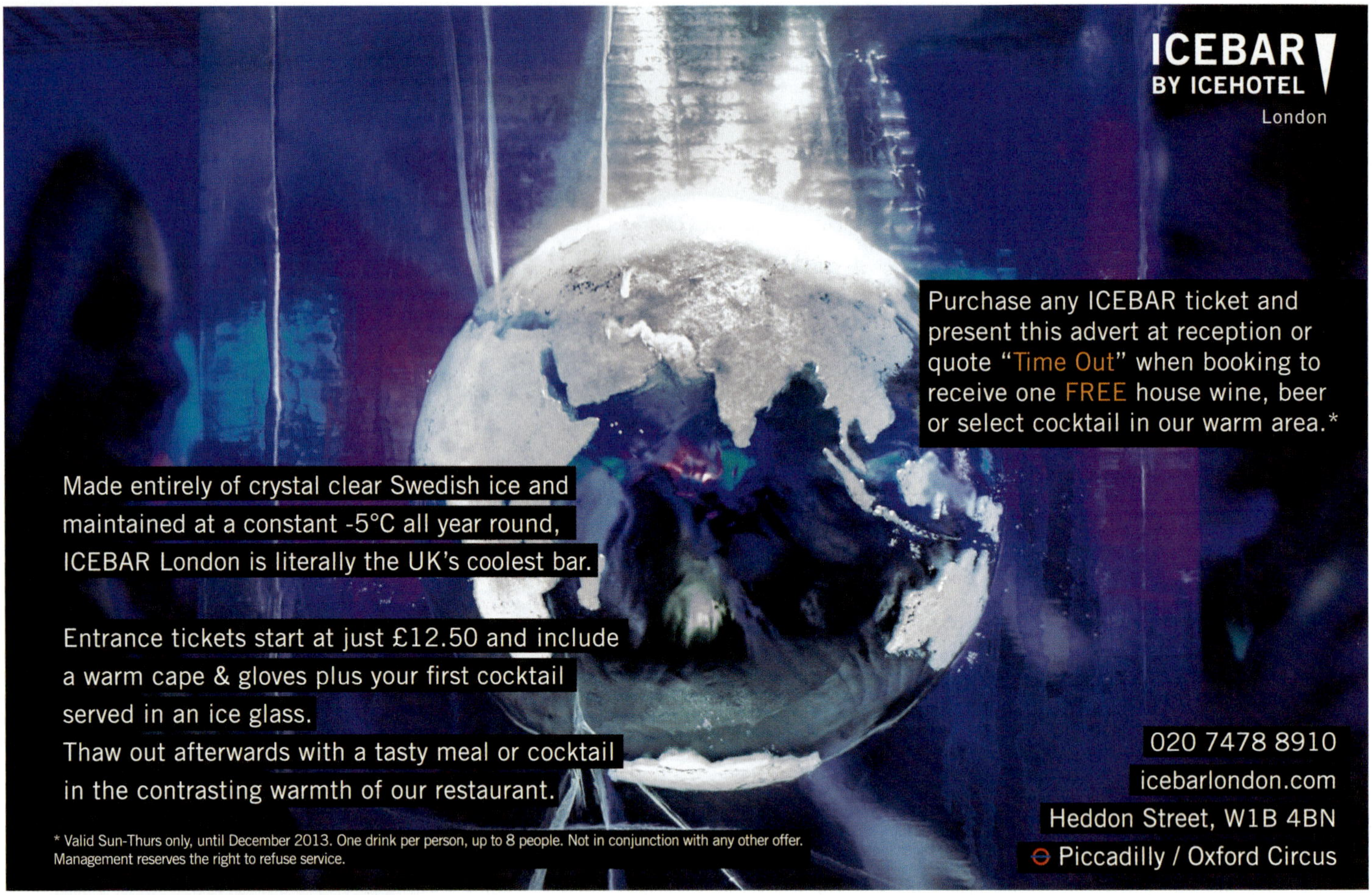

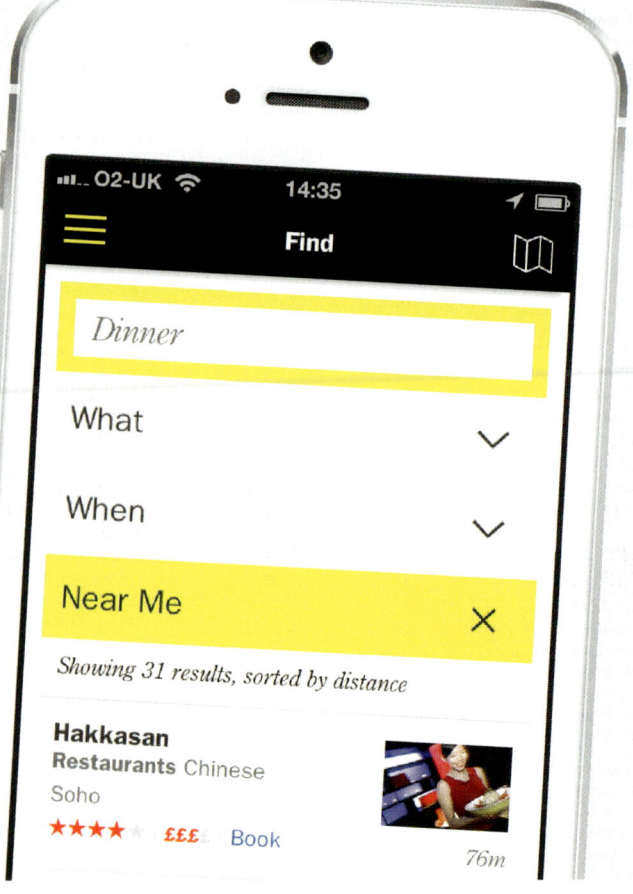

In addition to the venues listed below, the **Barbican Centre** (*see p107*), the **Southbank Centre** (*see p106*) and the **Royal Albert Hall** (*see p106*) also stage regular gigs.

Alexandra Palace
This hilltop landmark venue, adorned with sculptures and frescoes, opened in 1873 as the People's Palace and was devastated by fire twice – once only 16 days after opening, and the second time in 1980. Bar and toilet provision for some of the big shows remains patchy thanks to the layout, but the sound system is beloved of audiophiles – the Pixies chose it for the first London shows when they reformed, and James Murphy for the last UK appearances of LCD Soundsystem.
Alexandra Palace Way, N22 7AY (8365 2121, www.alexandrapalace.com). Alexandra Palace rail or W3 bus. Tickets vary; the promoters rather than the venue sell tickets.

Eventim Apollo
This 1930s cinema doubles as a 3,600-capacity all-seater theatre (popular with big comedy acts and children's shows) and a 5,000-capacity standing-room-only gig space, hosting shows by major rock bands and others not quite ready for the O2.
45 Queen Caroline Street, Hammersmith, W6 9QH (8563 3800 information, 0844 249 4300 tickets, www.eventimapollo.com). Hammersmith tube. Box office In person 4-8pm performance days. By phone 24hrs daily. Tickets £10-£43.

The Forum
Originally constructed as part of a chain of art deco cinemas with a spurious Roman theme (hence the name, the incongruous bas relief battle scenes and imperial eagles flanking the stage), the 2,000-capacity Forum became a music venue back in the early 1980s. Since then, it's been vital to generations of gig-goers, whether they cut their teeth on the Velvet Underground, Ian Dury & the Blockheads, Duran Duran, Killing Joke or the Wu-Tang Clan, all of whom have played memorable shows here.
9-17 Highgate Road, Kentish Town, NW5 1JY (7428 4099 information, 7428 4099, www.mamacolive.com/theforum). Kentish Town tube/rail. Box office In person 5.30-9.30pm performance days. By phone 24hrs daily. Tickets £5-£30.

IndigO2
The little sister of the vast O2 Arena is only little in comparison with the huge expanses of its elder sibling. With a capacity of 2,350 (part-standing room, part-amphitheatre seating, sometimes part-table seating), IndigO2 is impressive in its own right. Its niche roster of MOR acts is dominated by soul, funk, pop-jazz and old pop acts, though it also hosts after-show parties for those headlining at the O2.
For listings, see right O2 Arena.

Koko
Koko has had a hand in the gestation of numerous styles over the decades. As the Music Machine it hosted a four-night residency with the Clash in 1978; the venue changed its name to Camden Palace in the '80s, whereupon it became home to the emergent new romantic movement and saw Madonna's UK debut. Later it was one of the first 'official' venues to host acid house events. Since a spruce-up in the early noughties, it has hosted acts as diametrically opposed as Joss Stone and Queens of the Stone Age, not to mention one of Prince's electrifying 'secret' gigs in 2014. Nonetheless, the 1,500-capacity hall majors on weekend club nights – Annie Mac Presents and Club NME – and gigs by indie rockers.
1A Camden High Street, Camden, NW1 7JE (0870 432 5527 information, 0844 847 2258 tickets, www.koko.uk.com). Mornington Crescent tube. Box office In person noon-5pm Mon-Fri (performance days only). By phone 24hrs daily. Tickets £3-£25.

O2 Academy Brixton
Brixton is still the preferred venue for metal, indie and alt rock bands looking to play their triumphant 'Look, ma, we've made it!' headline show. Built in the 1920s, this ex-cinema is the city's most atmospheric big venue. The 5,000-capacity art deco gem straddles the chasm between the pomp and volume of a stadium show and the intimate (read: sweaty) atmosphere of a club. Since becoming a full-time music venue in the '80s, it's hosted names from James Brown to the Stones to Springsteen, Dylan, Prince and Madonna, via the Red Hot Chili Peppers. And with its raked dancefloor, everyone's guaranteed a decent view.
211 Stockwell Road, Brixton, SW9 9SL (7771 3000 information, 0844 477 2000 tickets, www.o2academybrixton.co.uk). Brixton tube/rail. Box office In person 2hrs before doors on performance days. By phone 24hrs daily. Tickets £10-£40.

O2 Academy Islington
Located in a shopping mall, this 800-capacity room was never likely to be London's edgiest venue. Still, as a stepping stone between the pubs of Camden and the city's larger venues, it's a good place to catch fast-rising indie acts and re-formed '80s bands, not least because of the great sound system. The adjacent Bar Academy plays host to smaller bands, and also hosts club nights.
N1 Centre, 16 Parkfield Street, Islington, N1 0PS (7288 4400 information, 0844 477 2000 tickets, www.o2academyislington.co.uk). Angel tube. Box office In person noon-4pm Mon-Sat. By phone 24hrs daily. Tickets £5-£25.

O2 Arena
The national embarrassment that was the Millennium Dome has been transformed into the city's de facto home of the megagig. The 20,000-seater has outstanding sound, great sightlines and the potential for artists to perform 'in the round'; shows from even the world's biggest acts (Britney, Led Zep, even One Direction) don't feel very far away. IndigO2 (*see left*) is on the same site.
Peninsula Square, North Greenwich, SE10 0DX (8463 2000 information, 0844 856 0202 tickets, www.theo2.co.uk). North Greenwich tube. Box office In person 12.30pm-8pm daily. By phone 8am-8pm daily. Tickets £10-£100.

O2 Shepherd's Bush Empire
Once a BBC television theatre, the Empire's baroque interior exudes a grown-up glamour few venues can match. The environment lends a gravitas to the chirpiest performance, as Lily Allen demonstrated. So you can imagine the sensation of seeing the likes of David Bowie or Bob Dylan here. It holds 2,000 standing or 1,300 seated, sightlines are good, the sound is decent (with the exception of the alcove behind the stalls bar and the vertiginous top floor) and the roster of shows is varied, with acts at the poppier end of the scale joined by everyone from folkies to grizzled '70s rockers.
Shepherd's Bush Green, Shepherd's Bush, W12 8TT (8354 3300 information, 0844 477 2000 tickets, www.o2shepherdsbushempire.co.uk). Shepherd's Bush Market tube or Shepherd's Bush tube/rail. Box office In person 4-6pm performance days. By phone 24hrs daily. Tickets £10-£40.

Roundhouse
The main auditorium's supporting pillars mean there are some poor sightlines at the Roundhouse, but this one-time railway turntable shed (hence the name), which was used for hippie happenings in the 1960s before becoming a famous rock (and punk) venue in the '70s, has been a fine addition to London's music venues since its reopening in 2006. Expect a mix of arty rock gigs (the briefly re-formed Led Zeppelin played here), dance performances, theatre and multimedia events.
Chalk Farm Road, Camden, NW1 8EH (7424 9991 information, 0844 482 8008 tickets, www.roundhouse.org.uk). Chalk Farm tube. Box office In person 11am-7pm Mon-Fri; 9am-7pm sat, Sun. By phone 9am-7pm Mon-Fri; 9am-4pm Sat; 9.30am-4pm Sun. Tickets £5-£50.

Scala
Although the venue has vacillated between use as a picturehouse and concert hall, the Scala's one consistent trait has been its lack of respect for authority: its stint as a cinema was ended after Stanley Kubrick sued it into bankruptcy for showing *A Clockwork Orange*. Nowadays, it's one of the most rewarding venues to push your way to the front for those cusp-of-greatness shows by big names in waiting – names as varied as the Chemical Brothers and Joss Stone.
275 Pentonville Road, King's Cross, N1 9NL (7833 2022, www.scala-london.co.uk). King's Cross tube/rail. Box office 10am-6pm Mon-Fri. Tickets free-£15.

Wembley Arena
Wembley Arena may have seen its commercial heyday end with the arrival of the O2 Arena (*see left*), although it is beginning to carve out something of a niche for soul with the Show revue. Still, it's hardly anyone's favourite venue, not least because the food and drink could be better, but most Londoners have warm memories of at least one Arena megagig, and a £30 million refurbishment did much to improve this 12,500-capacity venue.
Arena Square, Engineers Way, Wembley, Middx, HA9 0DH (8782 5500 information, 0844 815 0815 tickets, www.livenation.co.uk/wembley). Wembley Park tube. Box office In person 10.30am-4.30pm Mon-Fri; noon-4.30pm Sat (performance days only); 1hr before performance start Sun (performance days only). By phone 8.30am-8pm Mon-Fri; 8am-6pm Sat; 9am-6pm Sun. Tickets £5-£100.

In addition to the venues listed below, a handful of nightclubs also stage gigs. Try the **Notting Hill Arts Club** (*see p99*), **Madame JoJo's** (*see p104*), **Proud** (*see p98*) and **XOYO** (*see p99*).

12 Bar Club
A London treasure, this easy-to-miss hole-in-the-wall venue set among the guitar shops of Denmark Street books a grab-bag of low-key stuff, though its tiny size (it has an audience capacity of 100 and a minuscule stage) dictates a predominance of singer-songwriters.
22-23 Denmark Place, Soho, WC2H 8NL (7240 2622, www.12barclub.com). Tottenham Court Road tube. Open Café 11am-7pm Mon-Fri; noon-7pm Sat. Bar 7pm-3am Mon-Sat; 7pm-12.30am Sun. Shows from 7.30pm; nights vary. Admission £5-£13.

93 Feet East
With three rooms, a balcony and a wraparound courtyard that's great for barbecues, 93 Feet East keeps ticking by maintaining an incredibly broad programme: swing dance classes in the main bar, tech-house DJs, a mix of indie-dance bands and various art-rockers, plus short films, ping pong and cocktails nights, and a variety of arty happenings.
150 Brick Lane, Spitalfields, E1 6QL (7770 6006, www.93feeteast.co.uk). Aldgate East tube. Open 5-11pm Wed, Thur; 5pm-1am Fri, Sat; 2-10.30pm Sun. Shows vary. Admission free-£10.

100 Club
The 100 Club is synonymous with punk, having hosted shows by the Sex Pistols, the Clash, Siouxsie and the Banshees and the Buzzcocks. One historic show, in September 1976, featured the Sex Pistols, the Clash and

Nightlife

the Damned. These days, though, the famous, 350-capacity basement room is more of a hub for blues and pub rockers, and trad jazzers, coming into its own for the odd secret gig by A-list bands such as Primal Scream.
100 Oxford Street, Soho, W1D 1LL (7636 0933, www.the100club.co.uk). Oxford Circus tube. Open Shows vary; check website for details. Tickets £8-£17.50.

Barfly
This 200-capacity venue is part of London's indie-rock fabric, a key player in the fusion of indie guitars and electro into a danceable row.
49 Chalk Farm Road, Camden, NW1 8AN (7424 0800 information, 0844 847 2424 tickets, www.mamacolive.com/thebarfly). Chalk Farm tube. Open 3pm-2am Mon, Thur; 3pm-1am Tue, Wed; 3pm-3am Fri, Sat; 3pm-midnight Sun. Shows from 7pm daily. Admission free-£15.

Bloomsbury Bowling Lanes
Offering a late-night drink away from Soho, BBL has been putting on bands and DJs for a while now – and the range of activities make it a playground for grown-ups. As well as the eight lanes for bowling, there's pool by the hour, table football, karaoke booths and, beside the entrance, a small cinema. Music includes regular funk party Funk and Bowl Club, with appearances by the likes of Hackney Colliery Band and DJ Craig Charles.
Basement, Tavistock Hotel, Bedford Way, Bloomsbury, WC1H 9EU (7183 1979, www.bloomsburybowling.com). Russell Square tube. Open 4pm-midnight Mon, Tue; 4pm-2am Wed; noon-2am Thur; noon-3am Fri, Sat; noon-midnight Sun. Admission varies.

Brooklyn Bowl London
See right **All-new Nightlife Nexus**.
O2 Arena, Peninsula Square, SE10 0DX (7412 8747, www.brooklynbowl.com). North Greenwich tube. Open/admission check website for details.

Blues Kitchen
The Blues Kitchen combines credible live music (roots blues, rockabilly and so on) with a rather smart interior. The food is spicy New Orleans fare and there's a huge range of American bourbon for sippin'. All in all, it makes for a pleasant weekend afternoon hangout as well as a late-opening gig venue.
111 Camden High Street, Camden, NW1 7JN (7387 5277, www.theblueskitchen.com). Camden Town or Mornington Crescent tube. Open noon-midnight Mon, Tue; noon-1am Wed, Thur; noon-3am Fri; 10am-3.30am Sat; 10am-1am Sun. Admission free; £5 after 9.30pm Fri; £6 after 9pm Sat.

Borderline
A small, sweaty dive bar and juke joint right in the heart of Soho, the Borderline has long been a favoured stop-off for touring American bands of the country and blues varieties, though you'll also find a range of indie acts and

Brooklyn Bowl London

King's Cross, Dalston… Greenwich? Few Londoners would have predicted the next clubbing hotspot would be a peninsula in the Royal Borough of Greenwich, but it might just happen. This is where Studio 338 (*see p99*), a vast dance-music venue that has the hallmarks of a future superclub, reopened after a multimillion pound refurb. It was immediately a much cooler proposition than before, as demonstrated by the underground credentials of the world-class techno and house DJs (Marc 'MK' Kinchen, Kevin Saunderson, Kate Simko) who played the grand first night in March 2014. A big draw is the all-night terrace, but the interior is just as appealing, leaning towards the industrial but colourful vibe beloved of so many Berlin nightspots.

Of course, much of the area's current vim is down to the success of the O2 Arena (*see p101*), at the moment without rival as London's key venue for stadium rock and dance acts. And the O2 might provide 338 with some local competition. What was Matter, and then Proud2, has now reappeared in a third incarnation on the site as Building Six (*see p99*), run by the team behind London Warehouse Events. There's a new gig space here too: Brooklyn Bowl London (*see left*). Brooklyn Bowl was born in New York in 2009, a Williamsburg warehouse that has stayed a hipster hotspot ever since. As well as bowling, it has a great sound system and ambitions to host some of the hottest gigs in town. Interestingly, BB London has direct access from the O2 Arena's backstage area, which could bode well for secret pre-gigs and after-parties. In addition, some O2 Arena shows will be streamed live to BB – to be enjoyed while you tuck into classic American nosh: sloppy joes, oyster po' boys, cajun catfish and fried chicken.

singer-songwriters going through their repertoire here. Be warned, though, that it can get very cramped.
Orange Yard, off Manette Street, Soho, W1D 4JB (0844 847 2465, www.theborderline.co.uk). Tottenham Court Road tube. Open hrs vary. Admission £3-£20.

Bush Hall
This handsome room has been a dance hall, soup kitchen and snooker club. Now, with original fittings intact, it plays host to big bands performing stripped-down shows, top folk outfits and rising indie rockers.
310 Uxbridge Road, Shepherd's Bush, W12 7LJ (8222 6955, www.bushhallmusic.co.uk). Shepherd's Bush Market tube. Shows from 7.30pm. Tickets £5-£8.

Cecil Sharp House
Headquarters of the British Folk Dance and Song Society, Cecil Sharp

House is a great place to visit, even when there isn't any music playing – there's a folk arts education centre and archive open during the day. But the Kennedy Hall performance space boasts a comfortably sprung floor and a well-informed and enthusiastic team of bookers ensuring all angles of trad music are well represented without being preserved in aspic. Events range from regular Scottish ceilidhs to more contemporary alt folk.
2 Regent's Park Road, Camden, NW1 7AY (7485 2206, www.cecilsharphouse.org). Camden Town tube. Open/tickets vary.

Corsica Studios
Corsica Studios is an independent, not-for-profit arts complex whose ethos is to breed creativity and culture. The flexible performance space is used as one of London's most adventurous live music venues

and clubs, supplementing bands with poets, painters and lunatic projectionists. Main nights include Trouble Vision, a mashing of different genres of dance music.
Elephant Road, Elephant & Castle, SE17 1LB (7703 4760, www.corsicastudios.com). Elephant & Castle tube/rail. Open hrs vary. Tickets £3-£15.

Garage
This 650-capacity alt-rock venue books an exciting and surprisingly wide-ranging calendar of indie and art rock gigs, from ancient punk survivors such as the Pop Group and Sham 69 to the poppier end of the indie singer-songwriter scale (Fran Healy in the smaller Upstairs, for example).
20-22 Highbury Corner, Highbury, N5 1RD (7619 6721 information, 0844 847 1678 tickets, www.mamacolive.com/thegarage). Highbury & Islington tube/rail. Box office By phone 24hrs daily. Tickets £3-£20.

Green Note
A stone's throw from Regent's Park, this cosy little venue and vegetarian café-bar was a welcome addition to the city's roots circuit back in 2005. Singer-songwriters, folkies and blues musicians make up the majority of the gig roster, with a handful of big names in among the listings.
106 Parkway, Camden, NW1 7AN (7485 9899, www.greennote.co.uk). Camden Town tube. Open 7-11pm Mon-Thur, Sun; 7pm-midnight Fri, Sat. Shows 8.30pm daily. Tickets £4-£15.

Hoxton Square Bar & Kitchen
This 450-capacity venue is more than just a place to be seen: the line-ups are always cutting edge and fun, with the HSB&K often hosting a band's first London outing. Get there early or be prepared to queue.
2-4 Hoxton Square, Shoreditch, N1 6NU (7613 0709, www.mamacolive.com/hoxton). Old Street tube/rail or Shoreditch High Street rail. Open noon-midnight Mon, Sun; noon-1am Tue-Thur; noon-2am Fri, Sat. Tickets free-£5 after 10pm Fri, Sat.

Jazz Café
Given its sterling reputation, you wouldn't think that the jazz café was such a newbie on the London music map, converted from a branch of Barclays in 1990. In those days, the support pillars famously boasted the command of 'STFU' – this was a venue that took music seriously. These days, though, the interpretation of jazz is pretty loose, stretching to intimate shows by US hip hop legends (such as De La Soul) and racing certainties (such as Aloe Blacc's incredible UK debut), as well as funk, soul and R&B legends such as Marlena Shaw and Mary J Blige.
5 Parkway, Camden, NW1 7PG (7688 8899 information, 0844 847 2514 tickets, www.mamacolive.com/thejazzcafe). Camden Town tube. Box office In person 10.30am-5.30pm Mon-Sat. By phone 24hrs daily. Tickets £5-£30.

Nightlife

Lexington

Effectively the common room for the music industry's perennial sixth form, this 200-capacity venue has a superb sound system in place for the leftfield indie bands that dominate the programme. It's where the hottest US exports often make their London debut: indie bandss such as the Drums and Sleigh Bells have cut their teeth here in front of London's most receptive crowds. Downstairs, there's a lounge bar with a vast array of US beers and bourbons, above-par bar food and a Rough Trade music quiz (every Monday).
96-98 Pentonville Road, Islington, N1 9JB (7837 5371, www.thelexington. co.uk). Angel tube. Open noon-2am Mon-Wed, Sun; noon-3am Thur; noon-4am Fri, Sat. Tickets free-£15.

Nest

Formerly the Dalston hipster institution Bardens Boudoir, the Nest retains much of its predecessor's eclectic, forward-looking booking policy, with the benefit of a big money 'distressed industrial' refurbishment and, crucially, much improved toilets.
36 Stoke Newington Road, Dalston, N16 7XJ (7354 9993, www.ilovethe nest.com). Dalston Kingsland rail. Open hrs vary Mon-Wed, check website for details; 9pm-3am Thur; 9pm-4am Fri, Sat. Tickets free-£10.

Shacklewell Arms

A Dalston location and a roster of sharp acts make the Shacklewell Arms the venue du jour in fashionable hearts. This quirkily decorated gaff has hosted the Horrors, Toy and Haim, among many others.
71 Shacklewell Lane, Dalston, E8 2EB (7249 0810, www.shacklewell arms. com). Dalston Kingsland or Dalston Junction rail. Open 5pm-midnight Mon-Wed; 5pm-1am Thur; 5pm-3am Fri; noon-3am Sat; noon-midnight Sun. Admission free-£8.

Underworld

A dingy maze of pillars and bars below Camden, this subterranean oddity is an essential for metal and hardcore fans who want their ears bludgeoned by bands with names such as the Atomic Bitchwax, Skeletonwitch and Decrepit Birth. Tickets are purchased from the World's End pub upstairs.
174 Camden High Street, Camden, NW1 0NE (7482 1932, www.the underworldcamden.co.uk). Camden Town tube. Box office In person 11am-11pm daily. By phone 24hrs daily. Shows hrs vary. Admission £5-£20.

Union Chapel

In 2012, readers of *Time Out* magazine voted Union Chapel their top music venue. The Grade I-listed Victorian Gothic church still holds services and runs a homeless centre, while doubling as an atmospheric gig venue. It made its name hosting acoustic events and occasional jazz shows, becoming a magnet for thinking bands and their fans. These days, you'll also find classy intimate shows from bigger artists such

as Paloma Faith. Watch out for the Daylight Music free Saturday afternoon concerts.
Compton Terrace, Islington, N1 2XD (7226 1686, www.unionchapel.org.uk). Highbury & Islington tube/rail. Open hrs vary. Tickets £6-£35.

Windmill

There's a free barbecue every Sunday afternoon in summer; a somewhat scary dog lives on the roof, frightening unsuspecting smokers; and an actual windmill stands in the adjacent park. The Windmill is certainly not your average music venue, but it's been revelling in its rough-around-the-edges eccentricity for years, its unprepossessing exterior a cloak for its dedication to new leftfield music. The Vaccines played here in 2013, though generally the programming is biased towards alt country, alt folk and alt punk. It's worth a visit just to pick up an 'I Believe in Roof Dog' T-shirt.
22 Blenheim Gardens, Brixton, SW2 5BZ (8671 0700, http://windmill brixton.co.uk). Brixton tube/ rail. Open Shows 8-11pm Mon-Thur; 8pm-1am Fri, Sat; 2-11pm Sun. Admission free-£10.

Jazz & improv

These are exciting times for the city's homespun jazz scene. Inspired by freewheeling attractions at the **Vortex** (*see p104*) and the sporadic, unhinged **Boat-Ting Club** nights (www.boat-ting.co.uk), acts such as Portico Quartet, Led Bib and Kit Downes Trio have won Mercury Prize nominations with recent albums, and the F-IRE and Loop Collectives are busy nurturing future stars.

In addition to the venues below, the **100 Club** (*see p101*) hosts trad groups, while the **Spice of Life** at Cambridge Circus (6 Moor Street,

W1D 5NA, 7437 7013, www.spiceof lifesoho.com) has solid mainstream jazz. The **Jazz Café** (*see p102*) lives up to its name from time to time; there's a lot of very good jazz at the excellent **Kings Place** (*see p105*); and both the **Barbican** (*see p107*) and the **Southbank Centre** (*see p106*) host dozens of big names. For the increasingly excellent **London Jazz Festival**, *see p14*.

606 Club

Since 1976, Steve Rubie has run this spot, which relocated to this 150-capacity club in 1987. Alongside its Brit-dominated bills, expect informal jams featuring musos who've come from gigs elsewhere. There's no entrance fee as such; bands are funded from a music charge added to bills at the end of the night.
90 Lots Road, Chelsea, SW10 0QD (7352 5953, www.606club.co.uk). Imperial Wharf rail or bus 11, 211. Shows 8.30pm Mon, Thur, Sun; 7.30pm, 10.15pm Tue, Wed; 9.30pm Fri, Sat. Admission (non-members) £8-£12.

Bull's Head

This venerable, ancient Thames-side pub won a reputation for hosting modern jazz in the 1960s but today specialises in mainstream British jazz and swing, with guests such as the Humphrey Lyttelton band. A facelift has added posh pub food and quirkily appealing decor.
373 Lonsdale Road, Barnes, SW13 9PY (3437 0134, www.thebullshead. com). Barnes Bridge rail. Open noon-11pm Mon-Sat; noon-10pm Sun. Jazz Club 8-11pm Mon-Sat; 1-3.30pm, 8.30-11pm Sun. Admission £5-£12.

Café Oto

Opened in 2008, this 150-capacity café and music venue can't easily be categorised, though its website offers the tidy definition that it specialises

in 'creative new music that exists outside of the mainstream'. That means Japanese noise rockers ('Oto' is Japanese for 'sound'), electronica pioneers, improvising noiseniks and artists from the stranger ends of the rock, folk and classical spectrums.
18-22 Ashwin Street, Dalston, E8 3DL (7923 1231, www.cafeoto.co.uk). Dalston Junction or Dalston Kingsland rail. Café Open 8.30am-5.30pm Mon-Fri; 9.30am-5.30pm Sat; 10.30am-5.30pm Sun. Shows 8pm. Admission £4-£12.

Charlie Wright's International Bar

When Zhenya Strigalev and Patsy Craig began programming here in 2006, London's jazz fans were given a reason to visit what had been merely a rather good after-hours boozer. Now this agreeably scruffy venue stages a fine jazz programme every night of the week bar Saturday. Gigs don't usually start until 10pm, and run late on Thursdays and Fridays.
45 Pitfield Street, Hoxton, N1 6DA (7490 8345, www.charliewrights. com). Old Street tube/rail. Open noon-1am Mon-Wed; noon-4am Thur, Fri; 6pm-4am Sat; 6pm-1am Sun. Shows from 8pm daily. Admission free-£10.

Forge & Foundry

Run by a non-profit community organisation, this innovative music/restaurant space hosts concerts of various sizes and formalities. The programme is skewed heavily to jazz, but also features a carefully curated selection of roots and classical shows. There's an on-site restaurant, the Foundry; you can dine while you listen on a Friday, and there's an interesting Sunday brunch programme.
3-7 Delancey Street, Camden, NW1 7NL (7383 7808, www.forgevenue.org). Camden Town tube. Open hrs vary. Admission free-£12.

Pizza Express Jazz Club

The upstairs restaurant (7437 9595) is jazz-free, but the 120-capacity basement is one of the best mainstream jazz venues in town. Singers such as Kurt Elling and Lea DeLaria join instrumentalists from home and abroad on the nightly bills.
10 Dean Street, Soho, W1D 3RW (0845 602 7017, www.pizzaexpress live.com). Tottenham Court Road tube. Shows hrs vary, check website for details. Admission £15-£25.

Ronnie Scott's

This jazz institution was completely refurbished in 2006. The capacity was expanded to 250, the food got better and the bookings became drearier. Happily, though, Ronnie's has got back on track, with jazz heavyweights dominating once more – from trad talents such as Chick Corea to hotly tipped purists such as Kurt Elling to futuristic mavericks such as Robert Glasper. Perch by the rear bar or get table service at the crammed side-seating or more spacious (but noisier) central tables in front of the stage.

Oslo. See p98.

*47 Frith Street, Soho, W1D 4HT
(7439 0747, www.ronniescotts.co.uk).
Leicester Square tube. Shows 7.15pm-
1am Mon-Sat; noon-4pm, 8pm-
midnight Sun. Admission £20-£50.*

Vortex Jazz Club

One of the few venues in the city you could visit on spec and be guaranteed to hear something interesting. Along with nearby Café Oto, the Vortex is one of London's most lovingly curated venues. Jazz is the order of the day, but the Vortex serves it up in kaleidoscopic variety. For the less daring, there's a regular calendar of big band, piano trio, vocal, free improv, world music and folk-oriented sounds each month, as well as some poetry gigs. The Vortex hosts its own strand of the London Jazz Festival and various other forward-thinking events. *Dalston Culture House, 11 Gillet Street, Dalston, N16 8JN (7254 4097, www.vortexjazz.co.uk). Dalston Kingsland rail. Shows 8pm daily. Admission £5-£18.*

Cabaret

To see the best cabaret, head to **Soho Theatre** (*see p108*) downstairs space, host to excellent international performers ranging from European chanteuses to American alternative drag acts; the always interesting **Bethnal Green Working Men's Club** (*see below*); and the even more alternative **RVT** (*see p97*). A recent trend has been for cabaret in posh venues. **The Savoy** (*see p113*) has hosted evenings in the Beaufort Bar mixing burlesque, variety and song; **Brasserie Zédel** (*see p72*) puts on shows at its Crazy Coqs venue; and the **Hippodrome** (www.hippodrome casino.com), now a casino, also hosts music and cabaret in its dedicated performance rooms.

Bethnal Green Working Men's Club

Sticky red carpet and broken lampshades perfectly suit the programme of quirky lounge, retro rock 'n' roll and fancy-dress burlesque parties here. You might get to watch a spandex-lovin' dance duo or get hip with burlesque starlets on a 1960s dancefloor. The mood is friendly, the playlist upbeat and the air full of artful, playful mischief. *42-44 Pollard Row, Bethnal Green, E2 6NB (7739 7170, www.workers playtime.net). Bethnal Green tube. Open hrs vary; check website for details. Admission free-£8.*

CellarDoor

Some staggeringly clever design means that although there's room for just 60 in this subterranean converted Victorian loo, CellarDoor never feels claustrophobic. Musical-theatre cabaret crooners and drag queens are the order of the day, giving this sleek establishment a vintage feel. Nearly all shows are free and often great fun – EastEnd Cabaret regularly appear and

Champagne Charlie's Trash Tuesday open-mic night is an institution. *Zero Aldwych, Covent Garden, WC2E 7D (7240 8848, www.cellardoor.biz). Covent Garden tube. Open hrs vary; check website for details. Admission varies.*

Madame JoJo's

The red and slightly shabby basement space at JoJo's is a beacon for those seeking to escape the West End's chain pubs. The most treasured nights tend towards variety – Kitsch Cabaret is every Saturday night – but its long-running Tuesday nighter, White Heat, still books up-and-coming bands and DJs for a largely indie and student crowd. *8-10 Brewer Street, Soho, W1F 0SD (7734 3040, www.madamejojos.com). Leicester Square tube. Open 7.30pm-3am Tue-Sun. Admission £3-£15.*

Pheasantry

The successor to the institution that was Pizza on the Park, this jazz and cabaret venue is also part of the Pizza Express stable. The bright, spacious basement space has something of a cruise-ship feel and sightlines aren't always great, but it's the city's premier platform for New York-style jazz singing and musical-theatre-influenced cabaret work, often attracting big names from the West End and across the pond. *152-154 King's Road, Chelsea, SW3 4UT (0845 602 7017, www.pizza expresslive.com). Sloane Square tube. Shows 8.30pm, days vary, check website for details. Admission varies.*

St James Studio

When it opened in 2012, an integral part of St James Theatre was its downstairs Studio space, a cosy room that plays host to a range of work towards the classic end of the cabaret spectrum, as well as comedy, music and fringe work. Recent highlights have included runs from Barb Jungr and Peter Straker's barnstorming tribute to the songs of Jacques Brel. *12 Palace Street, Victoria, SW1E 5JA (0844 264 2140, www.stjamestheatre. co.uk). Victoria tube/rail. Open hrs vary, check website for details. Admission £15-£25.*

Comedy

The **Soho Theatre** (*see p108*) also hosts comedy acts.

Amused Moose Soho

Hils Jago's rosters are always strong, with names such as Bill Bailey and Eddie Izzard continuing to justify the club's multi-award-winning status. Jago has a lot of special guests who can't be named – in other words, top names trying out new material – and runs the Amused Moose Comedy Awards; finalists have included Jimmy Carr and Simon Amstell. *Moonlighting, 17 Greek Street, Soho, W1D 4DR (7287 3727, www.amused moose.com). Leicester Square tube. Shows Sept-May 7.45pm Sat. Admission £10-£14. No credit cards.*

Boat Show

The line-ups aboard this floating comedy club situated opposite the London Eye are consistently strong. A nightclub follows the comedy every Friday and Saturday at no extra charge. *Tattershall Castle, Kings Reach, Victoria Embankment, SW1A 2HR (07932 658895, www.boatshow comedy.co.uk). Embankment tube. Shows 8pm Fri, Sat. Admission £11-£15. No credit cards.*

Canal Café Theatre

This charming little theatre, perched on the edge of a canal, offers a number of shows a week. Past performers include Stewart Lee and Pete Firman, and it's a good place to catch young comics and sketch acts, as well as NewsRevue, who have a residency performing their topical sketches and songs every Thursday to Sunday. *Delamere Terrace, Little Venice, W2 6ND (7289 6054, www.canalcafe theatre.com). Royal Oak or Warwick Avenue tube. Shows vary; check website for details. Admission £8.50-£12.50.*

Comedy Café

The Comedy Café is another purpose-built club set up by a comedian. Noel Faulkner mainly keeps to the back room but, with the emphasis on inviting bills and satisfied punters, his influence can still be felt. The atmosphere is fun and food is an integral part of the experience. *68 Rivington Street, Shoreditch, EC2A 3AY (7739 5706, www.comedycafe. co.uk). Old Street tube/rail. Shows 8pm Tue-Sat. Admission £7-£12; free Wed.*

Comedy Store

Alternative line-ups at this, the daddy of British comedy clubs, helped to launch jokers such as Alexei Sayle, Dawn French and Paul Merton. The legendary King Gong show, in which would-be stand-ups are given only as much time as the audience will allow, is on the last Monday of the month. *1A Oxendon Street, Soho, SW1Y 4EE (0844 871 7699, www.thecomedy store.co.uk). Leicester Square tube. Shows times vary, check website for details. Admission £9-£23.50.*

Downstairs at the King's Head

Founded in 1981, this venue is still run with huge enthusiasm by its immensely knowledgeable promoter Pete Grahame. It's an easygoing place where comedians can experiment and play around with new material. It's popular with comics doing warm-up shows for TV and tours. *2 Crouch End Hill, Crouch End, N8 8AA (8340 1028, www.downstairsat thekingshead.com). Finsbury Park tube/rail then bus W7. Shows 8pm Tue, Thur, Sat, Sun. Admission £3-£11.*

Etcetera Theatre

This intimate black box theatre is a great place to catch Edinburgh previews, comedy in August's Camden Fringe, and big names such as Russell Brand warming up for tours.

The Oxford Arms, 256 Camden High Street, Camden, NW1 7BU (7482 4857, www.etceteratheatre.com). Camden Town tube. Shows vary; check website for details. Admission £3-£10.

Feature Spot

Feature Spot's monthly comedy nights often feature in critics' choices lists. Previous acts include Russell Howard, Stephen Merchant, Adam Buxton and Tim Minchin. *The 100 Club, 100 Oxford Street, Soho, W1D 1LL (07956 834135, www.featurespot.co.uk). Oxford Circus tube. Shows vary; check website for details. Admission £10-£15.*

Funny Side of Covent Garden

An enjoyable club upstairs in a mock Tudor pub. Well-known comedians such as Felix Dexter, Josie Long and Phil Kay have all performed here. *Upstairs at The George, 213 the Strand, WC2R 1AP (0844 478 0404, www.thefunnyside.info). Temple tube. Shows 8pm Sat. Admission £12.50.*

Hen & Chickens

This dinky, black-box theatre above a cosy Victorian corner pub is well known as the place to see great solo shows, especially from those warming up for a tour. Acts have included Jenny Eclair, Frankie Boyle, Rhona Cameron and Jimmy Carr. *109 St Paul's Road, Highbury Corner, Islington, N1 2NA (7704 2001, www.thehenandchickenstheatrebar. co.uk). Highbury & Islington tube/rail. Shows times vary. Admission £4-£12.50. No credit cards.*

The Invisible Dot

Probably the hippest comedy club in London, the Invisible Dot programmes gigs across London – and also runs a terrific programme at this anonymous-looking former workshop. *2 Northdown Street, King's Cross, N1 9BG (7424 8918, www.theinvisibledot. com). King's Cross tube/rail. Show times vary. Admission £6-£10.*

Leicester Square Theatre

With a mixture of mixed-bill shows and solo offerings, the theatre programmes comedy names in the main house, and rising stars in the basement. A favourite of many big-name American comics. *6 Leicester Place, Soho, WC2H 7BX (0844 873 3433, www.leicestersquare theatre.com). Leicester Square tube. Shows vary; check website for details. Admission £5-£47.*

Up the Creek

Set up by the late and legendary Malcolm Hardee, this purpose-built club remains one of the best places to enjoy comedy. It's renowned for its lively, not to say bearpit atmosphere, but there's a more chilled-out feel on Sundays (www.sundayspecial.co.uk). *302 Creek Road, Greenwich, SE10 9SW (8858 4581, www.up-the-creek. com). Greenwich DLR/rail. Shows 8.15pm Thur; 8.45pm Fri; 8.30pm Sat; 7.30pm Sun. Admission £5-£14.*

Performing Arts

Swan Lake, **Royal Ballet**. See p108.

Matilda the Musical

Critic's choice

1 **National Theatre** The absolute powerhouse of subsidised theatre in London, creating a string of West End hits. *See p107.*

2 **Kings Place** Superb venue for classical, jazz and world music, and spoken word performances. *See p105.*

3 **Matilda the Musical** Laugh, cry and believe the world can be a better place. *See p107.*

4 **Shakespeare's Globe** Experience the Bard's masterpieces in authentic surroundings. *See p107.*

5 **Southbank Centre** A must-visit for the gigs and concerts, and the free events. *See p106.*

Making a song and dance about it

Sample London's world-class theatre, classical music and dance scenes.

London's classical musicians seem unusually open-minded, with classical nights in pubs and jazz strands at august classical auditoriums. But as well as this mix-and-match aesthetic, passionate purists remain – the Barbican and Royal Festival Hall still deliver a big orchestral punch with the traditional repertoire. Music, of a different stripe, dominates the West End theatre scene too: the biggest attractions remain the indomitable musicals. That's not to say there's no 'proper' drama in the capital, with a couple of current successes having begun life in the National Theatre, the city's flagship publicly funded theatre. And London remains a hub for dance in a way few other cities can match, with even the 80-year-old Royal Ballet producing groundbreaking new work.

See the free *Time Out* magazine for the performing arts highlights of the week, or check out the cultural listings at www.timeout.com.

Classical Music & Opera

London's classical scene has never looked or sounded more current, with the **Southbank Centre** (*see p106*), the **Barbican Centre** (*see right*) and **Kings Place** (*see right*) all working with strong programmes.

Classical venues

In addition to the major venues below, you can hear what tomorrow's classical music might sound like at the city's music schools. Check the websites of the **Royal Academy of Music** (7873 7373, www.ram.ac.uk), the Royal College of Music (7591 4314, www.rcm.ac.uk), the **Guildhall School of Music & Drama** (7628 2571, www.gsmd.ac.uk) and

Trinity College of Music (8305 4444, www.tcm.ac.uk). There's also a trend for top-class classical and contemporary classical music in relaxed – for which read 'alcohol-friendly' – settings (*see p107* **Booze and Baroque**).

Barbican Centre

The London Symphony Orchestra remains in residence at Europe's largest multi-arts centre. The BBC Symphony Orchestra also performs an annual series of concerts, and there's a laudable amount of contemporary classical music. Beyond classical, programming falls into a wide range of genres: from Sufi music to New York rock legends. A brand-new concert hall opened in 2014 barely 100 yards from the main external entrance to the Barbican. Milton Court (1 Milton Street, EC2Y 9BH, 7638 8891, www.gsmd.ac.uk) is run by the Guildhall School of Music & Drama and combines a 608-seat concert hall and two smaller theatres.

Silk Street, the City, EC2Y 8DS (7638 4141 information, 7638 8891 tickets, www.barbican. org.uk). Barbican tube or Moorgate tube/rail. Box office 10am-9pm Mon-Sat; noon-9pm Sun. Tickets £8-£65.

Cadogan Hall

The programming at the austere yet comfortable 900-seat hall is dominated by classical. The Royal Philharmonic are resident; other orchestras perform, and there's regular chamber music. *5 Sloane Terrace, off Sloane Street, Chelsea, SW1X 9DQ (7730 4500, www.cadoganhall.com). Sloane Square tube. Box office Non-performance days 10am-6pm Mon-Sat. Performance days 10am-8pm Mon-Sat. Tickets £15-£50.*

Kings Place

The 400-seat main hall is a beauty; there's also a versatile second hall and a number of smaller rooms for workshops and lectures. The programming is tremendous and includes curated weeks featuring

Performing Arts

artists as wide-ranging as Schönberg and jazz band AIR. Other strands include chamber music and experimental classical, and there are spoken-word events too. *90 York Way, King's Cross, N1 9AG (0844 264 0321, www.kingsplace. co.uk). King's Cross tube/rail. Box office 10am-5pm Mon; noon-7pm Tue-Sun (performance days only). Tickets £9.50-£51.50.*

LSO St Luke's
This Grade I-listed church, built by Nicholas Hawksmoor in the 18th century, was beautifully converted into a performance and rehearsal space by the LSO several years ago. The orchestra occasionally welcomes the public for open rehearsals (book ahead); the more formal side of the programme takes in global sounds alongside classical music, including lunchtime concerts every Thursday that are broadcast on BBC Radio 3. *161 Old Street, the City, EC1V 9NG (7588 1116 information, 7638 8891 tickets, www.lso.co.uk/lsostlukes). Old Street tube/rail. Box office 10am-9pm Mon-Sat; noon-9pm Sun. Tickets free-£37.*

Royal Albert Hall
In constant use since opening in 1871, with boxing matches, motorshows and Allen Ginsberg's 1965 International Poetry Incarnation among the headline events, the Royal Albert Hall continues to host a very broad programme. The classical side is dominated by the superb BBC Proms (*see p12*). *Kensington Gore, South Kensington, SW7 2AP (0845 401 5034, www.roy-alalberthall.com). South Kensington tube or bus 9, 10, 52, 452. Box office 9am-9pm daily. Tickets £13-£275.*

St James's Piccadilly
This community-spirited Wren church holds free lunchtime recitals (Mon, Wed, Fri at 1.10pm) and offers regular evening concerts in a variety of fields. *197 Piccadilly, Piccadilly, W1J 9LL (7381 0441, www.sjp.org.uk). Piccadilly Circus tube. Box office 10am-5pm Mon-Sat. Tickets free-£27.*

St John's, Smith Square
This 18th-century church hosts concerts more or less nightly, and Thursday lunchtime recitals too, with everything from symphony orchestras to solo recitals making the most of good acoustics. Down in the crypt are two bars and a restaurant. The church marks its 300th anniversary in 2014. *Smith Square, Westminster, SW1P 3HA (7222 1061, www.sjss.org.uk). Westminster tube. Box office Non-performance days 10am-5pm Mon-Fri. Performance days 10am-6pm Mon-Fri. Tickets free-£28.*

St Martin-in-the-Fields
One of the capital's most amiable and populist venues, hosting performances of the likes of Bach, Mozart and Vivaldi by candlelight, jazz in the crypt's café and lunchtime recitals (1pm Mon, Tue, Fri) from young musicians.

SHADOW PLAYS
The new way to see historic theatre.

Sam Wanamaker Playhouse

'I'm told it would take a flamethrower to even char the walls,' says Dominic Dromgoole, the artistic director of **Shakespeare's Globe** (*see p107*), proudly. We're standing in the Sam Wanamaker Playhouse, London's newest, sexiest theatre and the intimate indoor sibling to the boisterous open-air Globe. It is made entirely of wood and lit entirely by candles, but rigorously engineered so that its exquisitely decorated oak frame could withstand even the fieriest conflagration. That's good: it was fire that did for the original, Elizabethan Globe.

What the first Globe didn't have was a bijou indoor venue. But Shakespeare and his King's Men theatre troupe did have one just down the road, on which the Wanamaker is modelled. They moved there in 1609, by which time Elizabeth's golden age was over and the unpopular James I had the throne. Shakespeare's plays got darker and weirder, and the new generation of Jacobean playwrights were writing claustrophobic, blood-soaked revenge tragedies for candlelit indoor spaces. Foremost is John Webster's bleak 1612 masterpiece *The Duchess of Malfi*, which made the perfect opener for the new theatre, a long-delayed cornerstone of Wanamaker's original plans.

The rest of the inaugural season was delightfully unfamiliar, taking in 1607 meta-comedy *The Knight of the Burning Pestle* and 1645 opera *L'Ormindo*, a hook-up with the Royal Opera House (*see below*). Notably, there was no Shakespeare, and the prices mark this as a more exclusive venue than the £5-to-stand Globe – tickets for *L'Ormindo* topped out at a hearty £100 (still not bad for opera).

There's no denying it's exclusive,' says Dromgoole. 'But our prices are still lower than the commercial sector. In fact, it's a f**king bargain!'

Trafalgar Square, Westminster, WC2N 4JJ (7766 1100, www.st martin-in-the-fields.org). Charing Cross tube/rail. Box office In person 8am-5pm Mon, Tue; 8am-9.45pm Wed; 8am-8.30pm Thur-Sat. By phone 10am-5pm Mon-Sat. Tickets free-£30.

Southbank Centre
The centrepiece of the cluster of cultural venues collectively known as the Southbank Centre is the 3,000-seater Royal Festival Hall, which was renovated acoustically and externally to the tune of £90m back in 2007; now the neighbouring 900-seat Queen Elizabeth Hall and attached 365-seat Purcell Room are due a little TLC – plans for refurbishment are in the pipeline. All three programme a wide variety of events – spoken word, jazz, rock and pop gigs – but classical is very well represented. The RFH has four resident orchestras (the London Philharmonic and Philharmonia Orchestras, the London Sinfonietta and the Orchestra of the Age of Enlightenment), and hosts music from medieval motets to Messiaen via Beethoven and Elgar. The foyer stage puts on hundreds of free concerts each year. For the **Hayward Gallery**, third leg of the Southbank Centre's tripod, *see p16*. *Belvedere Road, South Bank, SE1 8XX (7960 4200 information, 0844 875 0073 tickets, www.southbankcentre. co.uk). Waterloo tube/rail. Box office In person 10am-8pm daily. By phone 9am-8pm daily. Tickets £7-£75.*

Wigmore Hall
Built in 1901 as the display hall for Bechstein pianos, this world-renowned, 550-seat concert venue has perfect acoustics for the 400 concerts that take place each year. Music from the classical and romantic periods are mainstays, usually performed by major classical stars to an intense audience, but under artistic director John Gilhooly there has been a broadening in the remit: more baroque and increased jazz, including late-night gigs. Monday lunchtime recitals are broadcast live on BBC Radio 3. *36 Wigmore Street, Marylebone, W1U 2BP (7935 2141, www.wigmore-hall.org.uk). Bond Street tube. Box office Non-performance days 10am-7pm Mon-Sat; 10am-2pm Sun. Performance days 10am-7pm daily. Tickets £10-£35.*

Opera venues

In addition to the two big venues below, look out for performances at the Linbury Studio, downstairs at the **Royal Opera House**, **Cadogan Hall** (*see p105*), summer's **Opera Holland Park** (*see p11*), sporadic appearances by **English Touring Opera** (www.englishtouring opera.org.uk) and much promising work, often directed by big names, at the city's music schools. A small but lively fringe opera scene has sprung up with **OperaUpClose** branching out from its King's Head Theatre base in Islington (www.kingsheadtheatre.com) to play up west at the Soho and Charing Cross Theatres; and the **Charles Court Opera** company doing fine operetta in various small theatres (www.charlescourt opera.com).

English National Opera, Coliseum
Built as a music hall in 1904, the home of the English National Opera (ENO) is in fine condition following a renovation back in 2004. Under the stewardship of music director Edward Gardner, it has offered some fascinating collaborations over the last few years. All works are in English, and prices are cheaper than at the Royal Opera. *St Martin's Lane, Covent Garden, WC2N 4ES (7845 9300 tickets, www.eno.org). Leicester Square tube or Charing Cross tube/rail. Box office In person 10am-6pm Mon-Sat. By phone 24hrs daily. Tickets £20-£115.*

Royal Opera, Royal Opera House
Thanks to a refurbishment at the start of the century, the Royal Opera House has once again taken its place among the ranks of the world's great opera houses. Critics sometimes suggest that the programming can be a little spotty, especially so given the famously elevated ticket prices. The spine of the programme is, of course, fine productions of the classics. Productions take in favourite composers (Donizetti, Mozart, Verdi) and some modern (Benjamin Britten, Harrison Birtwistle). The Royal Ballet is also based here; *see p108*. *Covent Garden, WC2E 9DD (7304 4000, www.roh.org.uk). Covent Garden tube. Box office 10am-8pm Mon-Sat. Tickets £6-£215.*

Performing Arts

Theatre

The West End has managed to ride out the recession on a tide of song – in other words, those big-production musicals, the most ancient of which had been hoofing it on the London stage since the late 1980s. Although many of those old-timers have now gone, the format is still hugely popular, thanks to the arrival of a bunch of lively, thoroughly modern new musicals – including smash Broadway hit *The Book of Mormon*. Drama is making a very real comeback too, led by the success of National Theatre transfers such as *War Horse* and *The Curious Incident of the Dog in the Night-Time*, as well as a spate of excellent Shakespeare productions.

THEATRE DISTRICTS

The West End refers to London's traditional theatre district, a busy area bounded by Shaftesbury Avenue, Drury Lane, the Strand and the Haymarket. Most major musicals and big-money dramas run here, alongside transfers of successful smaller-scale shows. However, the 'West End' appellation is now also applied to other major theatres elsewhere in town, including subsidised venues such as the **Barbican Centre** (in the City), the **National Theatre** (on the South Bank) and the **Old Vic** (Waterloo).

Off-West End denotes theatres with smaller budgets and smaller capacities. These venues, many of them sponsored or subsidised, push the creative envelope with new writing, often brought to life by the best young acting and directing talent. The **Bush** is good for up-and-coming writers, while the **Almeida** and **Donmar Warehouse** offer elegantly produced shows with the occasional big star.

THE FRINGE

The best places to catch next-generation talent include **Theatre 503**, above the Latchmere pub (503 Battersea Park Road, SW11 3BW, 7978 7040, www.theatre503.com) and the **Finborough** (118 Finborough Road, SW10 9ED, 0844 847 1652, www.finboroughtheatre.co.uk), above a pub in Earl's Court.

Other venues that are worth investigating include the **Yard** (Queen's Yard, Hackney Wick, E9 5EN, www.theyardtheatre.co.uk), a new 130-seat venue near the Olympic Park; the **Southwark Playhouse** (77-85 Newington Causeway, Southwark, SE1 6BD, 7407 0234, www.southwark playhouse.co.uk); and the **Menier Chocolate Factory** (53 Southwark Street, Southwark, SE1 1RU, 7378 1713, www.menier chocolatefactory.com), which, like the **Union Theatre** (204 Union Street, Southwark, SE1 0LX, 7261 9876, www.union theatre.biz) has a knack for musicals up-close.

BUYING TICKETS

If there's a specific show you want to see, book ahead. And, if possible, always try to do so at the theatre's box office, at which booking fees are generally smaller than they are with agents such as **Ticketmaster** (0844 844 0444, www.ticketmaster.co.uk).

If you're more flexible about your choice of show, consider buying from the TKTS booth (*see below* **Going Cheap**) or taking your chances with standby seats .

The West End

MAJOR THEATRES

Barbican Centre

The annual BITE (Barbican International Theatre Events) season continues to cherry-pick exciting and eclectic theatre companies from around the globe. Watch out, too, for imaginatively leftfield family-friendly theatre and installations during school holidays. *For listings, see p105.*

National Theatre

This concrete monster is the flagship venue of British theatre, and no theatrical tour of London is complete without a visit. At the time of writing, one of the theatre's three auditoriums was out of action (the Cottesloe is being refurbished and will reopen as the Dorfman Theatre). In the interim, the big, red, temporary Shed is hosting performances of adventurous work from young writers. Productions range from top-notch Shakespeare to reworked foreign classics, and British revivals. *South Bank, SE1 9PX (information 7452 3400, tickets 7452 3000, www.nationaltheatre.org.uk). Embankment or Southwark tube, or Waterloo tube/rail. Box office 9.30am-8pm Mon-Sat. Tickets Olivier & Lyttelton £12-£48.*

Old Vic

Oscar-winner Kevin Spacey has been the artistic director here since 2003, and the theatre continues to have commercial success. The Old Vic is a beautiful venue, where programming runs from grown-up Christmas pantomimes to serious drama. *The Cut, Waterloo, SE1 8NB (0844 871 7628, www.oldvictheatre.com). Southwark tube or Waterloo tube/rail. Box office In person 9am-7.30pm Mon-Fri; 9am-7pm Sat. By phone 9am-7.30pm Mon-Fri; 9am-4pm Sat; 9.30am-4pm Sun. Tickets £11-£52.*

Open Air Theatre

The verdant setting of this alfresco theatre lends itself perfectly to Shakespeare romps – *A Midsummer Night's Dream* is a regular here. But it's not just the Bard – you'll also find classic American shows, such as hit musical *Porgy and Bess* and Arthur Miller's 1947 drama *All My Sons*.

Regent's Park, Inner Circle, Marylebone, NW1 4NR (0844 826 4242, www.openairtheatre.com). Baker Street tube. Tickets £15-£55.

Royal Court Theatre

From John Osborne's *Look Back in Anger*, staged in the theatre's opening year of 1956, to the many discoveries of the past decade, among them Sarah Kane, Joe Penhall and Conor McPherson, the emphasis at the Royal Court has always been on new voices in British theatre. *Sloane Square, Chelsea, SW1W 8AS (7565 5000, www.royalcourt theatre.com). Sloane Square tube. Box office 10am-6pm Mon-Sat. Tickets £10-£32.*

Royal Shakespeare Company

Britain's flagship company hasn't had a London base since it quit the Barbican in 2002, although it is turning its mind to finding one now the £100m redevelopment of its home theatres in Stratford-upon-Avon has reached completion. In the meantime, it continues its itinerant existence, sometimes popping up in smaller venues to stage new plays. Recent successes have included David Tennant in *Richard II*, staged at the Barbican in winter 2013/14. *Information 01789 403444, tickets 0844 800 1110, www.rsc.org.uk. Box office By phone 10am-6pm Mon-Sat. Tickets £5-£67.50.*

TOP TIP!
Going Cheap
The TKTS booths (Clocktower Building, Leicester Square, Soho, WC2H 7NA, www.tkts.co.uk) sells tickets for big shows at much-reduced rates.

Shakespeare's Globe

Sam Wanamaker's dream to recreate the theatre where Shakespeare first staged many of his plays has become a successful reality. Comedy is usually what the Globe does best, but the venue's been on great form for a while under Dominic Dromgoole, with the Shakespeare classics paralleled by new plays on similar themes. The open-air, standing-room Pit tickets are excellent value, if a little marred by low-flying aircraft. A new 340-seater indoor Jacobean theatre, called the Sam Wanamaker Playhouse, opened its doors in January 2014 (*see p106* **Shadow Plays**). For tours, *see p18*. *21 New Globe Walk, Bankside, SE1 9DT (7401 9919, www.shakespeares globe.com). Southwark tube or London Bridge tube/rail. Box office In person 10am-5pm Mon-Sat; 10am-4pm Sun. By phone 10am-6pm Mon-Sat; 10am-5pm Sun. Tickets £5-£100.*

LONG-RUNNERS & MUSICALS

Billy Elliot the Musical

The combination of Elton John's music and a heart-melting yarn about a northern working-class lad with a talent for ballet has scooped more awards internationally than any other British musical and launched the careers of dozens of young Billies. *Victoria Palace Theatre, Victoria Street, Victoria, SW1E 5EA (0844 248 5000,* www.billyelliotthe musical.com). *Victoria tube/rail. Box office 10am-8.30pm Mon-Sat. Tickets £20.50-£96.*

The Book of Mormon

South Park creators Trey Parker and Matt Stone's smash musical about the absurdities of Mormonism is not as shocking as you might expect. There's lots of swearing and close-to-the-bone jokes, but beneath it all, this is a big-hearted affair that pays note-perfect homage to the spirit and sounds of Broadway's golden age. And it's funny. *Prince of Wales Theatre, Coventry Street, Soho, W1D 6AS (0844 482 5115, www.bookofmormonlondon.com). Piccadilly Circus tube. Box office 10am-8pm Mon-Sat. Tickets £37.50-£152.*

The Curious Incident of the Dog in the Night-Time

Another hit West End transfer from the National Theatre, this adaptation of Mark Haddon's best-selling novel about a boy with Asperger syndrome is illuminating, touching and consistently surprising. With a wonderful graph-paper set, imaginative choreography and a strong young cast, it's deservedly garnered seven Oliviers and heaps of critical praise. *Gielgud Theatre, 35 Shaftesbury Avenue, Soho W1D 6AR (7492 1548, 0844 482 5130, www.delfontmackin tosh.co.uk). Piccadilly Circus tube. Box office 8am-8pm Mon-Fri; 9am-7pm Sat. Tickets £32-£108.*

Jersey Boys

A Broadway import that tells the story of Frankie Valli & the Four Seasons, through their songs. The well-trodden storyline of early struggle, success and break-up is elevated by pacy direction. *Piccadilly Theatre, 16 Denman Street, Soho W1D 7DY (0844 412 6666, www.jerseyboyslondon.com). Piccadilly Circus tube. Box office In person 10am-8pm Mon-Sat. By phone 24hrs daily. Tickets £22.50-£114.*

Les Misérables

The RSC's version of Boublil and Schönberg's musical first came to the London stage in 1985 – and no fewer than three celebratory versions ran simultaneously on one October night in 2010. This version should manage a few more anniversaries, as the voices remain lush, the revolutionary sets are film-fabulous, and the lyrics and score (based on Victor Hugo's novel) stand the test of time. *Queen's Theatre, 51 Shaftesbury Avenue, Soho, W1D 6BA (0844 482 5160, www.lesmis.com). Leicester Square tube. Box office In person 10am-7.45pm Mon-Sat. By phone 24hrs daily. Tickets £14.50-£97.*

Matilda the Musical

Adapted from Roald Dahl's riotous children's novel, with songs by superstar Aussie comedian Tim Minchin, this RSC transfer received rapturous reviews on its first outing in Stratford-upon-Avon and has been going strong ever since, winning multiple Olivier awards.

Performing Arts

Cambridge Theatre, 32-34 Earlham Street, Covent Garden, WC2H 9HU (0844 800 1110, www.matildathe musical.com). Covent Garden tube. Box office In person 10am-8pm Mon-Sat. By phone 10am-6pm Mon-Sat. Tickets £5-£97.50.

The Mousetrap

Running in the West End since 1952, Agatha Christie's drawing-room whodunnit is a murder mystery Methuselah.
St Martin's Theatre, West Street, Cambridge Circus, Covent Garden, WC2H 9NZ (0844 499 1515, www.the-mousetrap.co.uk). Leicester Square tube. Box office 10am-8pm Mon-Sat. Tickets £17.50-£65.

War Horse

Transferred from the National Theatre, *War Horse* is a moving piece of theatre (and a massive critical and popular hit). The play is based on Michael Morpurgo's children's novel about a horse separated from his young master and spirited off to World War I. The real stars are the extraordinary puppet horses.
New London Theatre, Drury Lane, Covent Garden, WC2B 5PW (0844 412 2708, www.nationaltheatre. org.uk/warhorse). Covent Garden tube. Box office In person 10am-7.30pm Mon-Sat. By phone 24hrs daily. Tickets £15-£90.

Off-West End

Almeida

Well groomed and with a funky bar, the Almeida turns out thoughtfully crafted theatre for grown-ups. Rupert Goold took over as artistic director in 2013 and immediately made his mark with *American Psycho*, a musical adaptation of the Bret Easton Ellis novel starring *Doctor Who's* Matt Smith.
Almeida Street, Islington, N1 1TA (7359 4404, www.almeida.co.uk). Angel tube. Box office In person & by phone 10am-6pm Mon-Fri. Tickets £10-£69.50.

Battersea Arts Centre (BAC)

Housed in the old Battersea Town Hall, the forward-thinking BAC hosts young theatre troupes; expect quirky, fun and physical theatre from the likes of cult companies Kneehigh, 1927 and Forced Entertainment.
Lavender Hill, Battersea, SW11 5TN (7223 2223, www.bac.org.uk). Clapham Common tube, Clapham Junction rail or bus 77, 77A, 345. Box office In person & by phone 10am-6pm Mon-Fri; 3-6pm Sat. Tickets £5-£25; pay what you can.

Bush

The Bush punches well above its weight, with well-designed productions and an impressive record of West End transfers.

7 Uxbridge Road, Shepherd's Bush, W12 8LJ (8743 5050, www.bush theatre.co.uk). Shepherd's Bush Market tube. Box office In person & by phone noon-7.30pm Mon-Sat (performance days); noon-8pm Mon-Fri (non-performance days). Tickets £10-£19.50.

Donmar Warehouse

The Donmar's combination of artistic integrity and intimate size, with audience right alongside the stage, has proved hard to resist, with many high-profile film actors appearing: among them Nicole Kidman, Gwyneth Paltrow, Ewan McGregor and Tom Hiddleston.
41 Earlham Street, Covent Garden, WC2H 9LX (0844 871 7624, www.donmarwarehouse.com). Covent Garden tube. Box office In person 10am-6pm Mon-Sat. By phone 9am-10pm Mon-Sat; 10am-8pm Sun. Tickets £7.50-£35.

Gate Theatre

A doll's house of a theatre, with rickety wooden chairs as seats, the Gate is the only producing theatre in London dedicated to international work.
Prince Albert, 11 Pembridge Road, Notting Hill, W11 3HQ (7229 0706, www.gatetheatre.co.uk). Notting Hill Gate tube. Box office By phone 10am-6pm Mon-Fri. In person 6.30-8pm Mon-Fri; 2-4pm, 6.30-8pm Sat. Tickets £20; £15 reductions.

Lyric Hammersmith

The building is undergoing a major facelift (due for completion in spring 2014), which will add a two-storey extension including drama, dance and recording studios, a cinema and a new café and bar.
Lyric Square, King Street, Hammersmith, W6 0QL (8741 6850, www.lyric.co.uk). Hammersmith tube. Box office By phone 10am-5.30pm Mon-Sat. In person 9.30am-7.30pm on performance days. Tickets £12.50-£35.

Soho Theatre

Its cool blue neon lights and front-of-house café help it to blend into the Soho landscape, but this theatre has made a name for itself since opening in 2000. It attracts a young, hip crowd and plays very effectively to the theatre/comedy/cabaret crossover scene.
21 Dean Street, Soho, W1D 3NE (7478 0100, www.sohotheatre.com). Tottenham Court Road tube. Box office In person 9am-9.30pm Mon-Sat. By phone 10am-10pm Mon-Sat. Tickets £5-£37.50.

Theatre Royal Stratford East

The Theatre Royal Stratford East is a community theatre, with many shows written, directed and performed by black or Asian artists. Musicals are big here.

Gerry Raffles Square, Stratford, E15 1BN (8534 0310, www.stratfordeast. com). Stratford tube/rail/DLR. Box office In person & by phone 10am-6pm Mon-Sat. Tickets £5-£24.

Tricycle

Passionate and political, the Tricycle consistently finds original ways into difficult subjects.
269 Kilburn High Road, Kilburn, NW6 7JR (information 7372 6611, tickets 7328 1000, www.tricycle.co.uk). Kilburn tube. Box office In person & by phone 10am-9pm Mon-Sat; 2-9pm Sun. Tickets £8-£29.

Wilton's Music Hall

London's last surviving example of the giant music halls that flourished in the mid 19th century, Wilton's is still a theatre, offering an atmospheric stage for everything from situation-specific Bach to immersive theatre to magic.
Graces Alley, off Ensign Street, Whitechapel, E1 8JB (7702 2789, www.wiltons.org.uk). Aldgate East or Tower Hill tube. Box office 10am-6pm Mon-Fri. Tickets £13-£25.

Young Vic

As the name suggests, this Vic (actually now in its forties) has more youthful bravura than its older sister up the road. Recent winners have included hard-hitting race musical *The Scottsboro Boys*, and the theatre has been attracting some starry acting talent, with both Chiwetel Ejiofor and Gillian Anderson having appeared.
66 The Cut, Waterloo, SE1 8LZ (7922 2922, www.youngvic.org). Waterloo tube/rail. Box office 10am-6pm Mon-Sat. Tickets £10-£35.

Dance

London is the home of two classical dance companies: the **Royal Ballet**, founded in 1931 and resident at the **Royal Opera House** (*see p106*), and (friendly) rival **English National Ballet**, a touring company founded in 1950 that performs most often at the **Coliseum** (*see p106*) and, for the regular *Swan Lake* 'in the round', at the **Royal Albert Hall** (*see p106*). On the contemporary side, London is the base for internationally acclaimed choreographers including Akram Khan, Hofesh Shechter and Wayne McGregor.

Barbican Centre

The Barbican attracts and nurtures experimental dance, especially in the intimate Pit Theatre.
For listings, see p105.

Coliseum

The English National Ballet performs here, along with the likes of the Peter Schaufuss Ballet and visiting Russian ballet companies.
For listings, see p106.

The Place

The theatre is behind the biennial Place Prize for choreography, which rewards

the best in British contemporary dance as well as regular seasons of new work.
17 Duke's Road, Bloomsbury, WC1H 9PY (7121 1100, www.theplace. org.uk). Euston tube/rail. Box office In person & by phone 10.30am-6pm Mon-Sat; 10.30am-8pm on performance days. Tickets £11-£14.

Royal Opera House

For the full ballet experience, nothing beats the Royal Opera House, home of the Royal Ballet. There's edgier fare in the Linbury Studio Theatre.
For listings, see p106.

Sadler's Wells

Purpose-built in 1998 on the site of a 17th-century theatre of the same name, this dazzling complex is home to impressive local and international performances of contemporary dance in all its guises. The Lilian Baylis Studio offers smaller-scale new works and works-in-progress, and the Peacock Theatre (on Portugal Street in Holborn) operates as a satellite venue.
Rosebery Avenue, Finsbury, EC1R 4TN (0844 412 4300, www.sadlers wells.com). Angel tube. Box office In person & by phone 10am-8pm Mon-Sat. Tickets £8-£60.

Southbank Centre

From international contemporary dance to hip hop to physical theatre to South Asian dance, there's an eclectic programme on offer.
For listings, see p106.

Other venues

Laban Centre

In 2005 the Laban Centre joined forces with Trinity College of Music to create the first ever UK conservatoire for music and dance. The centre was designed by Herzog & de Meuron of Tate Modern fame and features a curving, multi-coloured glass frontage. The stunning premises include a 300-seat auditorium and are home to Transitions Dance Company. Also in Deptford, the Albany (Douglas Way, SE8 4AG, 8692 4446, www.thealbany. org.uk) specialises in hip hop theatre.
Creekside, Deptford, SE8 3DZ (8305 9300, 8463 9100 tickets, www.trinity laban.ac.uk). Deptford DLR or Greenwich DLR/rail. Open In person & by phone 10am-5pm Mon-Fri. Tickets £4-£15 for the centre's own events.

Rich Mix

A cinema and arts centre that offers regular dance events (often in the street dance and hip hop genres) alongside music, comedy, spoken word and theatre. Quality can be variable, but enthusiasm levels are high.
35-47 Bethnal Green Road, Shoreditch, E1 6LA (7613 7498 box office, www.richmix. org.uk). Shoreditch High Street rail. Box office In person & by phone 9am-11pm Mon-Fr; 10am-11pm Sat, Sun. Tickets free-£18.

Performing Arts

Hotels

London's best beds: budget, boutique and blowout

Number Sixteen. See p117.

Snooze? You choose

With homegrown boutiques and funky imports, our hotels just keep improving.

It's a sign of London's massive financial pulling power that, even in these lean times, luxury hotels continue to flourish. The **London Edition** is perhaps the most striking addition in terms of expensive good looks, though the **Ace Hotel** wins out when it comes to hipster credentials. Things are also lively among the Victorian and Edwardian grandes dames, with the recently refitted **Savoy** and **St Pancras Renaissance** now joined by the **Great Northern Hotel**. Elsewhere, there's action in the field of modish, moderately priced hotels – finally following the pioneering **Hoxton** – such as **Z Soho**, **citizenM** and **Qbic**. On the whole, though, room prices remain high. Significantly, **Dean Street Townhouse**, its slightly younger sibling **Shoreditch Rooms** and **One Leicester Street** offer 'tiny' or 'post-supper' rooms at lower-than-you-might-fear rates. The popularity of hip new B&Bs and no-frills hotel concepts speaks to the same need.

Our listings

Hotels in this chapter are classified according to the average price of a double room. You can expect to pay more than £300 a night for hotels in the Deluxe category, £200-£300 for Expensive hotels, £100-£200 for Moderate properties and under £100 a night for hotels listed as Budget.

The classifications we use are just a guide. A hotel's rates can vary widely, both top to bottom and over the course of the year. As a rule, it's best to book as far ahead as possible, and always try hotels' own websites first: many offer special online deals throughout the year. If you do arrive in town without a bed booked, staff at **Visit London** (1 Lower Regent Street, 0870 156 6366, www.visitlondon.com) will be happy to help you out. Be aware that a few hotels don't include VAT in the rates they quote. And watch out for added extras.

The South Bank & Bankside

MODERATE

Bermondsey Square Hotel
This is a deliberately kitsch new-build hotel on a newly developed square. Loft suites are named after the heroines of psychedelic rock classics (Lucy, Lily and so on); some have private terraces or a hammock, or Japanese baths. Rooms have classic discs on the walls, and you can kick your heels from the suspended Bubble Chair at reception. But, although occupants of the Lucy suite get a multi-person jacuzzi (with a great terrace view), the real draw isn't the gimmicks – it's well-designed rooms, with free Wi-Fi, for competitive prices. The restaurant-bar, Gregg's Bar & Grill, which serves British food, can be a bit hit-or-miss, but the bar's lounge area is a good spot to relax in and the hotel's staff are happy and helpful. *Bermondsey Square, Tower Bridge Road, SE1 3UN (0870 111 2525, www.bespokehotels.com). Borough tube or London Bridge tube/rail. Rooms 80.*

citizenM London Bankside
This casual new-build is a superbly well-designed addition to London's affordably chic hotels. See p117 **Cheap, Not Nasty**. *20 Lavington Street, SE1 0NZ (3519 1680, www.citizenm.com). Southwark tube or Blackfriars tube/ rail. Rooms 192.*

Premier Inn London County Hall
Its position right by the London Eye, the Thames, Westminster Bridge and Waterloo Station is a gift for out-of-towners on a bargain weekend break. Extra points are garnered for its friendly and efficient staff, making this newly refurbished branch of the Premier Travel chain the acceptable face of budget convenience. Check-in is quick and pleasant; rooms are spacious, clean and warm with decent bathrooms with very good showers. Breakfast, a buffet-style affair in a comfortable dining room, is extra. Wi-Fi costs £3 a day, but guests get a 30-minute free session. *County Hall, Belvedere Road, SE1 7PB (0871 527 8648, www.premierinn.com). Waterloo tube/rail. Rooms 314.*

The City

EXPENSIVE

South Place Hotel
D&D runs some of the swankiest restaurants in London, so much was expected of its first hotel. South Place delivers. It manages the difficult balance of sufficient formality to keep expense-accounters satisfied their needs are being attended to, with enough levity for you to want to spend the evening indoors. The muted top-floor Angler restaurant is a superbly oiled operation, there's a pretty interior courtyard garden bar, and the ground-floor 3 South Place bar-diner segues neatly from smooth breakfast operation to boisterous bar. The attention to detail impresses: from conversation-piece art (wire high-heels in one cabinet, a light feature of suspended aeroplanes, steampunk drawings) to touch controls in the rooms, or the Bond-themed pool room and library complete with vinyl and turntable. *3 South Place, EC2M 2AF (3503 0000, www.southplacehotel.com). Moorgate or Liverpool Street tube/ rail. Rooms 80.*

NUMBER SIXTEEN: SIMON BROWN

Threadneedles

Threadneedles boldly slots some contemporary style into a fusty old dame of a building in the heart of the City; it was formerly the grand Victorian HQ of the Midland Bank, bang next to the Bank of England and the Royal Exchange. The etched glass-domed rotunda of the lobby soars on columns over an artful array of designer furniture and shelving that looks like the dreamchild of some powerful graphics software – it's a calm space, but a stunning one. The bedrooms are individual, coherent and soothing examples of City-boy chic, in muted beige and textured tones, with limestone bathrooms and odd views of local landmarks: St Paul's, Tower 42 and the Lloyd's building. Drinks are served under the stained-glass central dome, and the pillared restaurant is an impressive space too. It's all well run and well thought out.
5 Threadneedle Street, EC2R 8AY (7657 8080, www.hotelthreadneedles. co.uk). Bank tube/DLR. Rooms 74.

MODERATE

Apex London Wall

The mini-chain's second London hotel shares the virtues of the first (Apex City of London, 1 Seething Lane, 7702 2020). The service is obliging, the rooms are crisply designed with all mod cons, and there are comforting details – rubber duck in the impressive bathrooms, free jelly beans, free local calls and internet, kettle and iron provided. The City of London branch

Ace Hotel Shoreditch

Critic's choice

1 **Ace Hotel Shoreditch** A funky import from the States. *See p118.*

2 **Covent Garden Hotel** Classy and relaxed – the perfect treat. *See p113.*

3 **CitizenM London Bankside** Cheap, chic and lots of fun. *See p110.*

4 **Dean Street Townhouse** Great Soho location, stylishly played-down interiors. *See p113.*

5 **One Leicester Street** Ace food, ace bar, and just off the square. *See p115.*

has the better location for tourists, a short walk from the Tower of London, but this one is handier for business. Prices are decent for the City location, but book well ahead to get the best deal.
7-9 Copthall Avenue, EC2R 7NJ (7562 3030, www.apexhotels.co.uk). Bank tube or Moorgate tube/rail. Rooms 89.

Holborn & Clerkenwell

EXPENSIVE

Malmaison

Malmaison is deliciously located, looking out on a lovely cobbled square on the edge of the Square Mile, near the bars, clubs and restaurants of the East End. This being design-conscious Clerkenwell, it's no surprise that the decor throughout makes a cool statement. The rooms overlooking the square are the pick of the bunch, with the best of the views and morning sunshine that pours through sash windows on to big, white firm beds.
Charterhouse Square, EC1M 6AH (7012 3700, www.malmaison.com). Barbican tube. Rooms 97.

Rookery

Sister hotel to Hazlitt's (*see p113*), the Rookery has long been something of a celebrity hideaway deep in the heart of Clerkenwell. The front rooms can be noisy, but the place is otherwise as creakily calm as a country manor house. Guests enjoy an atmospheric warren of rooms, each individually decorated in the style of a Georgian townhouse: huge clawfoot baths, elegant four-posters, antique desks, old paintings amd brass shower fittings. Modernity isn't forgotten though: there's free Wi-Fi. There's an honesty bar in the bright and airy drawing room at the back, which opens on to a sweet little patio. The ground-floor suite has its own hallway, a cosy boudoir and a subterranean bathroom. Topping it all is the huge split-level Rook's Nest suite, which has views of St Paul's Cathedral.
12 Peter's Lane, Cowcross Street, EC1M 6DS (7336 0931, www. rookeryhotel.com). Farringdon tube/rail. Rooms 33.

Zetter

Zetter is a fun, laid-back, modern hotel with some interesting design notes. There's a refreshing lack of attitude and a forward-looking approach, with friendly staff and firm eco-credentials (such as free Brompton bikes for guests' use). The rooms, stacked up on five galleried storeys around an impressive atrium, look into an intimate and recently refreshed bar area. They are smoothly functional, but cosied up with choice home comforts such as hot-water bottles and old Penguin paperbacks, as well as having walk-in showers with REN smellies. The superlative Bistrot Bruno Loubet downstairs, and the fabulous Zetter Townhouse in a historic building just across the

Great Northern Hotel

square – with its excellent ground-floor cocktail bar (*see p71*) – have only served to widen the place's already considerable appeal.
86-88 Clerkenwell Road, EC1M 5RJ (7324 4444, www.thezetter.com). Farringdon tube/rail. Rooms 59.

MODERATE

Fox & Anchor

Check in at the handsome attached boozer (*see p70*) and you'll be pointed to the separate front entrance, with its lovely floor mosaic, and a handful of well-appointed, atmospheric and surprisingly luxurious rooms. All are different, but the high-spec facilities (big flatscreen TV, clawfoot bath and drench shower) and quirky attention to detail (bottles of ale in the minibar, the 'Nursing hangover' privacy signs) are common throughout. Expect some noise in the early mornings, but proximity to the historic Smithfield meat market also means you get a feisty fry-up in the morning in the pub.
115 Charterhouse Street, EC1M 6AA (7250 1300, www.foxandanchor.com). Barbican tube or Farringdon tube/rail. Rooms 6.

Bloomsbury, King's Cross & Fitzrovia

DELUXE

Charlotte Street Hotel

A fine exponent of Kit Kemp's much imitated fusion of flowery English and avant-garde, this gorgeous hotel was once a dental hospital. Public rooms have Bloomsbury Set paintings by the likes of Duncan Grant and Vanessa Bell, while bedrooms mix English understatement with bold flourishes. The huge, comfortable beds and trademark polished granite and oak bathrooms are suitably indulgent, and some rooms have unbelievably high ceilings. The Oscar restaurant and bar are classy and busy with a

smart crowd of media and ad people. At 5pm on Sundays the mini-cinema holds screenings.
15-17 Charlotte Street, W1T 1RJ (7806 2000, www.firmdale.com). Goodge Street or Tottenham Court Road tube. Rooms 52.

Sanderson

No designer flash in the pan, the Sanderson remains a statement hotel, a Schrager/Starck creation that takes clinical chic in the bedrooms to new heights. The design throughout is all flowing white net drapes, gleaming glass cabinets and retractable screens. The residents-only Purple Bar sports a button-backed purple leather ceiling and fabulous cocktails; in particular, try the Vesper. The 'billiard room' has a purple-topped pool table, surrounded by strange tribal adaptations of classic dining room furniture.
50 Berners Street, W1T 3NG (7300 1400, www.morganshotelgroup.com). Oxford Circus tube. Rooms 150.

EXPENSIVE

Great Northern Hotel

Designed by Lewis Cubitt, the city's first railway hotel opened in 1854, part of the Victorian railway explosion. It has had plenty of rough times since then, not least the 12 years it was dark, but almost £40m of renovation have recreated a classic. The furniture is by artisans and, in many cases, bespoke: witness the Couchette rooms, each with a double bed snugly fitted into the window to echo sleeper carriages; the neatly upholstered bedside cabinets; or the ceiling lights raised and lowered by fabulously steampunk pulleys. You're not expected to suffer the privations of a Victorian traveller, though: free Wi-Fi, film and music libraries on the 40in TV, Egyptian cotton sheets and walk-in showers are all standard. There's no room service but each floor has a simply charming pantry, full of jars of vintage sweets, a stand of fresh cakes, tea and coffee, books and newspapers – even a USB printer. There's also Plum + Spilt Milk,

Hotels

a grand restaurant with a quiet bar, on the first floor, while the busy ground-floor Great Northern Bar has direct access to the station.
King's Cross St Pancras Station, Pancras Road, N1C 4TB (3388 0800, www.gnhlondon.com). King's Cross tube/rail. Rooms 91.

London Edition

The London Edition makes a big impact as you walk into its grand hall of a lobby, complete with double-height rococo ceilings, floor-to-ceiling windows and marble pillars. And there's more to the space: it's the setting for the lobby bar, with an eclectic mix of comfortable, snazzy seating: sofas with faux-fur throws and wing-backed chairs, plus a blackened steel bar, a real fire and a colossal silver egg-shaped object hanging where you might expect a chandelier. Off on one side is the equally opulent Berners Tavern (*see p56*), where Jason Atherton is executive chef. With banquette seating and many paintings, it has the vibe of a grand café and a brasserie-style menu to match. Hidden away at the back of the public area is the clubby, wood-panelled Punch Room bar where the speciality is – you've guessed it – punch. Bedrooms are a contrast: akin to lodges or dachas, with matte oak floors, wood-panelled walls and more faux-fur throws tossed on luxurious beds. Larger rooms come with sofas, some have large furnished terraces and all have rainforest showers, Le Labo toiletries (with the hotel's woody signature scent), iPod docks and free Wi-Fi.
10 Berners Street, W1T 3NP (http://edition-hotels.marriott.com/london). Oxford Circus or Tottenham Court Road tube. Rooms 173.

St Pancras Renaissance

A landmark hotel in every sense of the word, the St Pancras Renaissance is the born-again Midland Grand, the pioneering railway hotel designed into the station's imposing Gothic Revival frontage. It opened in 1873 but fell into disuse in the 20th century (except for appearances as a Harry Potter backdrop and in the Spice Girls' 'Wannabe' video, among other screen roles). The Renaissance group has done a beautiful job of restoring it to its breathtaking, Grade I-listed best while adding modern comforts. The 120 rooms and suites in the historic hotel (there's a new wing too) have high ceilings, original features and awesome views over the station concourse or forecourt. Facilities are high-spec – Bose stereo, Nespresso machines, REN toiletries, marble baths – and the furniture is modern classic in style. The subterranean spa includes saunas, a steam room and a Victorian tiled relaxation pool. Public areas, including both restaurants (for the Booking Office, *see p 71*) and the gorgeous grand staircase, are similarly splendid. London loves it.
Euston Road, NW1 2AR (7841 3540, www.marriott.com). King's Cross tube/rail. Rooms 245.

FLAMING GROOVY
The hottest new hotel in town.

Chiltern Street Firehouse

It's been a long time coming. We've had the Chiltern Firehouse – or 'the new hotel in Marylebone', as we then knew it – on our 'coming soon' list ever since there were rumours André Balazs was in London looking for property.

Why the anticipation? Balazs, one of the world's most eligible bachelors, with a net worth estimated at $450 million, has built a hotel empire that began with Chateau Marmont in Hollywood and progressed through the Mercer in New York City, among many others. All of them are united by that rare combination of supreme quality and must-book-there buzz. But this, his first hotel outside the United States never quite arrived: until now.

Chiltern Firehouse (1 Chiltern Street, W1U 7PA, 7073 7676, www.chilternfirehouse.com) is in a lovely 1889 Grade II-listed Victorian Gothic fire brigade building, rebuilt from the inside out. It now has a discreetly gated garden as the entrance. The 26 suites are stunning, and a trip up the firehouse's watchtower to admire the view is a real treat. The staff's aura of professionalism and sincerity hits you immediately – they're uniformly well drilled and rarely go off-script – and the restaurant, taken over by the superb chef Nuno Mendes, is a thing of joy.

MODERATE

Academy

The Academy goes for the country intellectual look to suit Bloomsbury's studious yet decadent history. It's made up of five Georgian townhouses, and provides in all its rooms a tranquil generosity of space that's echoed in the Georgian squares sitting serenely between the arterial traffic rush of Gower Street and Tottenham Court Road. There's a restrained country-house style in the summery florals and checks and a breath of sophistication in the handsome, more plainly furnished suites. The library and conservatory open on to fragrant walled gardens where drinks and breakfast are served in summer.
21 Gower Street, WC1E 6HG (7631 4115, www.theacademyhotel.co.uk). Goodge Street tube. Rooms 49.

Harlingford Hotel

An affordable hotel with tons of charm in the heart of Bloomsbury, the perkily styled Harlingford has light airy rooms with evident boutique aspirations, and free Wi-Fi. The decor is lifted from understated sleek to quirky with the help of vibrant colour splashes from coloured glass bathroom fittings and mosaic tiles – overall, the hotel has something of a Scandinavian feel. The crescent it's set in has a lovely and leafy private garden.
61-63 Cartwright Gardens, WC1H 9EL (7387 1551, www.harlingfordhotel.com). Russell Square tube or Euston tube/rail. Rooms 40.

Morgan

This brilliantly located, comfortable and reasonably priced hotel is done out in neutral shades. The rooms are well equipped and all are geared up for the electronic age with wireless, voicemail, flatscreen tellies with Freeview, and air-conditioning. A good, slap-up English breakfast is served in a good-looking room with wood panelling, London prints and blue and white china plates. The spacious flats are excellent value.
24 Bloomsbury Street, WC1B 3QJ (7636 3735, www.morganhotel.co.uk). Tottenham Court Road tube. Rooms 21.

Rough Luxe

In a bit of King's Cross that's choked with ratty B&Bs and cheap chains, this Grade II-listed property takes shabby chic to extremes with artfully distressed walls, torn wallpaper, signature works of art, and old-fashioned TVs that barely work. It even retains the sign for the hotel that preceded Rough Luxe: 'Number One Hotel'. All rooms have free wireless internet, but otherwise have totally different characters: there's the one with the free-standing copper tub, the one with the rose motif and so on. The set-up is flexible, too: rooms with shared bathrooms can be combined for group bookings, and the owners are more than happy to chat with guests over a bottle of wine in the back courtyard where a great breakfast is served. A place to stay if you're looking for somewhere different from the norm.
1 Birkenhead Street, WC1H 8BA (7837 5338, www.roughluxe.co.uk). King's Cross tube/rail. Rooms 9.

BUDGET

Clink78

Located in a listed ex-courthouse, the Clink set the bar high for party-style hosteldom when it opened a few years back. There was the setting: the hostel retains the superb original wood-panelled lobby and courtroom where the Clash once stood before the beak. Then there's the urban-chic ethos that permeates the whole enterprise, from the streamlined red reception counter to the Japanese-style 'pod' beds. A thorough redesign of the public areas and licensed café/bar downstairs, with computer screens for internet access (£2/hr), has given things a new rock 'n' roll fillip, with street-art decor and more comfortable furniture to enhance the place's good-time vibe. Clink261 – a rebrand of the nearby Ashlee House, which had its public areas pepped up in 2010 – might be a better choice for older and calmer hostellers.
78 King's Cross Road, WC1X 9QG (7183 9400, www.clinkhostels.com). King's Cross tube/rail. Beds 717. Other location Clink261, 261-265 Gray's Inn Road, Bloomsbury, WC1X 8QT (7183 9400).

Jenkins Hotel

This well-to-do Georgian beauty has been a hotel since the 1920s, and was refurbished in 2013. It still has an atmospheric, antique air, although the rooms have mod cons enough – TVs, mini-fridges, tea and coffee, and free Wi-Fi. Its looks have earned it a role in Agatha Christie's Poirot, but it's not chintzy, just floral. The breakfast room is handsome, with snowy cotton tablecloths and Windsor chairs.
45 Cartwright Gardens, WC1H 9EL (7387 2067, www.jenkinshotel.demon.co.uk). Russell Square tube or Euston tube/rail. Rooms 19.

YHA London Central

The Youth Hostel Association's newest hostel is one of its best – as well as being one of the best hostels in London. The friendly and well-informed receptionists are stationed at a counter to the left of the entrance, in a substantial café-bar area. The basement contains a well-equipped kitchen and washing areas; above it,

five floors of clean, neatly designed rooms, many en suite. Residents have 24hr access and the location is quiet but central.
104 Bolsover Street, W1W 5NU (0845 371 9154, www.yha.org.uk). Great Portland Street tube. Beds 302.

Covent Garden & the Strand

DELUXE

Corinthia
Firmly in the grand hotel tradition, the Corinthia became a hotel after years as government offices. The colossal, modish chandelier (with 1,000 clear crystal globes, plus one in red) in the expansive lobby complete with central dome; the dark wood and silk-covered walls in the high-spec rooms; the luxurious bathrooms with pool-like oval baths: everything is as you would expect for a hotel in this price range, and it's done well and with a light, modern touch. The Espa spa and subterranean pools (with jacuzzi, steam room, sauna and hot seats) form a complex over two floors. Espa products are in bathrooms too. Afternoon tea is a stylish affair, served in the lobby. The Bassoon bar is an intimate, after-dark space, while the Northall restaurant serves British food in a dramatic circular space with floor-to-ceiling windows.
Whitehall Place, SW1A 2BD (7930 8181, www.corinthia.com). Embankment tube or Charing Cross tube/rail. Rooms 294.

Covent Garden Hotel
The excellent location in the heart of London's theatre district and tucked-away screening room of this Firmdale hotel ensure that it continues to attract starry customers, with anyone needing a bit of privacy able to retreat upstairs to the lovely panelled private library and drawing room. In the guest-rooms, Kit Kemp's distinctive style mixes pinstriped wallpaper, pristine white quilts and floral upholstery with bold, contemporary elements; each room is unique, but each has the Kemp trademark upholstered mannequin and granite and oak bathroom. On the ground floor, the 1920s Paris-style Brasserie Max and its retro zinc bar retain their buzz – outdoor tables give a perfect viewpoint on Covent Garden boutique life in summer.
10 Monmouth Street, WC2H 9HB (7806 1000, www.firmdalehotels.com). Covent Garden or Leicester Square tube. Rooms 58.

ME by Meliá London
London's first ME by Meliá is a beauty. Designed by Foster + Partners, the finishes are expensive and carefully modelled on what was there before – respecting the lines of Marconi House, the first BBC radio broadcaster. But it now contains a genuinely breathtaking internal atrium, a pyramid nine floors tall, coolly minimal in style – and starting not at ground floor, but from the first. Here guests can sit and sip champagne as they're checked in by personal 'Aura managers'. In the rooms, the tech and textile details are all taken care of, naturally, but idiosyncratic design touches include triangular windows you can't resist stepping into to peer up and down the Aldwych. The social spaces have different moods: from a bling American steakhouse and a basement events space into which cars can be driven, via a more relaxed Italian restaurant, up to Radio, the elegant tenth-floor roof terrace bar, where Thames-side seats and exceptional views are in demand.
336-337 the Strand, WC2R 1HA (0845 601 8980, www.melondonuk.com). Covent Garden or Temple tube. Rooms 157.

St Martins Lane Hotel
When it opened over a decade ago, the St Martins was the toast of the town. The flamboyant, theatrical lobby was constantly buzzing, and guests enjoyed Philippe Starck's playful decor. The Starck objects – such as the giant chess pieces and gold tooth stools in the lobby – remain, but the space, part of the Morgans Hotel Group, lacks the impact of its heyday. There's still much to be impressed by: the all-white bedrooms have comfortable minimalism down to a T, with floor-to-ceiling windows, gadgetry secreted in sculptural cabinets and sleek limestone bathrooms with toiletries from the spa at sister property Sanderson (*see p111*).
45 St Martin's Lane, WC2N 4HX (7300 5500, www.morganshotelgroup.com). Leicester Square tube or Charing Cross tube/rail. Rooms 204.

Savoy
The superluxe, Grade II-listed Savoy reopened after more than £100m of renovations in autumn 2010. Built in 1889 to put up theatregoers from Richard D'Oyly Carte's Gilbert & Sullivan shows, the Savoy is the hotel from which Monet painted the Thames, where Vivien Leigh met Laurence Olivier, where Londoners learned to love the martini. The famous cul-de-sac at the front entrance now has a garden of new topiary and centrepiece Lalique crystal fountain, but the welcome begins before you arrive with a phone call to ascertain your particular requirements. There's a new tearoom with glass-roofed conservatory; the leather counter of the new Beaufort champagne bar is set on a stage that once hosted big bands for dinner dances; and the Savoy Grill is again under the control of Gordon Ramsay's company. Highlight of the fitness and beauty centre is a pool in its own atrium, with a jet-stream for those who choose to swim against the current. Traditionalists can relax, though: the American Bar remains unchanged.
The Strand, WC2R 0EU (7836 4343, www.fairmont.com/savoy-london). Covent Garden or Embankment tube, or Charing Cross tube/rail. Rooms 268.

Soho & Leicester Square

DELUXE

Soho Hotel
You'd hardly know you were in the heart of Soho once you're inside Firmdale's edgiest hotel: the place is wonderfully quiet, with what was once a car park now feeling like a converted loft building. The big bedrooms exhibit a contemporary edge, with modern furniture, industrial-style windows and nicely planned mod cons (digital radios as well as flatscreen TVs), although they're also classically Kit Kemp with bold stripes, traditional florals, plump sofas, oversized bedheads and upholstered tailor's dummies. The quiet drawing room and other public spaces feature groovy colours while Refuel, the loungey bar and restaurant, has an open kitchen and, yes, a car-themed mural.
4 Richmond Mews, W1D 3DH (7559 3000, www.firmdale.com). Piccadilly Circus tube. Rooms 91.

W London Leicester Square
The W brand has made its name with a series of hip hotels around the world that offer glamorous bars, classy food and functional but spacious rooms. The London W is no exception: Spice Market gets its first UK site within the hotel; Wyld is a large nightclub/bar space aiming to become the Met Bar for a new decade, and the W lounge aims to bring New York's cocktail lounge ethos to London. The rooms – 192 of them, across ten storeys – are well equipped and decent-sized, and FIT (the hotel's state-of-the-art fitness facility), next to the pale and serene Away spa on the sixth floor, offers fine views over Soho. Also of note is the W's gobsmacking exterior: the entire hotel is veiled in translucent glass, which is lit in different colours through the day.
10 Wardour Street, W1D 6QF (7758 1000, www.wlondon.co.uk). Leicester Square tube. Rooms 192.

EXPENSIVE

Dean Street Townhouse & Dining Room
This Grade II-listed, 1730s townhouse has been converted into another winning enterprise from the people behind Soho House members' club, Shoreditch Rooms and High Road House (for both (*see p118*)). To one side of a buzzy ground-floor restaurant are four floors of bedrooms that run from full-size rooms with Georgian panelling and reclaimed oak floors to half-panelled 'Tiny' rooms that are barely bigger than their double beds – but can be had from the website for as little as £100. The atmosphere is gentleman's club cosy, but modern types also get rainforest showers, 24hr room service, Roberts DAB radios, free wireless internet and big flatscreen TVs. Even the calm little library room behind reception manages to be both low-key and luxurious.
69-71 Dean Street, W1D 3SE (7434 1775, www.deanstreettownhouse.com). Leicester Square or Piccadilly Circus tube. Rooms 39.

Hazlitt's
Four Georgian townhouses comprise this absolutely charming place, named after William Hazlitt, the spirited 18th-century essayist who died here in abject poverty. With flamboyance and attention to detail the rooms evoke the Georgian era, all heavy fabrics, fireplaces, free-standing tubs and exquisitely carved half-testers, yet modern luxuries – air-conditioning, free Wi-Fi, TVs in antique cupboards and double-glazed windows – have been subtly attended to as well. It gets

Z Soho. See p115.

creakier and more crooked the higher you go, culminating in enchanting garret single rooms with rooftop views. Of seven new bedrooms, the main suite is a real knock-out: split-level, with a huge eagle spouting water into the raised bedroom bath and a rooftop terrace with sliding roof, it's a joyous extravaganza. Entertainingly, from the back alley outside, the extension has been made to look like 1700s shopfronts.
6 Frith Street, W1D 3JA (7434 1771, www.hazlittshotel.com). Tottenham Court Road tube. Rooms 30.

MODERATE

One Leicester Street

The first thing you'll probably notice about this hotel is the awning and streetside terrace of its fine restaurant – the hotel's discreet entrance is on Lisle Street. Through it you'll find a cramped reception area, with stairs up to a sweet little first-floor bar that serves excellent cocktails. The hotel was taken over in 2013 by Singaporean hotelier Peng Loh, who is also behind the Town Hall (*see p118*). Some touches are familiar from there – the nacreous tiles in the classy bathrooms, for instance – but otherwise the vibe is simple comfort, but with all essentials in place. The top-floor suite is a beautifully lit eyrie.
1 Leicester Street, off Leicester Square, WC2H 7BL (3301 8020, http://one leicesterstreet.com). Leicester Square or Piccadilly Circus tube. Rooms 15.

BUDGET

Z Soho

For the money, the Z is a cast-iron bargain. First, the location is superb: it really means Soho, not a short bus-ride away – the breakfast room/bar exits on to Old Compton Street. Then there's the hotel itself, which is surprisingly chic – especially the unexpected interior courtyard, with open 'corridors' stacked above it, and room to sit and drink or smoke at the bottom – and very cheerfully run, down to free wine and nibbles of an evening. The rooms are quite handsome, and have everything you need, from a little desk to free Wi-Fi, but not much more. Including space: expect beds (perhaps a little short for anyone over 6ft tall) to take up most of the room, a feeble shower, and no wardrobes or phones in the rooms. A great little hotel – in both senses.
17 Moor Street, W1D 5AP (3551 3700, www.thezhotels.com). Leicester Square or Tottenham Court Road tube. Rooms 85.
Other location Z Victoria, 5 Lower Belgrave Street, Victoria, SW1W 0NR.

Oxford Street & Marylebone

EXPENSIVE

Dorset Square

Grown-up greys are a backdrop for splashes of orange-red and midnight blue, with bold patterns completing a sophisticated modish meets traditional look – the hallmark of owners Firmdale. The Regency townhouse has comfortable, spacious bedrooms, many looking on to the leafy private square; bathrooms are in granite and glass, with Miller Harris products. Downstairs is a comfortable lounge with a fireplace and the Potting Shed restaurant and bar.
39-40 Dorset Square, NW1 6QN (7723 7874, www.dorsetsquarehotel.co.uk). Marylebone tube/rail. Rooms 38.

Montagu Place

A small, fashionable townhouse hotel, Montagu Place fills a couple of Grade II-listed Georgian residences with sharply appointed rooms graded according to size. The big ones are entitled Swanky, and have super king-size beds and big bathrooms – some have narrow front terraces. More modest in size, the Comfy category has standard double beds and, being at the back of the building, no street views. All rooms have a cool and trendy look, with cafetières and ground coffee instead of Nescafé sachets, as well as flatscreen TVs and free Wi-Fi. The decision to combine bar and reception desk (situated at the back of the house) means you can get a drink at any time and retire to the graciously modern lounge. Service is at once sharp and very obliging.
2 Montagu Place, W1H 2ER (7467 2777, www.montagu-place.co.uk). Baker Street tube. Rooms 16.

MODERATE

22 York Street

Bohemian French chic – white furniture, palest pink lime-washed walls, mellow wooden floors, subtly faded textiles and arresting objets d'époque – makes this delightfully unpretentious bed and breakfast in the heart of Marylebone a sight to behold. You feel as if you've been invited to stay in someone's arty home, especially when you're drinking good coffee at the gorgeous curved table that dominates the breakfast room-cum-kitchen. Guests are also given free rein with the hot beverages in a lounge full of knick-knacks upstairs, while a cluttered smaller room downstairs has an internet station (the Wi-Fi is free). All rooms are a decent size and have en suite baths, a rarity at this price and in this part of London.
22 York Street, W1U 6PX (7224 2990, www.22yorkstreet.co.uk). Baker Street tube. Rooms 10.

Sumner

The Sumner's cool, deluxe looks have earned it many fans, not least in the hospitality industry, where it has won a number of awards. You won't be at all surprised when you get here: from the soft dove and slatey greys of the lounge and halls you move up to glossily spacious accommodation with brilliant walk-in showers. The breakfast room is sunny, with a lovely, delicate buttercup motif and vibrant Arne Jacobsen chairs, and the stylishly moody front sitting room is also cosy.
54 Upper Berkeley Street, W1H 7QR (7723 2244, www.thesumner.com). Marble Arch tube. Rooms 19.

Paddington & Notting Hill

EXPENSIVE

Portobello Hotel

The Portobello is a hotel with approaching half a century of celebrity status, having hosted the likes of Johnny Depp, Kate Moss and Alice Cooper, who used his tub to house a boa constrictor. Taken over in 2014 by A Curious Group of Hotels, it remains a pleasingly unpretentious place, with a more civilised demeanour than its legend might suggest. There is now a lift to help rockers who are feeling their age up the five floors, but there's still a 24hr guest-only bar downstairs for those who don't yet feel past it. The rooms are themed – the superb basement Japanese Water Garden, for example, has an elaborate spa bath, its own private grotto and a small private garden – but all are stylishly equipped with a large fan, tall house plants, free Wi-Fi and round-the-clock room service.
22 Stanley Gardens, W11 2NG (7727 2777, www.portobellohotel. com). Holland Park or Notting Hill Gate tube. Rooms 21.

TOP TIP!
Buyer Beware
Many high-end hotels charge extra for services that you might assume will be free, most commonly internet access and breakfast. Always check in advance.

MODERATE

La Suite West

A typical row of west London townhouses on the outside, La Suite has been transformed on the inside by designer Anouska Hempel, with sleek lines and a black and white palette – the antithesis of her maximalist Blakes (see p356). A discreet side entrance leads into a long minimalist reception area with open fire and a zen-like feel. An Asian influence persists in the rooms, with slatted sliding screens for windows, wardrobe and bathrooms helping to make good use of space (which is limited in the cheaper rooms). Thoughtfully designed white marble bathrooms, with rainforest shower and bath, give a feeling of luxury despite not being huge. The large terrace running along the front of the building, with trees planted for an arbour-like effect, is a big summer asset for drinks, lunch or dinner, and the Raw vegetarian restaurant is an unusual take on hotel dining. All in all, clever design, a friendly vibe and – importantly – keen pricing make for a great hotel for this price range. Highly recommended.
41-51 Inverness Terrace, W2 3JN (7313 8484, www.lasuitewest.com). Bayswater or Queensway tube. Rooms 80.

Vancouver Studios

Step into the hall or comfortably furnished sitting room of this imposing townhouse and it feels like the gracious home of a slightly dotty uncle, with decor in the public spaces comprising colonial swords and historic prints. The studio or apartment accommodation is more modern in tone. Each room has its own style – from cool contemporary lines to a softer, more homely feel – and all are well equipped with kitchen appliances. There's free Wi-Fi and a pretty garden too.
30 Prince's Square, W2 4NJ (7243 1270, www.vancouverstudios.co.uk). Bayswater or Queensway tube. Rooms 51.

BUDGET

Garden Court Hotel

Once people have discovered the Garden Court Hotel, they tend to keep coming back, says Edward Connolly, owner-manager of this long-established hotel, with quiet pride. There aren't many places this close to Hyde Park and Portobello Market that give such excellent value for money and impeccable service. The rooms in this grand Victorian terrace have a bright, modern look and plenty of space, and the lounge, with its wood floor, leather-covered furniture, sprightly floral wallpaper and elegant mantelpiece, is a lovely place to linger.
30-31 Kensington Gardens Square, W2 4BG (7229 2553, www.garden courthotel.co.uk). Bayswater or Queensway tube. Rooms 39.

Pavilion

A hotel that describes itself as 'fashion rock 'n' roll' is never going to be staid, but Danny and Noshi Karne's Pavilion is quite mind-bogglingly excessive. The rooms have attention-grabbing names, such as 'Enter the Dragon' (Chinese themed) and 'Cosmic Girl' (way out there, man). They are frequently used for fashion shoots, and the website has an impressive list of celebrities who have rocked up here over the years. Bizarre and voluptuous choice of decor notwithstanding, this crazy hotel represents excellent value and has the usual amenities, including free Wi-Fi.
34-36 Sussex Gardens, W2 1UL (7262 0905, www.pavilionhoteluk.com). Edgware Road tube or Marylebone or Paddington tube/rail. Rooms 29.

Stylotel

Partly due to the young manager's enthusiasm, it's hard not to like this place. It's a retro-futurist dream: metal floors and panelling, lots of royal blue (the hall walls, the padded headboards) and pod bathrooms. But the real deal at Stylotel is its bargain studio and apartment (respectively, £120-£150 and £150-£200, with breakfast included), around the corner above a pub. Designed – like the rest of the hotel – by the owner's son, they suggest he's calmed down

with age. Here's real minimalist chic: sleek brushed steel or white glass wall panels, simply styled contemporary furniture upholstered in black or white.
160-162 Sussex Gardens, W2 1UD (7723 1026, www.stylotel.com). Edgware Road tube or Marylebone or Paddington tube/rail. Rooms 39.

Piccadilly Circus & Mayfair

DELUXE

Claridge's
Claridge's is sheer class and pure atmosphere, with its signature art deco redesign still simply dazzling. Photographs of Churchill and sundry royals grace the grand foyer, as does an absurdly over-the-top Dale Chihuly chandelier. Without departing too far from the traditional, Claridge's restaurant is actively fashionable (Simon Rogan has taken over from Gordon Ramsay), and A-listers can gather for champers in the bar. The rooms divide evenly between deco and Victorian style, with period touches such as deco toilet flushes in swanky marble bathrooms. Bedside panels control the mod-con facilities at the touch of a button. If money's no object, opt for a David Linley suite, in duck-egg blue and white, or lilac and silver.
55 Brook Street, W1K 4HR (7629 8860, www.claridges.co.uk). Bond Street tube. Rooms 203.

Connaught
This isn't the only hotel in London to provide butlers, but there can't be many that offer 'a secured gun cabinet room' for the hunting season. This is traditional British hospitality for those who love 23-carat gold leaf trimmings and stern portraits in the halls, but

all mod cons in their room, down to flatscreens in the en suite. Too lazy to polish your own shoes? The butlers are trained in shoe care by the expert cobblers at John Lobb. Both of the bars – gentleman's club cosy Coburg (*see p72*) and cruiseship deco Connaught – and the Hélène Darroze restaurant are very impressive. In the new wing, which doubled the number of guestrooms, there's a swanky spa and 60sq m swimming pool.
Carlos Place, W1K 2AL (7499 7070, www.the-connaught.co.uk). Bond Street tube. Rooms 121.

Dorchester
A Park Lane fixture since 1931, the Dorchester's interior may be thoroughly, opulently classical, but the hotel is cutting edge in attitude, providing an unrivalled level of personal service. With the grandest lobby in town, amazing views of Hyde Park, state-of-the-art mod cons and a magnificent spa, it's small wonder the hotel continues to welcome movie stars (the lineage stretches from Elizabeth Taylor to Tom Cruise) and political leaders (Eisenhower planned the D-Day landings here). You're not likely to be eating out, either: the Dorchester employs 90 full-time chefs at the Grill Room, Alain Ducasse and the wonderfully atmospheric China Tang. There's even an angelic tearoom in the new spa: the Spatisserie. A few years ago, the Dorchester opened an entirely new hotel, 45 Park Lane (7493 4545, www.45parklane.com), a buzzier, boutiquier spot.
53 Park Lane, W1K 1QA (7629 8888, www.thedorchester.com). Hyde Park Corner tube. Rooms 250.

Haymarket Hotel
A terrific addition to Kit Kemp's Firmdale portfolio, this block-size building was designed by John Nash, the architect of Regency London. The public spaces are a delight, with

Kemp's trademark combination of contemporary arty surprises and plump, floral sofas. Wow-factors include the bling basement swimming pool and bar (shiny sofas, twinkly roof) and the central location. Rooms are generously sized (as are bathrooms), individually decorated and discreetly stuffed with facilities, and there's plenty of attention from the switched-on staff. The street-side bar and restaurant are top-notch, the breakfast is exquisite.
1 Suffolk Place, SW1Y 4HX (7470 4000, www.firmdale.com). Piccadilly Circus tube. Rooms 50.

Ritz
If you like the idea of a world where jeans and trainers are banned and jackets must be worn by gentlemen when dining (the requirement is waived for breakfast), the Ritz is the place for you. Founded by hotelier extraordinaire César Ritz, the hotel is deluxe in excelsis. The show-stopper is the ridiculously ornate, vaulted Long Gallery, an orgy of chandeliers, rococo mirrors and marble columns, but all the high-ceilinged, Louis XVI-style bedrooms have been painstakingly renovated to their former glory in restrained pastel colours. But amid the old-world luxury, there are plenty of mod cons including free wireless in most rooms, large TVs and gym. An elegant afternoon tea in the Palm Court (book ahead) is the way in for interlopers.
150 Piccadilly, W1J 9BR (7493 8181, www.theritzlondon.com). Green Park tube. Rooms 134.

Westminster & St James's

EXPENSIVE

Eccleston Square Hotel
This Grade II-listed Georgian house has been transformed into a smart, urbane and rather masculine boutique hotel, in a palette of grey, black and white, with high-quality fittings such as Italian marble chevron flooring throughout the ground floor and black Murano glass chandeliers. Upstairs, the monochrome continues, with leather headboards, and silk wallpaper and curtains, all in shades of grey. It's in the rooms that the hotel's USP becomes apparent: it's all about the tech. Whether it's the underfloor heating in the bathroom, the lighting or the curtains, it's all operated by finger-tip control pads. The most snazzy is the one that turns the 'smart glass' of the white marble bathroom walls opaque for privacy. (Bath-lovers note that these are eschewed here in favour of rainfall showers.) In addition, every room comes equipped with an iPad (and the Wi-Fi's free). It's all super convenient and comfortable.
37 Eccleston Square, SW1V 1PB (3489 1000, www.ecclestonsquare hotel.com). Pimlico tube or Victoria tube/rail. Rooms 39.

Trafalgar
The Trafalgar is part of the Hilton chain of hotels, but you'd hardly notice. The mood is young and dynamic at the chain's first 'concept' hotel, for all that it's housed in the imposing edifice that was once the headquarters of Cunard. To the right of the open reception is the Rockwell Bar. It's the none-more-central location, however, that's the hotel's biggest draw – the handful of corner suites look directly into the square (prices reflect location). Those without their own view can always avail themselves of the little rooftop bar, which is open to the public during the summer months.
2 Spring Gardens, Trafalgar Square, SW1A 2TS (7870 2900, www.the trafalgar.com). Charing Cross tube/rail. Rooms 129.

MODERATE

B+B Belgravia
How do you make a lounge full of white and black contemporary furnishings seem cosy and welcoming? Hard to achieve, but the owners have succeeded at B+B Belgravia, which takes the B&B experience to a new level. It's fresh and sophisticated without being hard-edged: there's nothing here that will make the design-conscious wince (leather sofa, arty felt cushions, modern fireplace), but nor is it overly precious. A gleaming espresso machine provides 24/7 caffeine, and there's a large but somewhat dark garden out back.
64-66 Ebury Street, SW1W 9QD (7259 8570, www.bb-belgravia.com). Victoria tube/rail. Rooms 17.

Windermere Hotel
Heading the procession of small hotels that are strung out along Warwick Way, the Windermere is a comfortable, traditionally decked-out London hotel with, thankfully, no aspirations to boutique status. The decor may be showing its age a bit in the hall, but you'll receive a warm welcome and excellent service – there are over a dozen staff for just 19 rooms. There's a cosy basement restaurant-bar, where the breakfasts are top-notch.
142-144 Warwick Way, SW1V 4JE (7834 5163, www.windermere-hotel. co.uk). Victoria tube/rail. Rooms 19.

BUDGET

Morgan House
The Morgan has the understated charm of the old family home of a posh but unpretentious English friend: a pleasing mix of nice old wooden or traditional iron beds, with pretty floral curtains and coverlets in subtle hues, the odd chandelier or big gilt mirror over original mantelpieces, and padded wicker chairs and sinks in every bedroom, along with free Wi-Fi. Though there's no guest lounge, guests can sit in the little patio garden in better weather and, for Belgravia, the prices are a steal.
120 Ebury Street, SW1W 9QQ (7730 2384, www.morganhouse.co.uk). Pimlico tube or Victoria tube/rail. Rooms 11.

Hoxton Hotel. *See p118.*

HOXTON HOTEL: BRITTA JASCHINSKI

Chelsea

EXPENSIVE

Myhotel Chelsea

The Chelsea myhotel feels a world away from its sleekly modern Bloomsbury sister. The Sloane Square branch has an aesthetic that is softer and decidedly more English – with a floral sofa and plate of scones in the lobby, and white wicker headboards, velvet cushions and Bee Kind toiletries in the guestrooms. These feminine touches contrast nicely with the mini-chain's feng shui touches, Eastern-inspired treatment room and sleek aquarium. Breakfast and cold dishes are served in a bar-restaurant with a modernised farmhouse feel, while Pellicano serves Italian food. The central library, which is done out in conservatory style, is wonderful. Just pick up a book, sink into one of the ample comfy chairs and listen to the tinkling water feature.
35 Ixworth Place, SW3 3QX (7225 7500, www.myhotels.com). South Kensington tube. Rooms 46.

San Domenico House

San Domenico owes much of its tasteful, historic look to previous owner Sue Rogers, who transformed this former private residence into a boutique hotel masterpiece. All the categories of guestroom, including the split-level gallery suites and a new junior suite, feature original furnishings or antiques. Royal portraits, Victorian mirrors and Empire-era travelling cases are complemented by fabrics of similar style and taste, offset by contemporary touches to bathrooms. The spacious bedrooms enjoy wide-angle views of London, some from little balconies, and have free Wi-Fi. Breakfasts are taken up to guests or laid out in the room downstairs, while main meals may be taken in the sumptuous coffee room by the lobby.
29-31 Draycott Place, SW3 2SH (7581 5757, www.sandomenicohouse.com). Sloane Square tube. Rooms 17.

Knightsbridge & South Kensington

The **Lanesborough** hotel (7259 5599, www.lanesborough.com) at Hyde Park Corner is scheduled to reopen in October 2014.

DELUXE

Blakes

As original as when Anouska Hempel opened it in 1983 – the scent of oranges and the twittering of a pair of lovebirds fill the dark, oriental lobby – Blakes and its maximalist decor have stood the test of time. Each room is in a different style, with influences from Italy, India, Turkey and China. Exotic antiques picked up on the designer's

CHEAP, NOT NASTY
Reduce your budget – but not your expectations.

QBic

Back in the mists of time – you know… 2009 or so – a hip new hotel opened in arty but then down-at-heel Shoreditch. Its owner reckoned he could give guests all mod cons in small but stylish rooms – at competitive prices. We loved the Hoxton (*see p118*), weren't at all surprised it was a success – and awaited a splurge of copy-cat hotels.

A mere three years later, we got our challenger: citizenM London Bankside (*see p110*) arrived from the Netherlands. It was affordable, stylish, had a real buzz, and cleverly set itself in the thick of the arty action: right behind Tate Modern.

The ground floor is a slick yet cosy café-bar and reception area: self-check-in, but with staff on hand to help and, when higher-grade rooms are free, offer upgrades. Guests are invited to use it as their 'living room' and – thanks to the neat design – do so. The rooms themselves are tiny but well thought out: there are blackout blinds, free Wi-Fi, drench showers with removable sidehead, storage under the bed and free movies. The rooms are also fun: those blinds are automatic, controlled – like the movies, air-con and funky coloured lighting – from a touch-sensitive tablet.

What is it about the Dutch? In 2013, they were at it again, with the arrival of the sassy, well-located and very affordable Qbic Hotel London City (*see p118*), but the home team hadn't quite given up. It turns out the Hoxton is preparing a local fight-back with the opening of the Hoxton Holborn – very handy for the City – at some point in 2014.

travels – intricately carved beds, Chinese birdcages, ancient trunks – are set off by sweeping drapery and piles of plump cushions. Downstairs, the Eastern-influenced restaurant caters for a celebrity clientele enticed by the hotel's discreet, residential location.
33 Roland Gardens, SW7 3PF (7370 6701, www.blakeshotels.com). South Kensington tube. Rooms 47.

Gore

This fin-de-siècle period piece was founded by descendants of Captain Cook in two grand Victorian townhouses. The lobby and staircase are close hung with old paintings, and the bedrooms all have fantastic 19th-century carved oak beds, sumptuous drapes and shelves of old books. The suites are spectacular: the Tudor Room has a huge stone-faced fireplace and a minstrels' gallery, while tragedy queens should plump for the Venus room and Judy Garland's old bed (and replica ruby slippers). Bistrot 190

provides a casually elegant setting for great breakfasts, while the warm, wood-panelled 190 bar is a charming and elegant setting for cocktails.
190 Queen's Gate, SW7 5EX (7584 6601, www.gorehotel.com). South Kensington tube. Rooms 50.

Halkin

Set up by Singaporean fashion mogul Christina Ong (who also owns the Metropolitan), the Halkin marries Eastern charm, style and food with a quiet location in Knightsbridge. The rooms, all located off black curved, almost trompe l'oeil wooden corridors, are comfortable and full of Asian artefacts and clever gadgetry. Bathrooms are well equipped and heavy on the marble, and come stocked with a range of products from Ong's Shambhala spa. The Michelin-starred Basque restaurant Ametsa with Arzak Instruction is on the ground floor, and there's tapas and afternoon tea, as well as cocktails, served in the bar.

Halkin Street, SW1X 7DJ (7333 1000, www.comohotels.com/thehalkin). Hyde Park Corner tube. Rooms 41.

Milestone Hotel & Apartments

Wealthy American visitors make annual pilgrimages here, their arrival greeted by the comforting, gravel tones of their regular concierge, as English as roast beef, and the glass of sherry in the room. Yet amid the old-school luxury (butlers on 24-hour call) thrives inventive modernity (the resistance pool in the spa). Rooms overlooking Kensington Gardens feature the inspired decor of South African owner Beatrice Tillman: the Safari suite contains tent-like draperies and leopard-print upholstery; the Tudor Suite has an elaborate inglenook fireplace, minstrels' gallery and a pouffe concealing a pop-up TV. Afternoon tea is served in the Park Lounge, a glorious melding of library and boudoir.
1-2 Kensington Court, W8 5DL (7917 1000, www.milestonehotel.com). High Street Kensington tube. Rooms 56.

EXPENSIVE

Number Sixteen

This may be Kit Kemp's most affordable hotel but there's no slacking in the typical Firmdale hotel style stakes – witness the fresh flowers and origami-ed birdbook decorations in the comfortable drawing room. Bedrooms are generously sized, bright and very light, and carry the Kemp trademark mix of bold and traditional. The whole place has an appealing freshness about it, enhanced by a delicious, large back garden complete with a central water feature. By the time you finish breakfast in the sweet conservatory, you'll have forgotten you're in the middle of the city.
16 Sumner Place, SW7 3EG (7589 5232, www.firmdalehotels.com). South Kensington tube. Rooms 41.

MODERATE

Ampersand

In a Victorian stucco property, Ampersand has a strong design ethos, with dove greys and duck egg blues enlivened by splashes of purples, yellows and reds, bringing together a striking and distinctive look. A whimsical twist on the classic comes from the likes of tall purple padded headboards reaching nearly to the ceiling and dove drawings on the dove-grey walls in the ornithologically inspired deluxe rooms. In the corridors, botanical drawings and representations of scientific instruments reference the museums nearby, while the colourful lounge area – where afternoon tea is served – has deep sofas and studded armchairs in scarlet velvets and kingfisher blues and a multicoloured teapot collection in a wall cabinet. Breakfast and dining is found downstairs in the white-tiled Mediterranean-oriented Apero restaurant.
10 Harrington Road, SW7 3ER (7589 5895, www.ampersandhotel.com). South Kensington tube. Rooms 111.

Hotels

Vicarage Hotel

Scores of devotees return regularly to this tall Victorian townhouse, which has a great location, tucked in a quiet leafy square just off High Street Kensington. It's a comfortable, resolutely old-fashioned establishment. The refurbished entrance hall is wonderfully grand, with red and gold striped wallpaper, a huge gilt mirror and chandelier. A sweeping staircase ascends from there to an assortment of good-sized rooms, furnished in pale florals and nice old pieces of furniture. *10 Vicarage Gate, W8 4AG (7229 4030, www.londonvicaragehotel.com). High Street Kensington or Notting Hill Gate tube. Rooms 17.*

East London

EXPENSIVE

Ace Hotel London Shoreditch

The Ace Hotel – of New York, Palm Springs, Portland, Seattle and Panama – landed in London in early 2014. Most Aces convert buildings that were built for a different use, but in this case an old Crowne Plaza hotel was taken over; a byproduct is spacious rooms and wide corridors. The look of the rooms is comfortable, a bit bohemian, like a modern urban apartment, with wall-to-wall daybeds/ sofas, sturdy oak or metal storage units, round oak tables and beds (and sofas too) covered in luxury denim. Furniture and accessories reflect the Ace appreciation of artisanship, and everyone gets a cosy denim-covered quilt by APC and an individual artwork. The lobby vibe is egalitarian and informal, with a long communal table with computers and DJs every night. The wood-clad midcentury-look brasserie Hoi Polloi (*see p67*) serves modish British food until late, there's a cute juice bar, Lovage, a nook of a coffee shop, and a florist. *100 Shoreditch High Street, E1 6JQ (7613 9800, www.acehotel.com/ london). Liverpool Street tube/rail or Shoreditch High Street rail. Rooms 258.*

Boundary

Design mogul Sir Terence Conran's warehouse conversion has restaurants – Albion (*see p54*) and a basement fine-dining establishment – a rooftop bar, and 17 bedrooms, all beautifully designed. Each has a wet room and handmade bed, but all are otherwise individually furnished with classic furniture and original art. The five split-level suites range in style from the bright, fresh Beach to a new take on Victoriana by Polly Dickens, while the remaining rooms (the larger corner rooms have windows along both external walls) are themed by design style: Mies van der Rohe, Eames, Shaker. There's also a charming Heath Robinson room, decorated with the cartoonist's sketches of hilariously complex machines. *2-4 Boundary Street, Shoreditch, E2 7DD (7729 1051, www.theboundary. co.uk). Liverpool Street tube/rail or Shoreditch High Street rail. Rooms 17.*

Town Hall Hotel

A few years back, a grand, Grade II-listed, early 20th-century town hall was transformed into a classy modern aparthotel – despite its unpromising location between a council estate and a scruffy row of shops. The decor is minimal, retaining many features from its previous life, but jazzed up with contemporary art and a patterned aluminium 'veil' that covers the new floor at the top of the building. The pale-toned, spacious apartments are well equipped for self-catering, but hotel luxuries such as free wireless internet and TV/DVD players are also in place. The De Montfort suite is the size of most houses, stretching over three floors, with a living room as big as a council chamber. Under a conservatory roof, there's a narrow basement swimming pool. *Patriot Square, Bethnal Green, E2 9NF (7871 0460, www.townhallhotel.com). Bethnal Green tube/rail. Rooms 98.*

MODERATE

Hoxton Hotel

Famous for its low rates (including some publicity-garnering £1-a-night rooms), the Hoxton deserves credit for many other things. First, there's the hip Shoreditch location – hip enough for Soho House to have taken over the downstairs bar-brasserie a few years ago. Then there are the great design values (the foyer is a sort of post-modern country lodge, complete with stag's head). Finally, the rooms are well thought out, if rather small, with lots of nice touches – free fresh milk in the fridges, a cold snack for breakfast, free Wi-Fi. Nowadays, there are even three individually designed suites. The downside? Popularity. If you don't book well in advance and plan to visit during the week rather than at the weekend, you could pay as much as at one of the big chains. A major refurb here and a new branch in Holborn were in the pipeline at the time of writing. *81 Great Eastern Street, Shoreditch, EC2A 3HU (7550 1000, www.hoxton hotels.com). Old Street tube/rail. Rooms 208.*

Shoreditch Rooms

The most recent hotel opening from Soho House members' club (*see p113* Dean Street Townhouse; *right* High Road House) might even be the best, catching the local atmosphere with its unfussy, slightly retro design. The rooms feel a bit like urban beach huts, with pastel-coloured tongue-and-groove, shutters and swing doors to the en suite showers. They're fresh, bright and comfortable, even though they're furnished with little more than a bed, an old-fashioned phone and DAB radio, and a big, solid dresser (minibar, hairdryer and treats within, flatscreen TV on top). Guests get access to the fine eating, drinking and fitness facilities (yes, a gym, but more importantly an excellent rooftop pool) in the members' club next door. *Ebor Street, Shoreditch, E1 6AW (7739 5040, www.shoreditchhouse.com). Shoreditch High Street rail. Rooms 26.*

BUDGET

Qbic Hotel London City

The second prong of the Dutch invasion of stylish budget hotels (*see p117* Cheap, Not Nasty) is cheaper and more focused on community and sustainability: in fact, the hotel was created at the end of 2013 by the incredibly rapid fit-out of a former office building using modular 'Cubi' bedrooms. Rooms are sold at four levels – starting at £59 a night for no view. Prices are pegged by keeping down the numbers of staff, which means self check-in and no cash accepted – even vending machines are credit card only. Still, the essentials are covered: TVs in each room, free Wi-Fi throughout, free snack breakfast or £7.50 for a continental in the natty social space downstairs. The location is gritty but great: minutes from Brick Lane and the Whitechapel Gallery. *42 Adler Street, Whitechapel, E1 1EE (no phone, www.qbichotels.com). Aldgate East tube. Rooms 171.*

West London

EXPENSIVE

Bingham

Quality boutique hotel, destination restaurant and sun-filled cocktail bar in one, the Bingham makes excellent use of its superb riverside location by Richmond Bridge. Six of its individually styled and high-ceilinged rooms over-look the Thames; all of them are named after a poet, in honour of the Bingham's artistic past (lesbian aunt-and-niece couple Katherine Harris Bradley and Edith Emma Cooper lived here in the 1890s, regularly hosting members of the Aesthetic Movement). Each room accommodates an ample bathtub and shower, art deco touches to the furnishings and irresistibly fluffy duvets. Run by the Trinder family for the last 25 years, the Bingham manages to feel both grand and boutique. A treat. *61-63 Petersham Road, Richmond, Surrey TW10 6UT (8940 0902, www.thebingham.co.uk). Richmond tube/rail. Rooms 15.*

MODERATE

Garret

This idiosyncratic attic apartment is an absolute treat. High above the Troubadour, a 1960s counter-culture café that still hosts excellent poetry and music events, it's unjustly named: yes, the rooms are in the attic and have charming pitched roofs, but there are acres of space for two – at a push, you could even get the kids to sleep on the pull-out sofa in the lounge-kitchen. The huge, high main bed lies under a skylight; there's well-executed Arts and Crafts decor and a fully equipped kitchen area, right down to the cafetière and selection of wines. A new room, the Eleanor, has recently been added. *Troubadour, 263-267 Old Brompton Road, Earl's Court, SW5 9JA (7370 1434, www.troubadour.co.uk). West Brompton tube/rail. Rooms 2.*

High Road House

This west London outpost of Nick Jones's ever-fashionable Soho House stable (*see p113* Dean Street Townhouse; *left* Shoreditch Rooms) features guestrooms designed by Ilse Crawford, and a members' bar and restaurant above the buzzing ground-floor brasserie. Guestrooms are soothing, unadorned, white Shaker Modern with little fizzes of colour (and hidden treats), the bathrooms well stocked with Cowshed products. *162 Chiswick High Road, W4 1PR (8742 1717, www.highroadhouse.co.uk). Turnham Green tube. Rooms 14.*

Mayflower Hotel

After fighting on the front lines of the Earl's Court budget-hotel style revolution, the Mayflower's taken the struggle to other parts of London (New Linden in Bayswater, www.new linden.com, for example). But this is where the lushly contemporary house style evolved, proving that affordability can be opulently chic. The recent complete refurbishment of the hotel shows that it's not resting on its laurels. Hand-carved Asian artefacts complement the richly coloured fabrics. The facilities too are up to scratch, featuring marble bathrooms, Egyptian cotton sheets, free Wi-Fi and CD players in the rooms. *26-28 Trebovir Road, Earl's Court, SW5 9NJ (7370 0991, www.mayflower-group.co.uk). Earl's Court tube. Rooms 46.*

Rockwell

The Rockwell aims for relaxed contemporary elegance – and succeeds. The listed premises mean there are no identikit rooms: they're all different sizes and individually designed, but share gleaming woods and muted glowing colours alongside more sober creams and neutrals. Basement garden rooms have tiny patios and look up at the ground-level bridge that leads on to the garden terrace proper from the handsome bar-restaurant. Each room has a power shower, Starck fittings and bespoke cabinets in the bathrooms, and triple-glazing ensures you never notice the noisy road just outside. *181-183 Cromwell Road, Earl's Court, SW5 0SF (7244 2000, www.therockwell. com). Earl's Court tube. Rooms 40.*

Twenty Nevern Square

Only the less-than-posh location of this immaculate boutique hotel keeps the rates reasonable. Tucked away in a private garden square, it feels far from its locale. The modern-colonial style was created by its well-travelled owner. In the sleek marble bathrooms, toiletries are tidied away in decorative caskets, but the beds are the real stars: from elaborately carved four-posters to Egyptian sleigh styles, all with luxurious mattresses. Sister hotel is the Mayflower; *see above*). *20 Nevern Square, Earl's Court, SW5 9PD (7565 9555, http://www.20 nevernsquare.com). Earl's Court tube. Rooms 25.*

Directory

Everything you need to know

Directory

Getting Around

Arriving & leaving

BY AIR

Gatwick Airport *0844 892 0322, www.gatwickairport.com. About 30 miles south of central London, off the M23.*
Of the three rail services that link Gatwick to London, the quickest is the **Gatwick Express** (0845 850 1530, www.gatwickexpress.com) to Victoria; it takes 30mins and runs 3.30am-12.30am daily. Tickets cost £19.90 single or £34.90 for an open return (valid for 30 days). Under-16s pay £9.95 for a single and £17.45 for returns; under-5s go free.

Southern (0845 127 2920, www.southernrailway.com) also runs a rail service between Gatwick and Victoria, with trains every 5-10mins (hourly 2-4am and every 15-30mins midnight-2am, 4-6am). It takes about 35mins, and costs £14.40 for a single, £14.50 for a day return (after 9.30am) and £29 for an open period return (valid for one month). Under-16s get half-price tickets; under-5s go free.

If you're staying in King's Cross or Bloomsbury, consider trains run by **First Capital Connect** (0845 748 4950, www.firstcapitalconnect.co.uk) to St Pancras. Tickets are £10 single, £10.40 day return (after 9.30am); £19 for a 30-day open return.

A **taxi** to the centre costs about £100 and takes a bit over an hour.

Heathrow Airport
0844 335 1801, www.heathrowairport.com. About 15 miles west of central London, off the M4.
The **Heathrow Express** train (0845 600 1515, www.heathrowexpress.co.uk) runs to Paddington every 15mins (5.12am-11.48pm daily), and takes 15-20mins. Tickets cost £20 single (£5 more if you buy on board) or £34 return (£5 more if you buy on board); under-16s go half-price. Many airlines have check-in desks at Paddington Station.

The journey by **tube** into central London is longer but cheaper. The 50-60min Piccadilly line ride into central London costs £5.50 one way (£2.70 under-16s). Trains run every few minutes from about 6am to 12.30am daily (7am-11.30pm Sun).

The **Heathrow Connect** (0845 678 6975, www.heathrowconnect.com) rail service offers direct access to Hayes, Southall, Hanwell, West Ealing, Ealing Broadway and Paddington stations in west and north-west London. The trains run

every half-hour, terminating at Heathrow Central (Terminals 1 and 3). From there to Terminal 4 get the free shuttle; between Central and Terminal 5, there's free use of the Heathrow Express. A single from Paddington is £9.50; an open return is £19.00.

National Express (0871 781 8181, www.nationalexpress.com) runs daily coach services to London Victoria (90mins, 5am-9.35pm daily), leaving Heathrow Central bus terminal every 20-30mins. It's £6 for a single (£3 under-16s) or £11 (£5.50 under-16s) for a return.

A **taxi** into town will cost £45-£85 and take 30-60mins.

London City Airport *7646 0088, www.londoncityairport.com. About 9 miles east of central London.*
The **Docklands Light Railway (DLR)** now includes a stop for London City Airport. The journey to Bank station in the City takes around 20mins, and trains run 5.36am-12.16am Mon-Sat or 7.06am-11.16pm Sun. A **taxi** costs around £35 to central London.

Luton Airport *01582 405100, www.london-luton.com. About 30 miles north of central London, J10 off the M1.*
It's a short bus ride from the airport to Luton Airport Parkway station. From here, the **First Capital Connect** rail service (*see left*) calls at many stations (St Pancras International and City among them); journey time is 35-45mins. Trains leave every 15mins or so and cost £13.50 single one-way and £23.50 return. Trains between Luton and St Pancras run at least hourly all night.

By coach, the Luton to Victoria journey takes 60-90mins. **Green Line** (0844 801 7261, www.greenline.co.uk) runs a 24hr service. A single is £10 and returns cost £15; under-15s £7 single, £10 return. A **taxi** to London costs £100-£120.

Stansted Airport *0844 335 1803, www.stanstedairport.com. About 35 miles north-east of central London, J8 off the M11.*
The **Stansted Express** train (0845 748 4950, www.stanstedexpress.com) runs to and from Liverpool Street Station; the journey time is 40-45mins. Trains leave every 15mins, and tickets cost £23.40 single, £32.80 return; under-16s go half-price, under-5s free. Several companies run coaches to central London. **The National Express service** (0871 781 8178, www.nationalexpress.com) from Stansted to Victoria takes at least 80mins. Coaches run roughly every 30mins (24hrs daily), more at peak

times. A single is £10 (£5 for under-16s), return is £18 (£9 for under-16s). A **taxi** into the centre of London costs around £120.

BY COACH

Coaches run by **National Express** (0871 781 8181, www.nationalexpress.com), the biggest coach company in the UK, arrive at **Victoria Coach Station** (164 Buckingham Palace Road, SW1W 9TP, 0843 222 1234, www.tfl.gov.uk), a good 10min walk from Victoria tube station. This is where companies such as **Eurolines** (01582 404511, www.eurolines.com) dock their European services.

BY RAIL

Trains from mainland Europe run by **Eurostar** (0843 218 6186, www.eurostar.com) arrive at **St Pancras International** (Pancras Road, King's Cross, NW1 2QP, 7843 7688, www.stpancras.com).

Public transport

Public transport is straightforward but it's certainly not cheap.
For lost property, *see p122*.

INFORMATION

Details on timetables and other travel information are provided by **Transport for London** (0343 222 1234, www.tfl.gov.uk). Complaints or comments on most forms of public transport can also be taken up with **London TravelWatch** (3176 2999, www.londontravelwatch.org.uk).

Travel Information Centres
TfL's Travel Information Centres provide help with the tube, buses and Docklands Light Railway (DLR; *see p121*). You can find them in **King's Cross tube station**, (7.15am-8pm Mon-Sat; 8.15am-7pm Sun), and in the stations below. Call 0343 222 1234 for more information.

Euston Station 7.15am-7pm Mon-Thur, Sat; 7.15am-8pm Fri; 8.15am-7pm Sun.
Heathrow Terminals 1, 2 & 3 tube station 7.30am-7.30pm daily.
Liverpool Street tube station 7.15am-7pm Mon-Thur, Sat; 7.15am-8pm Fri; 8.15am-7pm Sun.
Piccadilly Circus tube station 7.45am-7pm Mon-Fri; 9.15am-7pm Sat; 9.15am-6pm Sun.
Victoria Station 7.15am-8pm Mon-Sat; 8.15am-7pm Sun.

FARES & TICKETS

Tube and DLR fares use a system of six zones, stretching 12 miles out from

the centre of London. A flat cash fare of £4.70 per journey applies across zones 1-3 on the tube, and £5.70 for zones 1-6; customers save up to £2.50 per journey with a pre-pay Oyster card. Anyone caught without a ticket or Oyster card is subject to a £80 fine (reduced to £40 if you pay within three weeks).

Oyster cards A pre-paid smart-card, Oyster is the cheapest way of getting around on public transport. You can charge up standard Oyster cards at tube stations, Travel Information Centres (*see below*), some railway stations and newsagents. There's a refundable £5 deposit payable on each card; to collect your deposit, call 0343 222 1234.

Visitor Oyster cards are available from Gatwick Express and National Express outlets, Superbreak, visitlondon.com, visitbritaindirect.com, Oxford Tube coach service and on Eurostar services. The only difference between Visitor Oysters and 'normal' Oysters is that they come pre-loaded with money.

A tube journey in zone 1 using Oyster pay-as-you-go costs £2.20 (80p for under-16s), compared to the cash fare of £4.70. A single tube ride within zones 2, 3, 4, 5 or 6 costs £2.70 (80p for under-16s); single journeys from zones 1 through to 6 using Oyster are £5 (6.30-9.30am, 4-7pm Mon-Fri) or £3 (all other times), or 80p for children. Up to four children under 11 can travel for free when travelling with an adult.

Day Travelcards If you're only using the tube, DLR, buses and trams, using Oyster to pay as you go will always be capped at the same price as an equivalent Day Travelcard. However, if you're also using National Rail services, Oyster may not be accepted: opt, instead, for a Day Travelcard, a standard ticket with a coded stripe that allows travel across all networks.

Anytime Day Travelcards can be used all day. They cost from £9 for zones 1-2 (£4.50 child), up to £17 for zones 1-6 (£8.50 child). Tickets are valid for journeys begun by 4.30am the next day. The cheaper **Off-Peak Day Travelcard** allows travel after 9.30am Mon-Fri and all day at weekends and public holidays. It costs £8.90 for zones 1-6 (there are no longer different off-peak day Travelcards for zones 1-2 and 1-4). However, Oyster now has a daily cap of £7 if you're travelling in zones 1-2 off peak, £7.70 in zones 1-4 off peak, and £8.50 in zones 1-6 off peak – in other words, prices that work out cheaper than a day Travelcard, making Oyster pay as you go the cheaper option.

Children Under-5s travel free on buses and trams without the need to provide any proof of identity. Five- and 10-year-olds can also travel free, but need to obtain a 5-10 Zip Oyster photocard. For details, visit www.tfl.gov.uk/fares or call 0343 222 1234.

An 11-15 Zip Oyster photocard is needed by 11- to 15-year-olds to pay as they go on the tube/DLR and to buy 7-Day, monthly or longer period Travelcards, and by 11- to 15-year-olds to use the tram to/from Wimbledon for free.

Photocards Photocards are not required for 7-Day Travelcards or Bus Passes, adult-rate Travelcards or Bus Passes charged on an Oyster card. For details of how to obtain 5-10, 11-15 or 16+ Oyster photocards, see www.tfl.gov.uk/fares or call 0343 222 1234.

LONDON UNDERGROUND

Delays are fairly common, with lines closing at weekends for engineering works. Trains are hot and crowded in rush hour (8-9.30am and 4.30-7pm Mon-Fri). Even so, the 12 colour-coded lines that together comprise the underground rail system – also known as 'the tube' – remain the quickest way to get around London (for a map of the Underground, *see p128*), carrying some 3.5 million passengers every weekday. Comments or complaints are dealt with by **TfL Customer Services** on 0343 222 1234 (8am-8pm daily).

Using the system You can get Oyster cards from www.tfl.gov.uk/oyster, by calling 0845 330 9876, at tube stations, Travel Information Centres, some rail stations and newsagents. Single or day tickets can be bought from ticket offices or machines. You can buy most tickets and top up Oyster cards at self-service machines. Some ticket offices close early (around 7.30pm); carry a charged Oyster card to avoid being stranded.

To enter and exit the tube using an Oyster card, simply touch it to the yellow reader, which will open the gates. Make sure you also touch the card to the reader when you exit the tube, or you'll be charged a higher fare when you next use your card to enter a station. On certain lines, you'll see a pink 'validator' – touch this reader in addition to the yellow entry/exit readers and on some routes it will reduce your fare.

To enter using a paper ticket, place it in the slot with the black magnetic strip facing down, then pull it out of the top to open the gates. Exiting is done in much the same way; however, if you have a single journey ticket, it will be retained by the gate as you leave.

Timetables Tube trains run daily from around 5.30am (except Sunday, when they start an hour or so later, and Christmas Day, when there's no

service). You shouldn't have to wait more than 10mins for a train; during peak times, services should run every 2-3mins. Times of last trains vary; they're usually around 12.30am daily (11.30pm on Sun). The tubes run all night only on New Year's Eve; otherwise, you're limited to night buses (*see right*). However, there are plans to introduce a limited 24hr weekend service (dubbed the 'Night Tube') from 2015.

Fares The single fare for adults across the network is £4.70 for journeys within zones 1-3; £5.70 for zones 1-6; £7 for zones 1-7; £8.10 for zones 1-9. Using Oyster pay-as-you-go, journeys within zone 1 cost £2.20; zones 1-2 costs £2.20 or £2.80, depending on the time of day. Under-5s travel for free.

RAIL & OVERGROUND SERVICES

Independently run commuter services co-ordinated by **National Rail** (0845 748 4950, www.nationalrail.co.uk) leave from the city's main rail stations. Visitors heading to south London, or to more remote destinations such as Hampton Court Palace, will need to use overground services. Travelcards are valid on these services within the right zones, but not all routes accept Oyster pay-as-you-go; check before you travel.

Operated by Transport for London, meaning it does accept Oyster, the **London Overground** is a fabulously useful new service. Originally the rail line ran through north London from Stratford in the east to Richmond in the south-west, with spurs connecting Willesden Junction in the north-west to Clapham Junction in the south-west, and Gospel Oak in the north to Barking in the east, as well as heading north-west from Euston. Then, in 2010, the reopened East London line was incorporated into the Overground network, connecting trains south of the river to trains to the north: effectively, Crystal Palace, West Croydon and New Cross are now connected (via useful, new intermediate stations such as Shoreditch High Street) to Highbury & Islington and the northerly extent of the Overground. Trains run about every 20mins (every half an hour on Sunday), more frequently on popular line.

Docklands Light Railway (DLR)

DLR trains (7363 9700, www.tfl.gov.uk/dlr) run from Bank station (where they connect with Waterloo & City and Central tube lines) or Tower Gateway, close to Tower Hill tube (Circle and District lines). At Westferry station, the line splits east and south via Island Gardens to Greenwich and Lewisham; a change at Poplar can take you north to Stratford. The easterly branch forks after Canning Town to either Beckton or Woolwich Arsenal. Trains run 5.20am-12.20am daily.

Fares Fares on the DLR are the same as for the tube.

BUSES

You must have a ticket or valid pass before boarding any bus in zone 1, and before boarding any articulated, single-decker bus ('bendy buses', which are in the process of being phased out) anywhere in the city. You can buy a ticket from machines at bus stops, although they're often not working – better to travel with an Oyster card or some other pass (*see p120*). Inspectors patrol buses at random; if you don't have a ticket or pass, you may be fined £80.

All buses are now low-floor vehicles that are accessible to wheelchair-users and passengers with buggies. The only exceptions are Heritage routes 9 and 15, which are served by the world-famous open-platform Routemaster buses.

Fares Using Oyster pay-as-you-go costs £1.45 a trip; your total daily payment, regardless of how many journeys you take, will be capped at £4.40. Paying with cash at the time of travel costs £2.40 for a single trip. Under-16s travel for free (using an Under-11 or 11-15 Oyster photocard as appropriate; *see left*).

Night buses Many bus routes operate 24hrs a day, seven days a week. There are also some special night buses with an 'N' prefix, which run from about 11pm to 6am. Most night services run every 15-30mins, but busier routes run a service around every 10mins. Fares are the same as for daytime buses; Bus Passes and Travelcards can be used at no extra fare until 4.30am of the morning after they expire, with Oyster day-capping in effect until then too.

Green Line buses Green Line buses (0844 801 7261, www.greenline.co.uk) serve the suburbs within 40 miles of London. Its office is opposite **Victoria Coach Station** (*see p120*); services run 24hrs.

TRAMLINK

In south London, trams run between Beckenham, Croydon, Addington and Wimbledon. Travelcards that cover zones 3, 4, 5 or 6 are valid, as are Bus Passes. Cash fares are £2.40 (£1.45 with Oyster pay-as-you-go).

WATER TRANSPORT

Most river services operate every 20-60mins between 10.30am and 5pm, and may run more often and later in summer. For commuters, **Thames Clippers** (0870 781 5049, www.thamesclippers.com) runs a service between Embankment Pier and Royal Arsenal Woolwich Pier; stops include Blackfriars, Bankside, London Bridge, Canary Wharf and Greenwich. A standard day roamer ticket (valid 9am-9pm) costs £15, while a single from Embankment to Greenwich is £6.50, or £5.85 for Oyster cardholders.

Westminster Passenger Service Assocation (7930 2062, www.wpsa.co.uk) runs a daily

service from Westminster Pier to Kew, Richmond and Hampton Court from April to October. At around £12 for a single, it's not cheap, but it is a lovely way to see the city, and there are 33%-50% discounts for Travelcards.

Thames River Services (www.westminsterpier.co.uk) operates from the same pier, with trips to Greenwich, Tower Pier and the Thames Barrier. A trip to Greenwich costs £12, but Travelcard holders get a third off.

Taxis

BLACK CABS

The licensed London taxi, aka 'black cab' (although, since on-car advertising, they come in many colours), is a much-loved feature of London life. Drivers must pass a test called 'the Knowledge' to prove they know every street in central London, and the shortest route to it.

If a taxi's orange 'For Hire' sign is lit, it can be hailed. If a taxi stops, the cabbie must take you to your destination if it's within seven miles. It can be hard to find an empty cab, especially just after the pubs close. Fares rise after 8pm on weekdays and at weekends.

You can book black cabs from the 24hr **Taxi One-Number** (0871 871 8710, a £2 booking fee applies, plus 12.5% if you pay by credit card), **Radio Taxis** (7272 0272) and **Dial-a-Cab** (7253 5000; credit cards only, with a booking fee of £2 plus a 12.5% handling charge). Complaints about black cabs should be made to the **Public Carriage Office** (0845 602 7000, www.tfl.gov.uk/pco). Note the cab's badge number, which should be displayed in the rear of the cab and on its back bumper.

MINICABS

Minicabs (saloon cars) are generally cheaper than black cabs, but can be less reliable. Only use licensed firms (look for a disc in the front and rear windows), and *always* avoid those that illegally tout for business in the street.

Trustworthy and fully licensed firms include **Addison Lee** (0844 800 6677), which will text you when the car arrives, and **Ladycars** (8558 9511), which employ only women drivers. Otherwise, text HOME to 60835 ('60tfl'). Transport for London will then text you the numbers of the two nearest licensed minicab operators and the number for Taxi One-Number, which provides licensed black taxis in London. The service costs 35p plus standard call rate. Always ask the price when you book and confirm it with the driver.

Driving

London's roads are often clogged with traffic and roadworks, and parking (*see p122*) is a nightmare. Walking or using public transport are better options. If you hire a car, you can use any valid licence from outside the EU for up to a year after arrival. Speed limits are 20 or 30mph on most city roads.

CAR HIRE

All the car hire firms listed below have branches at the airport; several also have offices in the city centre.

Alamo *UK: 0871 384 1086, www.alamo.co.uk.*
Avis *UK: 0844 581 0147, www.avis.co.uk.*
Budget *UK: 0844 544 3455, www.budget.co.uk.*
Enterprise *UK: 0800 800 227, www.enterprise.co.uk.*
Europcar *UK: 0871 384 9900, www.europcar.co.uk.*
Hertz *UK: 0843 309 3099, www.hertz.co.uk.*
National *UK: 0870 400 4581, www.nationalcar.co.uk.*
Thrifty *UK: 01494 751500, www.thrifty.co.uk.*

CONGESTION CHARGE

Drivers coming into central London between 7am and 6pm Monday to Friday have to pay £10, a fee known as the congestion charge. The congestion charge zone is bordered by Marylebone, Euston and King's Cross (N), Old Street roundabout (NE), Aldgate (E), Tower Bridge Road (SE), Elephant & Castle (S), Vauxhall, Victoria (SW), Park Lane and Edgware Road (W). You'll know when you're about to drive into the charging zone from the red 'C' signs on the road. Enter the postcode of your destination at www.tfl.gov.uk/road users/congestioncharging to discover if it's within the charging zone.

Passes can be bought from some newsagents, garages and NCP car parks; you can also pay online at www.tfl.gov.uk/roadusers/ congestioncharging, by phone on 0345 222 1234 or by SMS. You can pay any time during the day; payments are also accepted until midnight on the next charging day, although the fee is then £12. Expect a fine of £65 if you fail to pay, rising to £130 if you delay payment.

BREAKDOWN SERVICES

AA (Automobile Association) *0870 550 0600 information, 0845 788 7766 breakdown, www.theaa.com.*
ETA (Environmental Transport Association) *0845 389 1010, www.eta.co.uk.*
RAC (Royal Automobile Club) *0870 572 2722 information, 0800 828282 breakdown, www.rac.co.uk.*

PARKING

Central London is scattered with parking meters, but finding an unoccupied one is usually difficult. Meters cost upwards of £1 for 15mins, and in some areas are limited to 2hrs. Parking on a single or double yellow line, a red line or in residents' parking areas during the day is illegal, and you may be fined, clamped or towed.

However, in the evening (from 7pm in much of central London) and at various times at weekends, parking on single yellow lines is legal and free. If you find a clear spot on a single yellow line during the evening, look for a sign giving the local regulations. Meters also become free at certain times during evenings and weekends. Parking on double yellow lines and red routes is illegal at all times.

NCP 24hr car parks (0845 050 7 080, www.ncp.co.uk) are numerous but pricey.

Clamping & vehicle removal
The immobilising of illegally parked vehicles with a clamp is common in London. You'll have to stump up an £100 release fee and show a valid licence. The payment centre will unclamp your car within four hours. If you don't remove your car at once, it may get clamped again, so wait by your vehicle.

If your car has gone, it's either been stolen or, if parked illegally, towed to a car pound by the local authorities. A release fee of £200 is levied for removal, plus upwards of £21 per day from the first midnight after removal. You'll also probably get a parking ticket of £60-£100 when you collect the car (reduced by 50% if paid within 14 days). To retrieve your car, call the **Trace Service** (0845 206 8602).

Cycling

The **Transport for London** (0843 222 1234, www.tfl.gov.uk) cycle hire scheme (nicknamed **Boris Bikes** after the mayor who introduced them) has been popular enough to see extensions to east and west from the initial central zone of operations, even if suggestions it would be self-funding through sponsorship deals and hiring fees currently seem wide of the mark. The scheme allows when-you-want-it access to a string of bicycle stations across central London. To hire a bike, go to a docking station, touch the 'Hire a cycle' icon and insert a credit or debit card. The machine will print out a five-digit access code, which you then tap into the docking point of a bike, releasing the cycle, and away you go. £2 buys 24-hour access to the bike and the first 30 minutes are free. Serious cyclists should contact the **London Cycle Network** (www.londoncycle network.org.uk) and **London Cycling Campaign** (7234 9310, www.lcc.org.uk).

Despite a rash of cycling fatalities in 2013, riders shouldn't be scared of London's streets – 180 million journeys are made each year by bike. Ride calmly, assertively and obeying the rules of the road; avoid getting caught on the inside of a left-turning bus or lorry; and if you find a road intimidating, get off and walk until you find a quieter route. For TfL's advice, see 'Cycle safety tips' at www.tfl.gov.uk/roadusers/ cycling/11598.aspx.

Walking

The best way to see London is on foot, but the street layout is complicated. We've included street maps of central London in the Explore section of this guide, and an indicative map of the major central London districts. The standard Geographers' London A-Z and Collins' London Street Atlas are invaluable supplements. There's route advice at www.tfl.gov.uk/ gettingaround, and look out for the yellow-topped 'Legible London' information posts as you stroll around (www.tfl.gov.uk/microsites/ legible-london/).

Resources

Addresses

London postcodes are less helpful than they could be for locating addresses. The first element starts with a compass point – N, E, SE, SW, W and NW, plus the smaller EC (East Central) and WC (West Central). However, the number that follows relates not to geography (unless it's a 1, which indicates central) but to alphabetical order. So N2 is way out in the boondocks (East Finchley), while W2 covers the very central Bayswater.

Age restrictions

Buying/drinking alcohol 18. **Driving** 17. **Sex** 16. **Smoking** 18.

Disabled

As a city that evolved long before the needs of disabled people were considered, London is difficult for wheelchair users, though access and facilities are slowly improving. The capital's bus fleet is now low-floor for easier wheelchair access; there are no steps for any of the city's trams; and all DLR stations have either lifts or ramp access. However, steps and escalators to the tube and overland trains mean they are often of only limited use to wheelchair users. A blue symbol on the tube map (*see p128*) indicates stations with step-free access. The *Step-free Tube Guide* map is free; call 0843 222 1234 for more details. For London Overground, call 0845 601 4867.

Most major attractions and hotels offer good accessibility, though provisions for the hearing- and sight-disabled are patchier. Enquire about facilities in advance. *Access in London* is an invaluable reference book for disabled traveller. It's available for a £10 donation (sterling cheque, cash US dollars or via PayPal to gordon.couch@yahoo.com) from **Access Project** (39 Bradley Gardens, W13 8HE, www.accessin london.org).

Artsline *www.artsline.org.uk.* Information on disabled access to arts and culture.
Can Be Done *Congress House, 14 Lyon Road, Harrow, Middx HA1 2EN (8907 2400, www.canbe done.co.uk). Harrow on the Hill tube/rail.* **Open** 9.30am-5pm Mon-Fri. Disabled-adapted holidays and tours in London and around the UK.
Royal Association for Disability & Rehabilitation *250 City Road, EC1V 8AF (7250 3222, 7250 4119 textphone, www.radar.org.uk). Old Street tube/rail.* **Open** 9am-5pm Mon-Fri.
A national organisation for disabled voluntary groups publishing books and the bimonthly magazine *New Bulletin* (£35/yr).
Tourism for All *UK 0845 124 9971, www.tourismforall.org.uk.* **Open** *Helpline* 9am-5pm Mon-Fri. Information for older people and people with disabilities in relation to accessible accommodation and other tourism services.
Wheelchair Travel & Access Mini Buses *1 Johnston Green, Guildford, Surrey GU2 9XS (01483 233640, www.wheelchair-travel.co.uk).* **Open** 9am-6pm Mon-Fri; 9am-noon Sat. Hires out converted vehicles (driver optional) plus cars with hand controls and wheelchair-adapted vehicles.

Internet

Most hotels have free high-speed internet (though some of the more expensive ones still charge a fee) and establishments all over town, especially cafés, have wireless access, usually free. Even the tube is wired: see www.tfl.gov.uk/wifi.

Left luggage

AIRPORTS
Gatwick Airport *01293 502014 South Terminal, 01293 569900 North Terminal.*
Heathrow Airport *8759 3344.*
London City Airport *7646 0000.*
Stansted Airport *01279 663213.*

RAIL & BUS STATIONS
Security precautions mean that London stations tend to have left-luggage desks rather than lockers. Call 0845 748 4950 for details.

Charing Cross *7930 5444.* **Open** 7am-11pm daily.
Euston *7387 1499.* **Open** 7am-11pm daily.
King's Cross *7837 4334.* **Open** 7am-11pm daily.
Paddington *7762 0344.* **Open** 7am-11pm daily.
Victoria *7963 0957.* **Open** 7am-midnight daily.

Lost property

Always inform the police if you lose anything, if only to validate insurance claims. Only dial **999** if violence has occurred; use **101** for non-emergencies. Report lost passports both to the police and to your embassy (see p124).

AIRPORTS

For items left on the plane, contact the relevant airline. Otherwise, phone the following:

Gatwick Airport *01253 503162.*
Heathrow Airport *0844 824 3115.*
London City Airport *7646 0000.*
Luton Airport *01582 395219.*
Stansted Airport *01279 663293.*

PUBLIC TRANSPORT

If you've lost property in an overground station or on a train, call 0870 000 5151, and give the operator your details.

Transport for London
Allow two to ten working days from the time of loss. If you lose something on a bus, call 0843 222 1234 and ask for the numbers of the depots at either end of the route. For tube losses, pick up a lost property form from any station. The TfL office also deals with property found in registered black cabs.
Lost Property Office, 200 Baker Street, Marylebone, NW1 5RZ (0343 222 1234, www.tfl.gov.uk). Baker Street tube. **Open** 8.30am-4pm Mon-Fri.

Opening hours

Government offices close on bank (public) holidays, but large shops often remain open, with only Christmas Day sacrosanct. Most attractions remain open on the other public holidays.

Banks 9am-4.30pm (some close at 3.30pm, some 5.30pm) Mon-Fri; some also Sat mornings.
Businesses 9am-5pm Mon-Fri.
Post offices 9am-5.30pm Mon-Fri; 9am-noon Sat.
Pubs & bars 11am-11pm Mon-Sat; noon-10.30pm Sun.
Shops 10am-6pm Mon-Sat, some to 8pm. Many also open on Sun, usually 11am-5pm or noon-6pm.

Postal services

The UK has a fairly reliable postal service. If you have a query, you can contact Customer Services on 0845 774 0740. For business enquiries, call 0845 795 0950.

Post offices are usually open 9am-5.30pm during the week and 9am-noon on Saturdays, although some post offices shut for lunch and smaller offices may close for one or more afternoons each week. Some central post offices are listed below; for others, call the **Royal Mail** on 0845 722 3344 or check online at www.royalmail.com.

You can buy individual stamps at post offices, and books of four or 12 first- or second-class stamps at newsagents and supermarkets that

display the appropriate red sign. A first-class stamp for a regular letter costs 60p; second-class stamps are 50p. It costs 88p to send a postcard abroad. For details of other rates, see www.royalmail.com.

POST OFFICES

Post offices are usually open 9am-5.30pm Mon-Fri and 9am-noon Sat, with the exception of **Lower Regent Street Post Office** (11 Lower Regent Street, SW1Y 4LR, 0845 611 2970), which opens 8am-6.30pm Mon-Fri; 9am-5.30pm Sat; noon-4pm Sun. Listed below are the other main central London offices. For general enquiries, call 0845 611 2970 or consult www.postoffice.co.uk.

Smoking

July 2007 saw the introduction of a ban on smoking in all enclosed public spaces, including pubs, bars, clubs, restaurants, hotel foyers and shops, as well as on public transport. Smokers now face a penalty fee of £50 or a maximum fee of £200 if they are prosecuted for smoking in a smoke-free area. Many bars and clubs offer smoking gardens or terraces.

Telephones

DIALLING & CODES

London's dialling code is 020; standard landlines have eight digits after that. You don't need to dial the 020 from within the area, so we have not given it in this book.

If you're calling from outside the UK, dial your international access code, then the UK code, 44, then the full London number, omitting the first 0 from the code. For example, to make a call to 020 7813 3000 from the US, dial 011 44 20 7813 3000. To dial abroad from the UK, first dial 00, then the relevant country code from the list below. For more international dialling codes, check the phone book or see www.kropla.com/dialcode.htm.

Australia 61; **Canada** 1; **New Zealand** 64; **Republic of Ireland** 353; **South Africa** 27; **USA** 1.

MOBILE PHONES

Mobile phones in the UK operate on the 900 MHz and 1800 MHz GSM frequencies common throughout most of Europe. If you're travelling to the UK from Europe, your phone should be compatible; if you're travelling from the US, it may not be. Either way, check your phone is set for international roaming, and that your service provider at home has a reciprocal arrangement with a UK provider.

The simplest option may be to buy a 'pay-as-you-go' phone (about £10-£200); there's no monthly fee, you top up talk time using a card. Check before buying whether it can make and receive international calls.

OPERATOR SERVICES

Call 100 for the operator if you have difficulty in dialling; for an alarm call; to make a credit card call; for information about the cost of a call; and for help with international person-to-person calls. If you need to reverse the charges (call collect) or if you can't dial direct, dial 155 (international operator); this service is expensive.

DIRECTORY ENQUIRIES

This service is now provided by various six-digit 118 numbers. They're pretty pricey to call: dial (free) 0800 953 0720 for a rundown of options and prices. The best known is 118 118, which charges £1.59 per call, then £1.99 per minute thereafter; 118 888 charges 59p per call, then £1.99 per minute; 118 811 charges 50p per call. Online, the www.uk phonebook.com offers ten free credits a day to UK residents; overseas users get the same credits if they keep a positive balance in their account.

Yellow Pages This 24-hour service lists phone numbers of businesses in the UK. Dial 118 247 (£1.50p connection charge plus 70p/min) and identify the type of business you require, and where in London. Online, try www.yell.com.

Tipping

In Britain it's accepted that you tip in taxis, minicabs, restaurants (some waiting staff rely heavily on tips), hotels, hairdressers and some bars (not pubs). Around 10% is normal, but some restaurants add as much as 15%. Always check whether service has been included in your bill: some restaurants include an automatic service charge, but also leave space for a gratuity on your credit card slip.

Tourist information

In addition to the tourist information centres listed below, there are travel information centres, selling tickets for travel and London attractions, at King's Cross St Pancras, Liverpool Street and Victoria stations, and at Piccadilly Circus tube station.

City of London Information Centre
St Paul's Churchyard, the City, EC4M 8BX (7332 1456, www.city oflondon.gov.uk). St Paul's tube. **Open** 9.30am-5.30pm Mon-Sat; 10am-4pm Sun.
Greenwich Tourist Information Centre
Discover Greenwich, Pepys House, 2 Cutty Sark Gardens, SE10 9LW (0870 608 2000, www.visit greenwich.org.uk). Cutty Sark DLR. **Open** 10am-5pm daily.
Holborn Information Kiosk
Kingsway, outside Holborn tube, Holborn, WC2B 6BG (no phone). Open 9am-6pm Mon-Fri.

Twickenham Visitor Information Centre
44 York Street, Twickenham, Middx, TW1 3BZ (8734 3363, www.visit richmond.co.uk). Twickenham rail. Open 9am-5.15pm Mon-Thur; 9am-5pm Fri.

Websites

www.bbc.co.uk/london
News, travel, weather, sport.
www.britishpathe.com
Newsreels, from spaghetti-eating contests to pre-war Soho scenes.
www.classiccafes.co.uk
Fascinating archive of the city's best 1950s and '60s caffs.
http://diamondgeezer.blogspot. com Superb blogger.
www.filmlondon.org.uk
London's cinema organisation.
http://greatwenlondon.word press.com Fun, engaged, often thought-provoking blog, by the author of our London cab feature.
www.hidden-london.com
Undiscovered gems.
www.londoneater.com
Passionate food reviews.
www.london-footprints.co.uk
Free walks and event listings.
www.london.gov.uk The Greater London Assembly's official website.
http://londonist.com
News, culture and things to do.
http://london.randomness.org.uk
Review site-cum-wiki of interesting London places.
http://londonreconnections. blogspot.com Transport projects.
www.londonremembers.com
Plaques and statues.
http://londonreviewof breakfasts.blogspot.com
Start the day in pun-tastic style.
http://london-underground. blogspot.com Annie Mole's fun and informative daily tube blog.
http://mappinglondon.co.uk
Best maps – and ways of mapping – the city.
www.nickelinthemachine.com
Terrific blog on history, culture and music of 20th-century London.
http://spitalfieldslife.com Key London blog: focused, charming, informative and very human.
www.timeout.com A vital source: eating and drinking reviews, features and events listings.
www.tfl.gov.uk/tfl Information, journey planners and maps from Transport for London, the city's central travel organisation.
updownlondon.com Invaluable live-update guide to step-free Tube access.

Apps

Appy Parking (free) Terrific guide to where to park, showing which areas are free and which are metered, and giving an option to pay through your phone.
Diamond Street (free) Audio social history of Hatton Garden, triggered by GPS as you wander the area.

Directory

Hackney Hear (free) Hyperlocal – and totally brilliant – audio guide to London Fields in Hackney.
Hailo (free) Calls a black cab, tells you how long it will be, and deducts the meter fare from your account – but there's no call-out fee.
iCockneyDialect (free) Talk like a local – over 800 translations into London's traditional rhyming slang.
London Cycle: Maps & Routes (free) Most popular of many apps showing the nearest Boris Bike.
London Bus Live (free) Tells you how far away your next bus is.
London Jigsaw (69p) Excellent mix of puzzle and trivia challenge.
Mission:Explore London (free) Fun for kids and adults – very silly challenges around the city.
Soho Stories (free) National Trust audio guide to Soho, with nuggets of the area's fascinating history triggered by your phone's GPS.
Street Art London (£2.99) The city's graffiti artists and their work.
StreetMuseum (free) Brilliant Museum of London app – archive shots geolocated to where you're standing, with informative captions.
StreetMuseum Londinium (free) StreetMuseum, but for Romans.
Time Out London Magazine (free) Indispensable guide to the week's happenings in the capital.
Time Travel Explorer (£1.99) Overlays your location with any of four historic maps, the oldest from 1746; a slider blends old and new.
Toiluxe – central London (69p) Where's the nearest public loo?
Tube Deluxe (69p) There are free apps, but not with departure boards, travel news and journey planning.

Emergencies

In the event of a serious accident, fire or other incident where lives are at risk, call **999** – free from any phone, including payphones – or **112** from mobiles, and ask for an ambulance, the fire service or police. For non-emergencies, call **101**. For hospital Accident & Emergency departments, helplines and police stations, *see right*.

EMBASSIES & CONSULATES

American Embassy *24 Grosvenor Square, Mayfair, W1A 2LQ (7499 9000, http://london.usembassy.gov). Bond Street or Marble Arch tube.* **Open** 8.30am-5.30pm Mon-Fri.
Australian High Commission *Australia House, Strand, Holborn, WC2B 4LA (7379 4334, www. uk.embassy.gov.au). Holborn or Temple tube.* **Open** 9am-5pm Mon-Fri.
Canadian High Commission *38 Grosvenor Street, Mayfair, W1K 4AA (7258 6600, www.canada. org.uk). Bond Street or Oxford Circus tube.* **Open** 9.30am-4pm Mon-Fri.
Embassy of Ireland *17 Grosvenor Place, Belgravia, SW1X 7HR (7235 2171, 7373 4339 passports & visas, www.embassyofireland.co.uk).* Hyde Park Corner tube. **Open** 9.30am-5pm Mon-Fri.

New Zealand High Commission *New Zealand House, 80 Haymarket, St James's, SW1Y 4TQ (7930 8422, www.nzembassy.com). Piccadilly Circus tube.* **Open** 9am-5pm Mon-Fri.

POLICE

London's police are used to helping visitors. If you've been robbed, assaulted or involved in a crime, go to your nearest police station. (Look under 'Police' in Directory Enquiries or call 118 118, 118 500 or 118 888 to find your nearest.)

In non-emergencies, call **101**; for emergencies, call **999**.

If you have a complaint, ensure that you take the offending officer's identifying number (it should be displayed on his or her epaulette). You can then register a complaint with the **Independent Police Complaints Commission** (90 High Holborn, WC1V 6BH, 0845 300 2002, www.ipcc.gov.uk).

LOST/STOLEN CREDIT CARDS

Report lost or stolen credit cards both to the police and the 24-hour phone lines listed below. Inform your bank by phone and in writing.

American Express *01273 696933, www.americanexpress.com.*
Diners Club *0845 862 2935, www.dinersclub.co.uk.*
MasterCard *0800 964767, www.mastercard.com.*
Visa *0800 891725, www.visa.com.*

Health

British citizens or those working in the UK can go to any general practitioner (GP). People ordinarily resident in the UK, including overseas students, are also allowed to register with a National Health Service (NHS) doctor. If you fall outside these categories, you will have to pay to see a GP. Your hotel concierge should be able to recommend one.

A pharmacist may dispense medicines on receipt of a prescription from a GP. NHS prescriptions cost £7.85; under-16s and over-60s are exempt from charges. Contraception is free for all. If you're not eligible to see an NHS doctor, you'll be charged cost price for any medicines prescribed.

Free emergency medical treatment under the NHS is available to:
● EU nationals and those of Iceland, Norway, Switzerland and Liechtenstein; all may be entitled to state-provided treatment for non-emergency conditions with an EHIC (European Health Insurance Card)
● nationals of New Zealand, Russia, most former USSR states and the former Yugoslavia
● residents (irrespective of nationality) of Anguilla, Australia, Barbados, the British Virgin Islands, the Falkland Islands, the Isle of Man, Montserrat, Poland, Romania, St Helena and the Turks & Caicos Islands
● anyone who has been in the UK for the previous 12 months, or who

has come to the UK to take up permanent residence
● students and trainees whose courses require more than 12 weeks in employment in the first year
● refugees and others who have sought refuge in the UK
● people with HIV/AIDS at a special STD treatment clinic

There are no NHS charges for:
● treatment in A&E wards
● emergency ambulance transport to a hospital
● diagnosis and treatment of certain communicable diseases
● family planning services
● compulsory psychiatric treatment

ACCIDENT & EMERGENCY

Listed below are most of the central London hospitals that have 24-hour Accident & Emergency (A&E) departments.

Charing Cross Hospital *Fulham Palace Road, Hammersmith, W6 8RF (3311 1234, www.imperial. nhs.uk). Barons Court or Hammersmith tube.*
Chelsea & Westminster Hospital *369 Fulham Road, Chelsea, SW10 9NH (8746 8000, www.chelwest.nhs.uk). South Kensington tube.*
Royal London Hospital *Whitechapel Road, Whitechapel, E1 1BB (3416 5000, www.bartshealth.nhs.uk). Whitechapel tube.*
St Thomas' Hospital *Lambeth Palace Road, Lambeth, SE1 7EH (7188 7188, www.guysandstthomas.nhs.uk). Westminster tube or Waterloo tube/rail.*
University College Hospital *235 Euston Road, NW1 2BU (3456 7890, www.uclh.nhs.uk). Euston Square or Warren Street tube.*

CONTRACEPTION & ABORTION

Family planning advice, contraceptive supplies and abortions are free to British citizens on the NHS, and to EU residents and foreign nationals living in Britain. Phone 0845 122 8690 or visit www.fpa.org.uk for your local Family Planning Association. The 'morning after' pill (around £25), effective up to 72 hours after intercourse, is available over the counter at pharmacies.

DENTISTS

Dental care is free for resident students, under-18s and people on benefits. All others must pay. To find an NHS dentist, contact the local Health Authority or a Citizens' Advice Bureau (*see right*).

Dental Emergency Care Service *Guy's Hospital, St Thomas Street, Borough, SE1 9RT (7188 8006). London Bridge tube/rail.* **Open** 9am-5pm Mon-Fri.
Queues start forming at 8am; arrive by 10am if you're to be seen at all.

PHARMACIES

Also called 'chemists' in the UK. Branches of Boots and larger supermarkets have a pharmacy. Staff can advise on over-the-counter medicines. Most pharmacies keep

shop hours (9am-6pm Mon-Sat) but the Boots store at 44-46 Regent Street, W1B 5RA, (7734 6126), opens until midnight (6pm Sun).

STDS, HIV & AIDS

NHS Genito-Urinary Clinics (such as the Centre for Sexual Health) are affiliated to major hospitals. They provide free, confidential STD testing and treatment, as well as treating other problems such as thrush and cystitis. They also offer counselling about HIV and other STDs, and can conduct blood tests.

The NHS website www.nhs.uk/worthtalkingabout also has information, including clinic locations.

HELPLINES

Alcoholics Anonymous *0845 769 7555, www.alcoholics-anonymous. org.uk.* **Open** 10am-10pm daily.
Citizens' Advice Bureaux *www.citizensadvice.org.uk.* The council-run Citizens' Advice Bureax offer free legal, financial and personal advice to all. Check the phone book or see the website for the address of your nearest office.
Missing People *0500 700 700, www.missingpeople.org.uk.* **Open** 24hrs daily. Information on anyone reported missing.
NHS Direct *111, www.nhs direct.nhs.uk.* **Open** 24hrs daily. A free, first-stop service for medical advice on all subjects.
Rape & Sexual Abuse Support Centre *0808 802 9999, www.rape crisis.org.uk.* **Open** noon-2.30pm, 7-9.30pm daily. Information and support.
Samaritans *0845 790 9090, www.samaritans.org.uk.* **Open** 24hrs daily. General helpline for those under emotional stress.
Sexual Healthline *0800 567 123, www.nhs.uk/worthtalkingabout).* **Open** 24hrs daily. Free and confidential.
Victim Support *0845 303 0900, www.victimsupport.org.uk.* **Open** 9am-9pm Mon-Fri; 9am-7pm Sat, Sun. Emotional and practical support to victims of crime.

Safety & security

There are no real 'no-go' areas in London, and you're much more likely to get hurt in a car accident than as a result of criminal activity, but thieves haunt busy shopping areas and transport nodes as they do in all cities.

Use common sense and follow some basic rules. Keep wallets and purses out of sight, and handbags closed. If you're on your mobile phone, make sure it can't be snatched out of your hand. Never leave bags or coats unattended, beside, under or on the back of a chair – even if they aren't stolen, they're likely to trigger a bomb alert. Don't put bags on the floor near the door of a public toilet. Don't take short cuts through dark alleys and car parks. Keep your passport, cash and credit cards in separate places. Don't carry a wallet in your back pocket. Be aware of your surroundings.

Index

CASS ART
MANIFESTO

LET'S FILL THE UK WITH ARTISTS

ART IS FREEDOM. CASS ART BELIEVES IN ART. WE KNOW THE FREEDOM AND CREATIVE PLEASURE IT BRINGS. SO WE WANT EVERYONE TO REALISE THEY CAN DO IT - AND AFFORD IT.

BEST MATERIALS. ARTISTS NEED THE CHOICE OF ALL THE BEST MATERIALS. WE STOCK THE TOP BRANDS FROM AROUND THE WORLD, AS FAVOURED BY THE UK'S ARTISTS.

BEST PRICES. WE NEGOTIATE DIRECTLY WITH ALL THE FAMOUS SUPPLIERS. THEY HELP US, SO WE CAN HELP YOU. THAT'S WHY OUR PRICES ARE AS LOW AS THEY CAN GO.

OUR SHOPS. THE SPACE IS DESIGNED TO HELP YOU AND INSPIRE YOU. MATERIALS ARE ORGANISED AND DISPLAYED JUST THEY WAY YOU WANT THEM. THE EFFECT IS THOUGHTFUL AND CONTEMPORARY.

OUR PEOPLE. OUR STAFF ARE ARTISTS. THEY KNOW ART. THEY ENJOY WORKING WITH WHAT THEY KNOW. THEY GIVE YOU INTELLIGENT AND THOUGHTFUL ADVICE — NO BLUFFING, NO HIDDEN AGENDA.

OUR NATION. WE ESTABLISHED OUR FIRST SHOP NEXT TO THE NATIONAL GALLERY IN 1984 AND REMAIN INDEPENDENTLY OWNED. FOR 30 YEARS WE HAVE BEEN ON A MISSION TO FILL THIS COUNTRY (ITS CITIES, TOWNS AND VILLAGES) WITH ARTISTS.

CASS PROMISE: BEST QUALITY, BEST BRANDS, BEST PRICES

ISLINGTON FLAGSHIP   CHARING CROSS   SOHO   HAMPSTEAD   KENSINGTON   KINGSTON

ONLINE @ CASSART.CO.UK

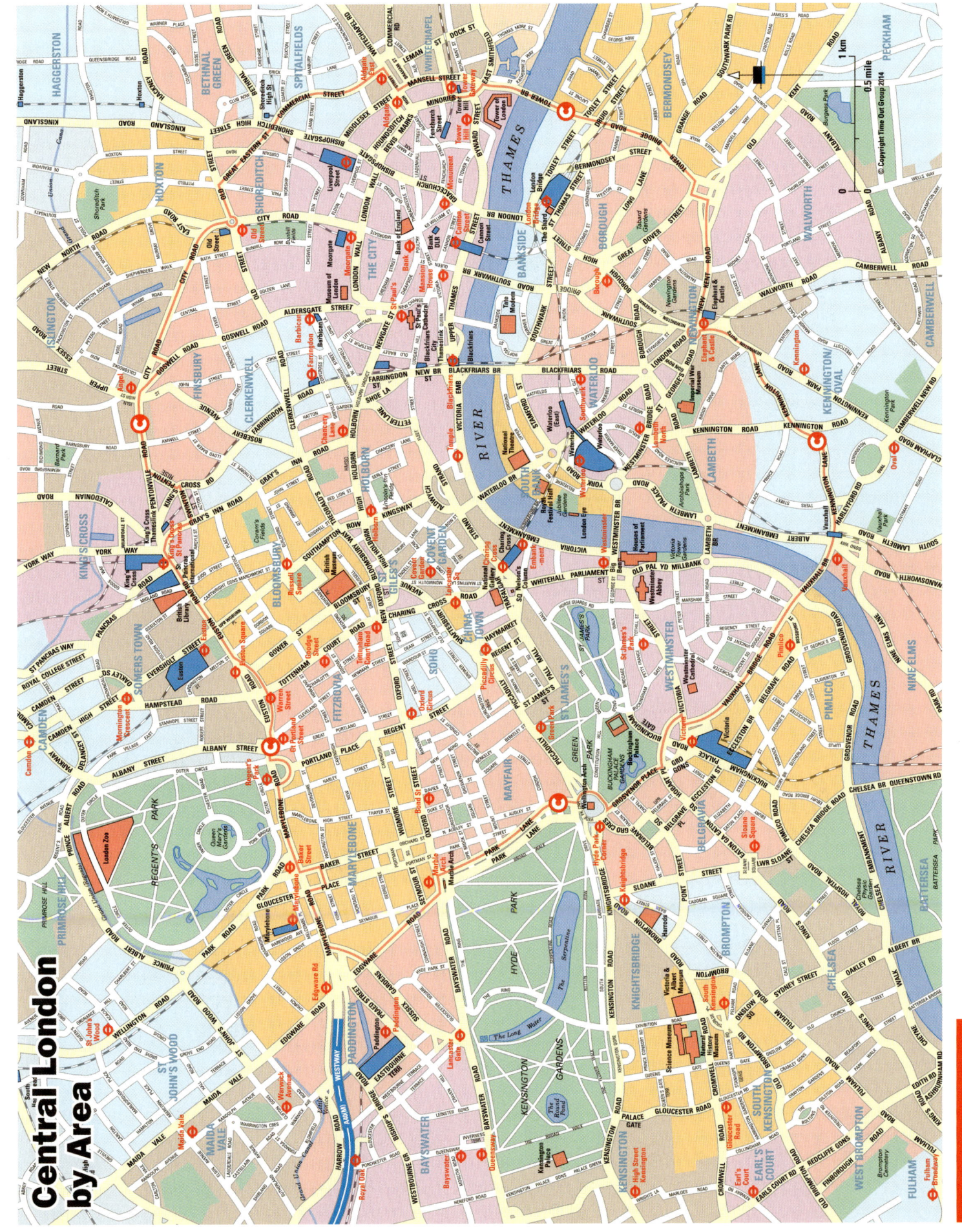

Central London by Area

© Copyright Time Out Group 2014

1 km
0.5 mile

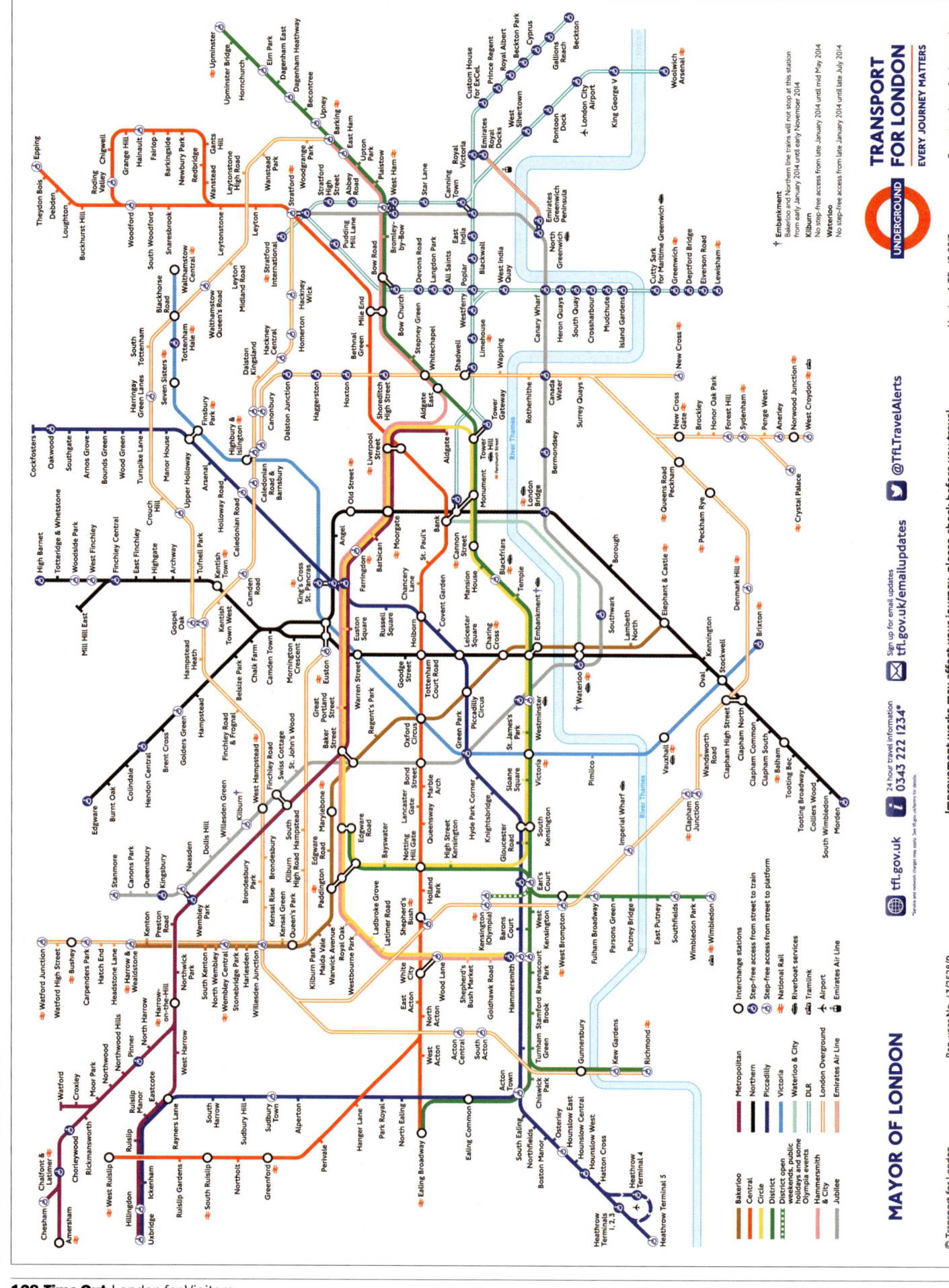